ADULT EDUCATION AND LIFELONG LEARNING

Theory and practice

4th edition

Peter Jarvis

R Routledge
Taylor & Francis Group

LONDON AND NEW YORK

First edition published 1983
by Croom Helm

Second edition published 1995
by Routledge

Third edition published 2004
by RoutledgeFalmer

This edition published 2010
by Routledge
2 Park Square, Milton Park, Abingdon, Oxon OX14 4RN

Simultaneously published in the USA and Canada
by Routledge
711 Third Ave, New York, NY 10017

Routledge is an imprint of the Taylor & Francis Group, an informa business

© 2010 Peter Jarvis

Typeset in Baskerville by Wearset Ltd, Boldon, Tyne and Wear

Printed and bound in Great Britain by TJ International, Padstow, Cornwall

British Library Cataloguing in Publication Data
A catalogue record for this book is available from the British Library

Library of Congress Cataloging-in-Publication Data
Jarvis, Peter, 1937–
Adult education and lifelong learning: theory and practice/Peter
Jarvis. – 4th ed.
p. cm.
Includes bibliographical references and index.
1. Adult education. 2. Continuing education. I. Title.
LC5215.J37 2010
374–dc22
2009034478

ISBN10: 0-415-49478-8 (hbk)
ISBN10: 0-415-49481-8 (pbk)

ISBN13: 978-0-415-49478-6 (hbk)
ISBN13: 978-0-415-49481-6 (pbk)

In memory of my Mother, Father and Jack

CONTENTS

CONTENTS

FIGURES

TABLES

PREFACE TO THE FOURTH EDITION

It is a rare privilege for an author to have a book appear in its fourth edition twenty-seven years after the first edition. A great deal has happened during that time, and this edition is profoundly different from the first edition. With all the changes it is easy to lose sight of our history and the history of the thoughts and ideas of scholars in our field and so I have tried to retain some of the historical records in this book without, I hope, being irrelevant to its main purpose.

In the first edition of this book I paid tribute to the students with whom I worked while I was preparing this book. Neither they nor I suspected that that year's course would last for quite so long! The book was and is still intended for students undertaking studies in the fields of lifelong learning, adult education and all forms of post-compulsory education, but it is not a basic 'how-to' book. Rather, it seeks to combine practice with theory and point the way beyond this introduction to further studies. It recognizes that practice precedes theory, although the field is often taught from its theoretical foundations.

Perhaps the change in the opening chapter is an indicator of just how much the field has changed: in the first three editions I wrote about the rationale for the education of adults but by this edition the first chapter is about the person as learner. Thereafter there is a new chapter on globalization since it has become obvious that the whole of the education of adults has been affected throughout the world by the recent trends in globalization. The third chapter is a major rewrite of the original second chapter. It is only when we move into the actual processes of teaching and learning that we can see that this is a revised edition of a previous work and the remaining chapters are updates of the third edition, apart from the sixth chapter, which is completely new.

Some material has been dropped from the third edition – some from each chapter – and the whole of the final chapter, on the United Kingdom. I have been privileged to share in the rich community of educators of adults both in the United Kingdom and worldwide over many years, and I have been an observer and learner wherever I have travelled and in whatever company I have shared. I may not always have been a good learner, but over the years this professional community has become very important to me. Not only sharing with colleagues but reading their work has been a source of genuine learning. While I got my inspiration for the first edition of this book from my students, and it is still the basis of the book, much of the subsequent material has been gained in and through the professional community. There is no single person to whom I can point and it would be invidious to attempt it, although I certainly have to acknowledge those colleagues with whom I worked while the first edition was being prepared – but now I just want to acknowledge the constant help and support of all of colleagues in my endeavours to understand the field. They have been my inspiration and the source of much of my knowledge, but the mistakes remain my own.

However, there is one person to whom I must acknowledge as a constant source of support: my wife, Maureen. Over the years she has put up with the demands of my writing and, therefore, the demands of the writer. Without her, I could have produced very little. She has been most gracious in understanding my lifestyle and to her I remain, as always, eternally grateful.

In addition, I am most grateful to Philip Mudd from Routledge, who has encouraged me to continue writing after my retirement from full-time university teaching – not only with this book but with a number of others, some of which are referenced throughout this text.

Earlier editions of this book have been translated into other languages, and this has been an indication to me of its usefulness. All that I can hope is that this edition will also be useful to those who read it – for that is its purpose.

Peter Jarvis
Thatcham, UK
August 2009

ACKNOWLEDGEMENTS

Figure 1.2: Maslow, A. H. *Toward a Psychology of Being, 3rd Edition.* Copyright © 1968. Reproduced with permission of John Wiley & Sons, Inc.

Figure 4.2: Kolb, D. A and Fry, R. 'Toward an applied theory of experiential learning' in C. Cooper (ed.) *Theories of Group Process,* pages 33–7. Copyright © 1975. Reproduced with permission of John Wiley & Sons Ltd.

1

THE PERSON AS LEARNER

When the first edition of this book was published, it was important to argue a strong case for the education of adults since it was still something that we did not take for granted, but that time was also the start of one of the most rapid periods of social change that we have witnessed, one that has, among other things, transformed our understanding of both education and learning. Now we assume that the person is a learner and that education is, if not a right, then an expectation. Indeed, the speed of change has been so rapid that it could be argued that this edition is an entirely different book as compared with the first edition, although there are still some parts that have changed little. There are three parts to this opening chapter: the person in an evolutionary and social context, being and learning, and social being – learning in relationship.

The evolutionary and social context of the person

At the heart of social living, it has been assumed in the West that people are born as individuals and that as they grow and develop, they learn to be social human beings – but this is one of the flaws in Enlightenment thinking (see Hall, 1976; Gray, 1995; Jarvis, 2008). In fact, the person is always part of society/group/family, and so, following Buber (1958), we start with the proposition that in the beginning is relationship and that we have to learn to become individuals and then social individuals after our birth. We also start with the assumption that, as a result of our birth, we are members of humankind – and once we make that assumption, we cannot escape from our evolutionary history. Humanity has evolved, and as part of that evolution we have changed and developed to become the human beings that we now are, and our recognition of this must affect our understanding of our learning. And so we could depict the place of the person (ego) in the wider society as shown in Figure 1.1.

The upward arrows in Figure 1.1 depict the process of time through which we have evolved, and in this sense we can now begin to locate one of the major contemporary debates: to what extent has humankind

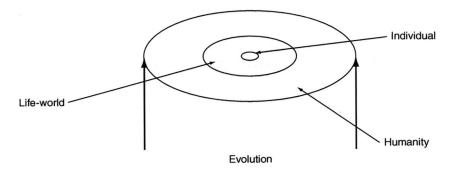

Figure 1.1 The social individual within humankind.

evolved and how does this question affect our understanding of the nature of culture? Do individuals have built into their brains (hard-wired) all the results of evolution so that the part that culture and learning play has a little less significance than we originally thought? Clearly, this is the beginning of a long and drawn-out debate which I do not want to explore here, although not to mention it would do a disservice to our quest in this study (but see Jarvis, 2009a). Throughout this book we will take it as read that we have evolved and that there are aspects of our evolution which affect our learning. Occasionally I shall refer to our having been hard-wired, but I do find Dawkins's (1976) idea of memes unconvincing – although there is a place for a biology of learning (see Jarvis and Parker, 2005). However, I shall also mention the idea of plasticity – that the wiring in our brains is not necessarily permanent. Consequently, this book assumes nurture still has a significant role to play, and this is where education and learning find their major role – and that they do so within a social context.

From before our birth we are in relationship, with our mothers in the wombs and, usually, in the earliest months of our lives. Additionally, from our birth we are almost certainly also in relationship with other people – significant others – and so, as infants, we begin our learning process in earnest. It is in the first three years of life that a major part of our learning for life occurs (see Tomasello, 1999; Nelson, 2007; Jarvis, 2009a). Early childhood learning is really beyond the remit of this book, although it is important to understand that we can really only begin to understand adult learning if we have a more complete understanding of the lifelong learning process.

One scholar whose work has recognized this and dominated our thinking on this matter in days gone by is Maslow (1968), who argued that we are born with needs. His well-known 'hierarchy' of needs is usually represented as in Figure 1.2.

This basic diagram has not gone uncontested since its publication. Dennis Child (1977:40ff.), for instance, suggested that the need to know

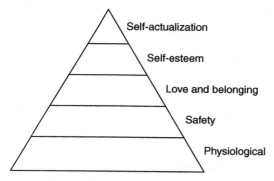

Figure 1.2 Maslow's hierarchy of needs.
Source: Maslow (1968).

should come at the top of the hierarchy, but in the third edition of his text he (1981:43) changed his mind and omitted his highest stratum. At the same time, he continued to highlight the significance of knowledge and understanding, and we will return to this shortly. Maslow (1968:60ff.) certainly considered the need to know but claimed that knowledge has a certain ambiguity about it, specifying that in most individuals there is both a need to know and a fear of knowing. However, the fear of knowing may be the result of social experiences rather than being basic to the person, but the need to learn is fundamental even if the consequences of that knowledge may be dangerous, as we will discuss in the next section. Is there a progression through the hierarchy so that movement upwards only occurs when the more preponderant needs are satisfied? Is it even a hierarchy? Argyle (1974:961) suggested that the main supporting evidence for the hierarchy comes from the lower end but that there 'is not such clear evidence about the upper part of the hierarchy'. However, even this is open to question since the upper end can almost overrule the lower end in such activities as extreme sports. Indeed, it could be argued that the desire to achieve overrules our more basic needs, but then it could be argued that as a result of advertising and creating desire in children from a very young age, we actually relegate our needs to a status below that of desire. Houston *et al.* (1979:297) claimed that the order of needs is itself arbitrary and that the exact order is not particularly important – only the fact that we, as human beings, have needs. Since we were born in relationship, one of our fundamental needs is to live in harmony with our society and environment (Maslow's third level), and this raises questions about disharmony and society's attempts to mould us into the social and cultural environment into which we are born.

The needs that Maslow depicts are a mixture of physiological and self-orientated, or needs of the body and needs of the mind, and so it is important that we look at the nature of the person since underlying theories of learning are theories of the nature of the person.

The nature of the person

The person can be regarded as an embodied self or as a dualism of body and self: that is the difference between I *am* my body and I *have* a body, so that this section contains three parts: the body, the self and the nature of the debate about body and mind.

The body

There has been considerable recent research about the nature of the body (e.g. Shilling, 1993), much of which lies beyond the focus of this study. Nevertheless, the body is a fundamental element in the person and cannot be omitted in any discussion about learning. At birth, the body is already the subject of evolutionary processes, carrying with it our genetic structures, and so on. Indeed, every experience from which we learn comes through the senses – seeing, hearing, feeling, and so on. However, we know that the fetus actually learns in the womb, which indicates that we can learn pre-consciously before birth. And then, we all know how the body can be programmed by constant repetition of an action – by a pianist, for instance, so that the sequence of music learned can be played almost automatically. The same is true when we drive a car. Consequently, any understanding of learners should begin with our understanding the nature of the person, and so we are going to touch upon a number of debates here, although I recognize that this is not the place to pursue them.

But all of our experiences of the world occur through our senses: we taste, touch, feel, smell, hear and see the external world. It is through our senses that we experience the world and learn about it. As O'Loughlin (2006:5) reminds us, 'The senses do not merely "make sense" of life, they are our means of furnishing intelligibility and ultimately our capacity to reason, judge and feel as we live our lives.' She goes on to point out that from the earliest of times, knowing has been associated with seeing – but that our experience of the world is wider than being simply vision-centred. The body, then, is at the heart of our experiences; it is the part of us that is seen and through which we learn and communicate.

However, the body also contains a brain – not a mind; but the brain, as Gardner (1983) points out, processes different bits of information in different parts of it. Greenfield (1999) shows that the brain responds to experiences in a physical manner and she (ibid.:112) defines consciousness, for instance, as 'an emergent property of non-specialised groups of neurons ... that are continuously variable with respect to an epicentre'. In addition, our construction and perception of our body influence our self-identity, which itself is a learned phenomenon. Gardner (1999) also illustrates how brain damage affects specific parts of the brain, which in turn relates to different human abilities, and so on. In addition, we are aware that the ageing processes do affect our bodies, and consequently our learning abilities, in different ways. It is clear, therefore, that new developments in learning theory might well come from neuroscience and biology – even from chemistry and pharmacology, if we think about the way that drugs affect our brain functioning.

Adult educators have been the only educationalists, until very recently, who have considered the ageing body within the educational processes. The physical capabilities of the adult do decline after they have reached a peak in late adolescence or in early adulthood. Verner (1964:18) summarized these as including 'sensory decline; loss in strength; lengthening of reaction time; decline in sexual capacity; changes in skin texture, muscle tone and hair colour; and a gradual decline in overall energy'. He suggested that there are some physiological losses that are very significant in the process of adult learning: loss in visual acuity, loss in audio acuity, loss of energy and the problems of homeostatic adjustment. Since these all affect adult learning, and therefore adult teaching, they need to be taken into consideration. However, these physiological changes may induce adults to underestimate their powers to learn and so reinforce the perception that education is something that occurs early in life. At the same time, learning can be used as a therapy, and I (Jarvis, 2001a) have argued elsewhere for the creation of an occupation of learning therapists who can assist the confused elderly redevelop some of their faculties and continue to learn despite some physical deterioration.

But what if the physical body and even the brain itself begin to deteriorate during adulthood? Until fairly recently it was thought that when human beings achieve biological maturity, they reach a plateau, on which they remain for a few years before beginning to deteriorate. Thorndike (1928), for instance, concluded that the ability to learn 'rises until about twenty, and then, perhaps after a stationary period of some years, slowly declines' (quoted in Yeaxlee, 1929:41). However, this argument has now come under considerable criticism, and Allman (1982) summarized some of these critical research findings nearly three decades ago. She recorded how Horn suggested that there are two forms of intelligence: fluid, which stems from the biological base, and crystallized, which is capable of growth through the major part of life since it is influenced by the social processes that the individual experiences. She pointed (ibid.:47) to Birran's 'discontinuity hypothesis', which states that 'the biological base ceases to be the primary influence on behaviour after physical maturation is complete and as long as the biological base does not enter into a hypothesized critical range of pathology, it will not regain supremacy of influence'. The value of the discontinuity hypothesis lies in the fact that when individuals disengage, they tend to be less engaged in physical activity, and it is the physical activity that stimulates the brain (Blakemore and Frith, 2005:134–137). Moreover, Blakemore and Frith (ibid.:8–9) make the point that 'research is beginning to show that this view of the brain [deterioration with age] is too pessimistic: the adult brain is flexible; it can grow new cells and make new connections, at least in some regions such as the hippocampus'. Other researchers, such as Cusack and Thompson (1998), have shown that the level of intelligence in older people can be altered by the amount of physical activity, since that activity is stimulating the brain. Yet the reverse is also true, as Hammond (Schuller *et al.*, 2004:78) argues when she suggests that 'positive experiences of learning develop psychosocial qualities that lead to both improved health outcomes and the motivation and opportunity to continue learning'. But the body does not continue to develop for ever! However, the person is more than a body.

The self

The self-concept is central to learning theory. Jarvis (1987, 1992), following George Herbert Mead, argued that the mind and the self are learned phenomena. The brain stores memories of experiences, almost certainly from the time when the baby is still in the womb and certainly from the time of birth, from which emerge the mind and then the self. However, the brain does not just grow from nothing in the womb; it contains within itself the results of our evolutionary process, which, suggests Donald (2001), goes through three stages: mimetic, oral and theoretic. These are very similar to what Nelson (2007:48) discovered in early childhood development – as if we re-enact our own evolutionary processes during the early months of life in interaction with others. Nelson (ibid.:105) writes:

> The development of inter-subjectivity towards the end of the first year entwines the self and other in a new relationship where the two are recognized by the infant as distinctively separable and interactive. By the middle of the second year a firmer representation of an objective self begins to emerge.

Through the processes of memory, meaning is created, but Nelson (ibid.:111) argues, '[E]verything that enters the memory is somehow meaningful to the individual. Thus memory *is* meaning.' Every memory is meaningful or significant to the child who is remembering it. So, that meaning develops as memory develops through the lived experiences of the child, and the body of individual memories (meanings) results in some way in an individuation of consciousness and, as Luckmann (1967:48–49) argues, the individual self becomes detached from its immediate experience in the interaction with other persons. We can see this in children as they first use their own names to refer to themselves, then they use 'me' and finally they employ 'I'; they have become a conscious self.

This, in turn, results in the person integrating the meanings that have evolved in response to the learning questions that have arisen from previous experience. Hence, ultimately, a self is formed that integrates the 'past, present and future in a socially defined, morally relevant biography' (Luckmann, 1967:48–49). There is, therefore, a sense in which the self transcends its biological body, reaching out to the socio-cultural environment and responding to pressures from it in a dialectical relationship in order to create a sense of meaning.

Thus, it may be seen that every new experience is interpreted by the mind and has a personal meaning given to it, which is then integrated into the meanings of past experiences already stored in the brain, which gives us a greater understanding of how we, as individuals, can behave and learn. This is ultimately the system of meaning or a body of knowledge that helps us interpret 'reality'. The system of meaning is significant to the individual and so the question needs to be raised as to whether that individual self is just an aspect of the physical brain or whether there is a separate mind that has emerged out of this complex early learning process.

The mind–body relationship[1]

From the earliest philosophical studies, the relationship between the body and the mind has constituted a problem which, although rarely discussed in the literature on human learning, has influenced the way that some scholars have understood learning. Even so, an existentialist position does not necessarily accept the crude mind–body dualism, whereas other scholars have maintained its validity. There is, indeed, no agreement between scholars about the nature of this relationship, and Maslin (2001) suggests five main theories:

1   dualism;
2   mind–brain identity;
3   logical or analytical behaviourism;
4   functionalism;
5   non-reductive monism.

Dualism

The dualist position is that the human being is a combination of two distinct entities: a physical body and a mind/soul. Clearly, when Descartes claimed that *I think, therefore I am,* he was reflecting the dualism of his age – but it may actually be better to claim that 'I am, therefore I think'. But rejecting Descartes' well-known dictum does not automatically rule out the possibility of some form of existence beyond life itself. This discussion, however, is beyond the remit of this study. Suffice it to say that there are a number of major problems with dualism:

- There is the fact of the existence of the brain itself – if there is a mind that has all the experiences, and so on, why do human beings have such complex neurological mechanisms that we call brains?
- When we act, our body and our mind perform in unison rather than each act being two distinct elements – the thought and the action. Ryle (1963 [1949]), for instance, forcefully criticized the idea that there are two distinct phenomena in every action.
- The idea that there is a 'little person' in the human being driving our actions now seems far-fetched; it is known as the homunculus fallacy.

We know that learning is more than just a mental act; it involves the whole person.

Mind–brain identity

Mind–brain identity is a monist theory which claims that only physical substances exist and that human beings are just part of the material world; therefore, mental states are identical with physical ones. The strengths of this position are clear:

- We are not faced with a dualistic position.
- We can understand why changes in the physical have mental effects.

Nevertheless, there are a number of problems with this approach:

- Being able to locate in the brain where a thought is occurring does not explain the meaning we give to that thought, or any intentions or plans that we might have as a result of it, or even rationality itself. Indeed, thoughts are different in type from neurological activity, and Bruner (1990:34) rightly, in my view, suggests that it is culture rather than biology that shapes human life, although I would not claim that biology has no influence at all.
- Mental states need not be identical with brain states. For example, an emotion or a pain (qualia) cannot be understood precisely from a brain scan.
- Intention cannot be understood from a brain scan.

There are also other objections to identity theory but I do not feel it necessary to pursue these further here. Nevertheless, while we can begin to understand how the brain functions, we can see that it does not overcome all the problems of how the mind operates, nor of the relationship between the two, and so it does not answer all the problems we have about understanding human learning.

Behaviourism

Behaviourism is a monistic theory within which a great deal of theory and policy about learning has been couched ever since the time of Pavlov. Maslin (2001:106) summarizes the behaviourist position thus: '[B]ehaviourism maintains that statements about the mind and mental states turn out, after analysis, to be statements that describe a person's actual and potential public behaviour.' Indeed, we frequently face the valid claim that 'I am, therefore, I act' – and this can, in some circumstances, be regarded as a behaviourist statement. Behaviourism does explain some of the outcomes of the learning process which can be measured, so that in an age where quantification is important, it is not surprising that behaviourism retains its attractions. Nevertheless, there are major problems with it theoretically:

- Behaviour is not the sole driving force of human being; there are others, such as meaning, or even thought itself.
- None of the objections to the mind–brain identity theory is overcome by postulating that everything can be reduced to behaviour.
- Behaviourism denies the common-sense assumption that I can actually think my own private thoughts and do not have to reveal them to anybody. To put it crudely, a good poker player could hardly be a convincing behaviourist.

While behaviourism can point to the outcomes of the learning processes, it is incapable of explaining the processes themselves.

Functionalism

Functionalism is another monistic approach which regards the mind as a function of the brain. It postulates that if we can understand all the inputs and outputs and also the state of the operating mechanism, we account for our understanding of mental states. In other words, the brain is seen as a complex computer – a picture that has become rather common in recent years. This theory has gained a great deal of currency recently because the analogy with the computer appears credible, especially now that we can also talk of artificial intelligence. But we might ask, is the human being really no more than a sophisticated computer – especially one that has been programmed to 'think'? If we were to accept this, then

9

learning could be reduced to a computer program. Indeed, Searle (1992) makes the point that thoughts have meaning and intentionality – something that a computer program performing its functions cannot have. Not only this, but computers are thoroughly rational machines that cannot deviate from their programmed logic, whereas human beings are not totally rational and they can and often do deviate from their original intentions! It was a computer specialist who invented the term 'fuzzy logic' to describe the way that we behave in contrast to the way computers function. In my own research into superstition many years ago, I discovered that all my respondents were in some way or another superstitious, or less than rational in their behaviour (Jarvis, 1980). Freudian psychology also points us beyond the bounds of rationality. Lowe (1992:99) argues that one of the problems with 'the computational approach is that it seeks to throw light on human visual cognition *without* invoking general intelligence' (*italics* in original). Maslin also raises a number of other objections, and despite the popularity of the analogy, this theory is not at all convincing. Nevertheless, it is one that has assumed a certain prominence as we have learned more about neuroscience. But if we reject it, then information processing theories of learning must automatically be seen as weak. Hence there are a number of weaknesses in this position – the major ones being that:

- Human beings are not computers – they are more than computers.
- Human beings are less rational than computers and have emotions.

Non-reductive monism

Non-reductive monism is also dualistic in terms of properties but not substances. Maslin (2001:163) describes it thus:

> It is non-reductive because it does not insist that mental properties are nothing over and above physical properties. On the contrary, it is willing to allow that mental properties are different in kind from physical properties, and not ontologically reducible to them. It is clusters and series of these mental properties which constitute our psychological lives ... property dualism dispenses with the dualism of substances and physical events, hence it is a form of monism. But these physical substances and events possess two very different kinds of property, namely physical properties and, in addition, non-physical, mental properties.

The relationship between the physical and mental properties might be described in terms of supervenience, which is 'the idea that one set of facts can fully determine another set' (Chalmers, 1996:32). There are, according to Maslin, three elements in discussions about the relationship of mind and brain:

1 Physical phenomena cannot always be reduced to mental and vice versa – there is an irreducibility.
2 The physical and the mental can vary simultaneously – co-variation.
3 The physical and the mental are not always dependent on each other.

Chalmers also makes the crucial distinction between logical and natural supervenience. A problem, then, with mental properties is that they cannot be located like physical substances – in this sense they are not a physical site and neither are they the processes that can be seen in brain scans. Consequently, Chalmers argues that consciousness per se cannot be logically reduced to a physical condition – that is, it is not logically supervenient upon the material. He has therefore ruled out the most common approach, as have others before him (see Bergson, 2004 [1912]), but he does not deny some form of dualism.

Having examined five different ways of looking at the mind–body relationship, we can find no simple theory that allows us to explain it. Exclusive claims should not logically be made for any single theory, although they are made quite widely in contemporary society. The monist and integrated theories all appear weak and this is unfortunate, since these are the ones most widely cited in contemporary society as the basis for learning. However, once we accept that learning is a matter both of the senses and of cognition, we have to accept some form of dualism, although the basic form discussed first seems to be as weak as the monist and integrationist theories in explaining the mind–body phenomenon and it may best be explained as a form of non-reductive monism. None of the theories can claim universal allegiance and in each there are problems that appear insurmountable. Nevertheless, I feel that non-reductionist monism is a relatively strong position. The human being is both physical and mental, but the mind–body relationship remains an unanswered problem.

Being and learning

Think of the beat of music, the beat of a drum – it is a universally appreciated sound, but why is it universal? Perhaps because while we were in the womb, we were exposed to the sound of the beat of our mother's heart; we learned it pre-consciously. How often do we hear of people who like a taste that their mothers liked during pregnancy? Perhaps it is because we learned to appreciate a taste while we were in the womb. We know, for instance, that the fetus's senses function as they develop in the womb, so that pre-conscious and pre-cognitive learning occur weeks before birth. Tremlin (2006:51) writes:

As early as the first trimester of a pregnancy, the fetus already possesses centers of balance and motion that respond to the mother's own movements. At the halfway point of gestation a fetus can hear. Sight remains severely muted; unlike the sense of hearing, there are few external stimuli in the uterus. But by the seventh month the eyelids are open and the fetus can see by diffused light coming through the abdominal wall. Taste, too, is working as the fetus takes in the amniotic fluid. In addition to these basic functions of sense and motor control, there is also clear evidence that the brain is busy *learning* in the womb. One example utilizes the fetus' well-developed sense of hearing. Clever experiments that chart the rhythm sucks on a rubber nipple reveal preferences for a mother's voice and other patterns of sound heard in the womb.
[*italics* in original]

We can see that from the outset, there is a sense in which learning is a biological phenomenon – but in the first instance it is pre-conscious. From before our birth we learn – not in the way that we tend to think about learning, but we still learn, and that learning continues after birth throughout our lives. This is not the place to discuss early childhood learning, but there is considerable research to show the extent of this (see Tomasello, 1995; Nelson, 2007). Moreover, we learn many of our emotions in these early months (Gerhardt, 2004) and we also learn to do things, as Tomasello and Nelson show. Knowledge, emotions and doing are all learned very early in our lives and they affect our growth and development throughout the whole of our lives. In a sense, we become aware of ourselves from very early on even though we may be incapable of conceptualizing it. This is part of what is now being called the theory of mind, because we also become aware of others as agents affecting our lives. We learn from our experiences with our mothers and with our other immediate families – for, as Buber (1958:22) claimed, 'in the beginning is relationship'.

The need to learn is more basic than the need to know; it is fundamental to our humanity, as Dewey pointed out:

> [L]ife means growth, a living creature lives as truly and positively at one stage as another, with the same intrinsic fullness and the same absolute claims. Hence education means the enterprise of supplying the conditions which insure growth, or adequacy of life, irrespective of age.
>
> (1916:51)

From the time of our birth we have to learn to function within our society or life-world. Our ability to learn develops with our development as human beings: it is through our living that we learn and through our learning that we live. We are not always conscious of our learning even though we are conscious beings; learning occurs pre-consciously, as we have already seen, and it also occurs incidentally. I once asked a group of nurse tutors to write down a definition of learning, and when they had done that, I told them to put aside their definition and I then asked them whether, when they are on a ward, they could recognize an illness by the odour that comes from an ill patient. They all said that they could, and when I asked them how they had acquired that knowledge, they said that they had learned it. But when I asked how many of them had included smell in their definitions of learning, it turned out that none had. Learning had occurred incidentally and they were unaware of the learning but they were aware of the outcome of their learning – their tacit knowledge. But this is no doubt true of all of us with sounds and smells and tastes, and so on. Learning almost becomes synonymous with consciousness, but we are not always consciously aware of the learning that takes place in our lives.

We might then ask whether there are times in our lives when we do not learn, and the answer might be that the only time when this might be the case is when people are in a vegetative state. There is some evidence that we do learn when we are asleep although these are still quite early days in research into sleep and learning. We learn because we are living human beings and much of our learning occurs through our conscious experiences, but we are forced to acknowledge that learning and consciousness are not synonymous.

We can see from this brief discussion that learning is more than a psychological phenomenon – it is a human, multidisciplinary phenomenon about which we can research and reflect, and so it also becomes a matter of philosophical debate. Later we will discuss the directions that learning theory and research are taking at this present time.

Learning social being: socialization

From our earliest days we learn to imitate; Tomasello (1999:52) regards children as 'imitation machines'. We need to be in relationship in order to learn how to do things that are fundamental to our social living. Indeed, copying is at the heart of our social learning and it is no bad thing! Think about the first time we visit a club or an organization, or even the first time we sit down at a smart meal or reception. We nearly always watch how others behave and try to copy their behaviour so that we can fit in. By imitation we begin to learn the subculture of the group, organization, etc. in which we find ourselves. Imitation is quite fundamental to our social living and basic to our learning processes, and there is a sense in which we are agents in our own socialization processes from the earliest days of our lives. In a classroom setting, one of the first jobs of teachers is to make explicit some of the patterns of behaviour that they want learners to adopt. Once the learners know what these are, they can relax a little and not have to look over their shoulders all the time to see what their fellow learners are doing.

Traditionally, every society has produced its own culture, which is carried by human beings and transmitted both through social interaction and through the educational system. Culture, in this context, refers to the sum totality of knowledge, values, beliefs, etc. of a social group. It is in the process of socialization that individuals learn their local culture. There is a sense in which some facets of education may be regarded as part of the process of socialization, although the former is usually viewed as a more formal process than the latter. Consequently, it is possible to understand precisely how Lawton (1973:21) could regard the curriculum as 'a selection from culture'. Obviously, the process of acquiring the local culture is very significant during childhood, both through socialization and education. However, sociologists regard socialization as a lifetime process having at least two aspects: primary socialization is 'the first socialization an individual undergoes ... through which he [*sic*] becomes a member of society; secondary socialization is any subsequent process that inducts an already socialized individual into new sectors of the objective world of his society' (Berger and Luckmann, 1966:150).

It is not difficult, however, to recognize that in a society where the rate of social change is very slow, such as pre-industrial Europe or a primitive tribe, it would be feasible for individuals to learn most of the cultural knowledge, norms and values necessary for them to assume their place in that society during childhood. In such societies it was only the elite, for example Plato's philosopher-kings, the priesthood, the upper classes, who continued to study esoteric knowledge during adulthood, while the remainder of the populace were regarded as having completed their education, except for the education necessary for them to assume more mature roles in society as they grew up and aged. Consequently, it is not hard to understand why a front-end model of education emerged, although it is equally obvious that such a model has little relevance to a society whose culture is changing rapidly.

From the onset of the Industrial Revolution, with the introduction of more sophisticated technology, the rate of social change increased. Indeed, change is endemic to technological societies. This means that primary socialization is insufficient. Secondary socialization becomes more significant and it is certainly more relevant for us as educators of adults. As we grow and develop, so we join other groups having their own subcultures, such as schools, leisure clubs and work, and in each of these we go through a process of secondary socialization. We learn to be a student, a club member and a worker; in other words, we learn specific behaviour associated with our position; new knowledge, new ideas, new values and

14

new practices all have to be confronted. However, as Turner (1962) showed, the process of secondary socialization is not merely a process of imitating the behaviour of other role players (behaviourist learning); we are also agents in this learning process. He (ibid.:38) showed that 'role behavior in formal organizations becomes a working compromise between the formalized role prescriptions and the more flexible operation of the role-taking process'. It is interactive rather than merely imitative and therefore we learn in more complex ways. This becomes a lifetime process and is part of the informal learning of lifelong learning. In this sense, secondary socialization continues throughout life since we frequently change jobs, change organizations to which we belong, change our status and lifestyle, and so on; it is part of our lifelong learning.

In Figure 1.3 the arc represents the all-encompassing culture into which we are born, socialized or live. The arrows represent interaction, with the direction denoting something of the process of dominance in the interaction. The inward arrows demonstrate that we internalize some of our external culture, and this comes as we learn in a number of ways ranging from personal interaction to more formal schooling to informal relationships – and we are exposed to many processes simultaneously. The outward arrows show that from very early on, we also externalize some of the things that we have learned, and so we are also change agents from the outset. This also happens in social interaction.

In primitive society it was possible to describe this arc as a single culture, but now this all-encompassing culture is what might also be described as multicultural. However, the issues are even bigger than this, as the generation gap signifies – as we age, we do not all keep up with all the cultural changes experienced by the young. Indeed, some of their primary socialization processes are learning experiences that their grandparents have never had! Now the young can teach the old about the new as well as the old teach the young about other aspects of culture; inter-generational learning is both a way of family life and a necessity in contemporary

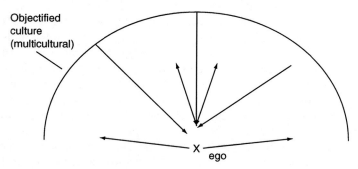

Figure 1.3 The socialization process.

15

society. Culture is really a problematic concept and merely describing it as all-encompassing does not obviate the problem, since it is not even the same phenomenon for all people in the same area. For instance, young people in the United Kingdom still grow up with their ethnic cultures even though they also acquire a sense of 'Britishness'; they may also have a sense of being a Muslim, say. The same is true for the United States and for every other country. We all have our own cultures and our own life-worlds, and it is perhaps better now to recognize that we all have our own life-worlds and they all reflect our individuality. Consequently, in this global society, individuals are exposed to many more local cultures; it is as if each was a subculture of a more global culture, and so it is easier to talk about our life-worlds. O'Neill (2003) has studied the way in which young males acquire their identities in a residential school and he has shown quite clearly that their self-identity is often not acquired through the culture of the school, but rather their social identity is formed by their wider social and family environment, although both combine to form their life-worlds. Consequently, we can see the process whereby people acquire multiple identities.

The fact that we are born into different cultural groups is indicative of the way in which there are pressures on all of us to conform to the groups of which we are members. Membership really implies conformity to the rules and regulations of the group, and we can see that education and social learning both exercise conformist pressures upon the group's membership – and especially during primary and secondary socialization processes. Those who exercise power in the group do have the ability to influence or control the content of what is transmitted; this is in the nature of power. It is not surprising, therefore, that throughout this book we will meet some more critical and radical perspectives.

Education has many purposes and functions (see Schuller *et al.*, 2004 on the hidden benefits of learning), but clearly it is an important agency in assisting individuals to respond to the rapid social change. Because it is so rapid, it is necessary for individuals to keep learning, so that they should not become alienated from the culture that engulfs them, but we can also understand that this is a way in which individualization emerges. The more technologically based the society, the easier it is for individuals to become alienated unless they keep on learning, but as they learn they become more differentiated individuals, and we note, for example, that more people are choosing to live alone as they develop their own individuality. All are affected by the changes in technology, as evidenced by the computer, the mobile phone, the iPod, and so on. Hence, individuals need to learn new knowledge to prevent the onset of alienation or anomie; lifelong learning – even lifelong education – helps them adjust to the cultural changes prevalent in their society, but, paradoxically, the more they learn, the greater the likelihood that they become individualized and perhaps alienated. (Given the fact that all people are born with a unique genetic inheritance, individualization is exacerbated by lifelong learning.) It is thus clear that many individuals have lost the security of a single dominant local subculture, which helped provide them both with a sense of membership of a community and with an identity. For some people this new situation is at the heart of identity crises, which Giddens (1991) refers to as 'existential anxiety'. He also notes how personal counselling has mushroomed as a result of these changes.

There is also resistance to the process of cultures merging and standardizing, and some local cultures are seeking to retain something of their difference in the fact of modern communications systems. Being exposed to other local cultures is now a lifetime process – a process of lifelong learning. Similarly, education may be regarded as a lifelong process, and further reference will be made to the concepts of learning and education and lifelong learning and life-wide learning later in this book.

Individuals do not just receive passively all of these changes; rather, they process and change them as part of the process of cultural change. Hence, human beings not only are born into a changing culture, but are part of the process. Their adaptation to this ever-changing society is a learning process, and all forms of education assist people in processing and adapting to these changes throughout the whole of their lives. In this sense human beings are lifelong learners. The provision of education for people of all ages is essential because it helps to facilitate this quest to understand our world, which is at the heart of humanity itself.

Conclusion

Learning, therefore, is an existential process – it is almost coterminous with life itself: it begins in the womb and probably finishes as we approach death. Learning begins with sense experience and is both individual and social, and we begin our social learning through imitation. At the same time, we acknowledge that the nature–nurture debate is an important one and that we have both an evolutionary and a social history. Conformity is, therefore, one of the natural outcomes of learning, although we recognize from the outset the need to resist it sometimes, and so it is necessary to see the significance of critical learning to resist the power inherent in group structures to force us to conform. But we also recognize that the society in which we live is changing rapidly, and so the next chapter examines that rapidly changing context within which we learn.

Note

1   This section summarizes the discussion in Jarvis (2006).

2

THE LEARNING SOCIETY

In the previous chapter I suggested that the individual's life-world reflects the changing culture of society and that there have been tremendous changes over the past few decades. It is these changes that have been a major reason for the changes in our attitudes towards, and practices of, education and learning. In this chapter we will examine these social changes and in the following one we will see how they have affected education, learning and educational policy. This chapter will have two major parts: globalization and the learning society.

Globalization

Globalization has become a buzzword with many different meanings and different interpretations placed upon it, and so it is first of all necessary to understand how we will use the term in this book. I shall then describe the process of globalization and provide an explanation for the process. Finally, in this first section we will look at the speed at which society has changed and try to explain why such rapid change has occurred.

Global change, as we know it today, began in the West at the end of the Second World War. Before then, each society had a great deal of territorial sovereignty, but in the past half-century things have changed quite fundamentally, driven by, among other things, industrial capitalism, information technology and even technology itself. There were a number of contributory factors at this time that exacerbated this process, such as:

- the oil crisis in the 1970s, which dented the confidence of the West;
- the demise of the Bretton Woods Agreement, which eventually enabled both free trade and the flow of financial capital to develop throughout the world;
- the development of sophisticated information technology, initially through the 'Star Wars' programme, through which the information technology revolution took off, with one development leading to another, as Castells (1996:51f.) demonstrates. He (ibid.:52) makes the

point that 'to some extent, the availability of new technologies constituted as a system in the 1970s was a fundamental basis for the process
of socio-economic restructuring in the 1980s';

- economic competition from Japan, which challenged the West;
- the use of scientific knowledge in the production of commodities in
the global market;
- the fall of the Berlin Wall and the democratization of the Eastern bloc
– for, from the time it occurred, there has literally been 'no alternative' (Bauman, 1992) to global capitalism, and so it reinforced the
process.

It was at this same period in the 1970s that theorists, recognizing these
processes, first began to suggest that there was actually a world economy
(e.g. Wallerstein, 1974) based on the capitalist system of exchange. His
approach was questioned in part by Robertson (1995), among others. Castells (1996) also argued that the state still had a place to play in a not completely free but extremely competitive global market. Nevertheless,
corporations began to relocate manufacturing and to transfer capital
around the world from about the early 1970s, seeking the cheapest places
and the most efficient means to manufacture, and the best markets in
which to sell, their products so that an international division of labour has
been created and a competitive international market generated. Additionally, the corporations have been able to locate themselves in countries
where they have to pay extremely low (even immoral) wages and less tax,
and thus underplay their responsibility to the world (see Cohen, 2002, for
a recent example), although some of them seek to persuade the world
that they are exercising social responsibility by establishing charitable
foundations or contributing some financial and intellectual assistance to
underprivileged peoples, or to other needy causes. As manufacturing was
relocated, new knowledge-based industries have taken their place in the
West, and this has had a phenomenal effect on the nature of education
and learning – but, significantly, it has also had an effect on those countries where manufacturing and service industries have been located.

It is as if these phenomena form the basis that has driven many countries in the world, since they are common to these countries; it is as if the
world has a common core, or substructure, and we see it when we travel
because we see the same adverts, the same goods for sale, and so on. This
global world with this common core can be depicted as shown in Figure
2.1 (Jarvis, 2007a, 2008).

The core running through all the different countries exercises a centralized power in each of the countries, and in this sense it is a force for
convergence between the different countries of the world. Those who control it exercise global power, and that control rests with large transnational
corporations and banks whose directors are unelected and very powerful.

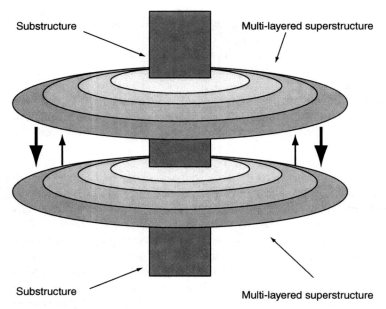

Substructure   Multi-layered superstructure

Substructure   Multi-layered superstructure

Figure 2.1 A global model of societies.

Note: Multi-layered governance is a concept first utilized by Held *et al.* (1999:62–77), although I have adopted it in a simpler manner here.

But these forces are supported by the one superpower, the United States, which is a part of the substructure. Monbiot (2007) illustrated the point nicely: the issue was breastfeeding or bottle-milk feeding of children in the Philippines. Mothers were always encouraged to feed their own children because using contaminated water – and much water in the Philippines is contaminated – in bottle-milk feeding is dangerous; 16,000 children a year die as a result of this inappropriate feeding practice. But powdered milk is produced in the rich Western nations and the incidence of children's disease has increased dramatically, which both the Philippines government and the United Nations blame on a decline in breastfeeding. In order to try to stem the incidence of bottle-feeding, the Philippines government drew up a series of rules designed to prevent the advertising of powdered milk (since there had been a misleading advertising campaign by industry, trying to persuade more women to give bottled milk to their children). Immediately, these rules were contested in court by the industry representatives, but their contestation was defeated. Then, as Monbiot (2007:33) puts it,

> ... the big guns arrived.
> The US embassy and the US regional trade representative

started lobbying the Philippines government. Then the chief executive of the US Chamber of Commerce – which represents 3m businesses – wrote a letter to the Philippines president … [claiming that] the new rules would have unintended consequences for investors' confidence.

Four days later the court decision was reversed and the Philippines government was unable to prevent companies from selling their products despite the danger to the children. The US government had acted as a part of the global substructure, giving it the political power that the corporations otherwise would not have had. At present the United States is part of the global substructure (through Americanization), although the situation may be changing. Power, political as well as socio-economic, resides in the global substructure but it can also be exercised between countries through political, trade, aid and other international mechanisms.

In Figure 2.1, each country is represented by one of the disks and may be depicted as shown in Figure 2.2.

At the heart of each society – certainly in the West – is the core, which exercises power over the whole society. The next most powerful group in most societies is made up of the international agencies – in the United Kingdom, one could say the European Commission, but in some other countries it is the World Bank and the International Monetary Fund. Only when we reach the third level do we come to national governments and then local and regional agencies. This means that the idea of national territorial sovereignty has long disappeared, and even national political leaders have only limited power. The two arrows represent democracy, with

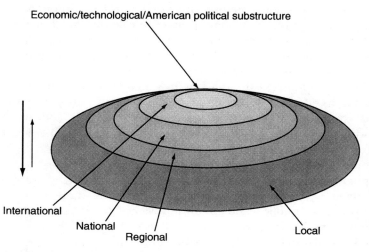

Economic/technological/American political substructure

International

National

Regional

Local

Figure 2.2 A multi-layered model of society.

the downwards-pointing arrow much more powerful than the upwards-pointing ones. However, it is significant that the credit crunch that started in 2007 has meant that the politicians actually gained some control of the financial markets once again, so that the third layer actually has regained power over the core temporarily, but whether there will be sufficient exercise of power from the politicians to continute to control the core is another matter.

When we look at these two figures we can see that the first thing to note is that the substructure is united and runs through all the different countries but the individual countries are not. There is an apparent unity in the core which means that its constituent members can agree on the aims and functions of the centre, although there is also internal competition since each constituent company or organization is competing with many others to produce products that can be marketed throughout the world. The fact that there is internal competition means that the speed of change within the core is fast, driven by the demands of the market which it is both creating and seeking to respond to. It is therefore changing faster than those aspects of the global system that are not so market driven and so it produces a driving force for change in each country. Additionally, it is necessary to recognize that change is neither gradual nor even, since new discoveries and huge advertising campaigns tend to generate change in fits and starts.

Since the transnational corporations in the core compete with each other to sell commodities, they have to generate new ones at the cheapest rates in order to be competitive throughout the world. Politicians, says Habermas (2006), were left behind, powerless, and they could either seek to catch up or endeavour to protect their people from the ravages of global capitalism. At that time neither appeared possible, although the strong welfare states did play a stronger protective role than weak states – such as the United Kingdom – during the period of neo-liberal economics. Because transnational corporations need to manufacture new commodities and to produce them most efficiently, they demand new knowledge and new skills appropriate to the markets in which they are competing, and this has had its effect on education at every level, since not all subjects are relevant to this global capitalist world. Kerr and his colleagues (1973:47), who propounded the logic of industrialism thesis, predicted this:

> The higher educational system of industrial society stresses the natural sciences, engineering, medicine, managerial training – whether private or public – and administrative law. It must steadily adapt to new disciplines and new fields of specialization. There is a relatively smaller place for the humanities and the arts, while the social sciences are strongly related to the training of managerial

groups and technicians for the enterprise and the government. The increased leisure time of industrialism, however, can afford a broader public appreciation of the humanities and the arts.

The arts and the humanities are distinguished from the really 'useful' subjects such as the sciences and social sciences; the transnational corporations consigned the humanities to leisure time, and for them education was to be the handmaiden of industry, taking the raw material of humanity and turning it into the human resources that would drive the world. This is precisely what has occurred since Kerr *et al.* wrote these words – and even post-school education has been placed within the ambit of the Minister for Business and Industry in the 2009 British government! Adult educators know that, in the United Kingdom at least, many of the liberal adult education subjects not only have been consigned to leisure time but have been priced at such an exorbitant fee that few people are able to afford to enrol in them. But as the market makes new demands, so it is necessary to learn new knowledge and new skills to produce new commodities, and so we have seen the development of lifelong learning – not lifelong education, as we will discuss in the next chapter. Learning, then, is a human process that we all undertake from the earliest times of our life, whereas education is a social process that controls and constrains our learning in a wide variety of ways. But those who control the educational process exercise the major power in teaching and learning since they control the content, so that those who have the greatest social educational needs – the industrialists – have now assumed a very powerful place in society. They are able to dictate what they expect their employees to learn, which places their demands at the forefront of the educational sector. Universities are expected to create a workforce through their teaching, as Lyotard (1984:48) wrote of universities, although it is much more widely applicable:

> In the context of delegitimation, universities and institutions of higher learning are called upon to create skills, and no longer ideals – so many doctors, so many teachers in a given discipline, so many engineers, so many administrators, etc. The transmission of knowledge is no longer designed to train an elite capable of guiding the nation towards its emancipation, but to supply the system with players capable of acceptably fulfilling their roles at the pragmatic posts required by its institutions.

However, during the time of writing this chapter a massive change occurred in the global world as a result of the credit crunch: no longer could the core of society be seen as the most powerful part of society; neo-liberal economic capitalism has failed and the large corporations can no

23

longer maintain themselves and dictate to the world. In a sense, the market is no longer sovereign. The credit crunch arrived and we had an over-production of debt! The states had to step in – the politicians have, in Habermas's language, been given a chance to catch up, and they have seized it eagerly. At the beginning of April 2009 the first G20 summit was called. Now for some countries, the third layer of society – the national governments – exerted its latent power and united, to some extent, to try to regulate neo-liberal economic capitalism. Yet while neo-liberal economics has failed, this does not mean that the demands that the core makes on education will change. If anything, because of the shortage of capital, non-vocational education will be even more starved of funds than it was previously, and more subject departments will close, and so on.

It is clear from this analysis that not only is education controlled by the economics of the situation, but it is also a political phenomenon, although few political studies of the education of adults exist (see Torres, 2009). Education will become even more functionally orientated – as part of the Ministry for Business and Industry – as the need to generate more goods and services in order to recreate consumerism.

During this same period, however, there has been a growing awareness that many of the poor of the world have largely been illiterate, and so UNESCO and the United Nations, and some other agencies, have introduced a literacy campaign. The argument has always been that only by being literate could the poor people play their part in the global world economy. Once education is seen in this way, it is politicized. It is not surprising, therefore, that the work of Paulo Freire became very popular at one time, but careful analysis of Freire's work is important to understand where and why it has been successful and where it has been less successful. Freire always presented his understanding of education as being a servant of the people or community in a time of political unrest, so that it was very successful in Latin America but less successful in Africa, where he also worked for a number of years. For instance, Oliveira and Oliveira (1976:49) suggest that

> [i]f the literacy campaign is to go beyond the celebration of the past [a political unrest generated by the people] and provide an opening towards the future ... the chosen region must be in the process of experiencing a socio-economic transformation. This point seems particularly important to us, for it is questionable whether learning to read and write corresponds to the real need of the peasant living in a rural area who continues to produce in traditional ways.
>
> (quoted in Torres, 2009:165)

The point Oliveira and Oliveira are making is precisely the same point as Kerr *et al.* made: education has to be relevant to the social demands of the society and to the desires of the people. Unless it is perceived to be relevant – not just theoretically so – the literacy campaign will not survive, as a number of research undertakings have shown. My own PhD student showed how in Nepal, once the UNESCO officials left any literacy endeavour, it soon died (Laksamba, 2005). Indeed, despite all the aid given to Nepal, while the literacy rate had improved, it was not presented to the people in the politically relevant terms of Freire. Had it been, it might have been more successful.

It is clear from the discussion thus far that society has a need for us to learn to be useful members, and so public education is designed to respond to the needs of society – both work and citizenship needs – so that it has to direct learning both through education and through the use of the mass media. During the period of market liberalism, the needs of the substructure of the global society have dominated, and even the needs of the state have had to play second fiddle, but as the state has been subservient to the needs of the market, it has directed the educational system to respond to these market needs. For, as Bauman (1999:156) noted:

> Once the state recognizes the priority and superiority of the laws of the market over the laws of the *polis*, the citizen is transmuted into the consumer, and a 'consumer demands more and more protection while accepting less and less the need to participate' in the running of the state. [*italics* in original]

In this sense, we can see the validity of Marx's analysis of the power of capital – even though the power is now vested in those corporations that control capital, technology and information technology, as I have argued elsewhere (Jarvis, 2008, 2009a).

Emergence of the learning society

As part of the process of globalization, we see the emergence of the information society, the knowledge economy and the learning society. In this section we will look briefly at all three, spending more time on the final one since we will also look at learning regions and so on.

The information society

The process of conveying information between people begins with language (first body and then verbal language), and this is enhanced as literacy is developed. This allows for written information to be conveyed between people at great distances through a variety of means of transport, but it was the invention of the wireless and the telegraph that made it possible for information to be conveyed at speed over vast distances. Conveyance of information, therefore, depended upon the level of technology developed and utilized for this purpose, and so it was with the development of the computer and electronic means of transfer that the information society, as we now know it, came into being, and with it what Castells (1996) called the network society.

However, we do have to recognize that the information carried and transmitted by technology almost always has use-value, and in this sense it is far from value-free – although those who provide that information and those who seek it are in a market exchange situation and so we see that the predominant culture of the capitalist system prevails and the information that has potentially the most use-value is the most valuable. In our model of globalization, we can see that technology, especially information technology, is at the heart of the substructure of the globalization process. But of the other two strands, we have the economic institution, namely advanced capitalism and the supporting might of the United States. Capitalism is the driving force of change and even for the introduction of advanced technology. The competition between transnational corporations means that the more cheaply they can produce commodities and the wider their markets, the greater their profitability. As Castells (1996:81) puts it, 'Profitability and competitiveness are the actual determinants of technological innovation and productivity growth.' Consequently, in the 1960s and 1970s we saw the introduction of the network society in which there was an internationalization of capital. Castells (ibid.:85) writes:

> By extending its global outreach, integrating markets, and maximizing advantages of location, capital, capitalists, and capitalist firms have, as a whole, substantially increased their profitability in the last decade, and particularly in the 1980s, restoring for the time being the preconditions for investment on which the capitalist economy depends.

The introduction of advanced technology, information technology, facilitated the further development of capitalism and legitimated the network, and therefore the information society. This movement towards technology led wrongly to a downgrading of industrial production, and so ideas such as the post-industrial society emerged. For Daniel Bell, for instance, 'knowledge and information ... [became] ... the strategic resource and transforming agent of the post-industrial society' (1973:531).

Webster (2002) suggests that there are five theories of the information society: technological, economic, occupational, spatial and cultural. He discusses all five approaches:

1 a vast array of innovatons that have appeared since the late 1970s;
2 the economic worth of informational activities;

3 the preponderance of occupations are to be found in knowledge work;

4 information networks that connect locations and consequently affect the way that time and space are organized;

5 contemporary culture, which is information-laden.

He concludes that as definitions they are 'either or both underdeveloped or imprecise' (ibid.:21). He suggests that while these descriptions are a useful device for exploring features of the contemporary world, they are unacceptable as definitions: Webster (ibid.:261) has 'quite forcefully rejected the concept of the information society, even though it is much used in and outside the social sciences'. He rightly acknowledges that it is not an entirely worthless concept but it is one that does not define today's society. Nevertheless, it does describe aspects of one of its dominant characteristics.

Webster (2002:141) also refers to the work of Schiller (1981:25), whose discussion comes very close to our model:

> What is called the 'information society' is, in fact, the production, processing, and transmission of a very large amount of data about all sorts of matters – individual and national, social and commercial, economic and military. Most of the data are produced to meet very specific needs of super-corporations, national and government bureaucracies, and the military establishments of the advanced industrial state.

Once these communication technologies have been established, a new information medium exists for the domination of society and its peoples: advertising. Basically, it offers information to people about the products that have been produced by the corporations, but it is very clear that its functions are more fundamental than this. Through psychological techniques, advertising creates desires and demands that create false needs; it serves as an agency for imposing lifestyles on people, and consequently for perpetuating the advanced capitalist system, since without consumption the system would collapse. It is in this society that we begin to understand that the education of adults is now occurring – but these changes have also caused us to rethink our understanding of knowledge itself.

The knowledge economy

During the process of globalization, transnational corporations looked for the cheapest ways of manufacturing commodities and we witnessed a massive transfer of manufacturing production from the West to less developed countries where the wages were a lot lower and the labour was neither organized nor unionized. This allowed corporations to exploit the poor in order to produce commodities for the more wealthy markets at the cheapest possible price. Over the years we have heard of sweatshop practices and see television programmes about the terrible exploitation of the poor while the corporations mouth mantras about their concern for the poor and how they are always doing their best for them. This is something that is rarely proven since none of the corporations is prepared to have an independent inquiry about the conditions under which its workers are expected to live. Bauman (1999:5–6) summarized a United Nations development report that illustrates these points:

- Consumption has multiplied by a factor of six since 1950, but 1 billion people cannot satisfy even their most elementary needs.
- Sixty per cent of residents in developing countries have no basic social infrastructures, 33 per cent no access to drinking water, 25 per cent no accommodation worthy of the name and 20 per cent no sanitary or medical services.
- The average income of 120 million people is less than $1 per day.
- In the world's richest country (the United States), 16.5 per cent of people live in poverty, 20 per cent of the adult population are illiterate and 13 per cent have a life expectancy of less than 60 years.
- The world's three richest men have private assets greater than the combined national products of the forty-eight poorest countries.
- The fortunes of the fifteen richest men exceed the total produce of the whole of sub-Saharan Africa.
- Four per cent of the wealth of the world's richest 225 men would offer the poor of the world access to elementary medical and educational amenities as well as adequate nutrition.

The poor do not often get wealthier as a result of a great deal of manufacturing that has been located in their countries – although a few individuals do, and the wealthy use and control knowledge for their own ends. Thus, we need to examine the nature of knowledge in these societies.

Stehr (1994) suggested that the knowledge society is based not on all forms of knowledge, but on scientific knowledge. But this knowledge has grown in volume and changes rapidly, so that Senge (1990:69) makes a significant point that perhaps for the first time in human history, humankind now produces more knowledge than people can absorb, but the knowledge economy fails to utilize a great deal of the knowledge that exists. Crudely, it divides knowledge into useful knowledge and the remainder, which is regarded wrongly as much less useful, and this has affected the way that we think about knowledge, since it is mainly only the 'useful knowledge' that is included in curricula and funded by governments. The types of knowledge necessary for us to learn in order to live together and care for the planet are omitted (see Jarvis, 2008, for a full discussion of this). This is precisely the point that Kerr *et al.* were making in the passage quoted earlier.

The learning society

We can divide knowledge into four types: fact, data, information and knowledge. Only the last is learned; the other three are objective and remain outside the person. Facts have no meaning but they can be data that contribute towards the building of meaning, while information can be another person's knowledge that the recipients have to learn in order for it to become their knowledge. The more rapidly knowledge changes, the more the recipients have to learn and the more society emphasizes this need to learn. The learning society – as a concept – is therefore the inevitable outcome of societies focusing on both information and knowledge.

The learning society, however, is both a confused and a confusing idea that requires some explication, but in this instance the learning society is associated with social change. The more prevalent or profound the changes that occur in a society, the greater the likelihood that it will be regarded as a learning society because its members have to learn in order to keep abreast with structural and work-based changes. There is a clear sense that there are two different types of knowledge: that necessary for social and cultural life, which once we have learned we can take for granted; and that which is work-based in order to increase consumption or that which is necessary for the military defence of the people. Knowledge necessary for social and cultural life often changes very slowly, a feature that is essential for social stability, whereas the demands of capitalism require new knowledge so that the latter changes very rapidly, thereby demanding a greater emphasis on learning. There must be both learning and non-learning in social living. To some extent, traditional society is premised on non-learning because we expect things to remain the same, whereas modern societies change rapidly and so learning societies have emerged.

However, Coffield (2000:28) suggests that as a result of the research projects for the learning society programme in the United Kingdom, for which he was the ESRC coordinator, 'all talk of *the* learning society will have to be abandoned rather than refined' (*italics* in original). He says that there are simply too many modern and post-modern readings of the term for any general agreement on one approach or model to be possible. He highlights ten different approaches to teaching and learning that can be detected in the various research projects on which he (ibid.:8) reports:

 1 skills growth;
 2 personal development;
 3 social learning;
 4 a learning market;
 5 local learning societies;
 6 social control;
 7 self-evaluation;
 8 centrality of learning;
 9 a reformed system of education;
10 structural change.

A number of things emerge from these. First, they are not different models of society but different emphases on the learning in the society being studied. Second, they may be describing something of the fragmentation of contemporary post-modern society. Third, they have neither a sophisticated nor an agreed model of learning on which to base the analysis, which prevents genuine comparison of the fourteen projects; this is something of which Coffield is acutely aware. Since all the ESRC projects were conducted in the United Kingdom, I want to argue that these projects have actually demonstrated that learning, in a variety of different forms, is becoming generally accepted in the culture of society – but whether there is enough evidence to say that fourteen projects are sufficient to indicate changes in the whole of society is debatable.

Coffield's ten approaches indicate that the forces of change do not produce standardized responses, but we should not expect this unless we have a deterministic model of society. Nevertheless, we can see that it is possible to reduce his number of categories to four:

1 *personal development* – personal development, self-evaluation, centrality of learning;
2 *utopian vision* – social learning, structural change;
3 *planned development* – social control, skills growth, a reformed system of education, local learning societies;
4 *market* – a learning market.

The personal development issues occur naturally in any learning process and so they are not distinctive to the learning society, but if the development is controlled and directed, then it involves planning and falls into the category of planned development, or strategy. The other two – vision and market – are distinctly different from each other.

However, one aspect of a learning society not touched upon in Coffield's report is that of everyday learning, which occurs in what Beck (1992) calls reflexive modernity. Coffield (2000:22) makes an implicit reference to this when he claims that the phrase 'We're all learning all the time' is anodyne. The fact that we are being forced to learn all the time is actually the very basis of a learning society, rather than an educative one, something that underlies many of the projects in this programme. Society is changing so rapidly that many of the traditional educative organizations are not able to keep abreast with the new demands, and so individuals are forced to learn outside of the education system. Much of this is either unplanned or uncontrolled, or both, but it is an aspect crucial to contemporary society – for the learning society is also reflexive. This form of everyday learning is a crucial dimension of the learning society but it is one that cannot be controlled, something that is very important when we consider the complex nature of teaching. Only those who have disengaged from society are not really being forced to learn a great deal, and even they are still exposed to some of the forces of change. However, one of the indicators that learning is embedded in the practices of society is the fact that organizations, regions and cities are all claiming the title of learning organization, learning region and learning city or town, and so on.

Learning organizations were slow to emerge because of the bureaucratic pressures of traditional organizational structures. Argyris and Schön (1978:26) claim that since the Second World War it has gradually become apparent not only to business firms but to all types of organizations that the requirements of organizational learning are growing. In the introduction to their book (ibid.:1–5) they produce a case study that shows how five workers at one level of a company were convinced that a product was a failure six years before the decision by senior management was taken to stop producing it. At first, the subordinates believed that the errors could be corrected by hard work but as they struggled, they realized that this was not sufficient, but senior management were still promoting the product as a winner. Eventually, they composed memos to middle management explaining the problems, but management found the memos too forthright. They also doubted them because previous studies had not predicted this situation. Having taken a 'reality check', they then wanted time to see whether they could correct the situation. When, finally, they decided that they had to communicate to senior management what they had discovered, they had to compose memos in carefully structured doses so that the bad news could gradually dawn upon senior management – but this actually took a lot of time. The learning of some individuals took nearly six years to permeate to the hierarchy because their learning had to be mediated through the power structures, which prevented changes occurring as rapidly as they should have done. Now Argyris and Schön rightly focus upon the need to change procedures, which they incorporate in the idea of organizational learning, but they actually play down discussion of the power relationships within the organization that prevented the lower hierarchical orders communicating rapidly to the upper levels without risking their own position. They write (ibid.:28):

Organizational learning occurs when members of the organization act as learning agents for the organization, responding to the internal and external environments of the organization by detecting and correcting errors in organizational theory-in-use, and embedding the results of their inquiry in private images and shared maps of organization.

The characteristics of this type of organization – the learning organization, as it has come to be called – are summarized by Clarke (2001:3):

- Team working and learning occur.
- It has a culture of cross-organizational working.
- It has a system of shared beliefs, goals and objectives.
- Individuals, teams and the organization all learn from experience.
- Individual, team and organizational learning are valued.
- The development of new ideas, methods and processes is encouraged.
- Risk-taking is encouraged.
- Responsibility and authority are delegated.
- Everybody is encouraged and expected to perform to their maximum ability.

But these characteristics are not the same as those suggested by other theorists. Pedler *et al.* (1997:15) suggest the following:

- a learning approach to strategy;
- participative policy making;
- informating;
- formative accounting and control;
- internal exchange;
- reward flexibility;
- enabling structures;
- boundary workers as environmental scanners;
- inter-company learning;
- a learning climate;
- self-development opportunities for all.

Neither are they the same as those given by Longworth (1999:215). For him, a learning organization is an organization that:

- needs to improve its performance through learning;
- invests in its future through education and training of its own staff;
- encourages its staff to fulfil their human potential;
- shares its vision of tomorrow with its people and stimulates them to respond to the challenge;

- integrates work and learning and inspires its people to seek excellence;
- mobilizes its human talent;
- empowers all its staff to broaden their horizons;
- applies up-to-date delivery technologies to create more learning opportunities;
- responds proactively to the needs of the environment;
- continues to learn and relearn.

While there are similarities between these three lists, there are also profound differences, but in none is power a major issue, and therefore for these and other reasons the analyses are open to question. Now it could be argued that Pedler *et al.* have a different audience, but they could also be describing different types of organization under the same title, so that these differences call into question the concept of learning as it is used here. We shall return to this point. However, we can also see from the above that different writers on learning organizations certainly produce different lists of characteristics, so that the very least we can say is that there is not only one type of organization to which the term 'learning' might be applied. In addition, a learning organization, if such a phenomenon actually exists, need not only be a work-based one; churches, for instance, might be learning organizations, as might other non-governmental organizations.

It is also the relationship between personal learning and the organization that Senge (1990) addressed in *The Fifth Discipline*. His first four disciplines are personal: how we think, what we want, how we interact and how we learn from one another (ibid.:11). His fifth discipline is systems thinking, which is social, when integration of thought and practice in a shared vision across the whole organization can stimulate change and efficiency in an organization. For Senge (ibid.:13), a learning organization is a place where individuals are 'continually discovering how they can create their reality' – it is a place of discovery, growth and development that results in more dynamic and creative solutions. In this sense, once again the organizational hierarchy has gone, as has the power inherent in it. There is an openness that encourages not only sharing of ideas but a genuine dialogue that can be really creative. However, Senge concludes that in order to create such procedures, what is required is a new type of management practitioner, more a leader than a traditional manager, and here Senge clearly recognizes the dimension of power. As he says (ibid.:139), 'Organizations learn only through individuals who learn [but] individual learning does not guarantee organizational learning', and implementing this learning ultimately rests with management, which has the requisite authority and leadership expertise to implement and carry through successfully the changes that it feels are necessary. Basically, then, learning in the learning

organization is personal and private and more open, but what are important are the social outcomes of learning that have been implemented in
the company in order to make it more competitive in the global market.

Senge's use of systems theory is important since it is a recognized sociological theory that has been discussed by many scholars over the years. It is
an organizational theory that has not commanded universal acclaim
among organization theorists in the way that Senge's book has acquired
fame among managers. Systems theory is open to critical discussion on at
least seven counts, according to Abercrombie *et al.* (2000:354–355):

1 It cannot deal adequately with conflict or change.
2 Its assumptions about equilibrium on society are based on a conservative ideology.
3 It is so abstract that its empirical references are hard to detect.
4 Its assumptions about value consensus are not well grounded.
5 It is difficult to reconcile assumptions about structural procedures
   with a theory of action.
6 The teleological assumptions cannot explain underdevelopment or
   underutilization.
7 It is tautologous and vacuous.

I have already highlighted some of these in the foregoing discussion, and
we could proceed to argue that the persons within the organization, and
their learning, are not really considered within the framework of power.
Indeed, change only happens when power is exerted within the organization itself – by managers! Hence, the learning organization appears to be
a management theory for managers but it is weak conceptually, sociologi-
cally and educationally.

It is necessary, therefore, to recognize that power is not the only issue
that needs to be understood in the learning organization; it is also necessary to understand who the trendsetters are and how innovations spread
through the company. People are important in the process, and it is
people, as actors – change agents – who are played down in these discussions. Thus, it is important to return to re-examine the relationship
between structure and action and learning.

What many writers on learning organizations do not focus upon is the
idea of human capital (Schultz, 1961) since they emphasize the way that
individuals might grow, not the way that they can be used. But those who
control organizations control workers, and if the workforce is to be
regarded as capital, then they control both the financial and the human
capital of the organization. Consequently, for organizations to become
Investors in People makes good sense in the knowledge economy, since it
is through ensuring that workers continue to learn that the organization
becomes more effective. But the reason for investing in the workforce is

not necessarily for the benefit of the worker; rather, it is for the gain of the organization. The recipients of the investment are not the reason for the investment; the profits are – although the individuals might well benefit themselves through the organized learning that they have undertaken. Some non-governmental organizations, however, which are Investors in People may, but need not, have made their investment mainly for the benefit of their workforce. Clearly, the workers may gain a lot from their learning, but if they are human capital, then they are not ends in themselves but means to other ends – something contrary to Kant's argument that people are ends and not means! Human capital, as a concept, implies power and suggests that learning by workers is a means to another end. Having a flexible workforce, able to respond to the demands of the management and of external forces, is essential to organizations that have to keep adapting to the pressures that global capitalism exercises.

The learning organization is different from bureaucracy, not because it does not have a hierarchy, but because the hierarchy have learned to create more open procedures for information processing so that they can facilitate or implement directly the outcomes that they and others in the organization have learned. The learning organization is the antithesis of the bureaucratic organization in the sense of having a more responsive management in implementing new procedures and, maybe, in creating a slightly flatter organization so that information can flow from bottom to top, and vice versa, more quickly. But it is not different in the oligarchic sense; the changes have been forced upon those who occupy places in the hierarchy by the forces of global capitalism, which demand that productive organizations become more competitive in order to survive. It is the hierarchy that has to implement new procedures and persuade the workers to adopt them, even to go to additional education and training so that they are better equipped to do so. But as most of the literature about learning organizations is written by management theorists for practising managers, the issues of power and control are not as significant since these can be assumed. Rather, their concern is in producing results, so that most of these studies concentrate on generating the procedures that will enable the organization to become more profitable – ultimately for their shareholders' benefit. Consequently, the emphasis now transfers to leadership! Nevertheless, one can note a fundamental weakness in these as academic studies of organizations. An interesting paradox emerges from this – that in order to be effective and efficient in a competitive world, those within the organization need to be open and share with each other. Perhaps it is a lesson that global capitalism needs to take unto itself as we contemplate the world that global capitalism is helping to create!

One of the other outcomes of globalization has been that we have become more aware of the local – a form of glocalization. Robertson (1995:31) makes the point that 'there is an increasingly globe-wide discourse of locality, community, home, and the like', and so it is not surprising that there should be a focus on the local. The information society and its network counterpart have also assisted in this development as the ideas of the learning region and the learning city have arisen, in which local information networks have been established. In fact, we might see the learning region and learning city as new forms of community education, and consequently we will discuss both of these together since they are very similar in structure.

In the same way as we noted that the concepts of society and organization are reified in the above discussions, so we see the same process happening with the learning city:

> A learning city is one which strives to learn how to renew itself in a period of extraordinary social change. The rapid spread of new technologies presents considerable opportunities for countries and regions to benefit from the transfer of new knowledge and ideas across national boundaries. At the same time global shifts in capital flows and production are creating uncertainties and risk in managing national and local economies.
> (Department for Education and Employment (DfEE), 1998b:1)

The DfEE definition of the learning city actually goes on to explain something of the origins of the idea – both global and local use of capital and technology. While many of the initiatives for learning cities and learning regions have come from adult educators, support is necessary from local government and local business and commerce. In fact, Longworth (1999:114) suggests that the network consists of:

- primary and secondary education;
- universities and tertiary education;
- industry, business and commerce;
- professional bodies and special interest groups;
- adult and vocational education;
- social services and voluntary organizations;
- local government.

The learning city idea also comes from the same period as many other concepts discussed in this book: the early 1970s. The purposes of the learning city are to support lifelong learning and to learn how to promote social and economic regeneration (Department for Education and Employment (DfEE), 1998b:1). The DfEE document sees the tasks of the learning city as partnership, participation and performance. But the first international meeting about the learning city did not happen until 1990, when one was organized in Barcelona. Thereafter, the idea grew, and it was one adopted and supported by the British government from the mid-1990s when the first local governments committed their towns and cities to become learning cities. A learning city network evolved, and the European Commission (2003) supported the development of networks to promote and support lifelong learning locally and regionally. This is about social capital rather than human capital: Field *et al.* (2000:243) suggest that social capital offers 'one way of apprehending and analysing the embeddedness of education in social networks'. But they go on to say that 'it also challenges the dominant human capital approaches ... which concentrate on narrowly defined, short-term results or tidy analytical devices'. The outset of their argument is that social capital actually provides many opportunities for informal learning but that it is inherently narrowing – which is precisely the same type of argument that has existed for years about the advantages and disadvantages of living in small communities. However, Field *et al.* produce considerable evidence.

Social capital takes us back to the ideas of the community and the community spirit, phenomena that have apparently declined tremendously as a result of the division of labour (Putman, 2000), although the same concern about the decline existed nearly a century ago. It might well be that this reflects the social process of constructing ideal communities, but we either see them as utopian and in the future or locate them in a dim and distant past! In both cases their function is to illustrate that we do not live in a perfect society – but then, we may never ever do so! What these studies have shown, however, is that there are community resources that can enrich human living, although they might have their drawbacks; these resources might aid informal learning, but through planning and learning we can create conditions and structures through which human living may be enriched. However, we cannot dictate that the community spirit will be created or learned.

Conclusion

The global society and the knowledge economy have generated a world of rapid social change: the environment within which people live is changing rapidly, and that change makes demands on individuals and groups to learn in order to keep abreast. It is not surprising that these social groupings are themselves regarded as learning societies, learning cities, and so on. However, they are not learning but changing; the people in them learn individually even though there might be a collective outcome. That outcome is usually achieved because those in power in the social group have put structures in place that are more likely to allow for the group to respond to the pressures for change. Among those structures which have changed is education itself and so we will look briefly in the following chapter at the way in which education has changed over the same period.

3

EDUCATION AND LEARNING

In the opening chapter I argued that learning is an existential phenomenon so that learning and life are almost coterminous – learning is intrinsic to our being – although it always occurs in a social context which, as I showed in the second chapter, is always undergoing change. These constant changes have affected the way that societies have provided learning opportunities (education) for their members. In this chapter we will examine two different ways of looking at learning and also the way in which education was itself renamed as learning towards the end of the twentieth century. The chapter consists of four sections: the concepts of learning and education, formal learning (education), non-formal learning and informal learning.

The concepts of learning and education

In this section I intend to distinguish between learning and education conceptually and then show how lifelong education became lifelong learning.

Learning is an existential phenomenon – it is intrinsic to our being – and to a great extent it is experiential, although in pre-conscious learning we have to recognize that some of our experiences may actually be pre-cognitive and pre-conscious, as we discussed in the first chapter. Fundamentally, however, learning is experiential – it is what we do with our experience – and so there is a sense in which its basis may also be found in phenomenology; that is, it is about our experience of everyday life. At the same time, we have to recognize that learning is more than phenomenal since our experiences are affected by the experience we have; it is also affected by the social structures within which we exist, and so on. In making the claim that learning is intrinsic to our being, we can see immediately that the study of learning has as many academic bases as there are disciplines that study the human being – that the study of learning must be multidisciplinary (Jarvis and Parker, 2005; Jarvis, 2009a).

At its very least, learning is the transformation of our experiences of living so that they affect us as persons – in this sense they become part of our biography – and so we can begin to see the parameters of learning. Elsewhere (Jarvis, 2009a:25) I have defined learning as

> [t]he combination of processes throughout a lifetime whereby the whole person – body (genetic, physical and biological) and mind (knowledge, skills, attitudes, values, emotions, meaning, beliefs and senses) – experiences social situations, the content of which is then transformed cognitively, emotively or practically (or through any combination) and integrated into the individual person's biography resulting in a continually changing (or more experienced) person.

In a sense, we are constructing our own biography whenever we learn. While we live, our biography is an unfinished product constantly undergoing change and development – either through experiences that we self-initiate or else through experiences which are initiated by others. We are always learning to be persons in society, and here we are confronted by paradox: the person is always complete whenever we consider a person whom we know, but we also know that the person is never complete and will not be so for as long as he or she can learn from conscious experiences. People are always *becoming*, and we develop our personalities in different ways as a result of our experiences.

Since learning is social, learners are not always free to learn what they would like; often the learners' learning is prescribed. Education, for instance, is the provision of learning opportunities, but these opportunities are often bound by parameters decided by what the providers wish the learners to learn. Hence, there is a fundamental need to help learners to develop a sense of criticality. State-provided education, for instance, has been traditionally something restricted to children, who are expected to learn what is prescribed, although religious institutions educated older people many centuries before children were educated. By contrast, state education occurred only during the formative years and when social maturity or adulthood was achieved, then education ceased. This approach may be found in many early writers on the subject. John Stuart Mill, for instance, claimed that the content of education was to be found in 'the culture which each generation purposely gives to those who are to be their successors' (quoted in Lester-Smith, 1966:9). Emile Durkheim, a French sociologist and educationalist, regarded education in a similar manner: for him it was 'the influence exercised by adult generations on those who are not yet ready for social life' (1956:71). But by the beginning of the twentieth century it was becoming more apparent in the West that an inter-generational perspective was not adequate to describe the educational process. John Dewey (1916:8), for instance, was forced to add the prefix *formal* to the term *education* in order to express the same sentiments as those specified by Mill and Durkheim if society was to transmit all its achievements from one generation to the subsequent one. Today, formal education refers to both institutionalized learning and a teaching method – to the structure and the process. In addition, and the term most likely to be used to convey the same idea, there is *initial education*; the idea was that by a given stage in the lifespan, individuals have stored away sufficient knowledge and skill to serve them for the remainder of their lives, so that their education is then complete. This is a front-end model of education but it is one that was to change rapidly after the Second World War.

Such a model of education, however, is also implicit in the writings of the well-known English philosopher of education R.S. Peters, who made a clear distinction between education and the educated man (a term that Peters used without gender bias). Peters (1972:9) regarded being educated – being an educated man – as a state that individuals achieve, while education is a family of processes that lead to this state. However, is the educated person an end-state or the end of the journey? Peters' writings tend to suggest that he considers it as a lifelong process which continues after an end-state plateau has been reached, for he claims that education 'was not thought of [previously] explicitly as a family of processes which have as their outcome the development of an educated man in the way in which it is now' (1972:7). An educated person is a social status in contrast to the uneducated person. Peters rightly claimed that to be an educated person is not regarded as having arrived but rather as travelling with a different view during life. Hence, for him, the educated person is both educated and being educated throughout the whole of his life. Indeed, if the state of being educated was achieved, the process would still need to continue or else it would be lost. Therefore, no initial nor inter-generation aspect may be considered intrinsic to the concept of education, since the educated person should always be in the process of being educated.

Peters (1966:23ff.), following Wittgenstein, claimed that the concept of education is too complex to define and so he suggested that there is a family of similar phenomena that may be regarded as education. He put forward three sets of criteria for consideration as a basis for education, but they were not regarded as totally satisfactory, so that other criteria were later suggested. For him, education must involve:

- a learning process which is institutionalized but should not be a single event;
- a planned rather than a haphazard process;
- an essentially humanistic process because knowledge is humanistic and because the process involves human beings as learners and, also, maybe as teachers.

Learning has to involve understanding, which is essentially a quality of critical awareness. Before a definition is offered, it is necessary to examine the term 'humanistic' here. Dewey claimed that knowledge is essentially 'humanistic in quality not because it is about human products in the past, but because of what it *does* in liberating human intelligence and human sympathy' (1916:230; *italics* in original). It is this human element that was reflected in the discussion in the opening chapter when knowledge was separated from information. Dewey went on to suggest that any specific matter that does this is essentially humane, so that in this context 'humanistic' has two facets: it is concerned about the welfare and humanity of the participants and it is humane. Hence, this implies that the educational process is normative and idealistic.

Education may now be defined as 'any institutionalized and planned series of incidents, having a humanistic basis, directed towards the participants' learning and understanding'. This definition is the common factor in the multitudinous branches of education, and the definition might be modified and adapted to reflect the branch of education to which reference is being made by adding a prefix, e.g. higher education. This basic definition of education does not restrict education to any specific learning process, to any time in life, to any specific location or to any specific purpose. At the same time, Biesta (2007) reminds us that focusing on learning rather than on educating presupposes that the learners know what they want and that education is now part of a learning market.

By the 1960s this was beginning to change in response to globalization, as an ACACE report illustrates, since

> going to school, including nursery school, [...] could go on full or part-time into the mid-20s. After compulsory schooling, 'initial' education takes a wide variety of forms: full-time study in sixth form, university, college, polytechnic, medical school, military academy and so on; part-time day release, evening classes and correspondence courses; on the job training in the factory.
> (Advisory Council for Adult and Continuing Education,
> 1979a:9–10)

Schooling is part of the formal education system, as are further and higher education, but there are other forms of education and learning, as we will discuss in the following pages. However, we can see at this point that learning is a wider concept than education – for education is but one system through which we learn. Coombs and Ahmed, for instance, sought to distinguish formal education from informal and non-formal education. They define formal education as 'the highly institutionalized chronologically graded and hierarchically structured "education system" spanning lower primary school and upper reaches of the university' (1974:8). Their

Type of learning

	Intended	Incidental
Type of situation		
Formal	A	D
Non-formal	B	E
Informal	C	F

Figure 3.1 Possible learning situations.

intention was to distinguish it from other forms of lifelong education occurring throughout the world, as the model shown in Figure 3.1 illustrates.

We can now illustrate the type of learning that might occur in each of the six different learning situations shown in Figure 3.1:

1   Box A is *formal education and training* that occurs in an educational institution and any other bureaucratic organization.
2   Box B can refer to the ongoing nature of learning that occurs in places such as the workplace, the community, and so on. Sometimes the learner is actually mentored in these situations.
3   Box C is both *learning in everyday life* and *self-directed learning*. It is the type of learning that we undertake when we decide to teach ourselves to use a computer program, and so on. It can be individual learning or part of a group project.
4   Box D refers to that *incidental learning* that occurs in formal situations, learning that is not always educational, but which the planners of the learning experience did not intend – for example, the realization that the instructor is not really as knowledgeable as we thought, or that the room is badly designed, or that the carer does not really treat me as an autonomous individual, and so on.
5   Box E also refers to *incidental learning* situations in non-formal and informal learning episodes.
6   Box F refers to *learning in everyday life* – to *pre-conscious and pre-cognitive learning*. It often results in tacit knowledge. This box is probably the most common learning situation of all, especially in rapidly changing

societies. In these we find ourselves in new situations and we have to learn how to cope – by thinking on our feet about our next action, and so on (Heller, 1984). If we fail to respond to this situation quickly, we usually have to plan our learning, and then the situation moves to Box C.

However, the degree of formality is not the only variable in the subcultures of social situations that might affect either the type of learning or the behavioural outcomes of such learning; the politics and culture of the social context, the social position of both learners and teachers (leaders, managers and so on) and even the status given to the knowledge being acquired will be among the factors that affect the type of experience from which the learners learn (Box C). Let us now examine these three forms of learning.

Formal learning

As was discussed in the previous chapter, the global capitalist expansion really occurred in the later 1960s and early 1970s. It was also at this time that we began to see tremendous changes in the education of adults, changes that were, in the first instance, a little unclear. Nevertheless, it was books like Daniel Bell's *The Coming of Post-industrial Society* (1973) that heralded these changes. Once information and knowledge were as significant to the economy as manufacturing, the nature of adult education was forced to change. Adult education had traditionally been outside the mainstream education – which had consisted of schooling to 16 or 18 years old; further education from 16 to 21 years old for initial job training; higher education from 18 to 21 years old for entry into the professions, with the occasional student studying for a higher degree such as a Master's or doctorate. At that time, adult education could have been classified as non-formal education. But almost the first pointer to the fact that some of it was being mainstreamed was that adult education became the education of adults, and in the early 1980s the University of Surrey introduced a Post Graduate Certificate in the Education of Adults (PGCEA) as a professional teaching qualification rather like the PGCE for school teachers, but without the same statutory rights. This was not apparently a great change but it did signify that adults could be in the formal education system in the United Kingdom. The significance was not the same in the United States, where *adult education* reflected both the formal and the non-formal aspects of the education of adults.

In this section we will briefly trace the development of formal lifelong learning by looking initially at the foundations of the idea and thereafter a number of developments, such as the introduction of continuing professional development, continuing education and recurrent education.

The foundations of lifelong education

The concept of lifelong learning was first adopted by the United Nations Educational, Scientific and Cultural Organization (UNESCO), although it was not a new concept:

> It is common place to say that education should not cease when one leaves school. The point of this common place is that the purpose of school organization is to insure the continuance of education by organizing the powers that insure growth. The inclination to learn from life itself and to make the condition of life such that all will learn in the process of living is the finest product of schooling.
>
> (Dewey, 1916:51)

While not everyone would agree with Dewey's understanding of the purpose of the school organization, they may well agree with the sentiments expressed in the remainder of the quotation:

> Since life means growth, a living creature lives as truly and positively at one stage as at another, with the same intrinsic fullness and the same absolute claims. Hence education means the enterprise of supplying the conditions which insure growth, or adequacy of life, irrespective of age.

For Dewey, education is one of the major foundations of a rich life, but it is also one that need not be laid at the beginnings of life or in childhood; it may be laid at any stage of life and then built upon. However, in the light of our current understanding, Dewey might actually have used the term 'learning' rather than 'education' to make his point more clearly. While he has not been overtly influential on a great deal of adult education in the United Kingdom, his influence has been far greater in the United States. Among his disciples was Lindeman, author of *The Meaning of Adult Education* (1961 [1926]), who became a major influence on Malcolm Knowles and other influential practitioners in the field.

Soon after Dewey's influential book, from which these quotations have been drawn, appeared in the United States, an important document about adult education was published in Britain. A.L. Smith, chairman of the committee that produced a famous 1919 report, wrote:

> [T]he necessary condition is that adult education must not be regarded as a luxury for the few exceptional persons here and there, nor as a thing which concerns only a short span of early manhood, but that adult education is a permanent national neces-

sity, an inseparable aspect of citizenship, and therefore should be both universal and lifelong.

(1919: introductory letter, para. xi:5)

This far-sighted statement, like many others in the report, was loudly acclaimed but never implemented, so that the idea of lifelong education remained an ideal, although the British Association of Adult Education was also founded about this time. Yeaxlee (1929:31), who served on the committee that drafted the 1919 report, returned to the subject in the very first book about lifelong education and claimed that

> the case for lifelong education rests ultimately upon the nature and needs of the human personality in such a way that no individual can rightly be regarded as outside its scope, the social reasons for fostering it are as powerful as the personal.

However, the major difference between all of these earlier orientations to lifelong education and the more current ones is that formal lifelong education is now regarded as something necessary for work rather than for the humanity of the learner. Clearly, this is not an either/or situation; it should be both/and, but the emphasis in recent years has been on work rather than the humanity of the learner. An ideal has been turned into a practical necessity with a pragmatic orientation.

It was not until after the Second World War that the term gained prominence and this was because organizations such as UNESCO adopted it, influenced by such individuals as Lengrand (1975). Thereafter, many publications emanating from UNESCO developed and expounded the concept. The Faure Report (1972) advocated that education should be both universal and lifelong, claiming that education precedes economic development and prepares individuals for a society that does not exist but which may do so within their lifetime. The report claimed that education is essential for human beings and their development, and that therefore the whole concept of education needs to be reconsidered. The sentiments of this report were echoed by the Delors Report (1996), in which it was claimed that learning has four pillars: learning to know, learning to do, learning to live together and learning to be. One pillar, however, was not discussed: learning to care for the planet.

In 1976, lifelong education appeared to have 'come of age' when the Lifelong Learning Act was passed into law in the United States, which authorized the expenditure of $40 million annually between 1977 and 1982 on lifelong education (Peterson and Associates, 1979:295). However, Peterson and his associates were forced to conclude that while 'lifelong education and learning policies are gaining favor in numerous foreign countries, notably Scandinavia, there are at the moment signs of slackening progress [in America]' (1979:423). Despite this rather gloomy assessment, lifelong education was established in the United States, although probably not in the same form as was intended by the Mondale Act.

Nevertheless, as developments occurred in post-school education in the following years, it was a process whereby formal education changed rapidly as it ceased to be full-time and even ceased to be award-bearing in the first few years of change. It was a process whereby the education of adults was absorbed into the formal education system in a system of work-life education which was shortly to be called lifelong learning.

Continuing professional development

Continuing professional development (CPD) was financed a great deal by the government through a number of differing agencies, e.g. the Manpower Services Commission, PICKUP and the local TECS (Training and Enterprise Councils). Later it was the Learning and Skills Councils that controlled the largest part of the budget, and in the first instance it was a matter of in-service or education-provided short courses for specific professions – but this was soon to change.

Continuing education

At that time there were considerable debates about the conceptual bases of each term and the differences between them. Indeed, a discussion paper published by the Advisory Council for Adult and Continuing Education stated, 'Continuing education has long been a popular idea among some people concerned with the education of adults. It has gone under a variety of names in different countries: *education permanente*, lifelong education, recurrent education' (Advisory Council for Adult and Continuing Education, 1979a:7). This report also made it clear that continuing education was not further education in the manner that it existed in the United Kingdom for a number of reasons: further education could have been post-compulsory but not necessarily post-initial; it implied a specific level of study whereas continuing education did not; and it was pre-vocational, vocational or academic while continuing education need not necessarily be directed towards any course assessment or award, although it usually was.

The confusion was typified at that time by a debate in which Venables (1976:19), for instance, defined continuing education as 'all learning opportunities which can be taken up after full-time compulsory schooling has ceased. They can be full-time or part-time and will include both vocational and non-vocational study', but McIntosh (1979a:3) (later Sargant) disagreed with the definition, suggesting rather that continuing education referred to post-initial rather than post-compulsory education. The logic of this suggestion is quite clear. Continuing education was growing in significance and this is to be seen by the fact that there were a series of government reports that came from the Advisory Council for Adult and Continuing Education. It was not long after the formation of this council that the national organization for the United Kingdom changed its name from the National Institute of Adult Education (NIAE) to the National Institute of Adult Continuing Education (NIACE).

Significantly, the professions used the term *continuing professional education* (CPE), and this became widely accepted for all forms of in-service training, although Houle (1980) referred to this as continuing learning. Cervero (1988), in the United States, however, regarded continuing professional education as a significant area of educational activity, introducing educators to those forms of continuing education that occurred in a number of different professions. In the United States, continuing professional education was defined by the Accrediting Commission of the Continuing Education Council of the United States as

> the further development of human abilities after entrance into employment or voluntary activities. It includes in-service, upgrading and updating education. It may be occupational education or training which furthers careers or personal development. Continuing education includes that study made necessary by advances in knowledge. It *excludes* most general education and training for job entry. Continuing education is concerned primarily with broad personal and professional development. It includes leadership training and the improvement of the ability to manage personal, financial, material and human resources. Most of the subject matter is at the professional, technical and leadership training levels or the equivalent.
>
> (Apps, 1979:68f.; emphasis added)

Professions provided their members with many updating programmes in continuing education and there was considerable debate about whether continuing education should become mandatory for registration as a member of a professional occupation – which it now is for the majority of professions. Higher education was also gradually changing its direction and beginning to practise policies of lifelong education, although this process was initially quite slow. Knapper and Cropley (1985) traced the implications of the idea of lifelong learning for higher education and Kulich (1982b) documented how Canadian universities were moving in this direction. Williams (1977) actually claimed that lifelong education was the new role for institutions of higher education. Nevertheless, with the gradual growth in part-time higher education and the introduction of schemes of accreditation of prior learning and credit transfer changes occurred, higher education institutions began to regard themselves as institutions providing opportunities for education throughout the lifespan – or at least throughout work-life. At this time there was a proliferation of Master's degree courses and many more students undertaking research degrees. Indeed, by 1974 Campbell (1984) suggested that in Canada the majority of new students on Canadian campuses were adults rather than undergraduate students, although they were part-time and often attending at weekends.

While it was the professions that emphasized continuing education in the first instance, paradoxically globalization led to the corporations being much more effective in introducing it not only for their knowledge workers but also to all their employees. This process began to emerge in the 1980s, with Eurich's (1985) book *Corporate Classrooms* being one of the earliest studies. Other studies were to follow quite rapidly (e.g. Castner-Lotto and Associates, 1989). At this stage it was recognized that the corporations, working with knowledge and changing rapidly to respond to the wider social forces, had to become learning organizations, and in both the United Kingdom (Pedler *et al.*, 1997) and the United States (Senge, 1990; Watkins and Marsick, 1993) this was the focus. Thereafter, there followed one innovative outcome: the corporations founded their own universities (Jarvis, 2001b; Meister, 1998) and the idea of corporate knowledge was developed (Tuomi, 1999). This was the beginning of the focus on human resource development, which will be discussed shortly.

Since continuing education offered no criticism of the current structure of education, it actually served to reinforce the status quo, so that it is inherently conservative. No such claims may be legitimately made about the next form of education strategy to be discussed in this chapter, for recurrent education has certainly had some radical claims made on its behalf.

Recurrent education

Recurrent education was the concept espoused most frequently by the Organisation for Economic Co-operation and Development (OECD) until the 1980s, when the term appeared to fall into disfavour. Brought to the attention of a wider audience in the late 1960s by Olaf Palme, it gained currency through the OECD publications and, in the United Kingdom from the mid-1970s, through the publications of the Association of Recurrent Education. There was some agreement about the definition of the term, which is perhaps summarized by the following, rather tautologous, suggestion that recurrent education is 'the distribution of education over the lifespan of the individual in a recurring way' (Organisation for Economic Co-operation and Development, 1973:7). This is a little broader than an earlier definition proposed by OECD: that recurrent education 'is formal, and preferably full-time education for adults who want to resume their education, interrupted earlier for a variety of reasons' (Organisation for Economic Co-operation and Development, 1971, cited by Kallen, 1974).

Unlike continuing education, which appeared to occur in a piecemeal manner in response to expressed or perceived needs, etc., recurrent educationalists regarded their approach to be a 'comprehensive alternative strategy for what are at present three unrelated sectors: a) the conventional post-compulsory educational system ... b) on-the-job training of all kinds c) adult education' (Organisation for Economic Co-operation and Development, 1973:25). Houghton (1974:6) actually claimed that recurrent education

> was the first new idea in education this century.... It represents one of those very rare shifts in the framework of thinking which Kuhn has described. Its emergence marks the beginning of the end of the dominant apprenticeship paradigm in education.

Clearly, this is a massive claim but, at the same time, recurrent education did offer a radical alternative system, one that its exponents claimed to be realistic in the light of contemporary society (e.g. Flude and Parrott, 1979).

Since some exponents of recurrent education presented it as a more radical approach to education and others have embraced the more moderate continuing education perspective, it is not surprising that some theorists extended this distinction to other respects of the curriculum. Griffin (1978), for instance, suggested that recurrent educationalists tend to be more student centred, have a more integrated approach to content and generally have a more romantic curriculum perspective, while those who had adopted a continuing education approach had a more classical perspective on curriculum issues. While he polarized continuing and recurrent education, he admitted that he had only undertaken a tentative exercise. However, he raised many valuable points about these two forms of education, and this might have been even more insightful had he also sought to incorporate some of the other philosophical issues espoused by many adult educators.

One of the most significant features of recurrent education was the belief that individuals should have a right to a specified amount of full-time formal education beyond compulsory schooling, and this need not have been taken during their formative years. Indeed, Gould (1979) not only regarded this as a moral argument about the equality of educational opportunity but also related it to a wider perspective on equality of occupational opportunity. Therefore, some of its exponents saw this as a radical, moral strategy for lifelong education since it suggested that everybody had the right to six years' full-time education after compulsory schooling.

Having a right to full-time education later in life is both inconvenient and expensive to employers and governments, and so it is hardly surprising that with the economic stringency of the 1980s and the advent of 'new right' politics, the idea of recurrent education disappeared from the political and educational agendas. Indeed, it even fell into disfavour with the OECD, and the Association of Recurrent Education in the United Kingdom also adopted a new name: the Association of Lifelong Learning.

One aspect of recurrent education that has survived, however, is the idea of paid educational leave. This was recognized in some of the early OECD literature (Organisation for Economic Co-operation and Development, 1973:70–72), where discussion occurred about the extent to which paid educational leave should be a statutory right or whether it should be the result of negotiations between employers and employees. By the time that the OECD had actually published this document, France had already introduced legislation that allowed for up to 2 per cent of a firm's labour force to take leave of absence at any one time and for 1 per cent of the wage bill, rising to 2 per cent by 1976, to be spent on employee education (ibid.:35).

Other European countries were also introducing similar legislation, and the International Labour Organization called for each member state to formulate and apply a policy of paid educational leave (Organisation for Economic Co-operation and Development, 1973). Killeen and Bird (1981) investigated the extent to which paid educational leave existed in England and Wales during this period and concluded that between 15 per cent and 20 per cent of the total workforce received some paid, or assisted, educational leave in the year of the study, 1976–7, which approximated to 6 days per person for courses organized by the employing organization and 12 days per person attending courses mounted by other organizations. They noted that this educational leave was not evenly distributed, younger workers being more likely to be released than older ones, and that the courses tended to be vocationally based and had a qualification as one of their end products. Bryant (1983) reported a similar research project in Scotland in which he recorded a similar picture to that discovered in England and Wales. Mace and Yarnit (1987) also recorded a number of examples of paid educational leave, including developments in London (Workbase), Sheffield (Take Ten – a day off to study each week for ten weeks) and Liverpool (Second Chance to Learn); this book of readings was an important one since it sought to address the issue of why low-paid and disadvantaged groups get fewer opportunities for educational development than do the more advantaged groups. In addition, the book reported on the 150-hour programme in Italy, which was an exemplar of what could be done with careful planning. Paid educational leave is still very important since corporations realize the importance of their employees keeping abreast with developments in their own field. However, the concerns of the 1970s and 1980s are recorded here as an example of how rapidly our attitudes towards education policy have changed with the advent of globalization. A new version of paid educational leave was promulgated at the UNESCO World Adult Education Conference in Hamburg in 1997, which was 'one hour a day of learning'.

Recurrent education, then, had two major strands: a more radical one that regarded it as a strategy for the reform of the whole education system and perhaps also the wider society, while the more conservative strand was less ambitious in its claims, preferring rather to see it as a reformist approach to implementing lifelong education. There is a marked difference in the philosophy of the two strands and yet they both recognize that while education may not be continuous after initial education, it should be lifelong, a right that all people should receive and that sufficient provision should be made for them to do so.

Non-formal learning

Among the major non-formal educational developments has been that known as human resource development but the most significant of all was the development of liberal adult education and, more recently, a branch of this: the education of senior citizens.

Human resource development

As we noted in the section on continuing education, the corporations began to develop their own education and training during this time. However, there had been another conceptual shift just a little earlier when Schultz (1961) introduced the term *human capital*. He pointed out that economists shied away from the use of this term because, while individuals actually invested in themselves, they might find it offensive to think of themselves in this manner. He (1961) wrote:

> Our values and beliefs might inhibit us from looking upon human beings as capital goods, except in slavery, which we abhor. We are not unaffected by the long struggle to society on indentured service and to evolve political and legal institutions to keep men free from bondage. These are achievements we prize highly. Hence, to treat human beings as wealth that can be augmented by investment runs counter to deeply held values.
>
> (quoted in Jarvis with Griffin, 2003, vol. 5:246)

However, it was not long before the idea of human capital development arose, and corporations opened their own human resource development (HRD) departments, some of which eventually turned into the corporate universities. HRD seeks to enhance the personal and work-related knowledge and skills of individuals, helping them to achieve their full potential. In more recent years, competence-based training and National Vocational Qualifications (NVQs) have been introduced. These involve work-based learning, and with it, systems of mentoring have also been introduced. Training officers, and even some personnel and welfare officers, have become human resource managers and trainers, and gradually HRD has assumed its own place in the learning society (see, for example, Brinkerhoff, 1987; Jayagopal, 1990; Hargreaves and Jarvis, 2000). In 1993 the Academy of Human Resource Development was founded in the United States by adult educators who had undertaken a great deal of their research in organizational settings, which illustrates that human resource development became a separate profession. The Academy has since run its own conferences and publishes its own books (see Redmann, 2000).

At the same time it must be recognized human resource development theories have implications that are nicely summed up by Baptiste (2001:197–198): 'human capital theory ... treats humans as lone wolves: radically isolated hedonists, creatures of habit (not intentions) who temper their avarice with economic rationality'. Baptiste suggests that these theories are apolitical, adaptive and individualistic and as such we may see that they actually make education the handmaiden of industry, as Kerr *et al.* (1973:47) suggest, something that belittles both education and, above all, human nature.

In the United Kingdom the system of HRD has been extended to the level of Master's degrees, and gradually some employers are beginning to expect their managers and senior personnel to undertake NVQs rather than releasing them to attend university courses, which are often regarded as not sufficiently work orientated. At the same time, universities and colleges have assumed a significant HRD role. It was also recognized that HRD training could have effects more widely, so that workers could take what they had learned and use it in the community (Dovey and Onyx, 2001). Accordingly, a number of analysts developed the concept of social capital (e.g. Coleman, 1990; Putnam, 2000).

By the mid-1990s all of these terms, except HRD, were to be subsumed in a new term, *lifelong learning* (European Commission, 1995), when, as we saw earlier in this chapter, the term 'education' actually began to take second place to learning. 'Lifelong learning' has remained the significant term in Europe ever since, although the European Commission (2006) started to use the term *adult learning* since it recognized that education and training and higher education had their own identities that could never be subsumed within the all-embracing term 'lifelong learning'. 'Adult learning' was a term already in use in the United Kingdom, although it has subsequently been recognized that 'learning' does not really incorporate education, and more recently the term *adult learning and education* (ALE) has come to the fore (NIACE, 2008), recognizing that there is no longer a free-standing liberal adult education sector in the United Kingdom (although we will examine that sector's history briefly in the following section).

The foundations of adult education

Adults have been educated by a wide variety of organizations for centuries but the 1919 report, mentioned earlier, became a benchmark for adult education. In many ways the University of Nottingham led the way by creating the first Department of Adult Education and the first Professor of Adult Education in the world. Universities, other adult education providers such as the Workers' Educational Association, the Women's Institute and local authorities all provided adult education courses. Many of these were of a relatively formal nature and developed quite strongly through to the 1970s in the United Kingdom. At the same time, adult education was growing and developing in the United States. It was during this time that Knowles introduced the term 'andragogy' to American adult education. It was a term well known in eastern parts of Europe; indeed, Knowles learned the term from the Serbian adult educator Dušan Savićević. In the first instance, Knowles (1970) sought to distinguish between adult education and children's education by giving the subtitle *Andragogy versus Pedagogy* to the first edition of *The Modern Practice of Adult Education.* However, the debate that followed resulted in the distinction between andragogy and pedagogy being downplayed. In the second edition the subtitle became *From Pedagogy to Andragogy.* In it, he suggested that andragogical techniques could be used with children and pedagogical ones with adults. During the time of this debate, Wiltshire (1976) also suggested that adult education might be understood as an educational process conducted in an adult manner.

Adult education, as post-school liberal education, reached a high point in the 1970s and 1980s, but this was also the time when, as we saw earlier, Kerr and his colleagues expected education to become work based – economically useful – and all other forms of adult education to become leisure-time pursuits, which the 2009 UK government White Paper (Department for Innovation, Universities and Skills, 2009) implicitly confirms. Significantly, libraries and museums, and other such cultural institutions, were regarded as adjuncts to adult education, but when liberal adult education became adult learning, they assumed a more significant place, so that by 2009 the government White Paper treats them as of equal significance in non-work education, which, as we shall see, has all been subsumed within the idea of informal learning. This adopts the OECD's approach, which emphasizes the work-based nature of lifelong learning. While we can safely claim that much work-based education is also non-formal, most of the adult education that existed prior to the impact of economic globalization – concerned with culture and the humanities – was to become regarded as a leisure-time pursuit. This approach to education, and the whole of culture in late-modern society, has been nicely summarized by Bauman (1992:17):

> Literature, visual arts, music – indeed the whole of the humanities – was ... set inside market-led consumption as entertainment. More and more the culture of consumer society was subordinated to the function of producing and reproducing skilful and eager consumers...; in its new role, it had to conform to the needs and rules as defined, in practice if not in theory, by the consumer market.

The term 'adult education' has carried specific connotations in the United Kingdom, connotations which imply that it is specifically liberal education, which has been stereotyped as a middle-class leisure-time pursuit. Underlying this implication is the idea that the adults' education has been completed and, during leisure time, adults improve or broaden their existing knowledge, skills or hobbies; it was regarded as a humanistic enterprise. It is hardly surprising, therefore, that adult education has become regarded as marginal in a global capitalist knowledge economy, although I shall argue that it is essential to the development of democracy.

One of the shining lights of this time was the foundation of Britain's Open University. Its first courses launched in the early 1970s but its charter was granted in 1969. In its earliest days the Open University emphasized a great deal of liberal adult education within a formal framework, but it has now been mainstreamed into the higher education system as distance education has become more acceptable in the contemporary world.

From this time onwards, adult education was regarded in the United Kingdom as a costly addition to formal education, although one in which the government had to be involved. During the 1980s, under a Conservative government, huge cuts in funding were introduced. Adult education was regarded as a sector of further education for funding purposes, and gradually local authority adult education institutes (AEIs) became subsumed within local further education colleges. Liberal adult education was provided locally and still partially supported by further education funding, although it was recognized that it was performing in a consumer market, just as Bauman predicted. However, the pressures of globalization and the continued need to pump funds into vocational education continued through the 1990s and into the new millennium. This resulted in further cuts in funding for non-vocational adult learning, which had potentially catastrophic results for adult education. Tuckett (2005:6), commenting on the UK scene, writes:

[I]f policies remained unchanged a million to a million and a half opportunities for adults will be lost over the next three years. And, as a result, once again questions are being raised about what public money should be spent on the field of adult learning.

Low taxation means that there are insufficient resources to spend on welfare provision, and the demands for an educated workforce mean that the government is being forced by industry and commerce to give priority to the latter, so that public money is selectively allocated in favour of economic interests. Naturally, governments can claim that they are doing this in the national interest since it is fundamentally important that there should be an educated workforce in the United Kingdom or else business and industry will go elsewhere and then the United Kingdom will not keep abreast of its competitors. But it is also the hegemonic power of the global substructure that produced the changes in the educational funding system in the first instance. At the same time as we have seen adult education decline and the closure of adult and continuing education departments in many universities in the United Kingdom, a similar scenario is being played out in a number of other countries in the Western world. At the time of preparing this edition of the book, the scene looks bleak for adult education in the United Kingdom despite the fact that a social movement, the Campaigning Alliance for Lifelong Learning (CALL), has been active in lobbying Members of Parliament and holding rallies. But it seems that for the British government, following – or perhaps leading – the European Commission's change in emphasis from lifelong learning to adult learning, the new emphasis is on adult learning of a specific kind: informal learning, which is certainly a much less costly option for the government. As we will see shortly, little money is offered, and that in a transformation fund.

Indeed, the British government admitted that there is a need to rethink the situation, as the 2008 consultation paper on informal learning makes clear:

As we freely acknowledge, prioritising adult education for those who require skills and qualifications for work, and for those who have not previously head the opportunity to enjoy a good level of education, has rightly stimulated a debate about the future of informal adult learning.

(Department for Innovation, Universities and Skills, 2008:9)

Indeed, there has been a great deal of debate and in places an angry reaction to the neo-liberal policies that the government has embraced. Nevertheless, the consultation paper asked some pertinent questions about the future of non-work learning, to which there were many responses, including a very full analysis from the National Institute of Adult Continuing Education (NIACE, 2008a:30–32) which called for the voluntary sector to be encouraged to engage more in the life of civil society; changes in social structures to encourage this; proper and reasonable funding; a focus on outreach and participation, but also a continued recognition of the priority of the workforce; and a new and slim-line infrastructure for adult learning. The final report to this publication (Department for Innovation, Universities and Skills, 2009) will be discussed later.

At the same time as there has been a major provision in the United Kingdom for adult education, especially in Scotland, there has also been another, less publicized activity, community education, which has also suffered considerable decline.

Community education

Occasionally a word appears in the English language that becomes ideologically acceptable for a period of time. 'Community' is such a word, becoming widely accepted in the United Kingdom in the 1960s and 1970s as something intrinsically good and right. Now sociologists talk about idealized communities, which is an extension of the original idea. Perhaps this is because a certain nostalgia exists for a world that is past, one we imagine or that we would like to see re-emerge. Not surprisingly, the idea of community education appeared to have been accepted with almost the same uncritical appraisal as the term *community*. This process was aided and abetted by the fact that it is a confused and multifarious concept.

Fletcher (1980a, b) suggested that there are three premises in community education:

1 The community has its needs and common causes and is the maker of its own culture.
2 Educational resources are to be dedicated to the articulation of needs and common causes.
3 Education is an activity in which there is an interplay between the roles of student, teacher and person.

He argued that certain implications follow from this in terms of centre or periphery activities, formality and informality, and democratic control. This, in turn, results in active and reactive processes. Perhaps Fletcher was guilty of reification of the concept of community in the first of these premises, but his second one – groups and categories of persons in the locality who have common causes – is increasingly significant, even more so as the United Kingdom becomes the host society for many refugees and migrants. The philosophy underlying this approach to community education is one of responding to certain forms of social inequality in order to produce a more equal society in which more people interact on an inter-personal basis, so that the locality begins to generate its own ethos. It would, therefore, be a matter of social policy and educational commitment to divert educational resources to the underprivileged and, as such, it would reflect the philosophy that led to the creation of educational priority areas in initial education.

Three distinct forms of community education can be distinguished:

1   education for action and/or development;
2   education in the community;
3   extra-mural forms of education.

But at the conceptual level, Lovett *et al.* (1983:36ff.) also sought to distinguish between different forms of community education, suggesting four types: community organization/education, community development/education, community action/education and social action/education. However, for the purposes of this analysis, three types of community education distinguished here will now be briefly discussed. Finally, I shall raise questions regarding the current debate about the decline of community education.

Education for community action and/or development

'Community education as a profession is rooted in the interests and experiences of people in communities and is committed to increasing the ability of individuals and groups to influence the issues that affect them and their communities' (Tett, 2008:25). Perhaps the best-known exponent of this position was Paulo Freire, who maintained that education can never be neutral. He formulated his ideas in Latin America against a background of illiteracy and poverty, and his thinking was a synthesis of Christian theology, existentialism and Marxism – one that underlay liberation theology. While his ideas developed in a Third World context, they are relevant to the United Kingdom and United States, as Kirkwood and Kirkwood (1989) showed (see also London, 1973). Even though much of Freire's work was written in Portuguese, it is widely available in English (see the bibliography), and even his posthumous works are widely available (see, for instance, Freire, 1996, 1997, 1998). He emphasized that education should make the learners critically aware of their false consciousness and their social condition. In becoming aware, they should reject many of the myths erected by the ruling elite that inhibit them (the learners) from having a clear perception of their own social reality. Having undergone a process of conscientization, learners should act upon the world to endeavour to create a better society. Understandably, Freire's radical, but moral, approach is one that has been criticized, especially by those who for varying reasons wish to see education as a neutral process, but over the years his stature has grown and his thinking has been much admired through-out the educational world. Freire was not alone in holding this perception of education, although few other writers have formulated it in such a sophisticated manner. Among those in the United Kingdom whose approach to education is similar to Freire's is Lovett (Lovett, 1975, 1980; Lovett and Mackay, 1978, etc.), who worked both in inner-city Liverpool and in Belfast in Northern Ireland. Lovett suggested that some adult educators see 'the role of adult education in community action ... as ... providing the working class with an effective educational service so that they can take full advantage of the educational service *and* make the best use of their individual talents and abilities' (1975:155; emphasis in original). In his work in Northern Ireland, Lovett (Lovett *et al.*, 1983) continued to work out these ideas and subsequently offered a model of different types of community education. While Lovett worked out his own ideas, Kirkwood and Kirkwood (1989) were applying Freire's concepts in a community education project in inner-city Edinburgh. They recorded how they adapted his educational techniques to their own situation, although the project was certainly less radical than some of Freire's ideas.

In the United States, perhaps the best-known institution organizing radical adult education is Highlander, which was founded by Myles Horton in Tennessee and worked with labour unions and citizenship groups. It played a significant role in the civil rights movement in the United States and its work is becoming increasingly well documented (Horton with Kohl and Kohl, 1990). In 1987, Horton and Freire came together at Highlander to 'talk a book' (Horton and Freire, 1990), in which they exchanged their understanding of radical adult education and produced a most insightful understanding of the place education might play in community development.

One of the clear distinguishing features about the education being described here is that these are not formalized educational systems; they are non-formal and occur beyond the boundaries of the traditional formal, bureaucratic educational system that exists in many societies in the world. But this form of radical education has declined in significance in recent days, to the concern of the authors of *The Edinburgh Papers* (2008), who rightly feel that the interests of the people are not well represented. They note that 'critical practices are being marginalised or eradicated and there is recognition of a growing co-option and corruption of practices to meet neo-liberal ends over associations, democratic and empowering community education' (Wallace, 2008:4). Community education is a necessary form of education if we are to enhance democracy, but in a society corrupted by neo-liberalism and parliamentary excesses it is hardly surprising that those in power welcome a form of education that stands for democracy; in fact, it is not only that there is no 'body capable of representing these concerns to government' (Wallace, 2008:4) – it is that there are few governments that will fund adequately an educational system that assumes a critical or an ethical perspective on society's practices.

Education in the community

Perhaps the earliest formal education of this type stemmed from the work of Henry Morris, who was responsible for the establishment of community colleges in Cambridgeshire before the Second World War (see Jennings, n.d.), and whose ideas were influential in their introduction in Leicester-shire shortly afterwards (Fairbairn, 1978). From these beginnings have grown larger urban educational and social complexes, such as the Abra-ham Moss Centre in Manchester and the Sutton Centre in Nottingham-shire, in which the school is regarded as the focal point of the community, in a similar manner to that of the parish church in medieval times, and it is held that adults, as well as children, should be able to attend classes in these centres. As a result of his work in Liverpool, Midwinter (1975:99) concluded that

> [e]ducation must no longer be open to caricature as a few hours at school for a few years in ... pre-adult life. It must be viewed as a total, lifelong experience, with the home and the neighbourhood playing important parts, and everybody contributing to and draw-ing on this educative dimension of the community.

However, he did not specify all the advantages of comprehensive schools including adults among their learners, but Mary Hughes (1977:226–232) saw many advantages in allowing adults to attend community schools at the same time as children, not the least being that it is education on the cheap. These large urban educational complexes have also been intro-duced in other parts of the United Kingdom, and a similar community school complex established in the suburbs of Grenoble, in France, was also influenced by these developments. Clearly, educational innovation is occurring throughout the world and much of it could be discussed under this sub-heading. Poster and Kruger (1990), for instance, brought together a number of examples from different countries in the Western world, highlighting some of the ways in which educationalists are reaching out into the community.

An innovation deriving from Henry Morris is the recent recognition in the United Kingdom that the day school is a community resource, and we are now beginning to see the concept of the extended school emerge. Schools now have an obligation to the community, and they are beginning to run courses for the parents of their pupils and for other people in the community. In addition, schools are using their premises for community education activities, so that a local historical society and a University of the

Third Age computer group both known to me regularly use the local comprehensive school's facilities.

Adult education beyond the walls

Extra-mural adult education is a term usually restricted to university adult education extension classes where academic staff from the universities teach in the community, or the universities employ part-time staff to teach liberal adult education classes under their auspices in the wider community. But with the advent of neo-liberal economic policies and practices, universities have had their funds curtailed to such an extent that they are ceasing to provide such education, and thereby impoverishing the civility of contemporary society (Stanistreet, 2009; Jones, 2009). Recently, the term has assumed some significance, with other educational institutions organizing educational classes in their local communities. However, these forms of educational outreach are rarely regarded as community education, even though they are examples of education 'beyond the walls' of the educational institution.

With the growing emphasis on practical knowledge, we have also seen the development of educational courses based in the home, the community, the workplace, and so on. These opportunities to learn might have been regarded as community education, extra-mural or placements within a more traditional course whereby learners could learn to apply theory to practice. Now this has changed, and even the idea of applying theory to practice has been thoroughly questioned (Jarvis, 1999). Hence, we shall deal with each of these approaches to learning in later pages of this study.

Education for senior citizens

In recent years there has been a tremendous growth in non-formal learning for seniors, with perhaps the two best-known organizations being the University of the Third Age in Europe and the Elderhostel Institute Network in North America. People are living longer, and Western Europe is now regarded as having a 'greying' population (The Stationery Office, 2006:11). It is the oldest region in the world (UNESCO, n.d.) – and the figures for the United Kingdom tend to confirm this. At the time of writing, there are as many people in the United Kingdom of 60 years of age and older as there are people under 16 years, and by 2021 it is estimated that the United Kingdom will have a population of 64,729,000, of whom 19.7 per cent will be 65 or older while 9.5 per cent will be 75 or older. Similar statistics can be found for the United States.

As early as 1962 the Institute for Retired Professionals was founded in the United States by Hy Hirsch and sponsored by the New York School for Social Research; this was ten years before the University of the Third Age

(U3A) was established by Pierre Vellas at the University of Toulouse in France, and it took another ten years for the latter idea to spread to the United Kingdom. Despite the fact that the founder in the United Kingdom, Peter Laslett, was a Cambridge don, the U3A in the United Kingdom has little connection with the university world. Each U3A in the United Kingdom is an independent non-governmental organization (NGO), although there is a Third Age Trust, which in some ways acts as a coordinating body.

The diversity of U3As in the United Kingdom is tremendous, with there being about 725 different ones in May 2009. Significantly, the difference in the way these two types of U3A (those in the United Kingdom and those following the French model) were founded reflects something of the difference in their approach to their activities. The ones that follow the continental European pattern are attached to universities and are much more academically orientated, while those in the United Kingdom tend to emphasize leisure as much as learning, and it is generally recognized that only through cooperation can these diverse and independent U3As run more sophisticated academic groups, except in the case of the larger groups that have sufficient members to run large and diverse programmes. A small U3A of which I am the founding chairman has, after four years of existence, a membership of just over 250, runs about thirty different regular interest groups and has about nine open lectures a year and engages in a number of social activities. There is another factor that affects the UK groups, namely the presence of Britain's Open University; since its foundation at about the same time as the U3As in France, it has offered formal education at a distance at undergraduate and postgraduate level to anybody, and many of its students have been seniors.

At the same time, this democratic and local approach to seniors' education has not been without its critics. For instance, Huang (2006) has suggested that the standard of teaching and learning in UK U3As could be improved by utilizing more university-trained teachers since its present mode of operation cannot control the level of education offered, and, at the same time, the locally based democratic system might be more efficiently organized. While the accusations have some justification, there is a sense in which the present U3A activities are performing two separate roles, those of leisure and learning – roles that are undertaken in the United States by the two separate arms of the Elderhostel Institute Network. Since the organizations in the United Kingdom are growing, it is clear that they are responding to local demands and so no incentive appears to exist in many local organizations to change.

Indeed, the University of the Third Age movement has spread more widely throughout Europe and beyond, and has its own International Association of Universities of the Third Age (AIUTA). This has not been very effective in recent years, although it has been in existence for many years. Now a new organization is appearing on the scene, a global internet network: the World Conference of Universities of the Third Age. This is due to hold its first conference in India in 2010.

In the United States the development of the Institute for Retired Professionals took a totally different route. It had begun under the sponsorship of the New School for Social Research in New York City but spread slowly. In 1976, however, a conference of interested parties led to these becoming known as Institutes for Learning in Retirement. At roughly the same time (1975), in New Hampshire, another movement was born: Elderhostel (www.elderhostel.org). This organized educational travel and grew extremely rapidly. By 2006 it offered some 8,000 programmes throughout the world to about 160,000 members. Its success once again reflects the significance of globalization and the wealth of current retirees.

However, in 1988 twenty-four Institutes for Learning in Retirement joined with Elderhostel to form the Elderhostel Institute Network. At about the same time locally they adopted the name Lifelong Learning Institute. The Network is a voluntary association of Lifelong Learning Institutes that are funded by Elderhostel. Lifelong Learning Institutes run a wide variety of teaching and learning programmes and they are often sponsored by their local universities, so that they approach the type of provision made by the Universities of the Third Age on the continent of Europe. It is significant that the cognitive interest motivation factor is dominant among its members, if the small-scale study conducted by Kim and Merriam (2004) is to be taken as representative. In contrast, Elderhostel clearly caters for the many seniors who want to travel and learn local knowledge at the same time. Elderhostel has also spread to Canada, where it is now known as Routes to Learning.

Another model that has emerged in Germany and Spain, among other places, is one in which universities open their classes to seniors. This certainly occurred in Germany in the 1980s, and in Spain the so-called Third Age Classrooms (the Spanish government would not permit the use of the term 'university') began to function as early as 1978 (Socias et al., 2004). By 1993 it was decided to open universities to older people, with the University of the Balearic Islands initiating an Open University for Seniors. Nine years after the universities opened classes to seniors, fifty universities had began to offer programmes specifically for seniors, and Socias et al. suggest that these programmes will become more institutionalized during the twenty-first century. In Japan there has been a similar movement, but Shirasha (1995) comments on the fact that many of the academic staff working in this area are untrained.

However, the Chinese, who have always had specialist universities – for instance, I visited a University for Banking a number of years ago – have also had schools and universities for seniors. The first began in 1993 and the number grew very rapidly (Leung et al., 2006; Li Herzhong, 1997). For instance, the TALIS conference in 2002 was held in the Wuhan University for Aged People. It is significant that the growth of these universities reflects the fact that under 'the Chinese 7 year Development Plan of Work on the Aged, all cities and counties should run schools or universities for the aged' (Li Zhi *et al.*, 1997).

Informal learning

This section has three sub-sections covering, respectively, learning in everyday life, self-directed learning and what the British government now calls informal learning (following the OECD) but which is basically all learning that is not part of initial or further and higher education.

Learning in everyday life

As I argued earlier, learning is intrinsic to being, and so we learn whenever we are conscious, although we are not always aware we are doing so. For instance, when my grandson comes home from school, we often ask him, 'What have you learned at school today?' And we expect a response! But if we ask adults, 'What have you learned from life recently?' we might well again get little or no response. This is precisely what I find when I conduct research into learning and when I run workshops on the topic of human learning. Many an adult when asked to write down a learning event finds it extremely difficult, and this is because a great deal of our everyday learning is incidental, pre-conscious and unplanned. In a sense, we respond to events in a living manner – but then, learning is about life. Indeed, for most people it is, or should be, lifelong. We all live in a social context (life-world) in which we learn (Jarvis, 1987).

Everyday life is a strangely unresearched subject when it comes to human learning – but see de Certeau (1984) and Heller (1984). While we will not delve deeply into these studies, we do need to recognize their significance if we are to really understand lifelong learning. Fundamentally, there are two states in this life-world: one in which we are in harmony with it and the other in which we are in disjuncture. Schutz and Luckmann (1974:6) describe this state thus:

> I trust that the as it has been known to me up until now will continue further and consequently the stock of knowledge obtained from my fellow men and obtained from my own experiences will continue to preserve its fundamental validity. We would designate this (in accordance with Husserl) the 'and so forth' idealization. From this assumption follows the further and fundamental one: that I can repeat my past successful acts. So long as the structure of the world can be taken as constant, and as long as my previous

experience is valid, my ability to operate on the world in this and that manner is in principle preserved. As Husserl has shown, the further ideality of the 'I can always do it again' is developed correlative of the ideality of the 'and so forth'.

In other words, we can take our world for granted because we are in harmony with it. But the world is not a constant and unchanging place and so there are times when we cannot take it for granted and we are forced to ask questions: Why? How? What does it mean? and so forth. This is disjuncture – we have to find new explanations, new knowledge, new ways of doing things. In other words, we must learn. These are the questions with which every parent and teacher is familiar when children keep asking questions, but they also adjust their behaviour to fit into that of their group or family, and so on. But often, as we grow older, we do not ask the questions so openly and we merely adjust our behaviour or our knowledge base, although there are times when we may not even notice that we are doing so. We actually take this process for granted, and so much of our learning is not only incidental but unrecognized.

And thus there are two conditions essential for learning in everyday life: social interaction and disjuncture. Interaction is the basis of social living: we nearly all live in families, are members of organizations, and so forth. Unless we are meeting with people whom we know intimately, it is hard to take for granted the whole of a process of interaction in which all our senses are operative. Even our nearest and dearest change as a result of their own learning and, as the old maxim tells us, the same water does not flow under the same bridge twice; situations never repeat themselves precisely. It is in meeting with others both within our life-world and beyond it that makes us aware of difference. Social interaction involves exploring difference and adjusting our behaviour (learning) to enable the interaction to proceed smoothly. People are different, and during interaction we learn to respond to those differences, accommodate them and even to learn from them. Disjuncture, then, is a normal experience in social interaction, but in some aspects of human living, ignorance is an acceptable response to disjuncture.

Self-directed learning

Until the 1970s, learning was usually regarded as something that occurred in the classroom, despite the fact that history is replete with stories of lifelong learners who spend months and years of their lives studying in order to understand the wonders of life itself. It came as something of a surprise to educators when Allen Tough (1979) reported research into adults' self-directed learning projects and suggested that self-directed education is common. Tough (1979:1) wrote that it

64

is common for a man or woman to spend 700 hours a year on learning projects. Some people spend less than 100 hours, but others spend more than 2000 hours in episodes in which the person's interest to learn or to change is clearly his primary motivation.

Tough was not concerned merely to count the odd hours of inquiry in which an individual might indulge, since he considered that these could not be described as learning projects. Rather, he defined a learning project as 'a series of related episodes, adding up to at least seven hours' (1979:6). Tough and his fellow researchers interviewed sixty-six people in depth in their initial research and discovered that all but one of them had undertaken at least one learning project during the year prior to the interview, that the median number of projects was eight and that the mean time spent on learning projects was 816 hours. A participation rate of 98 per cent was discovered – far higher than would have been anticipated from previous research (Johnstone and Rivera, 1965). But Tough and his colleagues employed a more intensive interview technique, and this method of research was one reason for the higher statistics. Additionally, Tough acknowledged that his sample was not random, so that it is not technically correct to claim that 98 per cent of the population of Canada, or even of Ontario (where the research was conducted), undertake at least one seven-hour learning project per annum. Indeed, his statistics may be a considerable overestimation (although they might actually be correct), but they do suggest that people have a need to learn, know and understand.

In the 1990s there was a series of self-directed learning conferences in the United States, organized by Huey Long (e.g. Long and Associates, 1988, 1993, 1997, 1998). Their success indicated that self-directed learning had become a significant feature of adult education in that country. But at this time, self-directed learning was also being used as a teaching method in such things as projects. In this sense, the teaching capitalized on both the good and the bad about self-directed learning. In a more recent article, Taylor (2009) examined self-directed learning in a modern political context and criticized the common assumption that self-directed learning is an uncomplicated good thing. He argued that 'self-directed learning is in part inspired by liberal humanism but very largely by a consumerist individualistic conception of the learner, operating within a perspective of a neo-liberal market place, and assumed to be motivated by an uncritical accepted market ideology' (ibid.:212). Yet the potentiality of self-directed learning still exists because learning is about the individual who can break away from the group and become a change agent.

Informal learning

Finally, the new UK government consultation paper (Department for Innovation, Universities and Skills, 2008) and White Paper (Department for Innovation, Universities and Skills, 2009) actually include almost all types of non-school, non-university, non-vocational accredited education under the banner of informal learning. The consultation paper recognizes that 'the greatest area of expansion in informal adult learning has been in self-directed and self-funded activities' (Department for Innovation, Universities and Skills, 2008:10). Throughout the consultation paper, informal learning is not clearly defined but it is regarded as all forms of 'part-time, non-vocational learning where the purpose isn't necessarily to gain a qualification' (Department for Innovation, Universities and Skills, 2009:11). In a sense, it includes everything that offers learning opportunities to citizens, whether state-funded or not, although it acknowledges that the greater part of it is not! That said, we can see immediately that what is being called here 'informal learning' is a combination of forms of all types of adult education and learning, and significantly there is a hidden bias in the term since it conveys the idea that all the important learning is formal – full-time, work orientated, accredited – whereas the remainder which is not so orientated can be lumped together as 'informal'. But this hidden message is not without significance. Indeed, the consultation paper actually acknowledges that the prioritizing of skills and work-related education has stimulated the debate about informal learning (Department for Innovation, Universities and Skills, 2008:9), as we noted earlier.

Conclusion

In this chapter we have examined some of the changes that have occurred in adult and lifelong learning – many of which have occurred since the first edition of this book was published. We have noted how the threefold typology with which we started has itself been conflated into two, reflecting the dominance of the formal structures but with just an acknowledgement of life-wide learning. Yet the prevalence of the latter demonstrates its social if not its political significance, although there is some recognition of its potential significance as Western Europe ages. But now we turn to the issue of what precisely is learning.

4

LEARNING

In the opening chapters of this book we have explored something about the social nature of individuals and the world in which we live and learn. We have seen how rapidly the world is changing and how we are constantly exposed to a society in which we have to keep on learning in order to feel at ease with our society, but so far we have not explored this process. We have, however, recognized that learning is intrinsic to our humanity and so we do not have to account for the fact that we learn; neither do we have to explain the social nature of our learning. However, it is now necessary to explore the nature of learning itself and we will do so in four sections covering, respectively, the nature of learning, theories of learning, an existential/experiential theory of learning that I have developed, and types and styles of learning.

The nature of learning

In the opening chapter we explored the nature of socialization and saw that individuals internalize an 'external' culture through interrelationship from very early in the lifespan. We noted that this process goes on in human relationships from birth, but in the second chapter we recognized the significance of information technology, and so we can see that this internalization process becomes less significant for social relationships as we age and receive more input from the media. However, the way in which we respond to the media will depend upon our previous experiences and our social situation.

These processes can be depicted in the form of a cyclic relationship between individuals and the wider world as learners both process and internalize the objectified culture of the wider society and thereafter externalize their learning through social interaction. It is now possible to develop a broad learning cycle. However, it must be emphasized that the learning cycle represents only one episode of learning and this repeats itself like a spiral, even like a double or triple helix, through the process of time as various attributes of the person – knowledge, skills, attitudes,

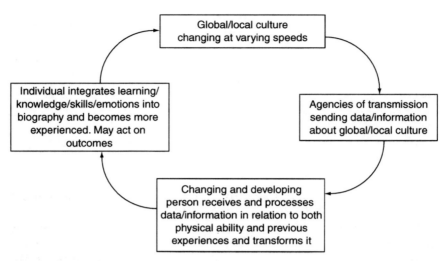

Figure 4.1 A transformative learning cycle.

values, emotions, beliefs and senses – are recipients of experiences from the wider global or local culture, which for simplicity I have called data or information.

Since it is the person who is the recipient of that data or information, it is natural that most learning theories start with the person; in other words, they can be located in the bottom and the left-hand boxes in Figure 4.1. Teaching and other forms of media transmission can be located in the right-hand box, although the nature of this transmission does not always imply a teacher since it can involve discovery learning.

Leaning must always be seen within the wider cultural context and it may be regarded initially as a process of receiving and transforming any element of culture, by whatever means it is transmitted. But even this definition is much wider than those frequently cited by learning theorists, such as that learning is 'a relatively permanent change in behaviour that occurs as a result of practice' (Hilgard and Atkinson, 1967:270) or learning is 'any more or less permanent change in behaviour which is the result of experience' (Borger and Seaborne, 1966:14). Both these definitions emphasize a change in behaviour as being the main focus of learning, but this is too restrictive because it necessitates the exclusion of the acquisition of new cognitive knowledge unless it results in behavioural change. The definition offered by Brundage and Mackeracher is much closer to that suggested here; they state that adult learning 'refers both to the process which individuals go through as they attempt to change or enrich their knowledge, values, skills or strategies and to the resulting knowledge, values, skill, strategies and behaviour possessed by each individual'

(1980:5). However, this definition, though it conveys many of the main ideas suggested in this section, does not actually capture the totality of the argument. These definitions each emphasize the orientations of the theorists concerned, and in order to criticize their definitions it is necessary to understand their understanding of human learning itself.

Theories of learning

Merriam and Caffarella (1991) have typified the variety of learning theories: behaviourist, cognitive, humanist and social. In many ways this is a useful framework within which to examine the theories that have been produced over the years, although it has to be recognized that these categories are not discrete and that considerable overlap exists between them. At the same time, it may be seen that there are ideological underpinnings to the different theories and there are implicit statements of the human condition to be discovered in each one. No theory is value-free, so theory cannot be divorced from the wider world of ideology and belief. In this section, behaviourist and cognitive theories will first be discussed and then experiential theories will be examined, which are both social and humanistic.

Behaviourist theories

Three forms of behaviourist theory are discussed here: imitation, connectionism and conditioning.

1   Imitation is perhaps the most fundamental of all learning. We all know the experience of going into a new environment, a club or a society and not quite knowing how to behave. We watch other people closely in the hope that we can see what is regarded as the correct behavioural pattern. It is an almost universal practice and it begins very early in our lives. As we see, it depends on human relationships, which are regarded by scholars of all persuasions as crucial to human development. Copying what we see and what we experience is basic to our human being. Dawkins (1976) considers this to be genetic and he (1976:15) calls it a replicator. He feels that any theory of the origin of life must have fundamental properties, namely self-replicating genetic entities (1976:269), and since learning is so closely related to life, replication is necessary. However, Tomasello (1999), who regards children as 'imitation machines', thinks that there is insufficient evidence for this genetic perspective. He (1999:83) claims that 'imitative learning ... represents infants' initial entry into the cultural world around them'. It is in the differing interpretations of culture that these two perspectives are antithetical and it seems to me that as yet the memetic

theory of Dawkins lacks sufficient proof to displace the traditional understanding of culture and learning. But imitation remains fundamental to living and to learning.

2   Connectionism was perhaps the first theory to gain recognition as 'trial and error' learning. This was first propounded by Thorndike (1928) towards the end of the nineteenth century, and as a result of his research with animals he expounded three laws, that of:

- readiness, which relates to the circumstances under which the learner is satisfied, annoyed, etc.;
- exercise, which refers to the process of strengthening the connection discovered between stimulus and response by practice;
- effect, which relates to the process of strengthening, or breaking, any connection as a result of the consequences of any action.

Basically, this theory focuses on a quite fundamental way of behaving: that if the learner discovers some act or explanation to be effective or valid, it will be repeated until such time as the consequences of the action no longer produce the desired or expected results. By virtue of starting with the learner, it is hardly surprising that Thorndike was able to pursue his work into adult learning.

3   Conditioning – in contrast to Thorndike's thinking – begins with the teacher. There are two basic theories. Perhaps the best-known of all psychological research into learning is that of Pavlov (1927), who proposed the theory of classical conditioning. Briefly stated, this asserts that the learner learns (is conditioned) to associate the presentation of a reward with a stimulus that occurs fractionally prior to it. Thus, Pavlov's dogs salivated at the sound of a bell since they had been fed when this had been rung on previous occasions. Operant conditioning, however, occurs when the response is shaped by the reward, so that after every action that approaches, approximates to or achieves the desired behaviour, the learner receives a reward. This form of conditioning was expounded by Skinner (1951), who later argued that 'man is a machine in the sense that he is a complex system behaving in lawful ways, but the complexity is extraordinary' (1971:197). Throughout his 1971 book, Skinner suggested that conditioning can explain all learning and that the exciting possibilities for the future lie in what human beings will create of humankind. He grappled with the philosophical problems of behaviourism but was not able to convince everyone that his perspective was quite so all-embracing as he suggested. Even so, there is a great deal of research evidence to support many of the claims of the behaviourists.

There are also a number of problems with the behaviourist approach, two of which are briefly discussed here. First, the definition is conceptually confusing: Hilgard *et al.* suggest that learning 'is a relatively permanent change in behaviour that occurs as the result of prior experience' (1979:217). However, the change of behaviour is a product while learning is the process that occurs before the change; process and product cannot be the same thing. Second, much of the behaviourist research into learning has been conducted on animals and small children, so it has not been possible to research the thought processes that occur during learning, and thus the research methodology is suspect for the claims that are made about the findings. This does not deny that there are behavioural changes as a result of learning; only that learning is the change process, not the behavioural outcome.

Not all conditioning may be intentional, nor is it all conscious, but it certainly occurs during the process of the education of adults. Lovell (1980:35), for instance, suggested that classical conditioning occurred when students chose an evening class or a subject because the tutor had created a warm, friendly atmosphere. By contrast, the process of grading assignments, or praising a reticent student for contributing to a group discussion, is in both cases an aspect of operant conditioning.

Cognitive theories

Cognitive theories will be outlined here: developmental, Gestalt, data processing, transformative and, finally, the work of Bruner.

1   As regards *developmental* theories, perhaps the most influential learning theorist in the West has been Piaget (e.g. 1929), who postulated a number of stages in the process of cognitive development which he related to the process of biological development during childhood:

    Stage 1 Sensori-motor, when infants learn to differentiate between themselves and objects in the external world. This occurs during the first two years of life.

    Stage 2 Pre-operational thought; children classify external objects by single salient features, and this spans the period from about 2 to 4 years.

    Stage 3 Intuitive, when children think in classificatory terms without necessarily being conscious of them, a stage that stretches from pre-operational thought to about 7 years of age.

    Stage 4 Concrete operations, between 7 and 11, when children begin to think using logical operations.

    Stage 5 Formal operational thinking, when children take early steps in abstract conceptual thought.

    Piaget's work has been very influential in education and it also provided a basis for two other well-known thinkers in this area: Kohlberg (1981), who has written about moral development, and Fowler (1981), who has focused on faith development.

71

However, Piaget's final stage is reached before adulthood, so his theories have not been influential among adult educators. Allman (1984), however, pointed to a number of pieces of psychological research which suggest that adult thought processes continue to change and develop through the lifespan. She concentrated on Riegel's (1973) idea of dialectic logic, which demands the ability to tolerate contradictions and which enables the tensions within them to generate new ideas.

Kohlberg's (1981) work on moral judgement is among the best-known developments of the Piagetian approach. He demonstrated how moral theorizing develops in stages with age, and his work has become increasingly significant as people begin to ask the ethical questions once again, including those surrounding adult education and lifelong learning. Kohlberg was clear, however, that each stage is not discrete. The basic premise is that learning is constructivist and that the knowledge gained through the process can be analysed thereafter, but that it is only at different stages in human development that the meaning of the moral concepts can be grasped and operationalized. Hence, younger children have a simpler conceptual understanding of moral knowledge than do those who have developed through a number of previous stages. Other theorists have been greatly influenced by Piaget, including Fowler (1981), who examined religious faith development using a similar framework. But, like that of Piaget, Kohlberg's and Fowler's work has thus far been applied to children far more than to adults, although its significance for the education of adults must be noted here.

In Eastern Europe, Vygotsky (1978, 1986) has had a similar influence, one that is beginning to spread to Western Europe and the United States. Like Piaget, his book *Mind and Society* (1978) focuses on children's development, but his concerns are slightly different. He acknowledges the debt psychology owes Piaget, and offers an extended analysis of his work (1986:112–157). But unlike Western thinkers, who were more concerned with stage in development, Vygotsky was concerned with potential, although he is clear that developmental processes do not coincide with learning processes. For him (1978:90), 'the developmental process lags behind the learning process'. He postulated that there is a level of actual development and also a zone of proximal development; the former he defines as 'the level of development of a child's mental functions that has been established as a result of already *completed* developmental cycles' (1978:85–86; *italics* in original), whereas the latter is 'the distance between the actual developmental level as determined by independent problem solving and the level of potential development as determined by problem solving under adult guidance or in collaboration with more capable peers'.

We see here an important factor in Vygotsky's work: he did not isolate the individual but recognized that development is dependent upon relationship and collaboration. However, Illeris (2002:51) argues that Vygotsky's approach opens itself to the adult controlling the process of development, and therefore to teacher-centred education.

Basing some of his thinking on Vygotsky's work, Engestrom (1987) regards the zone of proximal development as a space for creativity, and this he applies to all forms of activity and learning, in both adults and children. Engestrom has also developed his work with specific reference to activity theory in organizational settings, and in his book *Learning, Working and Imagining* (1990) there are twelve very carefully researched and analysed case studies.

2   *Gestalt* theorists, like the behaviourists, based their understanding on research with animals. The word 'Gestalt' actually means shape or form, and as early as 1912 Max Wertheimer postulated that individuals do not perceive the constituent elements of a phenomenon but perceive them as a totality. He formulated the 'Law of Prägnanz' in which there are four aspects of perception: similarity, proximity, continuity and closure. Similarity refers to the fact that people group phenomena by their similar salient features rather than by their differences; proximity refers to the fact that individuals group phenomena by their closeness to each other rather than by their distance from one another; continuity refers to the fact that objects are often perceived in relation to the pattern or shape that they constitute in their totality; and closure refers to the fact that there is a tendency to complete an incomplete representation, so that the whole is perceived, rather than the incomplete parts (see Child, 1981:73–74). From the holistic perspective, Köhler (1947) suggested that solutions to problems appear to come abruptly, as by a flash of insight, and that they are achieved because the insight emerges from the perception of the relationship between the different factors rather than in response to separate stimuli. While this theory has a number of attractive features, especially since it is recognized that some people are holistic learners, the idea of insight or intuition almost demands that it should be rooted in an earlier process, either socialization or an earlier learning experience, so that it would be unwise to regard all learning in such an inspirational manner.

3   Among the other cognitive approaches to learning is *data processing*, epitomized here by the work of Gagné (1977), who proposed an eight-phase model of learning that may be summarized as follows:

1   motivation – expectancy;
2   apprehending – attention: selective perception;
3   acquisition – coding: storage entry;
4   retention – memory storage;

5   recall – retrieval;
6   generalization – transfer;
7   performance – responding;
8   feedback – reinforcement.

This model has certain attractions in terms of its logical progression. However, it is that logic which seems to oversimplify the process slightly, as will be seen later in this chapter. Other aspects of Gagné's work are discussed more fully in the next chapter.

Gagné focuses upon memory in this model, and Child (1981:112–134) depicts the information-processing model of memory quite clearly when he suggests that learning begins with a stimulus which is partially picked up by a sensory register and processed through selective perception to the short-term memory. This memory has a limited capacity and so only some of the information is retained; some is lost at this stage. He then suggests that what is retained is coded and stored in the long-term memory, from where it can be recalled or rehearsed. Child's emphasis on memory loss here points to the fact that there is a sharp decline in what is remembered immediately after the event, with only 58 per cent being retained after 20 minutes, according to Ebbinghaus, 44 per cent being retained after an hour and only 33 per cent after a day (Child, 1981:119). The loss of memory in this manner indicates that rehearsing that which is stored soon after a learning event will almost certainly add to the amount of material that is remembered and that systematic repetition thereafter continues to aid recall.

4   The fourth groups of theories are concerned with *transformative* learning. As will be pointed out in the following chapter, Gagné also postulated that there are different types of learning, so he was not just concerned with recall of facts, etc. Another theorist who emphasized the distinction between rote learning and meaningful learning is Ausubel (Ausubel *et al.*, 1978). For him, learning is a process of constructing new meaning. This is a feature that Mezirow (1991) has also focused on in transformative learning, which is not surprising, as Mezirow's focus of attention is on adults rather than on the person as a whole. Dahlgren actually defines learning this way: 'To learn is to strive for meaning and to have learned something is to have grasped its meaning' (1984:23–24). Mezirow (1991:12) suggests that learning involves 'using a prior interpretation to construe a new or revised interpretation of the meaning of one's experience to guide future action'. We will look further at the work of Mezirow in the following chapters.

5   The final theorist to be examined here is Bruner (1990:104), who considered 'learning theory' dead, although he did not consider the study of the learning processes insignificant. He has argued for the significance of meaning and meaning-making in his later books, although

his earlier work (1979) was almost exclusively about the education of children. Here he focused on the idea that curiosity is innate, and his work on discovery echoes that discussed above in both behaviourist and cognitive terms. He suggested that to

the degree that one is able to approach learning as a task of discovering something rather than 'learning about' it, to that degree there will be a tendency for the child to work with the autonomy of self-reward or, more properly, be rewarded by discovery itself.

(ibid.:88)

Naturally, this points self-directed learning theorists in the direction of a cognitive strategy that underlies the motivation of some self-directed learners. Bruner also suggests that the main problem that individuals have is in memorizing what they have learned, and, echoing the early Gestalt theorists, he suggests that the way in which the material is organized is related to the amount that can be recalled.

It would be possible to review other theorists who have written about learning from a cognitive framework, but this introduction points to the fact that learning is viewed as a complex set of processes having different outcomes. Other theorists have adopted different approaches, although naturally their analyses overlap in some ways.

Social learning

Vygotsky (1978) clearly recognized the social nature of learning, and we are all well aware of learning through imitation, the adoption of role models, 'sitting by Nellie', and so on. Social learning theory emphasizes behavioural learning, and clearly relies on certain forms of reinforcement, but it is necessary to focus briefly on those researchers who have seen learning from a social perspective. The main social learning theorist has been Bandura (e.g. 1977, 1989), who has shown through numerous experiments that many of the behavioural patterns that we exhibit have been acquired through observing and copying others. I have already referred to this in the previous subsection. Indeed, we are probably all aware that we do it, especially when we enter new situations and are unsure about how to behave. We watch others and imitate their behaviour in order to feel safe in the strange environment. Bandura showed that children acquire aggressive behaviour in the same way, and so it seems strange to hear people putting forward arguments that children are not affected by the aggression that they observe on television!

'Sitting by Nellie' – watching the expert perform – gained a bad reputation in the days when practical knowledge was not emphasized. But this is perhaps because we tended to assume that it would result in unconsidered behaviour or ignorant practice; today we know that, while we might not acquire all the theory when we watch the expert, we rarely act mindlessly as a result of imitation. Indeed, as adults we choose to focus our attention on specific role models, whereas children may have less choice in their role models.

We can imitate in whatever situation we find ourselves, as Lave and Wenger (1991) show in their book *Situated Learning* and Wenger (1998) develops in his study of communities in practice. When we couple social learning with theories of conditioning we can see how we learn to fit in happily, and thus can begin to see how such a theory leads to a functionalist perspective on social groups – a theory that was discredited in sociological theory many years ago. Hence, we have to balance the idea of the social with that of functionalism. In addition, we cannot project this to a theory of group learning because not all groups function in such a harmonious manner. Also, some individuals learn to question the overarching culture of such dominated and conformist work groups and seek either to change the situation or to rebel against it. In this way, however, we can also see how it is possible to develop a sociology of learning.

Experience and learning

While Dewey was among the first educational theorists to advocate the centrality of personal experience, he was clear from the outset that the 'belief that all genuine education comes about through experience ... does not mean that all experiences are genuinely or equally educative' (1938:25). At the same time, it is important to note how foregrounding experience, especially practice experience, calls into question the primacy of theory over practice. Knowles (e.g. 1980a) focused our thinking on the centrality of experience in his work on andragogy, and this is not surprising in the light of the fact that adult education itself has traditionally been learner centred. This is something that Boud *et al.* (1983) also emphasized when they focused on the idea that learning was reflective experience. Many writers have focused on experience as a basis for human learning over the years. It has been Kolb's (1984) work that has become the popular focus of this work, although one of his main aims was building a theory based on the thinking of those who preceded him. The concept of experience is one that educators have taken for granted and so have not endeavoured to explore in the same manner as have philosophers such as Dewey (1938), Husserl (1973) and Oakeshott (1933). Oakeshott does make the point, however, that experience, 'of all the words in the philosophic vocabulary, is the most difficult to manage' (1933:9). Consequently, we shall now discuss the concept of experience as part of our approach to experiential learning.

Kolb's (1984) learning cycle has become one of the central images of experiential learning, although Kolb and Fry claimed from the outset that the learning cycle may begin at any stage and that it should be a continuous circle (see Figure 4.2). Note that there are elements of previous theories in this cycle, which is quite understandable since every theory is seeking to explain the same complex phenomenon. In addition, Kolb and Fry suggest that the movement in the vertical axis represents a process of conceptualization while that on the horizontal axis represents the variation between active and passive manipulation. They claim also that each quadrant represents a learning style, but we shall return to the idea of learning styles at the end of this chapter.

This cycle, which has become tremendously popular (probably because of its simplicity), does not do justice to the complexity of human learning. Jarvis (e.g. 1987, 2009a) has tested the cycle many times with a variety of groups of adult learners and on each occasion the participants have demonstrated that it is an over-simple description of the learning processes. We shall return to this shortly – but this work has become the springboard for future research.

But a great deal of vocational education has emphasized work experience, and even learning in the workplace (e.g. Marsick, 1987). Experiential learning consists of a number of different approaches: Weil and McGill (1989:4), for instance, suggest that there are four 'villages', representing the 'different meanings and purposes for experiential learning'. Their (ibid.:4–19) four villages are:

1   the assessment and accreditation of 'prior' experiential learning;
2   experiential learning and change in post-school education and training;
3   experiential learning and social change;
4   personal growth and development.

Unfortunately, the idea of practical experience (internship) is missing from this categorization, but in professional education it is a most important form

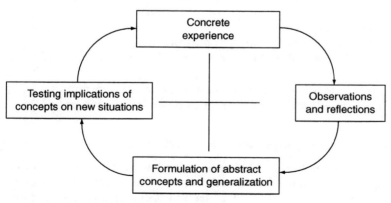

Figure 4.2 Kolb's experiential learning cycle.
Source: Kolb and Fry (1975:33–37).

of learning. While it may be included in the second village, it may also be the case that practical experience is not regarded by Weil and McGill as learning so much as the application, or transfer, of previous classroom learning into practice. However, the practice situation is actually one in which potential learning experiences do occur. Indeed, transfer is a misleading idea, since when students enter the practical situation for the first time, they are entering a new learning situation, and this is true irrespective of how much learning has occurred in the classroom before that new experience happened. The students are now having for the first time a primary, rather than a secondary, experience about practice, and they experience it differently. They are experiencing a new learning situation, so that the more they have learned from previous experiences, the more likely they are to have some knowledge that they can use in the present situation.

Weil and McGill endeavoured to provide a descriptive framework whereby it becomes possible to grasp the multitude of meanings that the term has acquired rather than providing theoretical perspectives to enrich our understanding of the learning processes. Indeed, in McGill's work with other collaborators he has also popularized action learning. Action learning is often a teaching form that uses active experiences as the basis of learning, but McGill and Beaty (1995:23) associate it with a positive approach to life. They write, 'Action learning is the antithesis of believing that we can do nothing about our situation. Whatever the context, people who use action learning believe that there is always something, however small, that can be done or positively not done.' In a later book, McGill and Brockbank (2004) develop this approach into a wider theory of teaching and learning, but it remains a clear form of experiential learning. Indeed, it lies at the heart of Boud's and Miller's (1996:9–10) five propositions upon which learning is based:

1. Experience is the foundation of, and stimulus for, learning.
2. Learners actively construct their own experience.
3. Learning is holistic.
4. Learning is socially and culturally constructed.
5. Learning is influenced by the socio-emotional context in which it occurs.

These points are written for animators of experiential learning, but they do provide a framework within which it can be understood more widely.

Wider perspectives on experiential learning

Even a cursory examination of books on experiential learning shows that the concept of experience is treated in a variety of ways by different authors. Sometimes, for instance, it is taken for granted (Boud et al., 1983; Fraser, 1995; Marton et al., 1984; Smith and Spurling, 1999; Tuijnman and van der Kamp, 1993; Vaill, 1996; Winch, 1998). Many writers imply that experiential learning is participatory. Elsewhere, Henry (1989, 1992) treats experience as having two modes: all learning is experiential, and experiential learning is about reflecting upon the experience (see also Eraut, 1994; Peterson, 1989). Others tend to use the term with reference to the sum of all past learning (Knowles, 1980a), which echoes Oakeshott's analysis.

Weil and McGill (1989:248) also make this distinction between the two phases of experience:

> Experiential learning is the process whereby people, individually and in association with others, engage in direct encounter and then *purposely* reflect upon, validate and transform, give personal and social meaning to and seek to integrate the outcomes of these processes into new ways of knowing, being, acting and interacting in relation to their world. [*italics* in original]

Here, their emphasis on the idea that experience is having a direct encounter with the world does not give due recognition to both perception and construction, but it does allow for sense experience as well as cognitive. At the same time, we can understand why the idea of a direct encounter arises since we are rarely consciously aware of the processes by which we construct our reality, and even less aware, as Freud taught us, of the effects of sublimation and repression (Hall, 1954). Indeed, it might well be that it was previous unpleasant experiences that were repressed, or that the experiences might have been traumatic – and, as Dewey (1938) pointed out, they can result in mis-education. This process, or these processes, of construction occur unconsciously and are influenced by both our biography and the situation within which the experience occurs. In other words, our biography – that is, the whole person – is involved both consciously and unconsciously in constructing the experience from which we learn, but it is also being changed throughout the lifespan by the experiences that it helps to construct. But as our life histories also include both our past constructed perceptions and our sublimations and repressions, it is difficult to regard all the thought processes as being entirely rational.

Crawford (2005) also recognizes the need to spend time on our experiences; she writes of attentive experience. In the same way, we can see that this is a matter of concentration on our experience so that we do not miss the innocuous little details that may actually determine the precision of an action. Sennett (2008) also discusses the attention to detail in skills learning; it demands both concentration and commitment.

Existential learning

Once we begin to focus on Freud, we can begin to understand just how complex is the human learning process. Indeed, it is such a complex process that

I do not think that we shall ever understand it fully, but in my own work I have tried to understand the process – a quest that I began in the mid-1980s and continued ever since. My first book on the subject (Jarvis, 1987) was published as a result of my initial research into learning.

Over a period of about fifteen months in 1985 and 1986, groups of adults participated in a project that did not actually begin as a research project, but as a series of workshops about learning. However, as they proceeded I recognized that they were generating research data and that I was actually a practitioner researcher (Jarvis, 1999). In each of the workshops, all the participants were first invited to write down a learning incident in their lives. They were asked to state what started the incident, how it progressed and, finally, when and why they concluded that it was completed. Having undertaken this exercise, they were then paired in order to discuss their different learning experiences, and it was suggested to them that they might like to examine the similarities and the differences in their experiences. Thereafter, two pairs were put together and they then discussed their four different learning experiences, and soon the groups were actually discussing learning rather than just their own experiences. At this stage they were introduced to Kolb's learning cycle (see p. 77), which I told them was probably not sufficiently sophisticated to do justice to their four experiences. I asked them to redraw it to fit their own experiences. We had all types of diagrams, many of them spirals. All were more complex than Kolb's diagram, but all were modifications of it.

This exercise was conducted on nine separate occasions both in the United Kingdom and in the United States, with teachers of adults and teachers of children, with university lecturers and adult university students who were teachers of adults in their full-time occupation, with younger people and with some not so young participants, with men and women. In all, about 200 people participated in the exercise, although the sample was middle-class and not tightly controlled. A complex model of learning was constructed by combining the many modifications of Kolb's diagram that the different groups of four produced. This model was subsequently tested in seminars, etc. over another nine-month period, again in both the United Kingdom and the United States, with some 200 or 300 people participating in these. The final model appeared, with a full description of this methodology, in a book (Jarvis, 1987). Subsequently, I have continued to use this model, adapting it as I realized how it was still not accurate. Even now I realize that the model below is still an oversimplification of the complexity of human learning and that we may never know sufficient to embrace all the processes in a single model.

I have continued that research until the present day and as I have done so, so I have altered my definition and my depiction of the processes to reflect my latest thinking on the topic. I now define it as the combination of processes throughout a lifetime whereby the whole person – body (genetic, physical and biological) and mind (knowledge, skills, attitudes, values, emotions, meaning, beliefs and senses) – experiences social situations, the content of which is then transformed cognitively, emotively or practically (or through any combination) and integrated into the individual person's biography resulting in a continually changing (or more experienced) person.

This process may be depicted as in Figure 4.3.

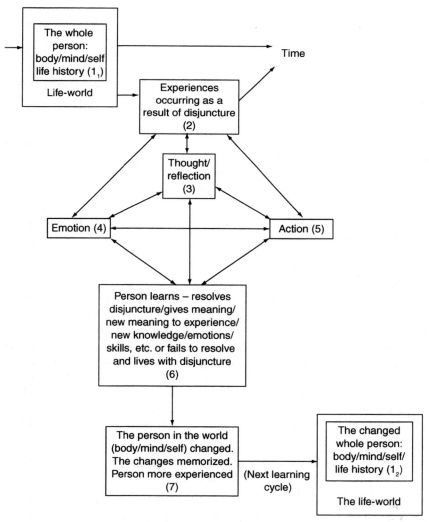

Figure 4.3 The transformation of the person through learning.

We need to follow Figure 4.3 through each point so that we can begin to appreciate the complexity of the processes of learning that are contained within this diagram.

Time

The horizontal arrows at the top and bottom of the diagram depict time – but we often live through time and presume on our life-world, apparently not learning. For as long as this occurs, we are not conscious of having an experience. In a sense, we are not changing, nor are we changing the world. For as long as we can presume upon the world, we do not consciously affect it, nor do we consciously learn – but this is an issue for learning; we may be internalizing some information unconsciously. It is only when, for various reasons, we cannot presume upon the world that we are forced to question it: why? what for? how? These are the questions that a young child asks at about the age of 4 years. They are questions that parents and teachers often dread – and yet they are the indicators of the need to learn; indeed, they are indicators of our own humanity. We continue to have these experiences throughout our lives, and the extent to which we pursue answers to the questions does depend to some extent on our personalities and the extent to which we are curious. It is at moments like this that we become conscious of time; it is almost as if time stands still and we become aware of the present.

The experience of time is an important factor in the adult's learning process and one that is often forgotten in discussions about learning, but it helps construct the way in which we interpret an experience. Brundage and Mackeracher consider that children and young adults 'tend to measure time as "time from birth"; adults past 40 tend to measure time as "until death"' (1980:35–36). Hence, as time becomes shorter, so the learning needs focus more acutely upon the problems of the immediate present, and previous experience becomes increasingly important to the older person. It may be, therefore, that certain subjects are more appropriate to the psychological orientations of different age groups: history, for instance, may be a more popular study for those whose orientation is already towards their past experiences than would be mathematics. However, more research is required to investigate the extent to which there is any correlation between preferred 'learning' topics, age and orientation towards time.

Person

We explored the concept of the person in the first chapter (and it has been more fully explored elsewhere; see Jarvis, 2009a). I pointed there to the significance of intentionality, and in this, Tomasello's dual inheritance model of our past is important. In common with the apes, we have both sociogenesis and cultural learning. Both of these have a common cognitive dimension, but human cognition has developed very rapidly – more rapidly than evolution would allow. This has enabled us to learn culturally, and we learn the subculture of our social world, but nonetheless we are all affected by our evolution and genetic inheritance. But even more significantly, Tomasello's model recognizes the place of the body and learning through the senses; learning is multi-sensorial.

Life-world

As we learn the subculture of the society into which we are born, so we construct our own life-world. We feel at home in this environment and we can take the world for granted, as we saw in the first chapter. However, the social world is not like a machine that operates in an unchanging manner. Because it is a world of human beings who can behave unpredictably and one in which social change is very rapid, we are constantly faced with unknown situations upon which we cannot presume, and then we are not sure how we cope with them. It is this that I have called disjuncture.

Disjuncture

It is possible to argue that for the most part people live almost unconscious of the passing of time; they act in a taken-for-granted manner. Bergson (Lacey, 1989) called this 'duration', which is the almost unconscious passing of time. However, he was clear that there is still a consciousness of the passing of time even when people act in an almost taken-for-granted manner, but it is at a low level. This taken-for-grantedness lies in the fact that people are in harmony with their socio-cultural environment; there is convergence between their perception of the world and their biography, and they do not have to think too deeply before they act because, almost instinctively, they seem to know how to act in those particular circumstances. It is not, however, intuitive but the result of previous learning experiences. They are bringing their past learning to bear upon a present situation and they experience it in a meaningful manner and appear to act instinctively. In many situations, however, we do act almost unconsciously; we are aware that we actually do have 'to think on our feet' and, having understood the situation, we act accordingly. This points us to the fact that we actually construct our experiences.

Disjuncture is a complex phenomenon and yet it is best described as the gap between what we expect to perceive when we have an experience of the world as a result of our previous learning (and, therefore, our biography) and what we are actually confronted with. The complexity of this experience may be depicted as shown in Figure 4.4.

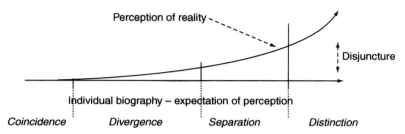

Figure 4.4 Disjuncture: the distance between perception of the reality and individual biography.

In the figure, *coincidence* is when there is no conscious experience because we can presume upon the world. *Divergence* is when there is a slight difference and we can adjust our behaviour to respond to the situation without changing our understanding of the world (our theory/ meaning), and can do so in an almost unconscious manner. *Separation* is when there is a larger gap between the two, and this is where the questioning begins and where our conscious learning starts. *Distinction* is when the gap is so wide that we know that in order to bridge it we have to undertake a great deal of learning, perhaps by undertaking a course of study. In the end the gap may grow so wide that we know that we can never bring the two together. This may be a meaningless or a very meaningful experience. Conscious disjuncture begins at the point of separation; we are aware of the situation and we consciously experience the world, but we do this cognitively, emotively and practically. Disjuncture occurs in all three dimensions of experience, and is often a combination, although sometimes it occurs in a single dimension.

Experience

Life might be described as a passage through time, so time must be the starting point of any discussion of experience. Human existence is situated within time and emerges through it, and I have argued elsewhere that learning is the process through which the human, as opposed to the biological, being grows and develops (Jarvis, 1992). In a simplistic sense, time is experienced as past, present and future. But the present is always problematic because immediately people try to conceptualize their present, it becomes a past event, so that, more realistically, people think about time as a matter of past and future, even though the act of experiencing is itself something that occurs at their intersection.

Since we do construct our experiences, we do so within our own lifeworlds – or cultural frameworks. Consequently, our reality is determined by our culture, and this, in its own way, affects not only our identity but also the way in which we learn. We do not all learn in precisely the same manner and we know, for instance, that Chinese learners approach learning in a different manner from Western learners (see Watkins and Biggs, 1996).

Experience involves being conscious of the world, aware of the specific situation and knowing that we are having an experience, even if we do not actually acknowledge it at the time. We are recipients of stimuli that originate externally to us but which we internalize through one or more of our senses, and we become aware of the situation and focus upon it. These stimuli may be regarded as primary experiences; we experience them directly and they are most frequently sense experiences, or mediated or secondary experiences (these are cognitive) in which we are told or read about something via a mediator, a teacher or via the media themselves. Nearly all traditional teaching is through the provision of secondary experiences – all theory is secondary! We will return to this in a later chapter on teaching. But we only learn from the internalized experience. However, these experiences can occur at any time in our lives and in any place, so that we do not learn only in educational institutions; we learn at work, at home, in the community, and so on.

Rogers captures something of the complexity of experience in experiential learning in a rather descriptive manner when he writes:

> Let me explain more precisely the elements involved in significant or experiential learning. One element is the quality of personal involvement: the whole person, both in feeling and in cognitive aspects. Self-initiated involvement is another element. Even when the impetus or stimulus comes from the outside, the sense of discovery, of reaching out, of grasping and comprehending comes from within. Another element is pervasiveness. It makes a difference in the behavior, the attitudes, even perhaps the personality of the learner. Yet another element relates to the learners' self-evaluation of the event. She knows whether it is meeting her need, whether it leads towards what she wants to know, whether it illuminates her dark area of ignorance. The onus of the evaluation, we might say, resides definitely in the learner. Its essence is meaning.
>
> (Rogers and Freiberg, 1994:36)

The idea is that 'significant learning' is experiential and that it occurs at the intersection of arrested experience and frozen time. Rogers' emphasis on the whole person is important since, at this point of intersection, individuals are aware of more than just cognitive phenomena. It is the whole person who is consciously aware of the situation – that is, it is the individual's skills, attitudes, values, feelings, emotions, beliefs as well as cognitions. It is all of these that help construct the experience itself. However, there is a problem with this wholeness since we may be consciously aware of an odour, for instance, which points us beyond the cognitive when we experience. Smell is a sense experience, but we must hold the sense in our mind. This is what Polanyi (1967) called tacit knowledge. We could not accurately describe a particular smell but we would recognize it on another occasion. The wholeness of the person demands a tacit dimension to most of our knowledge.

The concept of experience is most problematic, and books have been written about it (see Jarvis, 2009a for an introduction to the problem), since it is most important if we are really going to understand the nature of experiential learning – but as we are having, and after we have had, an experience, we think, feel and act upon that experience.

Thinking, feeling, doing

We deal with our experience by memorizing it, thinking about it, feeling it or doing something about it, and so on. Significantly, the content of our experience depends upon how long it lasts and what degree of attention we give to it. Crawford (2005) shows how attentiveness to our experiences helps us be aware of the senses, other than cognition, that affect our bodies and change our learning, and she suggests that it is during attentive experience that the more spiritual side of our being becomes more apparent. The fact that we try to bound our learning by time – often short amounts of it because of the pressure under which many of us live – means that we fail to appreciate the richness of our experiences. The outcome of the processes is that we learn about the content of the experience and/or we learn more about ourselves even though we are unable to learn from the content of the experience. As a result, we become changed individuals, as we see in box 7 of Figure 4.3. Then the process begins all over again, or indeed two or more processes might be going on simultaneously, and so Figure 4.3 makes it clear that the process is ongoing. Learning is an ontological process.

Types and styles of learning

Using Figure 4.3 as a basis, we will now look at some of the various types of learning that we engage in either consciously or unconsciously. It is necessary to point out that traditionally the different types of learning have been discussed from a cognitive perspective, but the following discussion is broader. Self-directed learning is not included here because the process can actually involve many different types of learning and it has been discussed already – and it will be discussed again when we look at some methods of teaching, such as project teaching.

Some people are rigid in their approach to learning, since once they have discovered a successful method, they always seek to apply that method. This creates its own difficulties, since problems emerge that cannot be solved by the normal approach.

Types of learning

Ten different types of learning are discussed in what follows. Note that I have not included problem solving as a separate type. There are a number of reasons for this, because disjuncture itself is a problematic situation and analytical thought is a form of reflection.

Non-learning

Non-learning occurs when we take a situation for granted and we act upon it in a taken-for-granted manner. It is depicted in Figure 4.3 as the time arrow, with the people in their life-world just continuing, unaffected by anything. In other words, there is no disjuncture since we all live patterned existences, and in this sense we 'fit into' the situation because this is what we have learned to do as a result of previous experiences. There is no new learning experience. I have called this presumption. Indeed, it is necessary that much of our daily living is so patterned or else it would not be possible for individuals to have social interaction and there could be no such thing as society; society has traditionally been premised on non-learning and so a rapidly changing society is one that might be called a learning society.

There are other forms of learning that I have called non-learning. Illeris (2007:160–175) regarded then as defences against learning when he adopted the idea of non-learning for his work; I called these non-consideration and rejection. While his discussion of the criteria for these positions is more elaborated than mine, he does not add to the basic points behind these two forms.

Non-consideration

Non-consideration occurs when we actually experience disjuncture and know that we need to learn something new and we are presented with the potentiality of a new learning experience – but we do not take it up. It may be because we do not have the time; we live in a rapidly changing world and we often do not have time to be attentive to our experiences, as Crawford (2005) points out, or because the gap between our biography and our perception is too large to be bridged, as we see in Figure 4.3, where the concept of distinction is introduced. Consequently, we can trace this in the learning model (Figure 4.3) as exiting at box 2. However, we are also presented with a question at this point: while we reject the opportunity to learn what was demanded as a result of the disjuncture, we may still reflect about the situation that has caused the disjunction and decide that we are too busy, and so on – so that we learn incidentally as a result of failing to consider an opportunity to learn. In other words, we still learn something about ourselves and so there is a secondary route through the diagram that takes us through boxes 3 to 6 and on to 7.

Rejection

A similar type of situation arises when we deliberately and consciously reject a new learning opportunity that has arisen as a result of disjuncture. This may be because we hold attitudes that protect our sense of self-identity and we feel threatened by the situation; it may be that we have repressed our suppressed experiences in our unconscious, which is causing us to reject the situation, and this rejection may express itself in an emotional reaction to the situation (see Illeris, 2007:161ff.). Once again, we exit at box 2 (Figure 4.3) but there is the possibility that we exit at either box 3 or box 4. But once we reject the opportunity to learn, we need to ask ourselves whether we actually learn more about ourselves as a result and then our learning follows the route box 3 → box 6 → box 7.

Ambivalence

In my work I have assumed ambivalence, but Illeris (2007:167–168) has extended the idea of non-learning to ambivalence in a most valid manner. His own discussion on this starts with the feminist literature (Becker-Schmidt, 1987) on the ambivalence experienced by many women between motherhood and productive labour. In a sense this is a situation that may be regarded as problem solving and at the heart of all learning. We are confronted with a disjunctural experience to which there is no ready answer and in which there may be a conflict in our emotions or between our rational thought and our emotions, and so on. In this sense, it is actually a form of reflective learning but always accompanied and influenced by our emotions (boxes 1 → 2 → 3/4 → 6 → 7).

Pre-conscious knowledge learning (incidental learning)

Pre-conscious knowledge learning is learning through the bodily senses. As I have pointed out already, this form of learning begins in the womb since the fetus is the recipient of movements, sounds, tastes and so on that occur during the latter half of pregnancy. We carry these bodily learned experiences into our later life in a variety of ways, although a great deal more research is needed for us to understand this phenomenon more fully. As a form of pre-conscious learning that occurs before birth, it does not find a route through my learning diagram (Figure 4.3), although we can see routes in the following discussion on memory. However, we also learn incidentally as we live our daily experiences, as epitomized in the above discussion on non-learning, and we only become aware of it when a subsequent experience brings to the level of consciousness what we have already experienced incidentally and, perhaps, unconsciously.

Memorization

Memorization is what many people traditionally considered as learning: a non-reflective cognitive skill in which we recall the 'facts' as we have learned them. A great deal of teaching in school has been based on this approach to learning, for example in the teaching of the sciences, history, and so on. This form of memorization is intentional and we can see the route through Figure 4.3 as boxes 1 → 3 → 6 → 7. However, there are many unintentional, or incidental, forms of learning that are a combination of pre-conscious learning and memorization. These occur when we have a sense experience and think about it at a later time. The significant thing about this approach to memorization is that the sense experience precedes the cognitive. Memorization, in the form of reminiscence, becomes very significant in seniors' learning (see Housden, 2007).

Emotional learning

Many of our emotions are hard-wired (see Turner and Stets, 2005) but there are others that we learn during the process of everyday living, and in this instance we follow the route 1 → 2 → 4/3 → 6 → 7 (Figure 4.3). This form of learning is essential to propel us to act upon our learning since cognition alone cannot do this (Goleman, 1998).

Action learning

We have already discussed action learning and we have noted that among the most common forms of learning are both imitation and trial and error. Both are action forms of learning and so for completeness they are included here. The learning route is boxes 1 → 2 → 5/4/3 → 6 → 7 (Figure 4.3). Action learning frequently occurs through bodily learning – that is, through sense experience. It is about skills learning, which Nyiri (1988) sees as being the way in which expertise is acquired. We try things out and drop them when they do not work, and the more that we do this over the years, the greater our expertise becomes; expertise is not an immediate process! It must be acknowledged that in some more mindless action learning the cognitive and the emotive dimensions play a less significant role.

Discovery learning

Trial-and-error learning (action learning) is a form of discovery learning but it is not the only one. Discovery learning occurs when we find the solution to a problem – active or cognitive – incidentally. It also occurs when we undertake a deliberate experiment, like testing a hypothesis, and thus many forms of scientific research are based on discovery learning.

Contemplation (reflective)

Reflective learning is the type of learning that occurs when philosophers and mathematicians reflect upon their problems. Indeed, problem-solving learning itself is often purely contemplative. Naturally, the spiritual contemplation that we all engage in as we think about profound questions concerning our existence all come within this form of learning – the route of which is $1 \rightarrow 2 \rightarrow 3/4 \rightarrow 6 \rightarrow 7$ (Figure 4.3).

The ten forms of learning listed above do not claim to be exhaustive but are listed to demonstrate the complexity of the learning process and illustrate why it is almost impossible to achieve a comprehensive theory of learning (Jarvis, 2006).

Learning and thinking styles

In the first part of this sub-section we will look at the traditional approaches to learning style and in the second we will examine two more recent approaches to thinking styles.

Learning styles

There has been considerable research over the years into what came to be known as learning styles, and in the summary that follows I have listed some of the main ones. There has always been a question as to whether these are different ways of learning or different personality characteristics. It has been widely recognized that we have different strategies for learning, but few educators have tried to match their teaching to these different approaches to learning, with the exception of the work undertaken at Lancaster (Entwistle, 1981). Some of the impetus for the work at Lancaster came from Marton and Säljö (Marton *et al.*, 1984:39–40), who examined the way that students learned from reading and discovered that those who focused on the text and tried to remember it never really learned what it was trying to convey. They called this a surface approach to learning. By contrast, those students who adopted a deep approach to learning tried to understand its meaning.

The following list summarizes some of the more traditional approaches to learning styles that have been adopted by different writers on the subject.

- *Active versus passive.* It will be seen from the learning cycle that some learners may actively initiate their experience and seek out information; these are self-directed learners. Others may be more passive in the receipt of information provided for them.
- *Assimilators versus accommodators.* Kolb (1984:78) described the assimilator as one whose dominant learning abilities are abstract conceptualization and reflective observation, and the accommodator as one whose strength lies in active experimentation and learning from concrete experience.
- *Concrete versus abstract.* Some learners like to start with the concrete situation, such as the experience, while others prefer to start from the abstract, theoretical idea. The distinction is similar to the preceding one.
- *Convergers versus divergers.* Convergers are best at abstract conceptualization and active experimentation, while divergers' strengths lie in reflective observation and concrete experience (Kolb, 1984:77).
- *Field dependence versus field independence.* According to Witkin, in the former mode 'perception is strongly dominated by the overall organization of the field, as fused' (1965:24). In the latter mode, 'parts of the field are experienced as discrete from organised background' (ibid.).
- *Focusing versus scanning.* If learners have a problem to solve, focusers will examine it as a totality and generate hypotheses that will be modified in the light of new information, while scanners will select one aspect of the problem and assume it to be the solution, until subsequent information disproves it, when they have to recommence the task. While not the same, this approach is similar to Marton and Säljö's approach to surface and deep learning.
- *Holistic versus serialistic.* This approach reflects Gestalt psychology; some learners see phenomena as a whole while others string together the parts.
- *Reflection versus impulsivity.* This is similar to focusing and scanning. Kagan, who undertook his studies with children, wrote that 'a child who does not reflect upon the probable validity of alternative solution sequences is likely to follow through the first idea that occurs to him. This strategy is more likely to end up in failure than one that involves reflection' (1971:54–57).
- *Rigidity versus flexibility.* Some people are rigid in their approach to learning; once they have discovered a successful method, they always seek to apply that same method. This creates its own difficulties, since problems emerge that cannot be solved by the normal approach.

Other people can change their approach depending on the situations in which they find themselves.

Thinking styles

However, there have also been other pieces of work that have avoided the terms 'learning' and 'style', and in drawing this chapter to a close, we will look at two of these: Belenky *et al.* (1986) used the phrase 'ways of knowing' and Sternberg (1997) wrote about 'thinking styles'.

Belenky et al.

The work of Belenky *et al.* has a number of major strengths, one being that their research comprised an intensive study of the lives of women, and so their discussion about 'ways of knowing' is quite existential. While their work was with women, they did not view this as an exclusively feminist study and recognized that these ways of knowing might be as relevant to men as to the women they studied, and this I believe to be true. They traced the life history of 135 women through in-depth interviews, and as a result of their analysis they suggested that there are five different ways of knowing (the fourth of which is subdivided into two): silence, received knowledge, subjective knowledge, procedural knowledge (separate and connected) and constructed knowledge.

SILENCE

Silence is described as being 'deaf and dumb' since some of the women in the study could not learn from the voices of others and they themselves felt voiceless. They felt passive, reactive and dependent, unable to speak out or protest. They did not feel that they could learn from their own experience and they depended on authority; the higher the authority, the more they accepted that authority. Consequently, secondary experience is by far the most important to their learning. They could only describe themselves in terms of how others described them; in a sense, they were alienated persons.

RECEIVED KNOWLEDGE

Some of the women learned to listen to the voices of others but had no confidence in their own ability to think. Once again, authorities (experts, teachers, professors, and so on) have the right answers; they know the 'truth'. The idea that there is no truth, probably merely conflicting perspectives, rarely crossed their minds. They believed what they were told. Knowledge always lay outside of them and so they always sought to learn from the expert – in a non-reflective manner. Belenky *et al.* describe these as 'selfless selves'.

SUBJECTIVE KNOWLEDGE

To reach the state of subjective knowing, individuals have to wrest control of their lives from others. This period of transition (which is not age-related, but about half of the interviewees were subjectivist) rarely had anything to do with learning in an educational setting, although it could be described as a transformative learning experience. However, it is described as a realization of failed authority (Belenky *et al.* specify failed male authority). Now the authoritarian position is no longer valid. For some, however, a return to education follows from reaching this stage of subjective knowing, but since they had considerable doubts about the authoritarian atmosphere of educational institutions, they found it hard to conform without retreating into a position of silent conformity while privately disputing much of what they heard and saw.

> Subjectivist women distrust logic, analysis, abstraction and even language itself. They see these methods as alien territory belonging to men. As we listened to subjectivist women describe their attitudes about truth and knowing, we heard them argue against and stereotype those experts and remote authorities whom social institutions often promote as holding the keys to the truth – teachers, doctors, scientists, men in general. It was as if, by turning inwards for answers, they had to deny strategies for knowing that they perceived as belonging to the masculine world.
>
> (Belenky *et al.*, 1986:71)

Now the primary experience is more important, since they have the confidence to know how to handle it; for these women, truth is experienced. They tended to be intuitive in the existential sense of just knowing what to do. Feelings played an important part; knowing what to do came from within but ideas came from outside, for these women.

PROCEDURAL KNOWLEDGE

The procedural knowledge approach sees the subjectivist approach as being in conflict with a recognition that there is external validity. This creates a major dilemma in education when teachers and professors tell students how to handle or describe data, since procedural knowing is the conflict between external authority and the subjectivist position.

Knowledge is acquired by systematic analysis, and the content becomes less important than the method by which the knowledge is acquired. It is now something that is gained objectively and dispassionately. Learners have to be critical thinkers, and there are two forms:

1   *Separate.* Knowledge becomes something that is objective, and information has to be treated with a degree of scepticism. Experts are now only as good as their arguments, but the doubting of information is still regarded as doubting the informer or teacher; it is personal rather than impersonal. Being critical in this way is not a congenial form of conversation, even between friends. There is still an underlying 'will to truth', as Foucault describes it (Sheridan, 1980). Since the knowledge is now important, the self has to be played down – for example, by writing in the third person.

2   *Connected.* In this form of procedural knowing, there is an attempt to understand the other's perspectives and points of view. Now empathy enters into the equation: 'If one can discover the experiential logic behind these ideas, the ideas become less strange and the owners of the ideas cease to be strangers' (Belenky *et al.*, 1986:115). No longer is the approach judgemental.

But

> in the institutions of higher learning most of these women attended, the subjective voice was largely ignored; feelings and intuitions were banished to the realm of the personal and private. It was the public, rational, analytical voice that received the institutions' tutelage, respect and rewards.
>
> (Belenky *et al.*, 1986:124)

There is a developing feeling at this stage that we are all connected in a common quest to gain knowledge. At the same time, academics who appear to let personal feeling enter into their judgement are a little bewildering to procedural knowers, because they have lost the sense of seeing knowledge as subjective.

CONSTRUCTED KNOWLEDGE

In the final stage, that of constructed knowledge, there is a realization that all knowledge is subjective and that the knowers construct their own knowledge. It is integrated and personal between those who can both listen and share in a collaborative manner. Knowledge about reality is complex, and experts are aware of the complexities of their subject. Now all knowledge is challenged but the process is intimately connected with caring. Constructivists become passionate knowers and emphasize the never-ending search for truth.

What we have seen in this typology is a developmental sequence, one that is not connected with age. It reflects different approaches to learning and thinking and illustrates something of the complexity of the person in box 1 and the interaction between the person, the situation and the experiences (boxes 1, 2 and 3 of Figure 4.3). We can also see, however, that it is the growing and developing experience of the women that takes them through these different ways of knowing.

Robert Sternberg

Sternberg also demonstrates something about the complexity of the person who enters situations, has experiences and learns and acts. For him, a thinking style is a 'preferred way of thinking ... but [w]e do not have *a* style but a *profile* of styles (Sternberg, 1997:19; *italics* in the original). He stresses that the style is a preference, not an ability, and that people have different styles which they use in relation to the situation in which they find themselves. His work is concerned with mental self-government (Sternberg, 1997:20–26), in which he argues that there are three *functions*:

1 legislative – people who like to decide for themselves, and are usually creative;
2 executive – people who like to follow rules and procedures and prefer pre-structured problems; they do what they are told;
3 judicial – people who like to evaluate rules; they also like problems.

However, there are four *forms* of mental self-government:

1 monarchic – people who are single-minded and driven;
2 hierarchic – people who have a hierarchy of goals and recognize the need to set priorities;
3 oligarchic – people who are motivated by several competing goals of perceived importance;
4 anarchic – people motivated by a pot-pourri of needs, who have trouble adapting to formal organizations.

But there are also *levels, scope* and *leanings*. There are two levels: global and local. Global thinkers like large, abstract problems, while local ones prefer concrete problems and working with detail. There are two scopes: internal and external. The internals tend to be introverted, task orientated, aloof and not socially aware, while external individuals tend to be extroverted, outgoing and people orientated. There are also two leanings: liberal and conservative. The liberal likes to go beyond existing rules, maximize change and seek ambiguous solutions, whereas the conservative individual likes to stick to existing rules, minimize change, avoid ambiguous situations and stay with familiar situations.

The strengths of Sternberg's approach are that his research is based on empirical research, that he tries to capture the person – both as a learner and as a doer – and that he recognizes that within the profile, he goes beyond the normal dichotomy of learning styles. He also recognizes that styles vary across the lifespan. Thinking styles are related to culture, gender, age, parenting and schooling, and occupation. While I think that his work could easily be extended to take in some of the dimensions of the whole person (which he does not explicitly refer to), it offers a realistic understanding of the person.

Earlier in this book, reference was made to self-directed learning (e.g. Houle, 1961; Tough, 1979; Long and Associates, 1988, 1993, 1997, 1998), and we can now see from Sternberg's studies the type of person who is likely to be self-directed. Additionally, we can see another framework by which we can analyse self-directed learning.

Conclusion

This chapter has covered a lot of ground about learning, looking at the characteristics of adult learners and basic theories of learning – especially the experiential and existentialist approaches to learning, in which the complexity of learning processes themselves was recognized. Finally, the complexity of the person's approach to learning has been discussed. Ultimately, it is argued that learning is the driving force of the individual, and that through learning, people grow and develop. Philosophically, learning is about both 'being' and 'becoming'.

We have examined adult learners and adult learning, but we have examined in detail few of the learning theorists. Consequently, the next chapter is devoted to elaborating upon the work of a number of the main ones.

5

PERSPECTIVES ON LEARNING THEORY

Having looked at a number of approaches to learning in the previous chapter, we now need to examine the fields of adult education and life-long learning more broadly and to investigate some of the writings about adult learning that have been produced in recent years. This chapter, which is closely linked to the previous one, highlights the work of seven major writers, each of whom, in their various ways, has contributed to our understanding of adult learning. I have omitted both Kolb's and my own work here because this was quite fully discussed in the previous chapter.

Five of the writers concentrate on adult education and the sixth is an educational psychologist; five assume a psychological and one a sociological perspective. They are Paulo Freire, Robert Gagné, Knud Illeris, Malcolm Knowles, Jack Mezirow and Carl Rogers; the main works of each referred to here are listed in the bibliography. These six have been selected because, in their differing ways, they have contributed to the theoretical knowledge of adult learning and their writings are examined here, comparing and contrasting their ideas to those presented in the previous chapters. Only Carl Rogers starts from the perspective of the nature of the person. Had more done so, they might have broadened their approach to learning and seen that it is possible to have a biology of learning, a philosophy of learning, a pharmacology of learning, and so on. I have begun this process in *Learning to be a Person in Society* but this is only the beginning, and so the next chapter points to where I think learning theory will develop.

Paulo Freire

The writings of Freire are very well known among adult educators, even though some have confessed to finding him difficult to comprehend. Freire's ideas emerged against the background of the oppression of the masses in Brazil by an elite that reflected the dominant values of a non-Brazilian culture. His writings epitomized an intellectual movement that

97

developed in Latin America after the Second World War, a synthesis of Christianity and Marxism that found its theological fulfilment in liberation theology; its educational philosophy was Freire's own work. From this background it may be seen that at the heart of his educational ideas lay a humanistic conception of people as learners, but also an expectation that once they had actually learned, they should not remain passive but become active participants in the wider world. Hence, for Freire, education could never be a neutral process; it is either designed to facilitate freedom or it is 'education for domestication' (Freire, 1973c:79), which is basically conservative.

In a sense, Freire never really distinguished learning from teaching, and so we will briefly return to him later when we discuss teaching theorists, but he is included here because of his emphasis on the learners and the ways that they can be emancipated from their socio-cultural milieu. This is only an implicit theory of learning throughout his work and it is this that we will try to focus on here.

In order to understand Freire's thinking, it is helpful to recall Figure 1.3, in which it was suggested that objectified culture is transmitted to the individual through the lifelong process of socialization. Since the culture that was transmitted was foreign to the values of the Brazilian people, who were its recipients, Freire claimed that this was the culture of the colonizers, and implicit in the process was the subordination of the culture of the indigenous people. He illustrated this in the following manner:

> It is not a coincidence that the colonizers refer to their own cultural practices as an art, but refer to the cultural production of the colonized as folklore. Similarly, the colonizers speak of their language, but speak of the language of the colonized as dialect.
>
> (1973c:50–51)

Since a construction of reality is contained within language, the common people have a construction of reality imposed upon them that is false to their own heritage. Thus, the idea of a false self-identify emerges, one that perpetually undervalues the indigenous culture, so that native people come to see themselves as subordinate. Hence, the oppressed are imprisoned in a cultural construction of reality that is false to them but one from which it is difficult to escape, since even their language transmits the values that imprison them.

Through the process of literacy education, Freire and his colleagues were able to design experiential situations in which the learners were enabled to reflect upon their own understanding of themselves in their socio-cultural milieu. It was this combination of action and reflection that he called praxis (Freire, 1972b:96). Herein lies the difference between human beings and the other animals, argued Freire: people are able to process their experiences and reflect upon them. Through the process of reflection, individuals may become conscious of realities other than the one into which they have been socialized. Freire wrote that conscientization 'is a permanent critical approach to reality in order to discover it and discover the myths that deceive us and help to maintain the oppressing dehumanizing structures' (1971, quoted in 1976:225). He then expressed it slightly differently: conscientization 'implies that in discovering myself oppressed I know that I will be liberated only if I try to transform the oppressing structure in which I find myself' (ibid.). Later, he claimed that he no longer used the term 'conscientization', and this may be because it had become too closely related to the Marxist idea of 'false class consciousness', which is much more restrictive than his understanding of the process. Nevertheless, Freire still regarded education as 'the practice of freedom' through which process learners discover themselves and achieve something more of the fullness of their humanity by acting upon the world to transform it.

In his later books he continually returned to the themes of his earlier ones. In *Pedagogy of Hope* (Freire, 1996) he continued to insist that educators understand the language of the oppressed, that they denounce the dominant elite practices and they understand the immense resilience of the poor, who need their voices to be heard in this capitalist world that continues to oppress them. Throughout his work it is possible to detect ideas contained in Figure 1.3. Having received and processed inputs from the objectified culture that engulfs them, learners can externalize and act back upon their socio-cultural milieu. Implicit, therefore, in Freire's formulation is a social theory of learning, although he never described it in this manner.

How do Freire's ideas differ from those suggested in earlier chapters? Fundamentally, there is one major difference and some minor ones. In the first instance the socio-cultural background from which his theory emerged has resulted in his depicting the objectified culture as being false and hostile to that of the indigenous learner, so that his approach was often viewed as being political rather than literacy education. However, this interpretation of culture is not something that was unique to Freire; many Marxist writers would concur that the dominant cultural knowledge and values, etc. acquired by most members of a society are the cultural perspectives allowed by an elite, so that some form of cultural hegemony exists. (See Westwood (1980) for a discussion in which this approach is applied to adult education, and Bowles and Gintis (1976) for their analysis of American schooling from a similar perspective.) Thus, Figure 1.3 actually allows for such an interpretation to be assumed, and, indeed, teaching might even be viewed as an activity that encourages it. Nevertheless, there is a significant difference between the model presented here and Freire's thought: he incorporated two opposing cultures into his understanding of the process – that of the ruling elite and that of the oppressed. This is the crux of Freire's argument that no education can be neutral since the culture of the oppressed is in opposition to that of the elite. Hence, literacy education can only assume a political perspective. The model produced earlier has not sought to analyse the culture of the United Kingdom in this way, although some sociologists and community educators might consider that such an analysis is necessary, and this will be discussed later in relation to the relevance of Freire's work for Western Europe and the United States.

I have pointed to some of the apparent differences between Freire's approach and that discussed in this book, but it must also be recognized that there are many similarities, including his emphasis on the humanity of the learners; his concern that learners should be free to reflect upon their own experiences and to harmonize their reflections and actions (he called this 'praxis'), and to act upon their socio-cultural milieu in order to humanize and transform it; his connection between the socio-cultural environment and individual learners; and his recognition that learners are able to create their own roles rather than become role-players performing roles prescribed by others. As a result of all these aspects, Freire maintained that education is always a political process since it is a social institution controlled by the social and political processes, which almost automatically ensure that social pressures are brought to bear on learners in order to make them conform to what is socially prescribed in both cognitive and behavioural terms.

Out of the political condition of Latin America emerged a Christian–Marxist approach to education that is both humanistic and radical. Yet the term 'radical' is often the 'kiss of death' to innovative approaches, as was seen with the concept of recurrent education. However, if there is not something radical about the educational process, the question needs to be posed as to how it differs from socialization. If education actually provides people with an opportunity to process and to reflect upon their experiences, it must allow them to reach different conclusions about them and to choose whether or not they will behave in a conformist manner.

Since Freire's ideas emerged in Latin America, do they have any relevance for contemporary Western society? This is a most important question to pose, since he could be dismissed as someone whose views are of significance only within the context in which they emerged. Yet this approach would be quite wrong, since many dominant ideas and values in contemporary society owe their origins to historical cultural milieux completely different from this one. London reflected upon Freire's work in the context of North America and he claimed that in that society adult education has adopted a 'bland approach ... [a] non-controversial stance, and [a] safe and respectable perspective' (London, 1973:59). But he maintained that a central problem for adult education is to undertake programming that will raise the level of consciousness of the American people so that they can become aware of the variety of forces – economic, political, social and psychological – that are afflicting their lives.

(ibid.:54)

Hence, it may be seen that from the earliest time when Freire's work became known in the United States, commentators were sympathetic to the adoption of his approach. At the same time, there were some who felt that his work was insurrectionary and that he should have been opposed (Berger, 1974). Perhaps his argument might have been even more compelling had he focused on the different cultures and subcultures in the United States as well, but his views emerged from the situation in Brazil, where the cultural and political power differences between rich and poor were much more pronounced even than in the United States, which illustrated his understanding of teaching and learning extremely clearly. The conditions of the poor there are caused by global capitalism, just as they are elsewhere in the world. Clearly, Freire's work is relevant throughout the world, and even more so as globalization is widening the gap between the rich and powerful and the remainder of the world's population.

Not all educators recognize the political significance of their role, although in the United Kingdom, for instance, community educators such as Lovett (1975) and Newman (1973, 1979) adopted similar perspectives, and Kirkwood and Kirkwood (1989) reported on a community education project carried out in Edinburgh using Freire's methods. However, a great deal of community education and literacy work has been much more instrumentalist and narrow, but it is still humanistic and valuable even though it has not assumed Freire's more radical approach. Indeed, it is possible to argue that many people in Western Europe and elsewhere are no more aware of the variety of forces that afflict them than are their counterparts in the United States. Consequently, it is important that the radical Christian perspective adopted by Freire is not lost from the world of lifelong learning as education and learning are being more closely related to employment.

Robert M. Gagné

Gagné (1977:284–286) developed a model for understanding a relationship between learning and instruction. He suggested that learning progresses through the following phases as the instructional process is undertaken:

- expectancy;
- attentiveness;

- selective perception;
- coding;
- storage entry;
- memory storage retrieval;
- transfer;
- responding;
- reinforcement.

This is a data-processing model of learning of the kind we have already discussed. There is a sense in which it lacks the concern for reflection and criticality that was to be found in Freire's work. In a later publication, Gagné suggested that there are nine phases in instruction:

1 gaining attention;
2 informing the learner of the objectives;
3 stimulating recall of prerequisite learnings;
4 presenting the stimulus material;
5 providing learning guidance;
6 eliciting the performance;
7 providing feedback about performance correctness;
8 assessing the performance;
9 enhancing retention and transfer.

(Gagné *et al.*, 1992:203)

As with Freire, Gagné's emphasis is twofold: teaching as well as learning may be found here, and it might even be claimed that it is really a theory of instruction and that he should be considered under theories of teaching. Nevertheless, there is another element of his work that is also significant to adult education, namely his types of learning. He proposed eight types, seven of which he regarded as a hierarchy, whereas the eighth may occur at any level. These are:

1 signal learning;
2 stimulus–response learning;
3 motor learning;
4 verbal chaining;
5 multiple discrimination;
6 concept learning;
7 rule learning;
8 problem solving.

He claimed that signal learning may occur at any level of the hierarchy and it may be understood as a form of classical conditioning, which was discussed in the previous chapter. Clearly, this happens with both children

and adults, and it is one of the ways in which everyone acquires many attitudes and prejudices throughout the whole of their lives. The remaining
seven types of learning are, according to Gagné, seven stages of a hierarchy, and we shall now discuss them.

Stimulus–response learning is the same as operant conditioning, in
which the response is shaped by the reward. The following two types of
learning, motor and verbal chaining, Gagné placed at the same level in
the hierarchy. The former refers to skills learning while the latter is rote
learning – both of which can be found in the model of learning discussed
in the previous chapter. With both, practice is necessary to achieve correctness, while reinforcement is necessary to ensure that the acceptable
sequence is maintained. In multiple discrimination learning, Gagné
moved into the area of intellectual skills; this, he suggested, is the ability to
distinguish between similar types of phenomena, so that the learners
themselves are able to decide which of similar types is correct for any specific situation. In contrast to discrimination is the ability to classify. Concepts are abstract notions which link together similar phenomena so that,
for instance, friendship is a concept but individual friendships are actual
occurrences; education is a concept but in actuality there are educational
processes. Gagné suggested that the ability to learn concepts is the next
order of the hierarchy, and it may be recalled that developmental psychologists, such as Piaget (1929), would claim that the ability to think in the
abstract commences mostly during adolescence, so that it is necessary to
recognize that the education of adults may be different from the education of children, since the levels of conceptual thought in the various
learning processes are different. This is implicit in Gagné's hierarchy of
types of learning but is important in relation to any consideration of adult
learning. One particular type of classification is that of rules, and he maintained that the ability to respond to signals by a whole number of
responses is successful rule learning. At this level of thought it is clear that
Gagné perceived the individual to be a little freer than did some of the
behaviourists, and this is quite fundamental to seeing his work in the context of the education of adults.

Problem solving is the highest order of learning in Gagné's hierarchy
and occurs when the learner draws upon his or her previously learned
rules in order to discover an answer to a problematic situation. Recall that
among the different styles of learning discussed in the previous chapter
was the dichotomy between the flexible and the rigid learner, in which the
former clearly has the mastery of more sets of rules than the latter. Problem solving is an approach to learning and teaching used frequently in the
education of adults, so the problem-solving sequence that Gagné proposed
is quite significant for adult educators. He suggested that the following
sequence occurs, in which the flexibility is apparent. Initially a learner
proposes one or more hypotheses concerning the problem, and these are

based upon the rules that have already been learned. These hypotheses are then tested against the actual situation, and once an answer has been discovered to the problem, the solution will be assimilated into the learner's repertoire of rules, so that the next time a similar situation arises, the learner will not experience it as a problem. There are similarities at this point between Gagné's approach and that of Schutz and Luckmann (1974) mentioned earlier. Another psychologist whose analysis is similar to Gagné's in this context is George Kelly (1955), who claimed that all behaviour may be regarded as a form of hypothesis testing to inquire whether the actual world is really like the perception of it constructed by the individual. If it is, then the experience merely reinforces the construct, but if it is not, then the construct (hypothesis) has to be modified in the light of experience. (See Candy (1981) for a direct application of some of Kelly's ideas to adult education.)

There are, however, a number of problems with this rather traditional approach to skills learning that we need to consider. First, the hierarchy of skills to intellectual is questionable. More recently there has been considerable focus on the arts of skills learning, and when it is studied carefully its complexity can be better understood. In a recent study, Sennett (2008) highlights the way that craftsmen learn their craft and, for instance, he suggests that there is a fivefold process of anticipation, contact, language cognition, reflection and evaluation in prehension and that the actual process of learning the skill is extremely complicated but involves trial-and-error learning, discovery learning and appreciation of correctness. Second, the fact that this is a data-processing model opens it to the criticisms of the mind–body relationship that we discussed previously. Third, the fact that problem solving is the highest point in his hierarchy begs the question about problem posing and even the recognition of the significance of disjuncture to learning. Fourth, at no point is there recognition of competence and the variability of perspectives in different cultures (Illeris, 2009b).

Knud Illeris

Illeris's work has had wide exposure in recent years, mainly because of his text *How We Learn* (Illeris, 2007), and in this and in two subsequent books he has brought together his own ideas about learning with those of other thinkers. Thus, his book *Contemporary Theories of Learning* (Illeris, 2009a) is similar in conceptualization to this chapter, although he actually takes and republishes previous writing rather than seeking to summarize other authors' positions, and his choice of thinkers differs from those selected here. This summary is based mainly on his chapter in this latter book. Learning, for him, is 'any process that in living organisms leads to permanent capacity change and which is not solely due to biological maturation or ageing' (Illeris, 2007:3). Clearly, the second half of this definition needs some discussion, but he is clear that biological change does affect learning and so he is trying to draw the boundaries of learning at the point when biological change alone does not cause learning. However, this is a contentious position upon which he does not really elaborate. In precisely the same way, his omission of ageing is extremely problematic since we can and do learn from our lives.

For him there are four major elements in learning: the learner (understood from biology, psychology and social science); the context or external conditions of the learning (learning space, society and objective situation); the internal process of the learning, which he calls internal conditions (dispositions, life age and subjective experience of the situation); and finally, the outcomes of the learning, which he regards as applications (pedagogy and learning policy). Learning occurs at the point of interaction between these basic elements in two processes: the learners and their social situation and an internal process of acquisition and elaboration. Consequently, he sees behaviourist, cognitivist and social learning elements in every human learning process. It is clear, however, that he does not wish to enter the wider debates about body, and this is a perfectly legitimate base for a theory of learning.

He claims that learning always has three dimensions: content, incentive and interaction. The content is about knowledge, skills, meaning, and so on. Incentive involves the drivers for learning such as motivation, emotion and volition, although it might be postulated that emotion and volition, for instance, are also learned, and so this is a rather arbitrary distinction. The third dimension, interaction, acknowledges the social context of learning and involves action, communication and cooperation. This in turn relates to the nature of the person since the content learned relates to the functionality of the person, the incentive relates to issues of sensitivity, and interaction relates to the manner in which the person integrates into the wider community.

Illeris's approach is a very neat way of summarizing learning, although it does not extend the debate to the many disciplines of learning, and neither does it discuss the way in which the sensitivity dimension is itself learned. Nevertheless, it does encapsulate many of the issues that occur in learning. He goes on to suggest that there are four types of learning that build upon the mental patterns:

1　cumulative learning;
2　assimilative learning;
3　accommodative learning;
4　transformative learning.

The mental patterns or schemes are constructed by the learners themselves and exist in the brain as dispositions. Thereafter, we accumulate, assimilate, accommodate our experiences as episodes of learning, or else we transform our previous patterns or schemes.

Illeris then discusses the barriers of learning, which he sees in terms of the Freudian defence mechanisms, and he also takes in the German psychologist Leithäuser's (1976) analysis of everyday consciousness. This latter idea is similar to the taken-for-grantedness (presumption) that we discuss in terms of non-learning. I do not see this, however, as a barrier to learning but as a social state that makes everyday life possible, or else it occurs in the situations which I call non-consideration and rejection – because we do not have sufficient time or inclination to take on board the possible learning that could arise as a result of disjunctural experiences. He regards ambivalence as another barrier whereas I regard it as a disjunctural problem that needs to be solved. Finally, Illeris has a category that he calls mental resistance but which I also see as falling within either non-consideration or rejection. In this sense, his analysis covers similar areas to mine, although he uses different sources.

One important critique that can be levelled at Illeris is that his is a narrow perspective since it lacks an in-depth philosophical analysis of the person and the implications of that for learning theory, so that there is little or no emphasis on the senses or on the body and the physical sciences and their application to learning theory.

One of the interesting things that Illeris (2007:257; 2009a) does is to try to locate all the scholars whose work he has studied within his own conceptual framework, and while we might not agree with his analysis of some of the scholars' work, this 'map of learning theories' does provide us with an introduction to the emphases of over thirty-five scholars who have written about learning, with Kegan, Jarvis and Wenger in the centre, as being the most holistic. This is a most useful introduction to a wide variety of work. However, even this many fails to cover the whole field, and some of his omissions are quite notable. Even so, Illeris's work is important in the context of contemporary thinking about human learning.

Malcolm Knowles

Knowles may almost be regarded as the father of andragogy because, while he did not actually invent the term, he was been mainly responsible for its popularization in the United States and Western Europe. Indeed, the term derives from the Greek *aner*, meaning man, and it was first used in an educational context in nineteenth-century Europe. Nevertheless, Knowles is most frequently associated with the concept, which he originally defined as 'the art and science of helping adults learn' (1980a:43). The significance of Knowles's thinking is simply that he helped learning theory to focus once again on the learners' experience, even though he failed to analyse the nature of experience.

Knowles (1978:53–57) initially distinguished sharply between the way in which adults and children learn and claimed that there are four main assumptions that differentiate andragogy from pedagogy. These are:

1   a change in self-concept, since adults need to be more self-directive;
2   experience, since mature individuals accumulate an expanding reservoir of experience which becomes an exceedingly rich resource in learning;
3   readiness to learn, since adults want to learn in the problem areas with which they are confronted and which they regard as relevant;
4   orientation towards learning; since adults have a problem-centred orientation, they are less likely to be subject centred.

However, in 1984 he added a fifth assumption about the motivation to learn (Knowles, 1984:12), and in his autobiographical book he added another one about the need to know (Knowles, 1989:83–85). Knowles had clearly given the idea a great deal of thought and frequently reconceptualized his understanding of andragogy. The fact that he reformulated the idea on a number of occasions illustrates the fact that each of the assumptions is open to considerable discussion. It might be asked, for instance, whether children are any less motivated than adults to learn about those phenomena that they regard as relevant and problematic to them, or whether Knowles had actually specified all the relevant points in any discussion about the differences in adults and children learning. The fact that Knowles had, to some extent, rethought his ideas is significant since the concept of andragogy has been, and is still being, accepted uncritically by many adult educators.

When Knowles's work was first published in the United States it stimulated considerable debate. Initially, McKenzie (1977) sought to provide Knowles's pragmatic formulation with a more substantial philosophical foundation and he argued that adults and children are existentially different – a point with which Elias agreed, although he suggested that this was not necessarily significant since men and women are existentially different but no one has yet suggested that 'the art and science of teaching women differs from the art and science of teaching men' (1979:254). To this point, McKenzie (1979) replied, without having undertaken the necessary research, that the differences between men and women, while pronounced, are not significant when related to their readiness to learn, nor are they important in relation to their perspective of time. He also argued that andragogy is similar to but not precisely the same as progressivism. Yet McKenzie did not really focus upon the point that children might actually have the same readiness to learn as adults, and indeed probably do, when they are confronted with a problem the solution to which they wish to know.

Another set of issues arose in the debate about andragogy. Label (1978) suggested that the education of the elderly should be known as gerogogy, since education should recognize the phases of adult development; but are there only two phases in adult development? Knox (1977:342–350) suggested otherwise, so that to include gerogogy as a separate element in the art and science of teaching would be the 'thin end of the wedge' in a multiplication of terms, which prompted Knudson to suggest that all of these should be replaced by a single concept of 'humanagogy', which is

> a theory of learning that takes into account the differences between people of various ages as well as their similarities. It is a *human* theory of learning not a theory of 'child learning', 'adult learning' or 'elderly learning'. It is a theory of learning that combines pedagogy, andragogy and gerogogy and takes into account every aspect of presently accepted psychological theory.
>
> (1979:261; emphasis in original)

Perhaps Knudson's position is a logical outcome of the debate, but the term 'humanagogy' has not gained any acceptance and, in any case, what makes humanagogy any different from the process of teaching and learning? It appears that Knudson has merely invented a new term for an old process, even though he has emphasized one aspect of the process that is regarded as significant to our understanding of the educational process: the humanity of the participant.

In 1979, Knowles chose to re-enter the debate. While he recognized that andragogy and pedagogy are not discrete processes, he claimed that 'some pedagogical assumptions are realistic for adults in some situations and some andragogical assumptions are realistic for children in some situations' (1979:53), and that the two are not mutually exclusive. However, since the debate was prolonged in the United States, and as a number of questions were raised throughout this discussion, it is worth inquiring whether Knowles's formulation is actually correct.

Knowles placed a tremendous emphasis on the self, something with which many adult educators would agree. Knox (1977) pointed out that the self undergoes development throughout the lifespan and that some aspects of that development may be related to physical age. However, it will be seen from the discussion on learning as an existentialist phenomenon in the previous chapter that to focus only on the self is too narrow; I would suggest that the emphasis should have been on the whole person. But other scholars, such as Riesman (1950), have pointed out that some adults are 'other-directed', so that when they come to the learning situation they may seek to become dependent upon a teacher. While it may be one of the functions of an adult educator to try to help dependent adults to discover some independence, it must be recognized that this may

108

be a very difficult step for some learners. But the fact that there are other-directed people suggests that Knowles's formulation was a little sweeping in this respect.

Knowles also claimed that adults have an expanded reservoir of experience that may be emphasized as a rich resource for future learning; but do not children and adolescents also have some experience that may be used as a resource in their learning? Do only adults learn from their relevant problems? What of those adults who study with the Open University or attend university extension classes? Once again, we see that because he differentiated between andragogy and pedagogy, he was forced into making rather difficult claims. Moreover, his treatment of the concept of experience is rather sketchy and yet it was a focal point for his theory of experiential learning.

It appears that Knowles was focusing upon something quite significant to adult learning, namely experience, but his formulation was rather weak, not based upon extensive research findings, nor was it the total picture of adult learning. Indeed, it was not a holistic analysis of the learning process, it did not describe why specific aspects of experience are relevant, nor did it generate a learning sequence for an adult, so some of the claims that Knowles made for andragogy now appear to be rather suspect. It is not surprising, therefore, that in his later work he made less all-embracing claims for this concept, nor is it surprising that many scholars have been rather critical of it. Day and Baskett, for instance, concluded that

> [a]ndragogy is not a theory of adult learning, but is an educational ideology rooted in an inquiry-based learning and teaching paradigm – and should be recognised as such.... It is not always the most appropriate or the most effective means of educating. This distinction between andragogy and pedagogy is based on an inaccurately conceived notion of pedagogy.
>
> (1982:150)

There have subsequently been many other criticisms of the concept of andragogy. Hartree (1984:209) concluded that while Knowles

> has done an important service in popularizing the idea ... it is unfortunate that he has done so in a form which, because it is intellectually dubious, is likely to lead to rejection by the very people it is important to convince.

Tennant (1986), writing from a psychological position, also rejected many of Knowles's arguments, although he did not reject the ideas of individual autonomy that underlie much of Knowles's work.

109

Yet despite its apparent conceptual weaknesses and the many criticisms being levelled at the concept, it became a popular term in adult education. So what are the strengths of the formulation that have resulted in its gaining support? Day and Baskett (1982) have perhaps located one of these when they suggested that it is an educational ideology, for clearly it is humanistic and liberal, which captured frequently expressed beliefs among adult educators. It also focused upon the self-directed learner and emphasized the place of the self in the learning process, both of which are very significant to learning theory. One of the worrying features about this term was that, because of its huge popularity in the United States and Western Europe in the 1980s, it is still being accepted uncritically by others – especially in the emerging countries of Eastern Europe at the start of the twenty-first century, without reference to the wider debate, and often without reference to the long history of the concept in the former Yugoslavia, among other places.

Additionally, it arose in a period of history in the twentieth century that B. Martin (1981) characterized as romantic, a period during which the value of the individual was emphasized and the boundaries of the institutions of society were weak. These boundaries resulted in an increased emphasis on integrated approaches to academic study and a wider acceptance of the ideological perception of progressive education. Indeed, the popularity of the concept in the 1980s reflects the fact that the education of adults needed a symbol as it became differentiated from school education, and so perhaps it is serving the same function at the present time elsewhere in the world.

Knowles's emphasis on self-direction resulted in his book on learning contracts (1986) assuming considerable importance in many circles. The learning contract is one made between teacher and learner, for the learner to undertake specific work by a given date. In a tutorial that precedes it, there may also be discussion about how the work is to be undertaken, which experts should be consulted, how the work should be presented and also the standard that should be achieved. This teaching and learning method has assumed a great deal of popularity among some sectors of adult education, possibly because it encourages individual autonomy and, maybe, because it appears less time-consuming for the teacher. But this latter assumption probably belies the reality of the situation! Another reason why learning contracts are popular at present is because of the current emphasis upon correct performance rather than correct academic knowledge, and the learning contract can be utilized in very practical ways.

Andragogy, then, was a theory that grew out of a specific period (Jarvis, 1984), although Knowles emphasized certain values, such as individual autonomy, that were to transcend the 1960s, the decade when Knowles first formulated the idea. By 1986, however, the andragogical teacher had become the manager and designer of the learning process, and the learning contract the agreement between the manager and the managed as to how the learning was to be undertaken. Knowles's work remains popular despite all its failings, and one of the main reasons for this is probably that it reflects popular ideological currents.

It may be concluded from this brief discussion that, despite the claims sometimes made on its behalf, andragogy is not a distinct approach to adult learning, but it does contain some elements of experiential learning theory. Neither is it a theory of adult teaching, even though its humanistic perspective might provide some guidelines for an approach to teaching adults. Is it a philosophy? Certainly, it includes within it an ideological perspective that is both idealistic and humanistic, so that it is not surprising that it has been found by many to be acceptable. However, 'andragogy' might also be employed as a term to denote the body of knowledge that is emerging about the education of adults, in the same manner as 'pedagogy' might be used to describe the body of knowledge about the education of children.

Knowles was, therefore, an important practitioner in the education of adults, and some of the points that he raised are based upon the humanistic ideals of education itself. It is significant that these points are discussed within this theoretical context since, while andragogy is not a theory of adult learning, its implications are quite profound for the practice of teaching adults.

Jack Mezirow

It was only in 1991 that Mezirow brought together thoughts that he had expressed in numerous articles and papers (1977, 1981) illustrating his insights into a number of established disciplines which he synthesized in an original manner. In *Transformative Dimensions of Adult Learning* (1991) he synthesized much of his earlier work, which he then extended in *Learning as Transformation* (Mezirow and Associates, 2000). In both of these he sought to synthesize perspectives and research from different academic disciplines to demonstrate how adults learn. In the former, he suggested that learning is the process of making meaning from experiences as a result of the learner's previous knowledge, so that learning is a new interpretation of an experience which has not changed greatly in the ensuing years. He went on to show how people make meaning in a variety of different ways and he also analysed the distorted assumptions that stem from prior experiences. Making meaning is an important element in learning, although, as I have pointed out, he restricts it to the cognitive domain, which is a pity since skills, emotions and even the senses are also learned from experience. This is an important study, although it is not unique, as the publishers claim on the dust jacket (see, for instance, Marton *et al.*, 1984, whose work Mezirow does not appear to know).

Mezirow's work on transformative learning has been well known in the United States for over twenty years now, and it has become more widely accepted than formerly. This section summarizes some of the ideas that he presents, although the emphasis of his work has changed in more recent years as he has endeavoured to produce a more complete theory of learning. We shall discuss his early work first, and thereafter make reference to his more recent publications.

Mezirow starts from the assumption that everyone has constructions of reality which are dependent on reinforcement from various sources in the socio-cultural world. He calls these constructions of reality 'perspectives' and notes that they are transformed when individuals' perspectives are not in harmony with their experience – a situation of disjunction. The individual's construction of reality is transformed as a result of reflecting upon experiences and plotting new strategies of living as a result of their assessment of the situation. Mezirow notes that life crises are times when this occurs, and his conclusion is in accord with both his own observations and those of Aslanian and Brickell (1980), who discovered that people tend to return to studying at times like this. Hence, the crux of Mezirow's analysis is that when a 'meaning perspective can no longer comfortably deal with anomalies in the next situation, a transformation can occur' (1977:157). He goes on to suggest that a learning sequence is established as a result of a discordant experience.

In a later work, Mezirow (1981:7) extends his thinking to include the following ten stages:

1 a disorientating dilemma;
2 self-examination;
3 critical assessment and a sense of alienation;
4 relating discontent to the experiences of others;
5 exploring options for new ways of acting;
6 building confidence in new ways of behaving;
7 planning a course of action;
8 acquiring knowledge in order to implement plans;
9 experimenting with new roles;
10 reintegration into society.

The extent to which this is actually a sequence is not clear since Mezirow suggests that there are two paths to perspective transformation – one sudden and the other gradual. However, he regards these transformations as 'a development process of movement through the adult years towards meaning perspectives that are progressively more inclusive, discriminating, and more integrative of experience' (1977:159). It is clear that there are a number of points now that perhaps require additional evidence since not all people develop as a result of their experience, nor do they necessarily learn from it. Additionally, do individuals' universes of meaning necessarily change in the same direction as other individuals' as they age? And do these processes not also happen with children?

It is this movement along a maturity gradient that Mezirow regards as a form of emancipatory learning, and here he draws heavily upon the work of Habermas (Mezirow and Associates, 1990). In his latest work (Mezirow and Associates, 2000:8) he also stresses the difference between instrumental and communicative learning. Even so, he had already used Habermas's third domain – emancipation – which is, according to Mezirow, 'from libidinal, institutional or environmental forces which limit our options and rational control over our lives but have been taken for granted as beyond human control' (1981:5). Hence, perspective transformation is an emancipatory process

> of becoming critically aware of how and why the structure of psycho-cultural assumptions has come to constrain the way we see ourselves and our relationships, reconstituting the structure to permit a more inclusive and discriminating integration of experience and acting upon these new understandings.
>
> (ibid.:5)

By 2000, Mezirow claimed that this related to both instrumental and communicative action. In this later book, there is considerably more reference to the emotional aspects of living than in his previous work, although his (Mezirow and Associates, 2000:5) definition of learning as 'the process of using a prior interpretation to construe a new or revised interpretation of the meaning of one's experience as a guide to future action' focuses on the cognitive domain and is rather narrow. He (Mezirow and Associates, 2000:19) claims that learning occurs in four ways:

1 elaborating existing frames of reference;
2 learning new frames of reference;
3 transforming points of view;
4 transforming habits of mind.

At the heart of Mezirow's work is meaning, which means that despite his references to emotional intelligence, and even to the spiritual, his is a rather restricted approach to learning. In addition, not all learning results in 'future action', as he claims. Nevertheless, this is an important attempt to understand the cognitive domain of learning, and it is clear that there are certain similarities and some differences between Mezirow's work and that of other theorists who consider the wider socio-cultural milieu. Both he and Freire regard education as a liberating force: Freire views it as releasing the individual from the false consciousness in which he has been imprisoned as a result of the dominance of the culture of the colonizers, but Mezirow regards the freedom from a more psychological perspective. Both Freire and Mezirow focus on the social construction of reality and regard learning as a method by which this may be changed. Like a number of theorists of adult learning, Mezirow focuses on the idea that learning occurs as a result of reflecting upon experience, so that much of his work is relevant to understanding the learning process in socialization and in non-formal learning situations. Perhaps his focus on adult learning as transformative finds its origins in his idea that there are different levels of reflection, of which he (1981:12–13) specifies seven – some of which he claims are more likely to occur in adulthood:

1   reflectivity: awareness of specific perception, meaning, behaviour;
2   affective reflectivity: awareness of how the individual feels about what is being perceived, thought or acted upon;
3   discriminant reflectivity: assessing the efficacy of perception, etc.;
4   judgemental reflectivity: making and becoming aware of the value of judgements made;
5   conceptual reflectivity: assessing the extent to which the concepts employed are adequate for the judgement;
6   psychic reflectivity: recognition of the habit of making percipient judgements on the basis of limited information;
7   theoretical reflectivity: awareness of why one set of perspectives is more or less adequate to explain personal experience.

The last three of these, Mezirow maintains, are more likely to occur in adulthood, but this claim might run into the same difficulties that Knowles ran into with his distinction between andragogy and pedagogy. Even so, the final one he regards as quite crucial to perspective transformation.

Indeed, there is a sense in which his approach is very similar to the phenomenological approach suggested in previous chapters. He also focuses on disjuncture – that is, if a person's stock of knowledge is inadequate to explain the experience, then the questioning process is reactivated. Additionally, his emphasis upon reflection is important since he has extended the analysis quite considerably by suggesting different forms. However, his idea of progress and development during the ageing process requires some further evidence, but it leads logically to the idea of the 'wisdom of the elders' and to the notion that the self-knowledge of the elders is always more mature than that of younger people (Jarvis, 2001a). Furthermore, the influence of social change plays little part in Mezirow's analysis, although sociologists of late modernity (Giddens, 1990, 1991) have written a great deal that would have enriched his analysis. Mezirow has, however, accepted some of the central tenets of Habermas's theory of communicative action without fully analysing the academic debate that the work has generated. Nevertheless, his approach is a significant contribution to recent literature on adult learning.

Carl Rogers

Carl Rogers is the final theorist to be discussed in this chapter. He was a humanistic psychologist who expounded this psychological approach in the fields of education and learning. Having this theoretical perspective, it is not surprising that he emphasizes the self-actualization of the learner and he (1969:279–297) argues that the goal of education is a fully functioning person. However, this orientation reflects the therapist in Rogers, and the distinction between education and therapy is occasionally blurred in his writings. Indeed, he uses therapeutic techniques for educational ends. His fusion of these two distinct activities is highlighted by Srinivasan's (1977:72–74) discussion of the curriculum distinctions between self-actualizing and problem-centred education, which are:

- emotional versus intellectual;
- involving the learning group in developing its own curriculum versus identification of appropriate subject matter;
- planning learning experiences so that learners can reassess their feelings versus building learning around a problem;
- support in active learning versus using prepared learning units;
- using a variety of audio-visual approaches versus standardized printed materials and group discussion;
- using the group's spontaneity versus a programmed learning text;
- decentralized educational opportunities versus formal educational provision;
- participatory techniques versus teaching;
- assessing personal growth versus assessing learning gains.

Clearly, Srinivasan has polarized the distinction since a number of the theorists mentioned in this chapter would focus upon the significance of some of the former elements in the dichotomies as significant aspects of their understanding of education. Certainly Rogers would not draw the distinction in quite the way that Srinivasan has done, but she has attempted to clarify an important conceptual issue. However, Rogers and Knowles are close in their emphasis on the self and the need for self-development and self-direction; indeed, Knowles acknowledged his debt to Rogers. Knowles (1980:29–33) specifies fifteen different dimensions of maturation and he certainly regards maturity as one of the goals of education. Recall that Mezirow, like Rogers and Knowles, was concerned about the maturation process of the learner, so for a number of theorists this plays a significant part in the education of adults.

Unlike some of the other writers discussed here, Rogers records the results of his approach to experiential learning in the context of graduate teaching in a university and he also records incidences of others in a formal setting who have attempted similar techniques. He suggests that experiential learning has a quality of personal involvement (though he recognizes that the teacher has a facilitating role); is pervasive inasmuch as it makes a difference to the learners; is evaluated by learners in terms of whether it is actually meeting their needs rather than in terms of its academic quality; and has an essence of meaning. It is perhaps significant to note that while Rogers regards experiential learning as self-initiated, he does not actually dispense with the teacher, although he does claim that teaching 'is a vastly over-rated function' (1969:103), so that he is describing a different form of self-directed learning from that discussed by Tough. In the third edition of his book (Rogers and Freiberg, 1994) there is a greater emphasis on schooling and also on teaching – yet the emphasis on whole-person learning still remains and the goal of learning is still a fully functioning person.

Like Srinivasan, Rogers (1969:157–164) regards experiential learning as being at one end of a spectrum, but at the other he places memory learning. He claims that experiential learning is typified by the following principles:

- Human beings have a natural potentiality to learn.
- Significant learning occurs when the learner perceives the relevance of the subject matter.
- Learning involves a change in self-organization and self-perception.
- Learning that threatens self-perception is more easily perceived and assimilated when external threats are at a minimum.
- Learning occurs when the self is not threatened.
- Much significant learning is acquired by doing.
- Learning is facilitated when the learner participates responsibly in the learning process.
- Self-initiated learning involves the whole person.
- Independence, creativity and self-reliance are all facilitated when self-criticism and self-evaluation are basic.
- Much socially useful learning is learning the process of learning and retaining an openness to experience, so that the process of change may be incorporated into the self.

His approach is clearly based upon the idea that the learner is the agent and that the social structure is not too oppressive to the learner. However, omission of any discussion about the wider socio-cultural milieu appears to be a weakness in this approach, so that while the above ten principles provide considerable insight into the learning process and offer some guidelines for the teacher, they do not present a comprehensive theory of individual learning in the wider socio-cultural environment.

Overall, Rogers' approach to experiential learning has much to offer and may provide inspiration for the teacher, as it did for Knowles, but it does not provide a comprehensive theory of adult learning. At its heart it reflects a humanistic belief system that has been quite fundamental to many individuals who work in adult education, but it also reflects the age in which he was writing, when a number of quite radical studies about schooling were published.

Conclusion

The work of six major theorists has been briefly examined in this chapter and the intention has been to highlight some of the similarities and some of the differences between them. Illeris's work is the most comprehensive as a theory of learning, although the others all emphasize different elements in the learning process, which is one of the strengths of Illeris's (2007:257) 'map of learning theorists' and their differing positions. Both Freire and Mezirow consider the socio-cultural milieu to be a significant factor in the learning process, in common with the model presented earlier, although they treat culture in rather different ways: Freire has a two-cultures model of society whereas Mezirow is content to regard it as rather static and homogeneous. The process of reflection plays a significant part in the work of a number of these theorists, since they recognize that human beings are able to sift and evaluate the external stimuli received from their experiences. Experiential learning is quite central to all of the writers' considerations, since they recognize that the adult learns most effectively when the learning process is in response to a disjunctural situation – a problem or a need. All of the writers, with the exception of Gagné, have placed considerable emphasis on the self and, although it is most exemplified in the works of Knowles and Rogers, it reflects the humanistic concerns of adult education. Even so, it is a much more debatable point as to whether the aims of education should be specified in terms of the development of the learner, because the success of the educational process is then being evaluated by non-educational criteria. The cognitive dimension of the learning process is insufficiently emphasized in some instances while in others the practical and the emotional are underplayed. The emphases that different writers put upon different elements of learning point to the need for a more comprehensive and integrated theory of learning, rather more like that offered earlier in this book.

Most of the theorists focus upon the human need to learn, Rogers being the most explicit about it being basic to humanity, but none of them except Illeris sought to incorporate it into such a comprehensive theory of learning. Mezirow and Freire have both developed theoretical perspectives but Knowles's andragogical approach appears to have achieved the status of a theory without having been systematically worked out. In all cases there are similarities with the model produced earlier in this study, but in each instance the theorists have emphasized those elements that are most central to their own concerns, so that there are naturally also a number of points of divergence.

At the same time, it is clear that our understanding of learning is developing all the time and in the next chapter we will begin to explore the directions in which I consider learning to be developing.

6

DEVELOPMENTS IN LEARNING THEORY[1]

In the previous two chapters we have examined different approaches to human learning but our understanding of the topic is growing at a very rapid rate and in this brief chapter we will look at some of these developments. Surprisingly, our understanding of human learning – something that we all do for all of our lives – is growing at a most rapid rate and we are already beginning to see developments into what is being called 'the science of learning' (e.g. Blakemore and Frith, 2005; Organisation for Economic Co-operation and Development, 2007). Both of these studies focus only on the brain and the science of learning, but learning is wider than this: it must include other scientific disciplines such as biology and pharmacology. Jarvis and Parker (2005) actually pointed in this direction in a book that brought together a number of academic disciplines to look critically at learning theory a number of years ago. In this chapter, we will examine seven areas in which we should see considerable developments in our understanding of human learning: action, cognition, emotion, experience, ageing, the whole person and a science of learning. It is this final one that returns to the academic disciplines.

Learning and action

Fundamental to a great deal of learning is learning by doing – that is, discovery learning, imitating and trial and error. In the book *Towards a Comprehensive Theory of Human Learning* (Jarvis, 2006) I listed behaviourism, social learning and action learning in this category. Behaviourism is best known from the work of Pavlov (1927) and the stimulus–response theories such as that of Skinner (1951); social learning theories include that of Miller and Dollard (1941), who claimed that all behaviour is learned in specific social, historical and cultural contexts. Among the classic social learning theorists is Bandura (1977), who, among other things, observed how children imitated adult behaviour, and more recently Lave and Wenger (1991), who were concerned about how individuals become socialized into organizations through learning from within their social context. Action learning was popularized by Revans (1980, 1982), who

119

developed the formula L = P + Q, where L = learning, P = programmed knowledge gained and Q = questioning insights. A great deal of research has gone into skill learning because of the primacy of work in the knowledge economy (Sennett, 2008). Additionally, Schön's work on the reflective practitioner can be regarded as a theory of action learning. Now, it would be possible to discuss each of these individually, but since I (Jarvis, 2006) have already done this, I do not feel it beneficial to repeat the exercise here. The question of how learning theory and action have developed in recent years (and what new I have discovered about this theme) is more important and I want to focus on two aspects here: early childhood learning and creativity. It is important to recognize that as we seek to understand learning, we cannot make the type of crude distinction previously made between children's learning and adult learning because there is a real sense in which 'the child is father of the man'.

Early childhood learning

Increasingly it is becoming apparent that it is false to try to separate adult learning from child learning and we will look at two issues here: play and imagination.

Play and imagination

First of all, it has always been recognized that play is important to child development; it is not just the aimless passing of time with or by children: 'simply running around without purpose or rules is boring and does not appeal to children' (Vygotsky, 1978:103). It is incorrect to regard play as action without purpose; there is a clear development in the way children play, and at the age of about 3 years a major transition takes place (Vygotsky, 1978:93, 97; Nelson, 2007:99–100). Prior to 3 years old, play serves several functions in the child's world, as set out by Nelson (2007:101–102):

> In summary, these various action modes – imitation, gesture, object and event play, category sorting – allow toddlers to represent their meanings, their knowledge of things and how they function in events in the child's world. The representations are external, 'in the world' and available for reviewing. They are also available for others who engage with the child and who may attempt to interpret or to share the child's meaning ... they are social steps towards shared meanings that become more precise as language enters more fully into the picture.

But thereafter, Vygotsky (1978:93) sees play as enabling children to create imaginary situations in which unrealizable desires can be realized. These situations are zones of proximal development because in play, children always behave beyond their average age. He claims that imagination is a new psychological process that is not present in the initial consciousness of children and it is at the heart of our understanding of play. However, play produces rules of behaviour in the situation, and children are sticklers for keeping to the rules. Thus, play helps children develop their imagination and learn rules and self-control. But imagination is not an end in itself: 'Creating an imaginary situation can be regarded as a means of developing abstract thought. The corresponding development of rules leads to actions on the basis of which the division between work and play becomes possible' (ibid.:103–104). If Vygotsky is right, then abstract thought begins to develop before Piaget's scheme suggests that it would.

It is during this time that the division between visual situations and the visual field occurs – that is, between situations of thought and real situations. It is this that led the political philosopher Kingwell (2000:68–74) to think that the universalism of imagination could be an alternative to Kant's universalism of rationality. He (ibid.:68) defines it as 'the capacity to see beyond the materials given'. It is a sense of challenging our own personal experience and empathizing with others; it is the opportunity to imagine a different and better world than the one in which we live, and in this sense it is at the heart of both empathy and desire. Kingwell also reminds us that this same imagination can lead to sadism, and so it is not intrinsically universally good. He (2000:73) concludes that '[i]maginative connections remind us, as nothing else can, that we are, as citizens embedded in cultures, neither entirely free nor entirely imprisoned'.

Play, then, is crucial to children's development, but during it we develop our imagination and learn to make and keep rules; we learn self-control and it assists us in the development of abstract thought. Imagination helps us empathize and to envision a better world, and I think that we will need to emphasize this even more in future generations. We will return to this when we look at creativity.

Creativity

When we think about being creative, we need to break the mean–ends syndrome of technical rationality. In fact, we must recognize that learning 'correct' skills and procedures might inhibit creativity. Creativity is not necessarily about *knowing how* or *knowing that*, but it might be: for instance, good creative artists may have learned all the skills of the artist before they become creative. But creativity is not necessarily about means, though it is about ends. Learning the skills might actually be a means to an end but it is not an end in itself. Moreover, creative doing is not something that can be hard-wired into the brain; it is cultural and even beyond traditional formulations of culture. Joas (1996) uses five metaphors that are most frequently employed about creativity: expression, production, revolution, life, and intelligence and reconstruction. All of these terms capture something of the nature of creativity and all refer to aspects of our doing, but they are not only about doing; they are about being.

We cannot be taught to be creative but we can learn to throw off some of the inhibitions that hinder our creativity. There are social conditions under which creativity is more likely to occur – and that is when the social structures that inhibit (that is, those we learn in our socialization) are lowered so that the social norms of behaviour are weakened. In this instance we enter liminality (Turner, 1969), a point that I (Jarvis, 2008) have discussed quite fully elsewhere. The point about liminality is that it does have specified goals, and in my study I note that the generation of *communitas*, when people relate to people without the inhibitions of social structures, is the end product. In a similar manner, Joas (1996) discusses the idea of creative democracy, and so we see how creativity and play may be linked together in this way.

Clearly, there are many other aspects of learning and action that I would like us to discuss, but there is insufficient space here. However, one of the significant developments is the new focus on early childhood learning.

Cognition

The category of cognition is very similar to Illeris's one on content, but clearly content can also include skills, and so it overlaps with my previous category 'action'.

Among the very first theorists of learning were Confucian scholars. Their work was initially based on memorizing what was being taught, but following this there were many theorists who focused on cognition, including the Gestalt theorists, Piaget, Vygotsky, Engerstrom, Marton, Gagné, Argyris and Schön, Mezirow, and Wildermeersch. Each of their theories has strengths and weaknesses, but primarily they examine neither the nature of the body nor the nature of the person as a whole in their formulations.

We have looked at all of these earlier in this book and we will return to them in the final section of this chapter, on the brain. Research into the brain has become much more possible as a result of recent technological advances – such things as electromagnetic scanners. We are now embarking upon a new area of research, one that is going to affect learning theory for many years to come. Now, what we can discover through brain science, it seems to me, is about the physiological mechanisms that occur in the brain when learning takes place; we can reinforce what we can learn about learning from our own experiences by scientific knowledge about the way that the brain functions. What Blakemore and Frith (2005) call implicit learning is what I (1987, *passim*) called pre-conscious learning; they show that we can learn without awareness.

Emotions

For many years, emotion did not constitute a major element in learning theories but in more recent years, especially as a result of Goleman's works (1995, 1998), it has come to the fore. In many ways it is also a precursor of neuroscience, and we will return to this point. Let me give you one simple example from my own experience: since 1987 I have researched and written about pre-conscious learning. But in recent years brain science has shown quite dramatically that there are brain mechanisms that illustrate this point, and it can be illustrated from studies of emotion and the brain.

Emotions have been divided into primary and secondary ones. The primary ones are those that have been built into us as a result of our evolutionary past – that is, they are hard-wired. This means that the emotions may be generated before conscious awareness because the seat of the emotions in the brain is the amygdala, which is part of the mammalian brain. While most sense experiences are transferred to the brain via the thalamus, some neurones take a short-cut to the amygdala, and so it receives the sensations milliseconds before the social brain. Thus, our immediate reactions are emotional before they are rational. Goleman (1995:16) regards this as an emotional sentinel that is able to hijack the brain. Moreover, this direct route to the brain can speed up reactions by minute fractions of a second that may have been significant for survival in our prehistoric past. Consequently, we may show some physical response to experiences just a moment before our cognition kicks in, and this is where sensitivity can occur in human interaction since we can read the non-verbal behaviours in the persons with whom we interact, and these influence the subsequent behaviour. However, as we grow and develop, we learn to control our emotions, a point to which we will return.

However, Goleman's (1995:80) conclusions about the place of emotion in learning are important:

> To the degree that our emotions get in the way of or enhance our ability to think and plan, to pursue training for a distant goal, to solve problems and the like, they define our capacity to use our innate mental abilities, and so determine how we do in life. And to the degree to which we are motivated by feelings of enthusiasm and pleasure in what we do – or even by an optimal degree of anxiety – they propel us to accomplishment. It is in this sense that emotional intelligence is a master aptitude, a capacity that profoundly affects all other abilities, either facilitating or interfering with them.

I am sure that there will be a great deal more research on the relationship between emotions and learning in the coming years.

Experience

It is now generally accepted that we perceive the world and learn from our perceptions rather than learning directly from the world. In this sense, experience is at the heart of human learning. Dewey (1938) was one of the major early thinkers about the place of experience in learning. He suggested that we live in a series of episodic experiences and so we learn from these episodes. However, there is a fundamental difference between single experiences that occur in episodes of time and events that are a continuity of episodes over a period of time, the progression of which cannot be predicted; it is possible to argue that we could be hard-wired for single episodes but it is not possible to argue for the hard-wiring for a continuity of episodes. Consequently, evolutionary theories are not sufficient and cannot replace cultural ones.

Experience is also open to philosophical analysis (Jarvis, 2009a), and it relates to consciousness, biography, episode/event, expertise. We can also see, for instance, how we have to be conscious of something in order to be conscious, and so it is intrinsically related to experience. From these four categories, for instance, we can begin to see how learning is related to life itself, which opens up for us a philosophical perspective on learning and the person. I suspect that there will be considerably more work in the area of philosophy and learning in the coming years.

Ageing

In the United Kingdom, by 2030 nearly half the population will be over the age of 50 years (Department for Innovation, Universities and Skills, 2009:25), and this has implications for both those who remain in work and those who are retired. Indeed, there is a growing body of evidence about what older people learn (Aldridge and Tuckett, 2008). Their learning covers a broad spectrum of subjects and, surprisingly, business studies does appear in the top ten! Educational gerontology is, consequently, becoming an increasingly significant area of study. In a brief survey of four years' publication of the journal *Educational Gerontology* (vols 30–33) (Jarvis, 2007b) I looked at forty issues (there were actually forty-two as volume 33 contained twelve issues). Ageing was by far the most frequent concern, and can be subdivided into three broad categories:

1   The ageing process – such as the physical and mental aspects (including mobility), learning (quite frequent – including older peer learning and educational courses), literacy, memory, intelligence. There

were a couple of papers about successful ageing and there was also a paper about ageing and HIV/AIDS.

2   The outcomes of the process – such as mobility, beliefs (spirituality was frequently mentioned), changing values, loneliness, gender and family.

3   Attitudes of the elderly towards ageing.

Few papers were about ageing from specific academic disciplines, other than gerontology, although there was one sociological and a few psychological ones. Given the nature of US academic and student bodies, it is not surprising that some of the papers were international and comparative studies.

The next most frequently cited issue was the training of professionals, which included discussions about geriatric education, training of doctors, social workers and nurses. Few other professional groups were specified, and one that I would have expected but was lacking was the clergy. There were surprisingly few profession-specific papers, and this may well be because they are published in other professional journals. Issues of initial preparation, continuing education and mentoring were all discussed in papers that I have classified in this section. There was also some focus on the non-professional: the family caregivers and the training that they need.

There is an increasing need for fully trained professionals to ensure that the environment in which older people live, especially if they are in care homes or rehabilitation hospitals, encourages learning. In fact, I advocated a new profession of learning therapist (Jarvis, 2001a) in order to advise on such learning environments. We will also research the whole issue of becoming confused, because insufficient stimulus is provided for elderly people to learn. Consequently, we should see new developments in situated learning.

Increasingly, then, we will look at learning in later life and see how older people age and continue to learn. Seniors certainly learn from their experiences (Jarvis, 2001a), and they bring all their biographical experience to future learning (see the work of Peter Alheit and his associates (e.g. 1995)). Studies on learning from our lives will also become increasingly significant (Dominicé, 2000; www.learninglives.org), as will the place of reminiscence in lifelong learning (Housden, 2007).

Withnall (2010) has recently completed a research project about the way that we can improve learning in later life, and it is significant that she felt the need to justify it in precisely the same way as I felt the need to justify adult education in the first edition of this book in 1983. She argues that continuing learning is successful ageing and that there are no limits to learning – but with the ageing society we are already beginning to see changing perspectives on learning and ageing (ibid.:100ff.).

While the focus in the past forty years has been third age learning, we are now moving into a situation where we will see developments in learning theory among the very old: fourth age learning.

The whole person

In Illeris's category of whole person there are really only a few theorists whom he would place here, namely Wenger, Kegan and myself. In the past year I have been developing this holistic perspective even further, and I feel that future work along these lines will possibly be within personality theory in psychology, or philosophical work along the lines of both my own work and that of a number of other scholars such as Cell (1986), Dominicé (2000) and the current research in the United Kingdom on learning from our lives (www.learninglives.org). I think that it is artificial to try to single out skills, say, or knowledge and make the learning of skills or knowledge the basis for understanding learning theory. When we learn a skill, we also learn knowledge, perhaps acquire confidence, and so on, and so it is important to look at the whole person.

Fundamentally, there is current concern about how we learn to be ourselves as a result of our own experiences, and I feel that this research will develop even further in the coming days, especially when the UK research is published. In a real sense, this is learning from our own experiences, and Cell's title *Learning to Learn from Experience* (1986) reflects this concern. In some ways there is a 'common-sense' element to this since it assumes that we learn from our experiences, but it is necessary to understand what experiences constitute the basis of our learning and how we reflect upon them when we use them in practice. In a sense there is an overlap here with andragogy, as defined by Knowles, but I think that these developments raise many profound questions for learning theory.

If we turn to personality theory we can see how complex is the concept, but this is not the place to talk about personality psychology. Suffice it to note that psychologists (Haslam, 2007:27) claim that personality is structured along five major axes, or dimensions:

1   extraversion–intraversion;
2   agreeableness–disagreeableness;
3   conscientiousness–irresponsibility;
4   neuroticism–stability;
5   openness to experience–conservativism.

Various personality traits find their place along these dimensions, and our personality, which is unique to each of us, is the combination of a multitude of traits that revolve around these five dimensions, which we learn and then exhibit. In this sense, personality psychology has two major strengths as far as I am concerned: it is about the whole person and it is about the uniqueness of that person.

When we perform any action, we impose our own personality about the act and we are recognized not only by our physical features but by our personality characteristics. Our identity is not just that we are a teacher but that I am this teacher – the 'I' is the unique me that I have learned from early childhood and which is still with me for as long as I exist as an independent human being. But how I play that role is, in a sense, unique: it has never been played that way before and so I cannot merely repeat past acts. I do something more: I impose myself upon the situation and play my unique role. In this sense, I am continually learning to play my role my way.

But it could be objected that I have previously made the point that because we can take for granted many of our actions, we have habitualized them such that we need not think about them; we simply act. It is only in disjunctural situations that we have to think about our actions. This is not an inconsistency in our argument; if we have played my unique role on many occasions in similar situations, we can assume that we will undertake that action in approximately the same way another time – until such time as a disjunctural situation occurs. Then we have to learn how to play our role afresh – but it is still the same 'I' who learns it and plays it. But herein is one of the major problems: we are no longer free to play that role in any way we wish since there are two sets of constraints. First, we have social identities, which means that we will consider how any new role performance will be perceived by our social life-world, and so we will feel constrained to act in accord with the way that we perceive others anticipate that we will act. Second, we have spent a lifetime developing our own personality characteristics and so, even if we could, we are unlikely to produce a different set of personality traits in any new action. Any fresh expression of my role is still recognizable as 'me'.

Now, there are a multitude of personality traits and it would be impossible to provide a definitive list. Indeed, it would be impossible to provide a definitive list of those that describe us when we act. We may be able to list a number of the major ones, which may well be orientated along one of the five major dimensions. However, these personality traits are not hardwired into the brain, but learned – and they reflect our individual differences along the lines of our habits, attitudes, beliefs, tastes, emotions, skills, and so on (see Jarvis, 2009a).

But the whole person is about body as well as mind, and we have to recognize the significance of the body in learning (O'Loughlin, 2006) since all of our experiences begin with a sense experience: we are more than just a 'cognitive personality'. That personality only finds expression through the use of our body and through speech – and, more significantly, our learning of each of these characteristics begins with bodily sensations.

We are both body and mind – and this takes us into mainstream philosophy. But more research will be carried out about the relationship between the body and learning.

But in just the way that we have learned to be different, we have all learned to be persons. In a sense, the term 'person' pulls us back from our individuality and locates us within humanity itself, and so we finally need to ask ourselves what it means to be a human person.

The science of learning

Throughout this brief chapter we have kept touching upon brain research, and there are three areas of development that we can include under the science of learning. The first comes from evolutionary biology. There are few academic articles of the biology of learning, although my colleague Stella Parker wrote a chapter under this title in our joint book, and there are even fewer papers on learning and evolution. The one person who has touched upon this is Richard Dawkins (1976), who has tried to reduce cultural learning to 'memetics'. The meme behaves like a gene, according to Dawkins (1976:192), and propagates itself by leaping from mind to mind through cultural transmission:

> Just as genes propagate themselves in the gene pool by leaping from body to body via sperms and eggs, so memes propagate themselves in the meme pool by leaping from brain to brain via a process which, in the broad sense, can be called imitation.

This theory is open to considerable debate since it lacks any hard evidence, and if we turn to the work of many early learning researchers, such as Tomasello (1999), who has studied young children's development quite extensively, we find that he concludes that children are 'imitation machines'. However, Tomasello is concerned with mimesis, not memetics. I think that the debate about evolution and learning will continue to grow in the next few years and that biology and learning will be a major subject in the future.

The second area comes from pharmacology. In a recent article in the *Times Higher Education*, Melanie Newman (2009) reports that some academics are calling on the government to make drugs available that will improve the functioning of the brain. There is certainly a great deal of research that demonstrates that cognitive functioning can be improved by taking certain drugs. This is another area that seems likely to affect the development of learning theory in the coming years, and I think that it will be related to developments in neuroscience and learning.

Finally, then, I want to point to neuroscience. There is a growing body of literature (e.g. Rose, 2005; Blakemore and Frith, 2005; Organisation for

Economic Co-operation and Development, 2007) that utilizes research from neuroscience to help us understand human learning, and I have already pointed to some of it in this chapter. Neuroscience will help reinforce many more subjective forms of research into learning, as I illustrated with my work on pre-conscious learning (which neuroscientists are now calling implicit learning). This work will also affect the development of cognitive psychology, which will, I think, play a significant role in new learning theory.

Like the previous section, this one has pointed to the expanding place that all the academic disciplines that appertain to the person play their part in helping us to understand human learning (Jarvis and Parker, 2005).

Conclusion

In this brief chapter I have tried to present a wide overview of the state of learning theory and also pointed in the direction in which I expect some of the debates in the future will take place. It is necessarily very broad since there are a lot of people working on a very great number of different topics that fall within the field of learning. However, it is now necessary for us to turn to teaching.

Note

1   This chapter is a revision of a lecture that was originally given at the School for Adult and Continuing Education at the University of Hong Kong (SPACE) and then published in its journal *International Journal of Lifelong and Continuing Education*.

7

TEACHING ADULTS

Teaching may be an overrated activity, as Rogers (1969:103) maintains, but it remains at the heart of the educational process, so that consideration needs now to be given to it. Hirst and Peters (1970:78) defined it as the intention to bring about learning, and if this broad definition is adopted, it may be seen that any activity that is performed in order to produce learning, however it is conducted, may be considered to be teaching. Hence, it is clear that Rogers and Hirst and Peters used the term in different ways and it is, therefore, essential to clarify its use at the outset.

It was Hirst and Peters' approach that was to be found in the Dearing Committee's report (1997) on higher education when we read that:

- We recommend that, with immediate effect, all institutions of higher education give high priority to developing and implementing learning and teaching strategies which focus on the promotion of students' learning. (Recommendation 8)
- We recommend that institutions of higher education begin immediately to develop or seek access to programmes for teacher training of their staff, if they do not have them, and that all institutions seek national accreditation of such programmes from the Institute for Learning and Teaching in Higher Education. (Recommendation 13)

Teachers could adopt a variety of approaches to the performance of their role but they had to be trained in what they were doing. It is also necessary to recognize that the world in which teachers perform their roles today is different from that in which they performed a generation or two ago. In that world, the teacher's role was primarily about enabling the learners to learn, as we defined it above, and this was normally undertaken by didactic methods. In today's global society there has been a division of labour within teaching itself. The following list indicates some of the different roles that teachers now perform:

Group 1
- Teacher/facilitator
- Teaching assistant
- Supervisor
- Trainer/coach
- Mentor
- Counsellor/adviser
- Administrator
- Assessor.

Group 2
- Researcher
- Trainer of teachers/trainers
- Author of learning materials
- Programme/curriculum planner
- Educational policy maker
- Programme administrators
- Programme technical staff
- Consultants and evaluators
- Retailer/marketer.

The first group of teaching roles are in direct contact with the learners whereas the second set are one stage removed, with the very last one recognizing that the knowledge-based economy has also produced a knowledge market. It might be claimed now that with the continuing development of e-learning, teaching through videoconferencing, teaching through the World Wide Web, and so on this list could be extended considerably. Indeed, in higher education in Singapore, it is expected that every new course produced will be put online – and government has given money to ensure that this happens. Education has become a very complex and multi-skilled business, and these are some of the skills that teachers and trainers need – both in their initial professional preparation and also in their continuing professional development, or in-service training – if they are to be regarded as professionals.

This now has serious implications for teaching itself, and since not all these roles can be performed by a single teacher, it is not unusual to see team-teaching occurring. Team-teaching can take a number of different forms: it can be two or more teachers teaching the same class at the same time, at different times on the same course, or a team of staff producing the learning material and using their different skills in order to transmit that material successfully. We shall return to this latter approach in Chapter 10 on distance learning. However, all forms of team-teaching need careful planning in order to be successful, which is also a time-consuming process, especially when courses or modules span more than one academic specialism. In times of financial constraint it is easy to overlook the amount of 'new' time spent in the preparation of teaching and learning.

Not only is collaboration between teachers occurring in the teaching and learning process, but new courses in adult education are being undertaken when the collaboration is between the academic staff and the students. In the University of Tennessee, for instance, a Master's degree in Adult Education is being undertaken entirely in this collaborative manner, in which part of the students' learning process is being undertaken in the collaborative process. Thus it may be seen that teaching and learning actually overlap in the contemporary world rather than being two separate processes.

The aim of this chapter, therefore, is to explore the relationships between learning and teaching and then to discuss the nature of teaching itself as moral interaction.

Conditions of learning and approaches to teaching

In the previous chapters a number of points have been raised about how adults learn effectively, and it is now necessary to draw many of them together and to relate them to various approaches to teaching. Table 7.1 summarizes many of these conclusions.

Whatever links are drawn between the conditions of learning and the approach to teaching, it is clear that teachers of adults do not always stand in front of the class and expound the wisdom that they consider the students need to know (see the exercise in Rogers, 1973:82–84). This is not to claim that there is no place for didactic teaching, but it does suggest an approach to teaching in which exposition is less significant than it often appeared to be in the past. However, it is clear that the teachers of adults, besides having either the relevant knowledge or experience, require certain other characteristics in order to help adults learn, including knowledge of the educational process, an appropriate philosophy and appropriate attitudes, and teaching and personal skills.

Teaching styles and teaching methods

Table 7.1 has not stipulated how teachers should perform their teaching role with adults, but it does imply that certain styles of teaching may be more appropriate than others. In most courses preparing individuals to become teachers of adults, considerable emphasis has been placed upon the variety of methods with which teachers should be familiar but much less has been placed on teaching styles. This is a major omission from teacher training since the style that the teacher adopts may play a considerable part in the outcome of the learning. Indeed, it may be even more important than the teaching method adopted. For instance, teachers may

132

Table 7.1 The conditions of adult learning and approaches to teaching

Conditions of adult learning	Approaches to teaching
Learning is a basic human need	Teaching is not essential to learning but may facilitate it
Learning is especially motivated when there is disharmony between an individual's experience and his or her perception of the world	Teachers and learners need to structure the process of learning together so that it may be relevant to the experience or problem that created the felt need to learn
Adult learners like to participate in the learning process	Teaching methods should be Socratic or facilitative rather than didactic in many learning situations.
Adult learners bring their own:	
• experiences to the learning situations	Teachers should use these experiences as a learning resource
• meaning systems to the learning situation	Teachers should try to build on the meaning system, rather than seek to be contrary to it, so that students may integrate their new knowledge with their old; methods should be used that enable students to use their previous knowledge as a resource
• needs to the teaming situation	Teachers should help students to be aware of the relevance of what they are learning; subject matter will be 'applied' rather than pure; learning will be individualized where possible.
Adult learners bring to the learning situation their own:	
• self-confidence	Teachers need to be empathetic and sensitive to the humanity of the learner at all times and, when appropriate, always anticipate a successful learning outcome
• self-esteem	Teachers should 'reinforce' all 'correct' knowledge and understanding in order that students are enabled to maintain a high level of self-confidence and self-esteem. Teachers should provide opportunities for adult students to reflect upon 'incorrect' knowledge, so that they can 'correct' it for themselves, where this is possible. Teachers should encourage self-assessment rather than teacher-assessment
• self-perception	Teachers should encourage self-assessment rather than teacher-assessment

continued

Table 7.1 continued

Conditions of adult learning	Approaches to teaching
Adults learn best when the self is not under threat	Teachers need to create an ethos in which no adult feels threatened or inhibited; this is especially true at the outset of any new course of learning. Cooperation rather than competition should be encouraged
Adult learners need to feel that they are treated as adults	Teachers should not regard themselves as 'the fount of all knowledge' but should attempt to create and facilitate a teaching and learning engagement between all the participants
Adult learners have developed their own learning styles	Teachers should recognize that different learning styles exist and encourage learners to develop effective and efficient learning. Hence, teachers also need to be flexible and adopt teaching styles relevant to the teaching and learning transaction
Adult learners have had different educational biographies so they may learn at different speeds	Teachers should encourage adults to learn at their own pace
Adults have developed a crystallized intelligence	Teachers should not be influenced by previous academic record, especially that from initial education
Adults bring different physiological conditions to the learning situation, e.g. declining visual and/or audio acuity, less energy, failing health	Teachers should ensure that the physical environment in which the teaching and learning occurs is conducive to adult learning

say that they are facilitative but their style might actually communicate that they expect learners to reach the outcome that they would have been taught had the session been didactic! There is an old maxim that teaching is about 'truth through personality', and while I do not now subscribe to it entirely, since it raises questions of 'truth', it does communicate the importance of teaching style.

Perhaps the most significant early piece of research that has affected thought about teaching styles was that developed by Lippett and White (1958) in a project directed by Kurt Lewin in the 1930s. They examined leadership styles of youth leaders in youth clubs with 10-year-old boys in the United States. Basically, they noticed three styles of leadership – authoritarian, democratic and *laissez-faire* – and discovered that group behaviour tended to be consistent with leadership style. They found that authoritarian leaders create a sense of group dependence on the leader, that their presence holds the group together and that in their absence no work is undertaken and the group disintegrates. *Laissez-faire* leadership results in little being done irrespective of whether the leader is present or absent. Democratic leaders achieve group cohesion and harmonious working relationships whether or not they are actually present. However, there are a number of problems in applying these findings to adult groups, or indeed to any other teaching and learning interactions: the subjects were children; the location was a youth club; and the task undertaken by the groups was a specific type of craft work. Even so, it may not be without significance that the democratic style of leadership achieved the types of results that it did.

Perhaps more significantly for educators of adults, McGregor's (1960) work has assumed greater importance. According to McGregor, there are basically two approaches to managing people, which he terms Theory X and Theory Y. The former assumes that average human being dislikes work, needs to be controlled, directed or coerced in order to do what is required and then prefers to be directed. The latter commences with the conception of self-motivated adults who seek to fulfil their own human potential. Hence, if teachers start with the perspective of Theory X, they will seek to manipulate the students either by a hard approach of threats or by a soft approach of rewards and permissiveness; but teachers who adopt a perspective that derives from Theory Y will be more concerned about the potentiality and growth of the students even though they may vary their approach and teaching method to suit the situation.

Hence, it is evident that the democratic approach in the research of Lippett and White and the Theory Y perspective in McGregor's work are most consistent with the philosophy of this book and with the picture of the educator of adults as seeking to aid adult learning and to develop the full potential of the learner. However, it must be borne in mind that neither of these approaches actually prescribes the manner in which teachers should perform their role, although they do circumscribe the number of methods that might be used. More recently there has been work on teaching styles (see, for example, Entwistle, 1981), although in some of it, especially in relation to schooling, there is a tendency to confuse teaching style and teaching method. Perhaps Kidd summarized the humanistic perspective on teaching adopted in this book. He, recognizing that there are differences between learners, pronounced his own decalogue for teachers of adults:

1 Thou shalt never try to make another human being exactly like thyself; one is enough.
2 Thou shalt never judge a person's need, or refuse your consideration, solely because of the trouble he causes.
3 Thou shalt not blame heredity nor the environment in general; people can surmount their environment [or perhaps some of their heredity].
4 Thou shalt never give a person up as hopeless or cast him out.

5 Thou shalt try to help everyone become, on the one hand, sensitive and compassionate and also tough minded.

6 Thou shalt not steal from any person his rightful responsibilities for determining his own conduct and the consequences thereof.

7 Thou shalt honour anyone engaged in the pursuit of learning and serve well and extend the discipline of knowledge and skill about learning which is our common heritage.

8 Thou shalt have no universal remedies nor expect miracles.

9 Thou shalt cherish a sense of humour which may save you from becoming shocked, depressed or complacent.

10 Thou shalt remember the sacredness and dignity of thy calling and, at the same time, 'thou shalt not take thyself too damned seriously'.

(Kidd, 1973:306–307)

Roby Kidd's creed summarizes much of the humanistic philosophy explicit in this discussion.

Now that we have examined some of the approaches to teaching, it is necessary to explore the teaching processes.

It may be seen from Kidd's ten commandments for an adult educator that they reflect the value of personal relationships in the teaching and learning process. Naturally, all relationships are moral ones, but teaching style is also important to what Goleman (1998) sees as working with emotional intelligence. Emotions are one of our most powerful components, and yet until recently they have been a neglected factor in teaching – although I have argued that we learn our emotions, and through them as well, often incidentally and pre-consciously. However, if we do this, then it is incumbent on teachers to provide the right situations for positive emotions to be learned.

This is most certainly to do with our teaching style; it is about our people skills. We have to provide situations in which learners feel cared for because their being matters, as much as their progress, to the teacher. This sense of care needs to be purveyed to the learners, not only through verbal communication but also through the non-verbal; as Goleman reminds us, this is an empathic relationship. But, at the same time, learners still have to own their own learning, so that teachers should never 'take over' the learning task; in modern parlance, learners are stakeholders in the teaching and learning process. Nevertheless, teachers are still concerned about correctness, so that we have to learn the art of being the friendly critic, and so on. Additionally, students must feel that they are being successful, or are going to be successful, in order for them to succeed. Teachers who convey to their students a sense of failure create a self-fulfilling prophecy, and so does communicating a sense of success. Belbin and Belbin (1972:167–168) record a discussion with the most successful London trainer of older men to become bus drivers: 'I never mention the word "fail". I always act as though I know they're going to pass.'

Learning is also a risk-taking business since as we learn, we question our past knowledge and even our previous attitudes, beliefs, values and emotions, so that teachers need to provide a safe environment for risks to be taken. It is crucial to all adult learners that they feel safe and supported as they launch out into the deep and learn new things. There is a growing body of evidence, including a doctoral study by one of my own students that shows how students who feel safe and supported get far higher grades than their contemporaries; this study was conducted with black underprivileged students in a Management Studies programme in a South African university. The fact that they are more successful underlines the significance of the human side of teaching.

Consequently, it can be seen that building a relationship with the students is a key to success in teaching. But more is the pity, in this instrumental age little time is allowed for teachers to do this part of their job properly, because it is not seen to have immediate effects. Perhaps it is time for all the people-based professions (nursing is another) to emphasize the human side of what we do and try to show, as Hesketh has done, that the longer-term outcomes are actually better if teachers are allowed to work with the emotions of their students.

Teaching style, therefore, is vitally important because it is through our styles – through the way that we manage the teaching and learning process – that we can enable more successful learning to take place.

The morality of teaching

Roby Kidd (1973), following Dewey, described teaching and learning as a transaction – and to an extent this is true. There is a sense in which both the teacher and the taught bring something to the classroom, and it is there that a transaction occurs. This appears to be a valid metaphor in contemporary society where education is viewed as a commodity to be marketed to potential learners, although it is intended to demonstrate here that such a metaphor is most problematic when applied to the educational process. Additionally, the idea of the transaction hides something of even greater profundity, and yet much more basic. What occurs between teachers and the taught is a human interaction; a relationship is formed between teacher and the learners. Of course, this is obvious, but the fact that the potentiality of human relationship occurs in this situation means that it is necessarily a moral interaction, for there can be no relationship between people that is not essentially moral.

Perhaps the crucial idea in teaching and learning lies in the word 'relationship'. Teaching and learning in the classroom situation, although not in all forms of distance education, involves a relationship between the teacher and the learner, and consequently it is with the work of some philosophers who have concentrated their analyses on 'relationship' that this part of the discussion begins. Of these, perhaps the best known is Martin Buber, after whom the adult education institute of the Hebrew University in Jerusalem is named, although there are many other eminent philosophers whose work is important to this discussion.

Buber, in a number of major works, explored the idea of relationship, especially in *I and Thou* (1959) and *Between Man and Man* (1961). In the former, he explored the idea of personal relationship, as opposed to I–It relationships. He might also have postulated a third form of relationship, I–Group relationship, since there are many occasions, especially in education, where individuals are confronted with a group, or an agglomeration of individuals. While such interaction might be regarded as impersonal, it is not the same as trying to interact with a tree, so it must be seen as a form of personal relationship.

For Buber, the personal relationship is conducted at three levels: with living beings, with individual persons and with spiritual beings. Each of these could be expanded upon here but only the second of them is relevant to the present discussion. People enter personal relationships through direct experience, usually because they share the same space at the same time, and through so doing they have opportunity to interact with each other, during which time they share a mutual bond. Before a relationship is formed, I exist in my world and the Other is a stranger, a significant idea since the stranger is free (Levinas, 1991:39), someone over whom I have no power. When I enter a relationship with the Other, it is usually through the medium of language in the first instance, although relationship is more than an exchange of words. When I and the Other are face to face, the distance between the Stranger and me recedes and some form of bond begins to be created, but the very formation of that bond impinges upon the freedom which is the prerogative of the Other. At the same time, my own freedom in respect to the Other is curtailed. The bond's existence, however weak, signifies that I am prepared to forgo some of my freedom in order to enter a relationship. This relationship may be only for a brief period of time, although there is potentiality for it to continue beyond the first interaction.

As teachers, we are able to enter into such a relationship with our students for whatever period of time the relationship exists because of our common humanity. Where there is no humanity, the relationship is of necessity an I–It one. Relationships with a group, because all its members are human beings, share many of the same characteristics but in this instance we tend to develop the bonds of community rather than those of the more exclusive personal relationship. (The exclusive personal relationship always puts at risk the community since it has the power to fragment the group.) The potentiality of individual personal relationships always exists in the educational situation. Herein lies a fundamental truth: when the I–Thou relationship is formed, the Stranger, or the group member, becomes a person with whom I, as a person, can share a human bond. My personhood can only be realized in relationship with another person – or, as Buber (1959:18) put it, 'In the beginning is relationship', and MacMurray (1961:17) suggested that 'the Self is constituted by its relation to the Other'. Elsewhere, MacMurray (1961:24) claimed that 'the idea of an isolated Agent is self-contradictory. Any Agent is necessarily in relation to Other. Apart from this essential relationship he [*sic*] does not exist.'

As the relationship becomes established, certain patterns of interaction begin to appear, and it is these that curtail freedom. Sociologists call these norms and mores, and some scholars, such as Heller (1988), regard these as the foundation of ethics, although it must be recognized that values, both moral and immoral, are manifest within norms and mores. Like the case studies, norms may not reflect the morality of the interaction for a number of reasons, including the fact that the norms of modernity were shown earlier in this section to be morally flawed in certain situations. Additionally, if there is an unequal power between the actors, the patterns of interaction may reflect the selfish desires of the more powerful actor even though they may not be presented to the less powerful, or even to the general public, in this manner. Hence, it appears that the actual location of morality lies with the intention of the actors rather than with the behaviour itself. One of the problems with this is that individuals can claim that they had good intentions even though their actions had unfortunate outcomes, and in other situations bad intentions can produce a good outcome – but in these latter situations the morality underlying the action has to be questioned. Consequently, ethics is not an empirical science! It is grounded in human intention, wherein the morality of action lies.

It is in a common humanity that the arguments for ethics lie, and in the formation of the relationship in which personhood may be realized rest the practicalities of ethics. Indeed, Levinas (1991:43) argues that ethics arise when an individual's spontaneity is inhibited by the presence of the Other, and if this position is accepted, then teaching must always be seen to be an occupation grounded in the moral debate. (He actually regards the bond that is established between the Self and the Other, the I–Thou relationship, as religion, and MacMurray develops his discussion in a similar manner with a discussion of the celebration of communion, although this point will not be developed further here.) However, it is clear that in the potentiality of personal relationship itself lies the basis of any discussion of the nature of ethical value. MacMurray (1961:116) would agree with this analysis, and claimed that the 'moral rightness of an action ... has its grounds in the relation of persons'.

It is for these reasons that it can be claimed that the basis of moral value is that it is universalizable. It may thus be seen why Kant claimed that values had to be generalizable in this manner, which is implicit in MacMurray's (1961:122) claim that

[t]o act rightly is ... to act for the sake of the Other and not of oneself. The Other ... always remains fully personal; consequently its objectives must be the maintaining of positive personal relations between all agents as the bond of community.

The underlying point here is that the intention behind the action is some form of care, or concern, for the Other. It is maintained that such an intention is never wrong in itself, except when the desire to care for one Other may put many others at risk, and this illustrates the distinction between the I–Thou and the I–Group relationship. Clearly, in this instance there is a major ethical debate about putting one's loved ones before unknown Others, or the teacher devoting more effort to favoured learners than to the class as a whole. Teachers must be concerned for all those with whom they work, and act for their sake rather than the teachers' own self-interest. At the same time, teachers interact with all members of the class individually, so that there is both an I–Group interaction and a potential I–Thou relationship with each individual member of the class. Since these are both personal in nature, the I–Thou relationship will constitute the basis of the following analysis and its significance for the I–Group relationship will be discussed in the conclusion.

There are many studies that have sought to demonstrate the significance of the moral relationship in teaching (e.g. Daloz, 1986; Freire, 1998; Palmer, 1998), and they recount the lengths to which teachers should go to help students achieve their own fulfilment through the processes of teaching and learning. This is the vocation of teaching. Included in the three books mentioned above are caring, commitment, humility and self-confidence, integrity, joy and pain in relating to learners and to their successes and failures, respect for the learners' autonomy and freedom, and tolerance. These show how committed teachers 'go the extra mile' for their students; they exemplify the morality of the teaching vocation. There is nothing more honourable nor sometimes more demanding than seeking always to help other human beings achieve their own potential.

Conclusion

In this brief chapter we have examined both the nature of teaching and the morality that underlies it: teachers have to employ their skill and expertise in order to provide situations that will enable learners to maximize their human potential. The skilled teacher is one who is aware of many of the methods of teaching and can utilize them in such a way as to enable the learners to gain mastery over the knowledge, skill, attitude or emotion that is at the heart of the teaching and learning transaction, and so the next chapter focuses upon teaching methods.

8

THE PROCESSES OF TEACHING

In contrast to initial education, adult learning has tended to emphasize the learner and learning more than the teacher and teaching. Traditionally, in initial education teachers and their skills have constituted a subject for discussion, but rarely has that discussion been sought to be related to the process of learning (but see Brookfield, 2009). Adult education has tended to regard the teacher as an adjunct to learning, often necessary and frequently important but not always essential to it. However, the focus of this chapter is on the teaching process in adult and continuing education. We will first discuss types of teaching, then methods of teaching, and finally teaching aids.

Types of teaching

Four types of teaching are discussed here: didactic, Socratic, facilitative and experiential. It is necessary to recognize that they are not totally different approaches. However, each of these four approaches will now be discussed in turn. Initially, therefore, an oversimplified model of didactic teaching is discussed.

Didactic teaching

Teaching has traditionally been regarded as the process of making a selection of knowledge, skills, etc. from the cultural milieu – those aspects which 'it is intended that pupils should learn' (Hirst and Peters, 1970:80) – and transmitting it to them by the use of some skilled technique. It has been assumed that such rewards as the teacher's approval, good grades in assignments and succession examinations (all forms of conditioning) will ensure that the pupil learns and is therefore able to reproduce that selection of culture thereafter. The content (selection from culture) may have been made by an examination board, an education committee of a profession, or an acknowledged expert in the field, and so on. Students are expected to learn that which is transmitted to them and to be able to reproduce it, which may equate with the lower order of Gagné's (1977) hierarchy of learning but is certainly no higher than the middle. In terms of Bloom's (1956) taxonomy of educational objectives, the students may be expected to have understood what was transmitted and, perhaps, be able to apply it but not necessarily to be able to analyse, synthesize or evaluate it. It might be argued that in university education expectations are higher than this, but, for instance, legal education may 'easily degenerate into mindless book learning ... any student of university calibre could obtain a comfortable honours degree by doing little more than memorising the set text book in each subject and doing the occasional problem' (Hegarty, 1976:81). The extent to which Hegarty's assessment is applicable to all undergraduate courses is another matter, and research into this question would certainly be welcome, especially in the light of the frequent claims about education being 'dumbed down'.

Not only does the level of learning not necessarily scale the heights of the learning hierarchies, but the selection of what is to be learned is made by agencies other than the learner, so that the relevance to the learner of what is learned may often be reduced to the rather instrumental end of being successful in the assessment procedures, rather than being able to learn and understand something relevant. This approach frequently results in the reproduction of the status quo, and while it might be argued that this is no bad thing in initial education, it is much less convincing in the education of adults. Yet following the philosophy of Freire, even this assertion might be considered dubious!

Is there, then, no place for didactic teaching in the education of adults? Such a claim would be too sweeping, but perhaps its place is less significant than it is generally assumed to be. An exposition can actually transmit knowledge and the students may:

- be encouraged to consider the validity of what has been presented to them;
- be provoked them to think;
- have their learning facilitated;
- be motivated to continue their learning, especially if it is superbly presented.

Hence, a didactic approach may prove very useful, especially if the students are encouraged to analyse what is transmitted to them, rather than merely reproduce it.

In the past decades, as the theory of the education of adults has developed, vocational education has assumed a greater relevance and it would be fair to say that training might be regarded by some as a form of didactic teaching, although many industrial trainers would claim, quite correctly, that they employ a variety of teaching and learning methods.

However, didacticism is also the traditional image of training since in many instances employers are only interested in their employees acquiring specific knowledge and skills, which has often resulted in this image. Studies such as those of Marsick (1987) and Casner-Lotto and Associates (1988) demonstrate the variety of approaches used in workplace learning, which would certainly deny this traditional image.

A variation on this theme is for teachers to encourage the learners to ask questions, so that they actually initiate the learning process but the teachers still provide the answers. By adopting this approach, teachers overcome one of the initial problems of didactic teaching: that it may not start from a diagnostic basis. Yet it is the teachers who still transmit knowledge and expect it to be received and learned by the students, who are still the receptacles of knowledge rather than the 'creators' of it. Frequently during the education of adults, students ask questions and teachers are left with a number of choices:

- Ask for the questions to be kept until the planned piece of teaching is over and in this way the continuity of the argument may be retained.
- Stop and answer the question. However, while this may satisfy the questioner, it may be less than satisfying for other learners who are following the argument, and it may also result in the teacher being led astray so that the argument or case is never made completely.

Teachers are sometimes frightened of questions since failure to be able to answer adequately may result in the teachers losing confidence and also losing face before their students. However, teachers who are unable to answer discover that they can confess their ignorance without losing credibility – provided it does not happen too often! Indeed, it is possible to argue that a display of fallibility may help to establish the teacher's position in the group, both as a teacher and as a human being. After all, why should the teacher know everything? No other profession expects its members to be omniscient! Many conscientious teachers, having admitted that they are unable to respond to the question, ask the class if anybody is able to answer. Here the experience and expertise of the group can be put to good use and teachers can learn from the class as well as contribute to the class learning. However, many very conscientious teachers, when confronted with a question that they cannot answer, tell the group that they will go and find out the answer. This they do, and they inform the students on a future occasion. A certain irony emerges in this situation: the student's question has revealed a teacher's ignorance. The teacher is made aware of a learning need and goes and learns in order to provide the students with an answer. Examine closely what has occurred. The student's question facilitated the teacher's learning! But what did the teacher do for the student's learning? The teacher merely made the students more dependent, but the teacher actually became a more independent learner. Two points emerge from this: first, perhaps the teacher should encourage the students to seek an answer as well; second, it is the questioning process that facilitates independent learning and so, perhaps, a good teacher leads students from question to question rather than from answer to answer. After all, that is how the learning need becomes apparent in children, as has been argued in earlier chapters, and it is also a way that effective learning may be facilitated with adults.

Socratic teaching

Socratic teaching introduces questioning into the teaching and learning process. It consists of the teacher directing a logical sequence of questions at the learners, so that they are enabled to respond and to express the knowledge that they have, but which they might never have crystallized in their own mind. However, unless teachers are very skilful in the use of questions and also perceptive in responding to the students, this approach is still likely to result in an expression of knowledge reflecting the accepted body of cultural knowledge and, therefore, a type of conformity. This method assumes that the learners have internalized a great deal of cultural knowledge incidentally and that the approach brings the answers to conscious awareness. However, conformity to and expression of the established body of knowledge is by no means wrong, and thus it is a useful method to employ, especially in teaching adults since it utilizes both their store of knowledge and their experience of life, which are essential learning resources in the education of adults. Yet if this method is used with great skill, it can and does help the learners 'create' rather than reproduce knowledge. Another advantage of its use is that the learners are always actively involved in the learning process.

There are a number of dangers when we lead sessions through questioning: first, that nobody will answer; second, that we intervene and direct the question at a student in the hope of getting an answer; third, that someone will dominate; and fourth, that there will be some who do not participate and we know that if we try to involve them in the discussion through asking them directly, we might embarrass them. Let us take each in turn:

- Teachers should not be embarrassed by silence, although when we watch inexperienced teachers we often see that having asked a question, if they do not get an immediate response they try to fill in the silence. Students will be aware of this and may deliberately not respond! But classes are not often as cynical as this. Teachers have to find techniques for coping with silence, such as going and finding a chair and deliberately sitting down – communicating that we (teachers) have plenty of time to await the answer.

- It is easy for us, as teachers, to overcome this silence by intervening and directing the questions at one or other students. This helps put us at ease but it does not necessarily help the students. In addition, we have to be aware of the ethical issues involved in this, since if we relieve our anxiety at the expense of the students, we are impinging upon their freedom not to answer, and this may be a misuse of our authority – it is the authority of office rather than that of the experts who have authority granted to them on the grounds of their own expertise.
- If one or more students dominate the answers then we might have to deliberately direct our questions to another area of the room so that we do not catch their eye, but without isolating another person who might be embarrassed to answer. If this does not work, then we might have to take such students aside privately and discuss with them how we appreciate their keenness to be involved, stress that we hope that they will always want to answer the questions, but say that we would like them also to allow or encourage others to participate by restraining themselves.
- In the same way, we might want to discuss with the student(s) who do not respond why this is the case. We might find that some feel that they learn best by reflecting on the process but not participating in it. Others might be too shy, and in that case we might find ways of helping them participate more fully.

All of these approaches are ways in which we, as teachers, can teach without communicating information.

Facilitative teaching

Teachers of adults may not always want to employ teacher-centred techniques in the performance of their role. They may seek to create an awareness of a specific learning need in the student; to confront students with a problem requiring a solution; to provide the students with an experience and encourage reflection on it. In all of these instances the outcome of the activity should be that learning has occurred, but teachers have performed their role differently: they have facilitated learning. Hence, it is possible to reconstruct the experiential learning cycle discussed in Chapter 4 in order to incorporate the teacher's role in the process.

It may be seen from my learning diagram (Figure 4.3) that learners function within their own life-world, and we know that learning experiences are often facilitated by others, such as teachers, but should they actually influence the process in this way? Dewey has suggested that, with children, teachers should be involved:

Sometimes teachers seem to be afraid even to make suggestions to members of the group as to what they should do. I have heard of cases in which children are surrounded with objects and materials and then left entirely to themselves, teachers being loath to suggest even what might be done with the materials lest freedom be impinged upon.

(1938:71)

Dewey went on to warn of the opposite extreme: of teachers who abuse their office and who channel children's work along the paths that suit the teachers' purposes rather than those of the children themselves. He maintained that teachers should be intelligently aware of the capacities, needs and past experiences of those under instruction, so that they may assist them in creating a cooperative learning exercise. Obviously, Dewey was writing about children learning in a progressive educational environment, but the same observations are relevant to the education of adults. Indeed, it might be recalled that McKenzie (1979) recognized the similarities between progressive education and andragogy.

Thus, we see that the teacher's role may be that of facilitator and/or guide, but not in this instance that of the director of the learning process, since that would detract from the adult's own autonomy and independence. Williams (1980) gave examples of the practical working out of some of the ideas presented here, but see Jarvis (1992, 2006) for a discussion about the concepts of self-direction and autonomy. Thus, facilitators assist the students' learning, even to the extent of providing or creating the environment in which that learning may occur, but should not seek to dictate the outcome of the experience. Consequently, it would be impossible for facilitators to set behavioural objectives for any learning experience that may be created, but they might be expressive ones. Because the learning experience is open-ended, facilitation is often a difficult role to play since the learners may reach conclusions other than those held by facilitators, but the latter should not seek to impose their opinions on the learners.

Teachers do have a role in the early stages of facilitative teaching and learning, but they cannot make any individual learn, and should play little part in the latter stages of the process; the creation of the autonomous learners is one of the aims of adult education. Even in distance learning, where adults may meet with tutors for an occasional tutorial after having learned from the teaching material, the teaching and learning cycle is only recreated with the students bringing more of their own learning from the initial stages. However, it might be objected that the teachers' involvement in the learning process, even as facilitator, inhibits the students' freedom to learn. But, it may be asked, what is freedom in this context? Boud and Bridge (1974:6), for instance, distinguish four types of freedom: pace, choice, method and content. By this they mean that students should be free to work at their own speed, choose to study particular aspects of a course, adopt whatever learning style suits them best and be free to choose what to learn. Boud *et al.* (1975:18) modified this slightly and suggested that the four types of freedom are pace, method, content and assessment. The extent to which any of these is achievable in any institutionalized course of study is open to question; the expectations of the educational organization and the influence of the teachers are never completely over-come. It is doubtful whether there can be complete freedom in any type of institutionalized learning.

Clearly, the traditional teaching role does not seem to fit easily into the teaching and learning process for adults if these freedoms are considered to be an important element in it, since class teaching seems to recede into the background. Indeed, one of the outcomes appears to be an individual-ized or small-group approach in which the participants are engaged in the pursuit of knowledge that is relevant to their own problems or experi-ences. Certainly, the class as a whole is perhaps a little less significant; small-group learning is frequently undertaken in adult education, and individualized learning has been developed both in adult basic education and in higher education. Considerable research has been conducted into individualized learning, and although it appears to have an idealistic per-spective, Crane noted that

> [u]nexpectedly perhaps, in view of the persuasive role played by committed Romantics in decrying the old and urging a renewed concern for the individual and individual differences, it was largely men with behaviourist training and outlook who actually produced innovations of value.
>
> (1982:33)

Certainly the group or class versus the individual is one of the problems that emerges logically from any analysis of this type of teaching and learn-ing. Students' learning should be regarded as their own, so the teaching and learning cycle must ultimately relate to individuals, although this does not preclude teachers interacting with the learners during the learning.

Experiential teaching

A great deal of teaching involves providing a secondary experience through which learners acquire cognitive knowledge consciously and, per-haps, emotions pre-consciously. The situation of the learning – the class-room – is actually something far removed from the reality of practice and daily living. Consequently, there has been an increasing emphasis on having a primary experience – entering a practice situation and learning through the senses – and so experiential teaching is becoming more popular. In professional preparation we are finding more work-based experiences provided, so that learners might actually learn in the workplace. In addition, role play and simulations are being devised so that learners can experience something at least of what it is actually like to be in a 'real' situation. It is not surprising, therefore, that we are gradually beginning to see such approaches as problem-based learning and even work-based learning being introduced.

The focus of this section has been upon the teaching process, and four types of teaching have been discussed: didactic, Socratic, facilitative and experiential. These may be seen as being either teacher centred or student centred, and it has been suggested that those approaches that are extremely teacher centred may be inappropriate for some education of adults.

Now that we have looked at the broad approaches to teaching, it is necessary to look at specific methods.

Teaching methods

It is impossible in the space available in this section to elaborate adequately upon every aspect of each teaching method that can be employed in the education of adults. Indeed, since the first edition of this book there have been many books on teaching in all types of education, for example Hargreaves (2003) for school education, Light and Cox (2001) for higher education and Jarvis (2002d) as a more general book. Consequently, it is intended only to highlight the variety of methods that can be used. Expert practitioners should be adept at using a wide variety of different approaches. Since there is such a wide range, it is initially necessary to classify them for the purposes of discussion, and a division between tutor-centred and student-centred approaches is maintained. However, it must be borne in mind that a variety of methods may be employed in any single teaching and learning process and that it might be more stimulating to the learner if more than one approach were used.

Teacher-centred methods

Before individual methods are itemized, we can see that tutors may lead a session and still adopt either of two basically different approaches: be didactic and teach the subject in the traditional method of providing the information, or be Socratic and seek to elicit the information from the students by careful questioning (see Freire and Faundez, 1989). The art of questioning is a technique that teachers should acquire, so that they are aware of how to gain the most effective response from the learners; but frequently it appears to be assumed that this is a skill that teachers have either naturally or as a result of their socialization process. This assumption may be false.

Seven frequently employed teacher-centred methods are discussed in this sub-section: demonstration, guided discussion, controlled discussion, lecture-discussion, lecture/talk/speech, mentoring and the tutorial.

Demonstration

Demonstration is one of the most frequent approaches to skills teaching. The teacher shows the student(s) how a specific procedure is undertaken and they are then expected to copy it. However, the demonstrator is usually very skilled so that the performance appears easy and effortless, but copying experts is not always easy because they have acquired their expertise through constant practice and trial and error as they work out the best way to undertake the action. In this process they may have also acquired tacit knowledge (Polanyi, 1967) which they cannot articulate but which can be learned. Practical knowledge is therefore extremely complex, and Nyiri, for instance, suggests that it has to be 'mined out of their [the experts'] heads painstakingly, one jewel at a time' (1988:21). (See also Baskett and Marsick (1992) for an edited volume that endeavours to outline a number of these significant issues.) However, Belbin and Belbin (1972:44–45) suggest that if a skill is broken down into a number of discrete stages and that if in both the demonstration and the subsequent practice sessions each sequence is initially performed slowly, it is possible for learners to acquire new skills fairly rapidly. They recognize that 'it takes time for someone who hitherto has been pressed toward greater speed, to accept that a really slow performance is ... required' (ibid.). In fact, Sennett (2008:172) suggests that it takes 10,000 hours of practice to become an expert and so when experts demonstrate, their demonstration contains a lot of learning! This approach is one that is often used in sports coaching, for instance. However, there is a possible danger in this approach if teachers present themselves as perfect role models. They need to explain to the students that their skills have been honed out of experience and that the students have to learn the skill through their own practice; coaches can only help them go through the trial and error of perfecting a skill in the way that is best for them. In the final instance, a skill can only be learned in practice, and expert coaches can only help by giving practical and analytical advice as a result of observation.

Guided discussion

The guided discussion approach has been separated from the more general discussion techniques because it is one of the approaches that epitomizes the Socratic method. It is sometimes called step-by-step discussion. In this approach the teacher has a carefully prepared sequence of questions that are directed towards the end of drawing from the learners the knowledge that they have implicitly but which they may not have articulated, crystallized or related to a wider theoretical perspective. It is a method that can be employed to elicit from students their own understanding of experiences that they have undergone. For instance, a teacher of theory may endeavour to draw from the students their understanding of some elements of a practical work experience in which they have already participated as part of their vocational education. However, the teacher should be careful not to artificialize the approach by being inflexible, since the students' responses may actually direct the discussion along paths other than those planned. If this is so, it might be wise for the teacher to follow the students' lead and redirect the questions, although there are times when the teacher has to ensure that the steps prepared should be followed. While this method sometimes appears simple and easy to prepare, it is one that requires confidence in the teacher as well as a great deal of knowledge and preparation.

Controlled discussion

In comparison to guided discussion, controlled discussion is quite didactic. In this approach the teacher sets the theme for the class and begins to talk about it, but the students are encouraged to contribute to the learning process or to elicit information. However, the teacher is still at the centre of the scene and is the focus to whom most of the questions or comments are directed. One of the problems in this approach is that there is a tendency for only the dominant or the confident to interject, so that the learning needs of the silent members of the group may not be met. If teachers want the learners to address each other, they must ensure that the environment is arranged so that there is no dominant seat, etc. and that the learners have eye contact with each other. Seating should be arranged in a circular formation (with or without desks). It is difficult sometimes for teachers to change the seating arrangements of a room, especially if they arrive after many of the students, and so it is often wise to ask a caretaker to have the room arranged in the required manner in advance. If this is impossible, it is useful to explain to adult students why the room should be rearranged, and in the majority of instances they will undertake the task themselves.

Lecture-discussion

The lecture-discussion is very similar to the previous method mentioned but it may assume a different form: a short lecture or address followed by discussion. Once again, however, it is self-evident that the teacher controls both the learning process and its content. By contrast to the previous method, the teacher has a larger initial input rather than merely focusing on the topic to be discussed, so the discussion may tend to develop or to demonstrate the weaknesses in the position taken in the lecture. It is worth remembering that unless the content of the lecture is controversial or provocative, the discussion may not be particularly valuable since it may merely rehearse the arguments previously presented.

All forms of discussion require careful preparation on the part of the teacher and a willingness to endure silence by the class, especially during the early part of the discussion. It is a common failing to try to prompt the class to talk by too much early tutor intervention. Confident and talkative adults are, consequently, useful allies during early phases of a discussion session but then it may be necessary for the teacher to draw other people into the debate and encourage the talkative members of the group to contribute a little less. It is, however, part of the human process that the teacher should facilitate both of these aspects without injuring the self-esteem of any of the class members, so that it is often unwise even to ask individuals directly either to participate or to contribute a little less to the discussion. Hence, the social skills of the teacher are as important to the teaching and learning process as are knowledge and teaching techniques (Legge, 1971a).

Lecture

Lecturing is perhaps the most frequently employed teaching technique despite all the criticisms that have been levelled against it at various times. Bergevin *et al.* define the speech, or lecture, as 'a carefully prepared oral presentation of a subject by a qualified person' (1963:157). However, many students know to their cost that the lectures they listen to are not necessarily carefully prepared for all occasions, nor is the presentation always given by an experienced person. Hence, this is more of a description of an ideal type. A lecture may thus be more accurately defined as 'an oral presentation of a subject', although this still leaves the definition of 'subject' open to question.

Thus far, the distinction between lecture, speech and talk has not been raised, but while Beard (1976) discussed the lecture in her work on higher education, neither Bergevin *et al.* (1963) nor Legge (1971a) concentrate upon it a great deal with respect to adult education. This separation has been to the detriment of higher education. Bergevin *et al.* clearly regard the speech as a rather formal presentation, while Legge's orientation towards non-examinable liberal adult education enabled him to focus upon the less formal concept of the 'talk'.

Many criticisms have been levelled at this particular approach to teaching but, despite these, nearly all teachers continue to use the lecture method. Perhaps it is important to put the lecture in perspective, and Bligh summarized the research on this topic when he argued that:

(1) with the exception of programmed learning, the lecture is as effective as any other method of transmitting information, but not more effective; (2) most lectures are not as effective as more active methods for the promotion of thought; and (3) changing student attitudes should not normally be the major objective of the lecture.

(1971:4)

Thus, it may be seen that only in the transmission of information is the lecture as effective as other methods of teaching, and then it must be borne in mind that most of this research was not conducted with adult students. However, Davies (1971:163) claimed that the lecture is a useful teaching method with less able adult students. Yet adult basic education has tended not to employ this method, so this raises questions about his claim. The lecture is no more effective than a variety of other teaching techniques, so why is it so frequently employed? This question certainly requires consideration.

It might be argued that since many educators of adults are not actually trained to perform the teaching role, they do not have evidence of the effectiveness of other approaches; or that they do not know how to teach apart from the lecture; or that they do not have the confidence to attempt other approaches. This may be an argument for introducing more teacher training into all forms of education of adults, including informal education – a point that will be developed in the final chapter. Additionally, it is clear that because students are familiar with this approach to teaching, or because it means that some of them may be passive learners, they prefer this approach. But these may be quite superficial and even wrong reasons; students may put pressure on a teacher to give a lecture because they may not want to reveal their level of knowledge or understanding of a topic, and they may feel threatened if they think that their lack of comprehension will become apparent for others to see. Teachers, or at least some tutors, may also obtain satisfaction from having given a 'good' performance, or they may simply like lecturing because it enables them to control the content of the session in such a way as to ensure that any gaps in their own knowledge may not become apparent – which might occur if the students directed the session. The maxim 'if you don't know a subject well, lecture it' is perhaps a reflection of a teacher's sense of insecurity, especially before a class of adults, and the lecture is perhaps a novice's approach to teaching, even though many lecturers are not novice lecturers. Programme planners also like the lecture method because of the ease of timetabling and room planning.

In addition, it might be argued that the lecture can be an instrument of motivation, and it may be true that the superb lecture may actually produce this result; but, perhaps, few teachers actually possess such oratorial skills, and so Legge's ironic comment that 'the really hopeless teacher, i.e. the one who fails to communicate at all, drives the good student to the library to do the work for himself' (1971a:57) may be closer to the real situation! Lectures, it has been claimed (e.g. Beard, 1976:101; Legge, 1971a), may be economical in teaching many students at the same time and ensuring that the whole syllabus is covered. While there may be some truth in these claims, it must be recognized that covering the syllabus without ensuring that the students learn it is far from efficient (Bligh, 1971:3), and since there is evidence that the level of concentration varies at different phases of the lecture (Legge, 1971a), it is difficult to ensure that learning actually occurs during the presentation. Additionally, individual learning needs may not be catered for, and unless the learners have an opportunity to question the lecturer, they may never actually interact with the speaker. Even if they are provided with the time to raise queries, individual students may not do so because they may not wish to reveal their ignorance or to hinder the remainder of the group. If a student does interrupt the speaker with questions, the rest of the class may become frustrated while they are answered. This is a dilemma that is intrinsic to the lecture method and it appears to have no resolution that would result in effective learning from every participant. The lecturer may seek to resolve the problems by not taking any questions, but this may result in reduced learning efficiency. But even if questions occur, they may interrupt the thought processes of other learners, who may then lose the flow of ideas with which they were grappling. Thus, it may be seen that many unresolved problems surround this approach.

Where the lecture method is employed, there are a number of errors in technique that should be avoided. For example, conscientious lecturers may prepare too much material for the time available but still endeavour to complete the self-appointed task by speeding up the presentation, so that they actually deliver all the content but to the detriment of the learner. Hence, out of the best intentions the lecturer may hinder rather than help learning. Additionally, lecturers may be bound to notes, even to reading them, so that little eye contact is achieved with the class, which results in teachers being unable to detect and respond to any of the students' manifest learning needs. Hence, it may be wise for teachers to reduce the volume of notes, even to headings, sub-headings and references, in order to ensure that they have both contact and fluency of delivery. This is one of the reasons why PowerPoint presentations might be useful, which is a topic we will return to later in the chapter. In a similar manner, teachers may wish to illustrate a point by writing on the blackboard, but if they continue to speak while they have their back to the class,

n deficient hearing, may be unable
nen a lecturer who is not bound to
speaking. Since the lecture has to
it may not always be sufficiently
needs of all the students and it may
the content of the presentation to
ual lecture.

sufficient opportunity for the adult
ll the ideas presented, neither may
lect upon the knowledge transmit-
useful to provide the opportunity
answers during the session, or for a
f the session in order to help adult
rms of audio-visual stimuli may also
ll the information and ideas with
which they have been presented.

I have raised a number of critical points about the lecture, but it is a
useful teaching tool, especially when it is well used, though only for the
transmission of knowledge. It should perhaps be employed a little less frequently than it is at present and used only by those trained in its use rather
than its being the basic technique used by those who are employed to
transmit ideas to others.

Mentoring

There are different interpretations of mentoring, although it is clearly a
significant teaching method in contemporary education and training.

In his excellent book on mentoring, Daloz (1986:215–235) suggests
some of the major things that good mentors do in the situations of mentoring adult students: support, challenge and provide a vision. Each of
these is subdivided into a number of different functions:

- support – listening, providing structure, expressing positive expectations, sharing ourselves, making it special;
- challenge – setting tasks, engaging in discussion, heating up dichotomies, constructing hypotheses, setting high standards;
- vision – modelling, keeping tradition, offering a map, suggesting new
  language, providing a mirror.

In a sense, in these instances the role of the mentor is to help the protégés
to reflect on their practice, to learn from their experiences and to improve
so that they gain more expertise. In mentoring, this is done through an in-
depth relationship – that is, a primary experience. Indeed, it is the relationship that makes mentorship so important – not just to professional

practice but to life itself. It is here that the mentor gains from the relationship – but the mentee should gain as much.

Murray with Owen (1991:5), however, point out that there are two schools of thought about mentoring: one suggests that it can be structured or facilitated, while the other maintains that it can happen only when the 'chemistry' between the two people is right. However, these alternatives are not automatically exclusive, since a facilitated relationship might actually develop into one where the chemistry appears to be right for the relationship to continue and to deepen. Clearly, in education and training, structured or facilitated mentoring is called for; but this is not something that can just be turned on and off with the passing of every two-month module, etc. This has already been discovered in nursing, when, as Barlow (1991) reported, short-term mentorship did not seem appropriate for clinical practice with students. Indeed, these mentors were often new staff nurses who would no doubt have benefited from being mentored themselves.

During studentship and early years of practice, however, beginners might benefit from having a mentor. The mentoring role might be performed by the personal tutor or a senior colleague – especially if the individual is acknowledged to be concerned about excellence in practice. Mentorship might also be facilitated for junior qualified staff, in the way that Murray indicates. She records a top-level executive as saying:

> I'm always mentoring, both formally and informally. My role is to help my subordinates make decisions. I let them bounce ideas off me and I give my input. But ultimately, I want them to make decisions. If I were making all the decisions for them, I wouldn't need them, would I? So taking on what you call an 'additional protégé' is no great hardship for me in terms of time. It's what I do anyway.
>
> (Murray with Owen, 1991:58)

Elsewhere, she cites a mentor from AT&T Laboratories who claims that 'having a protégé from a different department helps her to bring objectivity to the relationship that a supervisor might not have' (ibid.:61).

If the chemistry is right, however, it is the relationship that is important in mentoring; in Buber's (1959) words, it is an I–Thou relationship. But he takes it even further in his characterization of the educative relationship:

> I have characterized the relationship of the genuine educator to his pupil as being a relationship of this kind. In order to help the realisation of the best potentialities in the pupil's life, the teacher must really *mean* him as the definite person he is in his potentiality

and his actuality; more precisely, he must not know him as the mere sum of qualities, strivings and inhibitions, he must be aware of him as a whole being and affirm him in his wholeness. But he can only do this if he meets him again and again as his partner in a bipolar situation.

(Buber, 1959:131–132; emphasis in original)

Mentoring, then, may be seen in a variety of different ways. In all of them it is done in a one-to-one situation, where the mentor seeks to assist the learners to reflect upon their practice and improve it.

Tutorial

Tutorials are more likely to occur in the formal system of education than in informal adult education. However, it might be possible to classify some small classes in the latter as group tutorials. In addition, it must be remembered that in the university extension tradition a three-year course was referred to as a tutorial. But the normal use of the word refers to a teaching and learning method. According to Davies (1971:167–168), there are three basic types: supervision, group and practical.

The first type involves a student and a tutor. The former is often expected to read a prepared piece of work to the latter and then to defend the argument in the ensuing discussion. This is quite normal practice at Oxford and Cambridge Universities, but since it is labour-intensive it is not so widely practised elsewhere. Another similar use of this type of tutorial is for the student and tutor to meet after the latter has marked an assignment by the student and then the student may seek to clarify an argument or challenge the tutor's assessment grade, while the tutor may seek to explain comments, point out ways in which the work might have been improved and, even, to defend the grade that has been awarded.

By contrast, group tutorials employ one tutor to a number of students. Davies (1971:134–135) argues that the optimum number in the group depends on the ability of the tutor rather than a figure beyond which the group cannot function. Nevertheless, he suggests that six or seven is probably sufficient because of the number of possible relationships that can exist between the students.

Practical tutorials may be either individual or group and are often based in a laboratory, gymnasium, workplace, etc.

In all of these tutorials, the tutor's role may be either didactic or Socratic, although a tutorial may be more effective if the latter approach is adopted. Apart from teaching style, it must also be stressed that the tutorial requires a tutor who is trained and sensitive in human relationships, and in the group tutorial the tutor should have some understanding of the group dynamics, or else the tutorial may fail as a teaching method.

Thus far, all the teaching methods examined have been tutor centred, but in the education of adults the tutor should play a less dominant role than that generally assumed by the teacher, so that it is now necessary to discuss those teaching methods in which the tutor also acts as facilitator.

Student-centred group methods

In this section, student-centred teaching methods are considered. Each of the students referred to here brings to the teaching and learning situation a vast and unique experience of life. This is a major resource since they have knowledge, reflections on their experiences and an interpretation of meaning and purpose of life for them. Peer teaching is not, therefore, necessarily 'the blind leading the blind', as some people have claimed, since it can be an approach that capitalizes on the resources of the learners themselves, although it has to be borne in mind that there may be technical knowledge, etc. that none of the members of a group possesses, in which case the teacher may have a more didactic role. Generally, however, in student-centred teaching the teacher is a facilitator of the learning rather than a source of knowledge, and while they are responsible for creating the learning situation, teachers do not control the learning outcomes. Indeed, if they ever do this, they may actually be involved in indoctrination rather than education.

There are many different methods of teaching that might have been incorporated in this section but to discuss them all in detail would require a whole book, so sixteen different approaches have been selected here because they are frequently used, or have the potential for future use. Even so, the list does not purport to be exhaustive. It is: brainstorming; buzz-groups; debate; fishbowl; group discussion; interview, listening and observing; panel; problem-based learning; projects and case studies; role play, simulation and gaming; seminar; snowballing; therapy groups; visits and study tours; work-based learning; workshops.

Brainstorming

Bergevin *et al.* call brainstorming an 'idea inventory' (1963:195–196). It is an intensive discussion situation in which the quantity of ideas produced, or potential solutions offered to a problem, is more important than the quality. All the points made by the participants are recorded over the period of time mutually agreed by the group for the brainstorming to operate. No group member may criticize any idea or suggested solution during this initial period, irrespective of how strange or ludicrous it might appear, since this might create inhibitions in the learners contributing to the inventory. At the close of the agreed period the group is free to analyse the points raised and to arrive at a consensus, if possible, about potential courses of action or solutions to the problem under scrutiny. Clearly, this approach is an aid to creative thinking in decision making or problem solving – it does enable 'thinking outside of the box' – but Davies reported one study that raises questions about the effectiveness of this method since, it is claimed, the notion of expressing 'all ideas may have a deleterious effect on the group members' (1971:170). By contrast, he reports another study in which many good-quality ideas were produced, suggesting that some of the claims made for the method are valid. The construction of a list of ideas, or possible solutions, may be seen as the initial stage in the facilitative learning and teaching, and the next phase in the process is that of observing and reflecting upon the outcome of the first one. Since this is true of many of the methods discussed in this section, no further reference is made to the theoretical perspectives outlined initially.

Buzz-groups

In many ways, buzz-groups are similar to brainstorming, but in this approach smaller groups, usually between two and six members, are used for a short period of time during the process of a lesson in order to discuss a particular item or topic. Small groups encourage participation by all members of the class, and may help in the process of reflection. It is often a useful technique to use in conjunction with a lecture, especially to help divide the session and retain student concentration.

Debate

Debate is a more formal approach to teaching and learning and one that is not used so frequently in adult education, although it is often regarded by students in higher education as an enjoyable leisure-time pursuit. Nevertheless, Legge (1971b:87) claimed that the debate is a useful method of presenting students with sharply contrasting viewpoints and demonstrating how these different opinions can be analysed and assessed. In addition, he pointed out that because the debate is a staged performance in which two or three members support and an equal number seek to refute a prepared proposition, it provides certain protection for the point of view expressed by the participants, even though there may be quite fierce denunciation of it. Even so, Legge suggested that opinions may be modified as a result of reflecting upon the arguments presented during the performance, and this is important when there are strongly held opinions among the class.

Fishbowl

The object of the fishbowl method is to get as many people in the group as possible to participate and discuss their views on a given subject. It can be used in a variety of settings, although it is best used when the room is large enough for the chairs to be arranged such that all the members of the group can sit in one compact circle. At the same time, if there are too many in the group it is not a very useful method, and so it should be restricted to classes of under about twenty students, who can sit in the circle. There is then a small inner circle of chairs in which the individuals involved in the discussion sit. Those who sit in the outer circle must remain silent.

The idea of this approach is to get two or three members of a class discussing a proposition. They sit in the inner circle, with the remainder in the large outer circle. Once the discussion is under way, any member of the outer circle who wishes to participate in the discussion can do so by replacing a member of the inner circle. This is usually done by touching the shoulder of one of the inner group when that person is not speaking (!), replacing that person and participating in the discussion. There can be any number of moves between the inner and outer circle, with individuals coming into the inner circle as many times as they wish – but inner-circle participants must concede their place if they are not speaking when a member of the outer group wishes to replace them.

It is possible for the teachers to join in this discussion if necessary, perhaps early on to encourage others to participate, although they can do so later if they wish to redirect the discussion in specific ways. It is a useful discussion tool that allows as many people to participate as wish to while everybody is sufficiently close to the process to follow the debate.

It is often useful to put a time limit on the fishbowl – say about half of the session – so that it gives time afterwards for the class to consider and write up some of the points that they have gained from the discussion. It may be useful for the group to list the main points of the discussion in some form of feedback before they write it up.

Group discussion

Discussion reoccurs on the list because it is one of the most frequently employed teaching methods in the education of adults. Many aspects of group discussion exist, all of which could have been covered separately. Bligh mentions *free-group discussion*, which he defines as 'a learning situation in which the topic and direction are controlled by the student-group' (1971:126) and which the teacher may or may not observe. He suggests that this is a useful method in which attitude change may be produced in the participants. It may also enhance human relations and self-awareness, and create a willingness to consider new ideas. But if the group fails to function smoothly, these positive gains may not be achieved and problems of human relations, etc. may arise, which the teacher should not ignore.

In contrast to this, there is *problem-centred discussion*, in which the group has a task (which may have been set by the tutor) to perform. The outcome of this approach may be enhanced analytical thinking and the ability to make and evaluate decisions.

Bergevin *et al.* (1963:95) claim that a good discussion topic should meet four criteria:

1   The topic should interest all group members.
2   It should be possible for participants to acquire sufficient information to discuss it meaningfully.
3   The topic should be clearly worded and understood.
4   The topic should suggest alternative points of view.

These criteria are a useful guide since adult students may opt out of the discussion if it is not of interest or relevance to them, or if they do not think that they have anything to contribute to or learn from the discussion. Hence, it is important for the teacher to pick discussion topics with care and maybe to do so in conjunction with the students.

Although discussion groups are frequently organized in adult teaching, there are a number of weaknesses in the approach: the topic may not be suitable or relevant; the end product may not be regarded as useful; the technique relies heavily on the ability of the participants to articulate and to listen to each other; and dominant personalities tend to come to the fore and quiet people remain passive. By contrast, there are a number of strengths in this method: it encourages learners to accept responsibility for their own learning; it facilitates group sharing; it assists individuals to develop a sense of teamwork; and it helps people develop a sense of self-confidence. Legge claims that many 'of the weaknesses of discussion as an aid to learning ... result from the failure of the teacher to use the method with skill and the failure of the students to take the role of good discussion group members' (1971a:78). Hence, it is incumbent upon teachers to ensure that they understand the technique and are aware of group dynamics, so that they are able to help students prepare for the role that they play and to understand the reasons why this method is used in adult teaching. Perhaps teachers are less prone to inform students about why specific teaching methods are being used than they ought to be, especially in the case of adult students.

In recent years the discussion group has become a favourite teaching method for a number of reasons, including the fact that teachers realize the expertise of the adult learners with whom they are working; but this brings a danger: if the discussion group is used too often or unimaginatively, students can be heard to mutter, 'Not groups again!' Overuse of this, as of any method, is detrimental to the teaching and learning process.

One of the main problems with group discussion is the plenary session in which group rapporteurs report on the discussion of their group. There are a number of ways of making this more interesting: limit the time for the report and be firm about it; ask the group to prepare specific questions (for a subsequent panel or for all the participants); ask the group to prepare recommendations to be put to all the participants or to some external body.

Interview

The interview, sometimes called a witness session, is not employed quite so frequently in the education of adults as it might be, but it is a technique with considerable potentiality. In this instance, the resource person is the subject to be interviewed, so both the topic and often some of the questions are prepared in advance. However, it is not a scripted exercise since this would result in an artificial situation. The aim of the technique is for the interviewer to elicit information from the resource person by means of the questions that the learners want answered. Hence, the students often prepare the questions for, and submit them to, the interviewer in advance, so that the session is relevant to their interests and learning needs. This approach may help clarify issues, provide information, explore and analyse problems and even to stimulate an interest in a topic.

Advantages of the use of this method include the fact that it helps the resource person to communicate knowledge without having to present a lecture; it helps to articulate an idea in response to direct and relevant questions; it is relatively easy to employ; and it helps the less dominant members of the group because they are enabled to submit their questions before the session. It is a technique that might be used more often when visiting specialists are not trained educators. Bear in mind that the resource person need not be a visitor; it might even be one of the members of the class who has specific specialist knowledge that the remainder of the group consider relevant or interesting to them.

The interview does not allow for detailed presentation of an argument, and much of the success of the session depends upon the skill of the interviewer. If the latter talks too much, is unable to modify his approach or cannot stimulate the learners, then the interview may fail through no fault of the resource person.

Listening and observing

Listening and observing is a group technique that is designed to promote active listening and observing during a lecture, speech, film, etc. Each group, or each person in a group, is given a specific task to undertake. For example, one group may be given the job of listening for bias during a lecture while another is expected to assess the relevance of the presentation for a specific category of learners. Once the presentation is complete, the group members confer among themselves and reach decisions about the questions underlying the exercise that are then reported back to a plenary session. Plenary sessions are themselves teaching and learning periods, and in some instances they are similar to what Bergevin *et al.* (1963:83) call a forum.

Listening and observing has the advantages of encouraging active listening or active observation and then of helping students crystallize their ideas about the presentation, but it may have the disadvantage of the students missing other elements of the presentation because they have concentrated upon the task that they undertook to the exclusion of all else.

Panel

Like the interview, the panel can utilize the experience and expertise of visitors to the group or it may use the class members themselves. There are a number of slightly different approaches:

- Each member can deliver a short address to the whole group and at the end of three or four talks there can be a period of questions and answers.
- The panel members can discuss aloud a specific topic for a specified length of time while the class listens to their deliberations and then may be invited to raise questions.
- The discussion between panel members might occupy the whole time.
- A panel might be set up merely to respond to the questions of the class, without an initial input or stimulus. In this instance a considerable amount of preparation is necessary beforehand in order to ensure that the questions are forthcoming.

The panel technique may be used in order to present opposing views on a topic and to create a wider understanding of the subject. As a method, it is useful in stimulating interest and demonstrating to a class the validity of opposing perspectives. By contrast, it has a number of difficulties:

- The chairperson needs to be proficient in the arts of chairing.
- The class members might have to undertake considerable preparation beforehand in order to familiarize themselves with the complexities of some of the arguments.
- Class members should have sufficient confidence to pose questions, since there is a tendency to consider that students' queries are not worthy of an expert's consideration.

However, if these problems can be surmounted successfully, the panel session can be both a stimulating and a relevant teaching and learning method.

Problem-based learning (PBL)

Problem-based learning has grown in popularity over recent years with the gradual realization that the knowledge used in professional practice and, for that matter, in everyday life is not academic discipline based and neither is it theoretical. Indeed, the difficulties in relating theory to practice have become very great, and some (Jarvis, 1999) believe that it is no longer really possible to do so in the areas of social living and working, or in the social sciences in general. Theory is more likely to be constructed after the practice, and it is integrated knowledge rather than being based on a single discipline. Lyotard (1984), for instance, argued that a great deal of legitimated knowledge in the current age is performative. As learning occurs in practical situations, so the idea of setting learners practical and problem-orientated activities has grown in popularity. The method was pioneered in the Faculty of Health Sciences at McMaster University in Canada, but it is now popular in progressive educational establishments throughout the world.

Kwan (2000:137) summarizes problem-based learning (PBL) in medical education thus:

> In the traditional curriculum, preclinical disciplines, such as anatomy ... are a prerequisite for proceeding to paraclinical subjects and clinic specialities.... In contrast, in [a] PBL curriculum, health care problems are used to guide the direct learning from an integrative perspective.... Knowledge [from the disciplines] ... will come into place as long as they are of sufficient relevance to achieving the learning objectives.

In this method the learners work in syndicate groups on a problem that has been suggested – maybe by the tutor – and they define their problem and then seek to solve it. Groups are given a set period of time and then they can submit their report – even teach the other groups as a result of their own activities.

Some 'watered-down' approaches have also been used, when the tutors teach the disciplines in the first part of the course and then introduce learners to problem-based approaches, but this does not occur when PBL is fully implemented. At the same time, not every academic finds this method acceptable.

Projects and case studies

Projects and case studies are frequently employed in the education of adults, but it is widely recognized that they are difficult techniques to use in courses that are assessed, since grades are generally awarded to individuals rather than groups. Yet they do incorporate the highest level in Gagné's hierarchy of learning, so they are techniques that should be encouraged.

There are some notable examples of group projects in liberal and informal adult education. Coates and Silburn (1967) conducted, with their class, a sociological study of a deprived area of Nottingham, and after three years of research they had gathered enough data to write a book that was published. During the course of the project the students gained considerable knowledge of the discipline, of the area of Nottingham in which the research was conducted, of the social and political processes of society, and of research methods. Such approaches do not have to be restricted to the social sciences, for it would be just as possible to undertake such work with the environmental, health and natural sciences. It would also be very possible to use this technique in University of the Third Age groups. Fletcher (1980a) regarded community studies, such as that conducted by Coates and Silburn, as a form of practical adult education – almost the practice-based education discussed in the previous section – but if a class makes discoveries about a community, it might want to use the results in an active manner thereafter. Tutors mounting such project-type courses should be aware before they commence that this is a possible outcome of studies of this nature.

Case studies are very similar to group projects, but the group may seek to focus upon a specific phenomenon. If so, the case study may incorporate a multidisciplinary perspective.

Group projects and case studies can, therefore, assume an exciting and innovative ethos, in which the class learn by doing and then use the results in a practical manner. However, the attrition rate from such classes may be greater than average, especially if the activity becomes politically orientated in the community; but more research into this is necessary.

Role play, simulation and gaming

Role play, simulation and gaming are other approaches to teaching in which the student group actively participates. They are included together in this section because of their similarities but discussed separately for the sake of convenience.

Role play is similar to psychodrama and socio-drama, but it has educational rather than therapeutic aims. It can be employed when tutors wish students to experience something about which they are cognitively aware.

This is an approach that has difficulties, so it should not be used carelessly or thoughtlessly. It should be used naturally, and students should feel that what they are doing fits logically into a planned learning sequence. Rogers states that it 'often makes for a smooth, easy introduction to the techniques if at first role playing is done by the teacher' (1973:78), so that the students see the significance of what they are undertaking. Usually, role-playing is a brief episode acted from someone else's life or from the role for which an individual is being prepared. Hence, in vocational education it is possible to devise many learning situations in which role play would be a most natural method to employ, and when this has been done with adult students they are often most positive about the use of the techniques. Stock (1971:93) suggested that role play encourages active participation, enables problems of human behaviour and relationships to be presented, and extends the cognitive into the emotional. Rogers (1973:77–78) also indicates that students of any ability can be involved, that this approach helps to break down social barriers in the class, motivates students to learn more, telescopes time so that a longer procedure may be enacted in a brief period, and that it may be therapeutic. Hence, this method has much to commend it, especially in the education of people who are socially mature enough to participate seriously and then willing to reflect and to learn from their experiences.

However, some students may feel reluctant to participate, and it is wise for the teacher to leave them to respond to the situation in whatever way they wish, so that they will not feel over-embarrassed by it. Additionally, the technique has other disadvantages: there are difficulties relating role play to reality in some instances; role play cannot be predicted precisely, so the learning outcomes will vary with the role players; it may be time-consuming in preparation; it is hard to evaluate its effectiveness; and it may create emotional crises in individuals to which teachers, if not trained as counsellors, may be unable to respond competently. However, in order to help overcome this last potential problem there should always be a period of debriefing afterwards, during which students can readjust to their normal situation. Obviously, the more the emotional involvement demanded by the role play, the greater the need for a debriefing period. Indeed, if teachers do not provide it, they may discover that adult students request it. Such a period also provides an opportunity to reflect upon the experience, a stage in the facilitative teaching and learning cycle. Stock (1971:93) also claimed that role-playing should not be used when the educational objectives are complex or where there is any danger that they may be obscured by the involvement. He also notes that bad casting may destroy the learning situation.

Role play is often a constituent element of simulation, when the teacher may involve the students in a much more complex problem and even relate it to a future occupational role in vocational education. For instance, it is possible for trainee lecturers to simulate a complete board of examiners meeting, so that each member of the group learns something about the process before actually having to attend a meeting in a professional capacity. However, the preparation of a simulation is extremely time-consuming, and unless the simulated situation relates closely to reality, the point of the exercise might be lost. Since role-playing is also expected in these types of learning exercises, most of the problems noted above are significant here too. In addition, since simulations involve a specific number of actors, it may be difficult to involve all the students in any one exercise, so the learning experiences of participant and observer will vary. Simulation should also be followed by a period of debriefing, during which time the learning experience may be reflected upon and ideas be allowed to crystallize in the minds of the participants.

Unlike the previous two techniques, gaming may not involve role play in quite the same way, and so there might be a greater cognitive element to the initial learning experience. Since there are patterns of behaviour in human interaction and regulation in social living, it is possible to design games that highlight these patterns and regulations. Because the same is true of the physical universe, it is possible to learn about aspects of that through gaming techniques. Rogers (1973:78) noted the case of a Marxist economics lecturer who got his students to play Monopoly in order to demonstrate the working of the capitalist system. Other games are on the market covering a variety of topics, but one of the problems with educational games is that their potential sale may not be large enough to attract the volume games producers and thereby keep the price low, so that, while lecturers should be aware of the games that have been commercially produced in their own area of expertise, they might also consider producing their own. Davies (1971:169) points out that some business games have been produced that involve role play as well. He also notes an important fact that evaluation of the use of gaming is scarce, especially as regards the education of adults as opposed to children.

Seminar

Seminars are in complete contrast to the methods discussed above since there is usually an introductory statement or paper by one or more students or a visiting specialist and this forms the basis for a group discussion. The thesis of the paper should be sufficient to ensure, or provoke, discussion so that it may be controversial, provocative, topical and relevant. The method has all the advantages and disadvantages of the lecture-discussion but it also results in active learning by the presenter(s) of the topic as well as passive learning by the remainder of the group who are recipients of the presentation. However, the seminar may prove to be a method that is daunting to students if they are to teach their peers, and this may prove too off-putting to ensure success. This highlights the significant fact that this method is dependent upon the ability of the presenter to provoke discussion, otherwise the tutor may have to intervene to ensure that the session is a useful learning experience.

Snowballing

Snowballing is an approach that starts with each individual learner but then becomes a group process. Initially, individuals are asked to reflect upon a task, proposition, etc. and to reach some conclusions about it. Thereafter, they are asked to work in pairs and to reflect upon their original conclusions and reach a joint conclusion. Thus, each individual has the opportunity to share his or her own thoughts and ideas with another member of the class. When this process is complete, the pairs are asked to form groups of four and to repeat the process. There is a likelihood that all will join in the discussion, knowing that they have the support of their partner from the previous stage. Each group should then elect a rapporteur to report upon the group's collective findings in a plenary session.

Gibbs (1981) advocated this approach since, initially, the individual's own experiences are utilized and all members of the class actually participate in the process. Since this method actually assists in demolishing the barriers of interaction, it is a useful technique early in a course as an ice-breaking exercise and it can be used in nearly every discipline. However, there is an important point to note in this method: the timing is very significant and it is very easy to overrun, so that the plenary session is cut short. Tutors have also to beware in this type of teaching and learning session, especially when the time is restricted, that they do not seek to provide a summary of the group's reports in which they superimpose their own ideas upon them. Even so, this is a useful method which can be employed with large numbers of students and which encourages full participation by all of them.

Therapy group

The therapy group is 'a method of teaching self-awareness and interpersonal relations based upon therapeutic group techniques in which individual group members discuss their relationship with each other' (Bligh, 1971:128). It is a form of experiential learning. This approach may be employed in sensitivity training and in developing individual self-awareness, so it can be useful in certain forms of professional education where the trainees have to learn to work closely with other people in order to practise their profession effectively. However, this approach can result in situations in which the outcome is social disharmony within the learning group, disharmony that may continue for long after the learning session has been completed. Indeed, it is an approach that can, unless used with professional care, be damaging to an individual's self-esteem, and so it is unwise to use it unless all the participants have consented to participate and unless there is easy access to a trained counsellor.

Visits, tours and field trips

Adult education has a long history of arranging study tours both at home and abroad, and also of arranging field trips. The purpose of these has always been to provide personal experience for the learner; but it should be noted that it can also provide a common learning experience for a group and that this may become a resource for further learning activities. Not only does a visit provide a learning experience, but it may also help integrate a group, so that it may be a useful technique to use early in a course – although it might also constitute the whole of the course. It is significant that this approach is being used by the European Union to help create a common European awareness, through such programmes as Erasmas and Socrates.

It is often necessary to have some form of debriefing session, or group discussion, in order to ensure that the learning experiences are reflected on and shared. However, there are limitations to this approach: trips take a lot of time to organize and may be relatively expensive; they may preclude some people from participating in them, especially the handicapped or those who are extremely busy with many different activities; and they may have to be organized in conjunction with another party, and thus the tutor may not be totally responsible for the arrangements of the learning activity. More recently, study tours have been organized in continuing professional education, but the problems of organization are exacerbated when the applicants for the course have to gain study leave, paid or unpaid, in order to participate.

In order for these groups to be effective learning exercises, a great deal of preparation is required. The greatest danger is that they become leisure-time pursuits, which makes it hard to maximize the learning opportunities that they present. This is the technique that Elderhostel uses, and it is becoming much more popular as educational tourism is becoming more significant (Vignuda, 2009). Now it is becoming more important to train tour guides as facilitators of adult learning.

Workshops

The penultimate method to be examined in this section is the workshop, which has similarities to the project and case study method. Here a group of students are encouraged to relate theory to practice in some area of their interest or occupation. Students may actually design their own working programme or participate in one devised by a tutor. In the workshop situation, students are enabled to undertake a piece of work or research, either individually or in groups, and the product of the exercise may be subjected to the critical scrutiny of the class for discussion and appraisal. The end product of such a workshop may be improved skills, a product useful to professional practice, or merely additional learning. Hence, the workshop may be seen to provide a wide range of learning experiences and is a method that is attractive to adults, especially those who have some previous experience of a topic. Moreover, some workshops can have very practical outcomes.

Work-based learning

Work-based learning has become a major area of research in this neo-liberal age, and in these situations the worker's learning is the subject of research and practice. Work-based learning includes the practicum, the work placement, and so on. Following the discussion that has occurred throughout this book about the rapidity of change of artificial knowledge, the fact that learning comes from human experience and that legitimate knowledge is practical knowledge, it is perhaps not surprising that the work placement has assumed a major place in vocational preparation. In a real sense, the workplace is the classroom. This is a stage beyond problem-based learning because now the problems are being examined in the workplace itself by the workers. Consequently, some educational institutions have devised ways of helping work-based learners reflect on their learning and demonstrate the depth of their understanding. It is in situations like this that students should be encouraged to keep learning diaries in which they record what they do and what they have learned from it. Many institutions now send academic staff into the workplace in order to help both the staff and the students understand the situations in which the learners are working, and then they arrange evenings and weekends when the workers can come together to share their learning and also have some of the more theoretical elements explained to them to help extend their understanding. Now many institutions are awarding qualifications for work-based learning. Later in this book we shall also examine the idea of the practitioner researcher (Jarvis, 1999), which might also have been called work-based research.

While a considerable number of student-centred group methods have been examined in this section, no attempt has been made to ensure that the list is exhaustive. The main purpose has been to demonstrate that a variety of approaches exist, so that adult teaching should not always follow the same format. Additionally, a number of different methods may be employed in a single teaching session. Hence, it is necessary for the teacher to be proficient in the use of a variety of methods in order to provide stimuli to the students and to enable them to learn in ways to which they are best suited. Yet thus far the discussion has focused only upon student-centred group methods, and so it is now necessary to examine some individual student-centred methods.

Individual student-centred methods

In contrast to the previous sub-section, the focus in this one is on individual students and the methods that might be employed to facilitate their learning. There are a variety of approaches that can be employed, including both self-selected learning and tutor-set projects. The traditional adult education approach of self-directed learning occurs in one form or another in many of these. Significantly, self-directed learning in the way that Tough (1979) envisaged it stands outside the educational system, although educational programmes might be incorporated into the self-directed learning project. It is proposed, therefore, to discuss only eight methods in this section, chosen because of their significance to the education of adults: the assignment, computer-assisted learning, contract learning, experiential learning, personalized systems of instruction, the practical, the personal tutorial and self-directed learning. Each is elaborated upon briefly in the order just given.

Assignments

Assignments are a common feature of most courses of teaching and learning, and may involve, for instance, writing an essay, a case study, or a research project. In addition, assignments may have a more practical application, and students may be asked to produce a teaching aid, or some other piece of equipment relevant to their course or occupation. If more practical assignments are produced, it is necessary to ensure that expert assistance is available for consultation, but the remainder of the discussion in this sub-section will be based on the assumption that the assignment is a piece of written work – in whatever writing form it is produced. An advantage of encouraging students to work in media other than the written word is that adults bring to their learning their own interests and skills, which may stretch beyond the written word, and these may be used to the benefit of the learning process. The written word is only one method of communicating knowledge and it may be one that some few adults have not used extensively since their initial education. At the same time, writing an assignment is perhaps the most common method by which results of research undertakings are communicated, and so all students should seek to be proficient in the use of this medium. But the proficient use of the written word may be a skill that adults have never been taught, and so it may be necessary to diagnose adults' learning needs in the arts of writing prior to setting such assignments. If there is a learning need, tutors should help students acquire the necessary skills to undertake the task (see Sommer, 1989). Recently, many books have appeared offering guidance to students on the art of writing, preparing a thesis, and so on.

Once the tutor is sure that students are able to use the written form, assignments of this nature may be set. The title of any assignment may be tutor set or student set, or a choice of either may be given to the group. Advantages of tutor-set assignments include ensuring that the whole syllabus is covered and producing a standardization of grading at the end of the process. Yet grading is a subjective process affected by many variables, including handwriting, length and style, and so it is dubious whether the latter advantage could actually be substantiated. Encouraging students to select their own topic may mean that they are more likely to choose an area relevant to their learning needs, their interests, or both. However, there is also a tendency to choose subjects that are already known, especially if the assignment is to be graded, and this may partially defeat the object of allowing students to select their own assignment topic. Even if this disadvantage can be overcome, it is not always easy for students to select a subject which they can handle in the time or space available, and so the tutor may have to offer them help in getting sufficient precision into their titles to enable them to do justice to their topic within the limitations imposed upon them.

Essays are perhaps the most frequently employed method, which may be because the tutors themselves were expected to write them, although projects and case studies are assuming a more important place in adult learning and teaching. The use of these methods is significant because they enable students to follow the sequence of the learning cycle: engaging them in an analytical approach to the problem; discussing the title and its implications; collecting data to construct an argument in response to the analysis; planning a structure in which they can reveal the results of their reflections and evaluations of the data collected; showing something of the process of reflection during the sequence of the argument; and reaching conclusions and testing them against the wider reality. Hence, the preparation of the written assignment is a method of learning, and setting assignments is a technique of facilitating that learning.

Usually, written assignments are submitted to the tutor, who marks and returns them to the student. Tutors do need training in marking written assignments, so that the grading may also be seen as a teaching exercise. It is generally assumed that the tutor, as an expert in a subject, is able to assess and grade a piece of work. However, there are a number of problems about this assumption. It is necessary that the tutor is competent to assess both the structure and the content, that the completed assignment is the end product of the learning process and that there is some objective standard against which the work is judged. Clearly, some tutors do not assess the structure, only the content, of the argument, even though the structure may constitute an equally important element in the learning process and reveal the way in which the learners have been able to organize their thoughts and manage data. This suggests that tutors might need to be trained in the arts of marking assignments, which may be even more the case when the students are adults. We shall return to this point in a later chapter.

However, it is perhaps a totally false assumption that the completed assignment is the end product of the learning process, one that reflects the behaviourist psychology that has dominated education for so long. Many adult students continue to reflect upon what they have written, and tutors are often asked for feedback about work that they have marked. The written assignment therefore actually constitutes another medium through which teachers and learners engage in dialogue. Since marking may be regarded as part of that dialogue – and it is a delicate part – tutors may be required to correct misunderstandings that the adult students have acquired, and it is often useful to adopt a Socratic technique. Hence, tutors highlight strengths and weaknesses by means of questions, so that students are enabled to reflect upon what they have written and reach conclusions of their own, which may be more beneficial to their self-image and self-esteem than being corrected. In addition, the questions facilitate a continuing process of learning, whereas didactic comments might inhibit the learners from continuing to pursue ideas in the assignments that they have written. This is not to deny that there is a place for didactic comment, but only to claim that too much information may not be helpful, so that didacticism should play a less significant role in marking than it frequently does (Jarvis, 1978a). However, if grading is to be regarded as part of the teaching and learning process, perhaps the tick or the cross is the least helpful of all comments since it merely provides reinforcement, positive or negative, for what is written. Unless it is used in response to empirical fact, it suggests nothing necessarily about correctness, or otherwise; only agreement or disagreement on the part of the tutor.

Computer-assisted learning

With the growth in popularity of the personal computer, most people are familiar with its use. More learning packages are becoming available and it will be easier for educators of adults to use these. Even so, the popularity of the computer might well result in more privatized learning projects, such as those discussed by Tough (1979), being undertaken; no doubt there are already a multitude of such learning activities being undertaken in Western Europe and North America. Most educational institutions now have the facilities for adult teaching to be assisted by computer programs. The computer's potentiality for responding to the learning needs of students is great. Nevertheless, the lack of personalized contact with tutors may not always prove satisfying to learners, so that it does not necessarily mean that there will come a time when human teaching is redundant.

However, the computer is now much more significant in e-learning projects, which will be discussed in Chapter 10.

Contract learning

It was Knowles (1986) who helped to make contract learning well known. Adults bring a great deal of experience to learning situations, are highly motivated to learn and are capable of being self-directed in their learning, so that the idea of adult learners entering a contract to learn with their teachers is a logical step forward. Clearly, this approach recognizes that learning is an individual process; learners have different experiences and different motivations, so that classroom teaching and learning might not always be as effective and individualizing a process. Therefore, contracts are developed between teachers and learners, spanning a variety of aspects of what is to be learned. For example, teachers and learners may agree individually upon the aims and objectives of the learning, the resources and resource persons to be used, the date by which the learning is to be achieved and the mode by which the learners demonstrate that they have achieved the desired ends. The contract may be a written one or an informal agreement. Which form is chosen may depend upon whether the contract is made during a normal face-to-face course where there is frequent contact between teachers and learners, when it can be informal, or where there is less frequent contact, when it may be more advisable to write the contract. If it cannot be kept, it becomes the responsibility of the one who cannot keep it to renegotiate the terms with the other party. Thus, if students cannot achieve the desired end by the agreed date, for instance, then they take the initiative and renegotiate the contract.

It is also possible to enter a contract about the grade to be awarded for a piece of work, so that the criteria for each level are agreed upon in the contract and then students demonstrate that they have met those criteria when they present their work. If the tutors do not agree, then they have to demonstrate to the students why they wish either to lower or to increase the contracted grade.

In many ways this is an extremely attractive adult approach to teaching and learning, but it is very time-consuming for teachers if they have big classes, more so than teaching by more traditional methods, and so they should understand the commitment that they make at the outset as well as expecting this to be understood by the students.

Experiential learning

Experiential learning is included here as something entirely different from the previous discussions about experiential learning in the learning theory section. Here it is a teaching technique in which tutors provide students with an episodic experience of what they have been learning in the classroom or what they are about to experience when they enter the world of work. These experiences may be 'artificial' inasmuch as they are provided for the purpose of teaching only and the learners are not exposed to the actual social forces of the situation in everyday life. In a sense, it is an attempt to provide primary experiences, a sense of reality, to counterbalance the secondary experiences of the lecture theatre. In this sense, we see experiential learning as a teaching method.

Personalized systems of instruction

The personalized system of instruction refers to the Keller Plan (Keller, 1968; Boud and Bridge, 1974), which is perhaps the best known of the early programmed learning systems to emerge, and it is included here as an example of the way that these developed. Crane (1982), for instance, refers to Postlethwait's audio-tutorial system, individually prescribed instruction, programme for learning in accordance with needs and the personalized system of instruction. The Keller Plan consisted of units of work, or modules, which students studied at their own pace and in their own time without a teacher. Each unit had to be passed successfully before they proceeded to the next one, which is referred to as mastery learning. Lectures and other learning activities were provided but attendance was not compulsory since they were regarded as an additional and occasional stimulus. Keller summarizes his plan in the following five points:

1   the go-at-your-own-pace feature, which permits the student to move through the course at a speed commensurate with his ability and other demands upon his time;
2   the unit-perfection requirement for advance, which lets the student go ahead to new material only after demonstrating mastery of that which preceded;
3   the use of lectures and demonstrations as vehicles of motivation rather than sources of critical information;
4   the related stress upon the written word in teacher–student communication; and, finally,
5   the use of proctors, which permits respected testing, immediate scoring, almost unavailable tutoring, and a marked enhancement of the personal–social aspect of the educational process.

(1968:83)

This method was acclaimed by Taveggia as 'proven superior to conventional teaching methods with which it has been compared' (quoted by Holmberg, 1981:127). Rogers (1977) discusses British counterparts to this approach in her chapter on discovery learning, but it was Leytham who elaborated a set of principles for programmed learning when he suggested that:

- aims and objectives should be clearly specified;
- materials selected for learning should relate to aims and objectives;
- each new stage should only introduce sufficient new material to ensure that it is not too difficult so that students make few, or no, mistakes;
- the level of difficulty of new material should be commensurate with the students' previous experience;
- students should work at their own pace;
- students should be active learners;
- students should receive feedback;
- no new stage should be inserted before the previous one is mastered.

(1971:140)

Clearly, Leytham's principles are in accord with the points stressed by Keller, with the exception of the latter's use of proctors who undertake the administration of the tests and provide the feedback. While this approach to teaching can be instituted within the educational organization, it is also clear that many of the principles of modular and distance learning are encapsulated within these formulations. However, one of its drawbacks is that all the material that is taught and learned is selected by the teacher, and while the learner is left to learn it, it remains the teacher's choice, and the learner's need is not necessarily a determining factor in the selection of content. Perhaps this is one reason why it has found a niche in adult basic education (see Crane, 1982 for an example) and in higher education, but as yet it has only established a place in liberal adult education through distance learning. Yet this approach appears to offer considerable potential as disciplines become even more specialized and interests even more diverse.

Practicals

In many professions the teaching of practical skills was until recently a matter of the learner copying the demonstrator, and stress was laid on learning through experience. I have already pointed out that there has been a renewed emphasis upon the value of practice and the place of practical knowledge in recent times. New forms of apprenticeship are appearing, but one of the main problems with the UK government's policy of trying to get more school leavers into universities is that some of the highly skilled manual occupations are not getting sufficient recruits. These occupations demand prolonged periods of practical placements so that the practical skills can be learned under the guidance of a mentor, or an expert teacher of practice. Theory had assumed too great a significance to the detriment of practical skills in some cases, although it is possible that the pendulum might be swinging too far in the other direction, with certain government policies assuming that all relevant theoretical knowledge can be learned in the practical situation. At the same time, Beard has pointed out that 'there is some evidence that this method is unnecessarily slow since students have insufficient practice and feedback' (1976:147). Hence, there has been a gradual movement in some areas of education to teach practical skills in a simulated situation, so that students can practise the skills until they are mastered. Belbin and Belbin (1972) emphasize that most adult students, left to learn at their own pace, can master skills, especially if each skill is subdivided into separate elements and each element mastered separately. It is immediately noticeable that there are considerable similarities between skill teaching and the programmed learning discussed above: much of the learning is tutorless, students are left to work at their own pace and in their own time, and each phase is mastered before progression to the following one.

However, in some other forms of education for adults there is another aspect of the practical, and that is work undertaken in a laboratory. In this instance it is necessary for the tutor to decide whether the purpose of the exercise is merely to learn the use of experimentation by repeating other people's experiments or to undertake original work. Naturally, these are not mutually exclusive, but if one of the aims is to help students understand the process of experimentation, it is necessary to combine the practical with some other learning technique, such as a discussion or a tutorial, so that reflection upon the process can be stimulated and additional learning occur.

Personal tutorial

The tutorial has already been discussed from the perspective of the tutor but it can be used in order to respond entirely to the student's learning needs. In this instance the tutor plays the role of respondent to the questions and problems raised by the adult student about the content and method of what the latter is studying. Hence, the tutor is merely answering questions and the student is effectively guiding the progress of the tutorial, but when this occurs it is perhaps wise to agree beforehand upon the length of time to be allocated to the session.

Self-directed learning

Self-directed learning is potentially a very democratic way of learning and has traditionally been used in the education of adults in both the United Kingdom and the United States. It has been regarded as a high point of much teaching and learning – but see Taylor's (2009) political analysis of the topic. However, many of the methods discussed in this chapter employ self-directed learning strategies, so we can see that it is a significant teaching method in its own right.

It may well have become clear from the discussion on contract learning that self-directed learning might be regarded as a teaching technique and a development from andragogy (see Brockett and Hiemstra, 1991). Certainly, Knowles regarded self-directed learning as one of the manifestations of andragogy and a vital element in his understanding of contract learning. Underlying the whole idea is the idea that the individual is an autonomous learner. While there are degrees of autonomy, Jarvis (1992) demonstrated the paradox of this position. However, Candy (1991) also showed that however free the learner appeared to be within the framework of an educational institution, there is still a residue of teacher influence, and so he distinguished between autodidaxy and self-directed learning. Candy (ibid.:15) regarded autodidaxy as self-directed learning outside the educational institution in which the learners' autonomy is retained, which he (ibid.:108–109) claimed had a number of characteristics of autonomy, namely that the learners:

- conceive goals and policies independently of pressure from others;
- exercise freedom of choice and action;
- reflect rationally;
- are prepared to act fearlessly in accord with the foregoing;
- have self-mastery;
- perceive themselves as autonomous.

Candy recognized that there were threats to the idea of individual autonomy. However, for the purposes of this study the distinction between self-directed learning within an educational institution and that outside is of major significance since the influence of the teacher is never far removed from any form of student-led learning within the institution, and it is only with distance education that learners are apparently free from the immediate presence of teachers. But, and necessarily, distance education institutions are very centralized in many ways, so there is no genuine learner autonomy in this form of education either.

Thus far in this chapter there has been a division between tutor-centred and learner-centred methods. The division has been created for ease of discussion, but, clearly, in any teaching and learning session it is possible to combine a number of approaches, and it is often a useful technique in teaching adults to negotiate with them about aspects of both content and method. This is not relinquishing professional responsibility but rather exercising it in a mature manner with adult learners who may contribute greatly to the teaching and learning process. Finally, it is now necessary to move from methods of teaching to aids for teaching, and this constitutes the next section of this chapter.

Teaching aids

In the same way that teachers of adults should be aware of and able to employ a variety of teaching methods, they should also be aware of and able to use a variety of teaching aids. A multitude of different ones exist, and with the continuing growth of technology there is an increasing sophistication of equipment. Table 8.1 lists many of the teaching aids and much of the equipment about which teachers of adults should be aware, some of which they should also be competent to use in the classroom.

Many of the aids listed in what follows are in daily use, so require little comment here, although there are many publications that deal with the technological aspects of teaching which may be referred to as appropriate. Therefore, it is intended to raise only a few points here.

Initially, it is important for teachers of adults to know that such a variety of audio-visual aids exist and that it is useful to have some expertise in their use. Many teaching and learning aids are produced commercially and can be purchased either by individual teachers or by the educational institution in which they are employed. At the same time, most educational institutions have an audio-visual aids department and it is always worthwhile discovering precisely what services it offers, so that lessons may be enhanced by the technical help that such a department can render. Additionally, if the library facilities in the college or institution are limited, many public libraries are prepared to cooperate with teachers of adults in order to ensure that they have sufficient stocks of books on a specific subject to enable class members to borrow them. Local museums also are often prepared to loan boxes of teaching materials, such as relevant artefacts, on specific topics if they are approached. They are, of course, also pleased to receive class visits when it is appropriate.

In more recent years, probably the most frequently used audio-visual aid is PowerPoint. It has assumed a central place in many presentations and yet it is nearly always used in the same rather traditional manner – that is, having bullet points for the points to be raised, and occasionally variations on the theme. Yet PowerPoint can be used much more adventurously if the presenters are experts in its use. In addition, when Power-Point is used with a class or a group of learners not all of whom have the same first language, I have found that summarizing the whole of a

Table 8.1 Teaching and learning aids and equipment

Aids				Equipment	
Audio	Audio-visual	Visual	Learning aids	Basic	Technical
Audio cassettes	Films	Artefacts/models	Articles/journals	Chalkboard	Camera/cine camera
Audio recordings	Tapes	Charts	Books	Flannelgraph/ Feltboard	Cassette recorder
Radio	Slides	Diagrams	Computer programs	Flipchart	CD player
Records	Television programmes	Drawings	Handouts	Magnetic board	Closed-circuit television
	Video recordings	Graphs	Home experiment kits	Plasticgraph	Computer/ PowerPoint
		Illustrations	Games	Whiteboard	Epidiascope
		Photographs	Media programmes		Episcope
		Slides	Role play		Projectors
			Simulation exercises		• cine
			Study visits		• overhead
			Work books/sheets		• slide
					Radio
					Television
					Video recorder

presentation, including the full quotations, etc., helps them follow the presentation more easily because they can both hear and see the text.

When teachers of adults either prepare their own aids or use the services of the audio-visual aids department, it is wise to be aware of the laws of copyright, since infringement of these may occur out of ignorance. It is also worthwhile checking to see whether their employing educational institution has signed the copyright agreement, because this agreement allows them to photocopy specific materials for use as handouts, under certain conditions to which they must adhere, without reference to the publishers. Even if the educational institution has not signed the agreement, many companies and organizations are prepared to grant permission for the reproduction of their materials, given acknowledgement, and so it is often advisable to seek permission from them if they themselves are not included within the agreement. Moreover, some companies and organizations will also provide teaching resources to teachers who approach them.

Such a variety of teaching aids and equipment ensures that students may be able to learn in accordance with their preferred learning style. Indeed, the greater the variety of appropriate aids employed, the more likely it is that students' learning will be helped; but teachers should not employ too many aids in a single session for the sake of their performance, because this artificializes the learning environment and interferes with the learning process. Considerable research has already been conducted into the relationship between learning and audio-visual communications, and it is necessary for the teacher to be aware of some of this. For instance, Sless (1981) examined the relationship between learning and visual communications and, while he admitted that his own coverage was incomplete, he maintained that students were not trained in the use of visual stimuli, so that if teachers use them they must 'also show how people can learn from these forms' (1981:77). Nevertheless, the technologies have now been in common use for a number of years and many adults are adept in this use.

Thus, it may be seen that a wide variety of aids and equipment are available, and teachers will enrich the learning experience if some of the techniques are employed in their work. It is therefore the responsibility of teachers of adults to be aware of what provision is made by their own educational institution and by other institutions in the locality, so that they are able to perform their role effectively.

Conclusion

This chapter has reviewed a great deal of material about teaching adults. It began by seeking to draw relationships between learning and different approaches to teaching, in which it was recognized that the humanity of both the adult students and the teachers is paramount in the process. It was clearly seen that there are a wide variety of styles, methods and audio-visual aids available to teachers, who should be competent in all the domains, even if not with every method and aid, etc. Now it is necessary to examine the ideas about teaching that occur in some of the well-known writers on the education of adults.

9

THEORETICAL PERSPECTIVES ON TEACHING

In the previous chapters the processes of learning and teaching were discussed and it will have become apparent from the numerous methods mentioned that there are a diversity of approaches to teaching and many theoretical perspectives on it, so it is now necessary to examine some of the latter. This chapter will therefore focus on some of the major theorists of teaching: Brookfield, Bruner, Dewey, Freire, Illich, Knowles and Parker. None of the writers has actually developed a theory of teaching adults, although Brookfield's work contains a very clear guide to his understanding of teaching adults, while Bruner's *Toward a Theory of Instruction* (1968) is a systematic theory of teaching. The other five are all concerned with adults but none has an explicit theory. Knowles's theory of andragogy clearly relates learning and teaching in a much more integrated approach than most, and this is to its credit, although there are other problems with it. In the remainder of this section each of these seven is now discussed.

Stephen Brookfield

Much of Brookfield's considerable output has been directed at teaching and teachers of adults, and his work over the past years has enriched our understanding of both the practice and the theory of teaching. From the outset he has seen teaching as a process of enabling and enriching learning, and although he has tended to fight shy of the definitional debates, he has focused on the practice of teaching. He is more concerned about successful teaching than getting a 'correct' definition of the term. Brookfield's concerns have always been practical rather than theoretical, and he has argued that despite the emphasis on learning in the contemporary debates about lifelong learning, the place of teaching is of uttermost importance as 'the instigator of significant learning' in whatever learning site individuals find themselves (2009:221). At the same time, there is an implicit theory of teaching running through all his writing. Significantly, he has not been afraid to use his own teaching as a critical basis of learning about teaching (e.g. Brookfield, 1986:248–258; 1990:15–28). At the same time, his work is full of references to other teachers and their experiences; in a very constructive manner his work is an excellent synthesis of the work of the many scholars from whom he has also learned.

Brookfield's concerns in his writing about and the practice of teaching include the importance of respecting learner autonomy, so that facilitation, self-direction and other forms of student-centred learning have been at the centre of his work – but in order for learners to be autonomous and empowered, they have to be critical thinkers. But if learners are to be free to be critical, so too must the teachers be critical of themselves and their practices (Brookfield, 1995). Developing critical thinking is one of the major aims of teaching since adults should be challenged to think about alternative solutions to problems and different ways of practice. It is not surprising, therefore, that he welcomed Michael Newman's (2006) more recent study *Teaching Defiance*. For Brookfield, therefore, teaching has always been a moral exercise in which autonomous teachers and learners interact in a mutual learning process – with the teachers providing more input than the learners. Indeed, one of the themes that run through his writing is the need for teachers to be thoroughly professional and be prepared in terms of both content and method. But teaching is not just the provision of input; it is about the giving of oneself – it is an emotional practice.

Brookfield has always argued that educational programmes should be constructed around learners' needs, something which is important for informal learning since adults do not have to attend educational courses and only when it is relevant to them will they spend the necessary time on formal learning. Needs-meeting has always been central to adult education, and in the past there have been many debates about the nature of 'needs'. Knowles focused on a similar aspect: the relevance to the learner of what is taught.

Teaching has always been about a relationship in which the skilful teacher has to respond to the situation in which the learners find themselves. Good teachers have to have the ability to build relationships with the learners, and Brookfield (1990:164–175) outlines the ways that teachers can build trust:

- Do not deny your credibility.
- Be explicit about your organizing vision (what and how we want to achieve our ends).
- Make sure your words and actions are congruent.
- Admit your errors.
- Be prepared to reveal aspects of yourself that are beyond the teaching situation.
- Take the students seriously.
- Do not have favourites.
- Realize the power of your own role-modelling.

Here are some of his prescriptions for the moral relationship of teachers and learners: teaching is a human project and in order to be good teachers we have to know ourselves and understand our strengths and seek to overcome our weaknesses. In other words, we need to become critically aware of our teaching and critically reflective about our practice.

Underlying Brookfield's work there is a humanistic philosophy of teaching and learning. It is implicit in almost everything he has written about the subject, but is rarely discussed, merely assumed. His is a practical philosophy of teaching and his writing provides a textbook for what good, humanistic teaching entails.

Jerome S. Bruner

Bruner, in his classic study *Toward a Theory of Instruction* (1968), recognizes that the human being is a natural learner and he claims that schools often fail to 'enlist the natural energies that sustain spontaneous learning' (ibid.:127). This might appear to be an indictment of modern schools but it is also a recognition that they perform a socializing and moulding function to equip children to take their place in society as much as an educational one, or one that creates individuals who can perform an innovative role in contemporary knowledge society (Hargreaves, 2003). Bruner (1968:53), therefore, recognizes that any instruction that is given in school should be regarded as having an intermediate as well as a long-term aim, the latter being that the learner should become a self-sufficient problem solver. However, it might be claimed that any didactic process, such as formalized instruction, is actually helping to create a sense of dependency in the learner rather than one of independence, especially if the school-teachers are unable to detach themselves from the process and encourage independent learning in children. Consequently, by the time children grow into adults they will have learned to expect that teachers will instruct them. Indeed, adult students do exert considerable pressure upon educators of adults to conform to their expectations of teachers playing a didactic and, often, an authoritative role. It is against this discussion that Bruner's theory of instruction may be viewed. He (1968:40–41) claims that a theory of instruction should have four main features:

1 It should specify the experiences that most effectively implant in an individual a predisposition towards learning.
2 It must specify the ways in which the body of knowledge should be structured so that it can be readily grasped by the learner.
3 It should specify the most effective sequences in which to present the materials to be learned.
4 It should specify the nature and pacing of rewards and punishments in the process of learning and teaching.

Clearly, Bruner has positioned his theory against the background of initial education, so that some of the above points appear to be diametrically opposed to some of those already mentioned in the education of adults. Yet the first of these four points is quite significant since Bruner maintains that instruction should facilitate and regulate the exploration of alternatives, and a major condition for undertaking this is curiosity. Curiosity, in Bruner's work, is an outcome of disjunction, which was discussed earlier, and some psychologists relate the beginnings of curiosity in our lives to the point of separation of mother and child at birth. It will be recalled that curiosity is aroused in adults, as well as in children, when their interpretation of their socio-cultural environment no longer provides them with relevant knowledge to cope with their present experiences. Hence, in teaching adults it is possible for the teacher to provide experiences that arouse this questioning process, so that the adult students' questioning is orientated in a specific direction. Clearly, the structure and form of knowledge are significant in teaching adults, and Bruner recognizes that the mode of representation, the economy of presentation and the effective power of the representation vary 'in relation to different ages, to different "styles" among learners, and to different subject matters' (1968:44). Hence, this second point may be seen as relevant to adult teaching. The relevance of his third point is also clear since he claims that instruction 'consists of leading the learner through a sequence of statements and restatements of a problem or body of knowledge that increase the learner's ability to grasp, transform, and transfer what he is learning' (ibid.:49). Finally, all learners need some reinforcement, so the relevance of this is very evident in the education of adults. However, it must be recognized that Bruner is discussing only one type of educational method, instruction, or a didactic presentation of knowledge, and the relevance of his theory must be seen in relation to this.

There are also considerable similarities between Bruner's formulation and those in the personalized system of instruction discussed in the previous chapter, and it may be seen that Bruner has highlighted many of the points that underlie a theory of instruction. Instruction is obviously didactic and there is a sense in which, as a teaching method, it controls the amount of knowledge to be learned by the students, so that it is open to the accusations that some of the analysts discussed later in this chapter would make about it. Nevertheless, many of the more informal methods of teaching also include some teacher direction and guidance, so that they may not be quite so free of control as might appear on the surface. However, it might be true to claim that all teaching methods may be located on a continuum between student centred and teacher centred, and perhaps more are located towards the latter end of the continuum than adult educators might like.

While Bruner is clearly concerned about the humanity of the participants in the teaching and learning process, there is no explicit place within his principles for a humanistic perspective, although he does recognize the importance of the relationship between teacher and learner. Nevertheless, Bruner has outlined a set of principles that educators of adults should be aware of because they form part of the theoretical perspectives of teaching.

John Dewey

Perhaps Dewey is the most significant of all educationalists for the development of adult education, and so it is hardly surprising that he should be considered here. Many of his ideas have already been discussed in earlier chapters, so it is not intended to repeat them at length. However, Dewey was one of the major exponents of progressive education, and his earlier books were clear expositions of this position. Among his basic principles were that the concept of education had to be reconceived, so that it related to the whole of life rather than just its early years. For Dewey, the human being is born with unlimited potential for growth and development, and education is one of the agencies that facilitate it. Another tenet of progressivism significant to understanding Dewey's thought is the recognition that prominence is given to the scientific method; so the individual needs to start with a problem, develop hypotheses about it and test them out by examination of the empirical evidence. Hence, the problemsolving method, discussed in relation to Gagné's hierarchy of learning, is significant in the work of Dewey. He also recognized that this resulted in a changed relationship between teacher and taught, so that teachers might facilitate and guide the learning but they should not interfere with or control the process in the way that a didactic teacher would.

Some of the above ideas appear in *Education and Democracy* (1916), but in many ways the book that Dewey wrote on experience and education (1938) reflects some of his more developed thinking on teaching. He was concerned to contrast his approach with that of the more traditional schools of thought, and he considered freedom and experience to be significant. Additionally, he maintained that continuity of experience and interaction between young and old are both important to learning. While he was actually writing about initial education, some significant ideas for the education of adults are implicit in his work, so it is important for the educators of adults to be aware of theoretical approaches to children's education.

Dewey considered that since experience is at the heart of human living, and because continuity of experience leads to growth and maturity, then genuine education must come through experience. Hence, the teachers' role is to provide the right type of experience through which the learner may acquire knowledge and understanding, and this facilitates the process of growth and development. Learners mature without having a structure of knowledge and the body of social rules imposed upon them. However, it might be argued that if the teachers' main task is to provide the conditions in which the students learn, and if teachers are actually directing the process when the students require help (Dewey, 1938:71), then they are involved in a much more subtle process of control than that which occurs in traditional, didactic teaching. Dewey recognizes that this possibility exists and he condemns those who 'abuse the office, and ... force the activity of the young into channels which express the teachers' purpose rather than that of the pupils' (ibid.). According to Dewey, teachers' leadership responsibilities include:

- being intelligently aware of the capacity, needs and past experiences of those under instruction;
- making suggestions for learning but being prepared for the class to make further suggestions so that learning is seen to be a cooperative rather than a dictatorial enterprise;
- using the environment and experiences and extracting from them all the lessons that may be learned;
- selecting activities that encourage the learners to organize the knowledge that they gain from their experiences in subject matter;
- looking ahead to see the direction in which the learning experiences are leading to ensure that they are conducive to continued growth.

These points are collected from different pages of Dewey's work but they reflect some of his major points about teaching. It is clear that Dewey's work on teaching may be regarded as facilitative learning and that many of his ideas are similar to those expounded in earlier chapters of this work. It was Lindeman (1961 [1926]) who, influenced by Dewey, incorporated many of these ideas into adult education, so that theories of teaching in adult education reflect a progressive educational perspective that can be traced directly back to Dewey.

Paulo Freire

Freire's work was discussed in Chapter 5 in terms of the theory of learning implicit in his writing, but the theory of teaching is much more explicit. Three elements are discussed here, and these are summarized by Goulet (Freire, 1973a:viii), who suggests that the basic components of Freire's literacy method are:

- participant observation of educators 'tuning in' to the vernacular universe of the people;
- an arduous search for generative words;
- an initial codification of these words into visual images which stimulate people 'submerged' in the culture of silence to 'emerge' as conscious makers of their own 'culture';
- the decodification by a 'culture circle' under the self-effacing stimulus

of a coordinator who is no 'teacher' in the conventional sense, but who has become an educator-educatee in dialogue with educatee-educators too often treated by formal educators as passive recipients of knowledge;

- a creative new codification, this one explicitly critical and aimed at action, wherein those who were formerly illiterate now begin to reject their role as mere 'objects' in nature and social history and undertake to become 'subjects' of their own destiny.

Without raising issues of literacy education, the first significant point that emerges from this summary is that Freire advocates, and practises, going to those who have a learning need and listening to them, so that the educator can become the learner. While this serves a diagnostic function, it has more purposes than this because it enables the educator to learn the language of the potential learners and to identify with them. At the outset of the teaching and learning, the teacher bridges the gulf between him or her and the learners in order to create a genuine relationship and dialogue, without which humanistic education cannot occur.

The second significant point about this process is that the learners are encouraged to participate in dialogue and to problematize the reality in which they are immersed. This is a deliberate attempt to make the learners question what they had previously taken for granted, so that they can become aware that they have been socialized into the culture of the colonizers and that their construction of reality may be false within the context of their indigenous heritage. This occurs through the analysis and use of language, since language is a significant carrier of the universe of meaning, and through becoming aware of what has happened to them, the learners are enabled to reconstruct their universe of meaning. In this process the learners are not objects of a social process but creative subjects within it.

Finally, Freire does not regard the educator and the learner as having mutually distinct roles but thinks that in a genuine dialogue the teacher teaches the learners, who learn and teach the teacher as well. Hence, in the dialogue there is also a mutual planning of the teaching and learning, so that it is relevant to the needs of the participants. It is in this dialogue that the humanistic nature of Freire's teaching method is apparent since he (1972b:61–65) claims that it is essential to the educational process and that it requires an intense love for and faith in humankind. Perhaps Freire's philosophy of teaching is summed up by a Chinese poem:

> Go to people, live among them,
> Learn from them, love them,
> Serve them, plan with them,
> Start with what they have, Build on what they have.
>   (Author unknown)

Perhaps more than most theories of teaching, Freire's work emphasizes that the teacher has to reach out to the learners and learn from them in order to be able to contribute effectively to the teaching and learning process. As in other theories of teaching adults, the humanity of the learners is respected and emphasized.

Two significant points need to be made here. Clearly, Freire presents a radical approach to teaching, and he regards it as a method by which learners can act upon their socio-political environment in order to change it. Hence, the educator is the facilitator of learning, and education is a process of change. The educator is not the 'fount of all wisdom' trying to fill the empty buckets; education is not a process of banking received knowledge. Rather, education is an active process in which the teacher controls neither the knowledge learned nor the learning outcomes. Because of the politically radical elements in Freire, there is a danger that other aspects of his philosophy of teaching may be lost.

Freire offers a humanistic teaching method in which he recognizes education to be a political act. However, he highlights the fact that teachers have to break down the barriers between teacher and taught, should speak the same language as the learners, should be aware of how they construct their universe of meaning and what they see as their learning needs, and should start where the learners are and encourage them to explore and learn from their experiences.

From Freire's unique synthesis of Christianity, Marxism and existentialism he has produced a theoretical approach to teaching that is both inspiring and challenging. That he is regarded as a political radical should not discourage educators of adults from seeking to emulate elements of his method, since it epitomizes the high ideals of humanistic education. Many of his early ideas about teaching have been reinforced by later writing on teaching and democracy (Freire, 1998).

Ivan Illich

Like Freire, Illich was a radical Christian who presented an alternative approach to education. He is included here, however, not because of his radicalism but because one of his major ideas has found expression in the idea of much informal adult education in the United States, and to some extent it is being incorporated into the University of the Third Age in the United Kingdom. His approach also presents a warning to those adult educators who seek to professionalize their occupation.

In order to understand Illich thoroughly it must be understood that he offered a radical critique of some of the established institutions in Western society, including medicine, the Church and teaching, and so it is necessary to summarize his concerns before they are applied to education. Illich (1977) claimed that the professions dominate ordinary people – that they prescribe what the people need, often without genuine consultation, and institutionalize it within the professional's own territory. Hence, doctors determine when a person is ill, prescribe an acceptable remedy in relation to the need and ensure that health cure takes place in 'hygienic apartments where one cannot be born, cannot be sick and cannot die decently' (Illich, 1977:27). Similarly, teachers determine what children need to learn, and prescribe the educational remedy in a building that artificializes the real experiences of living. Professionals dominate people's lives, prescribing what they regard as right and proper, and the general populace are no more than the recipients of the process. This is the crux of Illich's position, and it is one that led to considerable changes in professional practice and even to the ethos of some professional practice.

Since education has fallen into the trap of institutionalization, Illich (1973a) proposed a radical critique of teaching in formal situations: that it was necessary to de-school society. He considered this essential because not only education but social reality itself had become schooled. Accepted knowledge and credentials for occupational advancement have become incarcerated within the institution of the school, but there is no equality of access to it, so that expenditure on education is unequally distributed in favour of the wealthy. Every time some other area of social living is incorporated into a school curriculum, a new class of poor is generated, so that, for instance, with the introduction of new training initiatives for young adults in the United Kingdom, a new class of poor who are unable to attend the courses and gain the advantages is generated.

In precisely the same way, Illich and Verne (1976) offer a critique of lifelong education. Continuing education specialists will generate the need for more learning, prescribe how and where it should be learned, and perpetuate the school system throughout the whole of the lifespan. They claim that in 'permanent education we are no doubt witnessing a further reduction of the idea of education, this time for the exclusive benefit of the capitalists of knowledge and the professionals licensed to distribute' (1976:13). Clearly, Illich offered a valid criticism of the process of institutionalization in Western society, and indeed in other societies as well. What, then, did he propose as a remedy for the malady that he diagnosed?

Illich (1973a) proposed that learning networks should be established and that resources are required to establish a web-like structure throughout a society. In short, long before the learning society became a common concept in lifelong education he was advocating learning zones, cities, and so on. He (1973a:81) proposed four different approaches that enable students to gain access to any educational resource which may help them to define and achieve their own goals: reference services to educational objects; skill exchanges; peer matching; reference services to educators at large. This clearly required organization, and some of the resources spent on the school system could be used for this purpose, and the professional teacher, liberated from the bureaucratic control of the school, would be free to provide a service to these learners who require it. Such a scheme is idealistic and revolutionary, so there is no likelihood of a society reforming its educational institution in this manner since it is investing even more capital in the school system than ever before, and education has become a marketable commodity. But the free university system in the United States appears to be fulfilling these criteria: a free university, according to Draves, is 'an organization which offers non-credit classes to the general public in which "anyone can teach and anyone can learn"' (1979:5). Some of the free universities are sponsored by traditional colleges, while others are sponsored by libraries and some others are independent. They exist to coordinate learning and teaching opportunities, to introduce potential students to potential teachers. There is a national conference of free universities each year and in 1979 there were over 180 free universities established in the United States, with over 300,000 participants. A similar approach is appearing in the University of the Third Age in the United Kingdom at present.

Illich, then, offered a radical critique of contemporary society and of the dominant position occupied by the professionals. While his radical alternative to schooling does not appear to have gained a great deal of support in initial education, there is evidence that some adult educators are seeking to respond to the learning need in people and to create networks where teaching and learning can occur outside the institutional framework. Nevertheless, such free institutions must run the danger of ossifying and becoming established, and so it remains to be seen whether learning networks will survive and multiply in the coming decades.

Malcolm Knowles

Like Freire, Knowles was discussed in the chapter on learning theorists but, unlike Freire, he is included again because he actually produced a textbook in which he specifically discussed the two processes. In addition, he produced a table in which he specified sixteen principles of teaching in response to conditions of learning. He demonstrated that he regards teaching as the process of designing and managing learning activities. His (1980a:57–58) principles indicate the process of teaching, and they can be summarized as follows. Teachers:

- expose learners to new possibilities for self-fulfilment;
- help learners clarify their own aspirations;
- help learners diagnose;
- help learners identify life-problems resulting from their learning needs;

- provide physical conditions conducive to adult learning;
- accept and treat learners as persons;
- seek to build relationships of trust and cooperation between learners;
- become co-learners in the spirit of mutual inquiry;
- involve learners in a mutual process of formulating learning objectives;
- share with learners potential methods to achieve these objectives;
- help learners to organize themselves to undertake their tasks;
- help learners exploit their own experiences on learning resources;
- gear presentation of their own resources to the levels of learners' experiences;
- help learners integrate new learning to their own experience;
- involve learners in devising criteria and methods to measure progress;
- help learners develop and apply self-evaluation procedures.

This list of principles clearly demonstrates the facilitative teaching style of a humanistic educator of adults. Knowles saw andragogy as embracing the process of teaching and learning rather than merely learning or teaching, and within this context it is perhaps important to understand that these principles embrace progressive education for adults, so that they are rather different in perspective from the other approaches that have been examined in this chapter.

Elsewhere in the same work, Knowles (1980a:222–247) applies these principles to the process of teaching, which he regards as having seven stages:

1 setting a climate for learning;
2 establishing a structure for mutual planning;
3 diagnosing learning needs;
4 formulating directions for learning;
5 designing a pattern of learning experiences;
6 managing the execution of the learning experiences;
7 evaluating results and re-diagnosing learning needs.

The climate of learning is perhaps more significant than many educators actually assume, and this reflects an emphasis on teaching style. Knowles included both the physical setting of learning and the psychological ethos. He recognized that the learning climate is also affected by the way in which teachers and the adult students interact. This is especially true in the early sessions, a point that many adult educators focus upon, so that it is significant that teachers endeavour to establish good relationships between themselves and the class, and between the learners themselves, from the outset of a course. Only within this climate can diagnosis occur, within which Knowles claimed that there are three stages: developing a model of the desired end-state of the teaching and learning; assessing the present level of knowledge; and assessing the gap between the two. Thereafter, learning objectives can be formulated by teachers and the learners together. Once this stage has been reached, Knowles advocated that the adult learners design the pattern of learning experiences, which should contain continuity, sequence and integration between different learning episodes. It is the teachers' role to manage the learning experience, and Knowles maintained that teachers should serve both as strong procedural technicians – suggesting the most effective ways in which the students can help in executing the decisions – and as resource persons, or coaches, who provide substantive information regarding the subject matter of the unit, possible techniques, and available materials, where needed (Knowles, 1980a:239). Finally, teachers should join with the students in both an evaluation of the process and a re-diagnosis of future learning needs.

Thus, it may be seen from the above sequence that Knowles clearly regarded the learners as active explorers in the learning process, participating in every stage, and the teachers as resource persons for both content and process. He is obviously in accord with many of the ideas that Dewey expounded, and so, unlike McKenzie (1979), I maintain that Knowles applied progressive education to the education of adults. Therefore, it may be seen that the ideology of andragogy is humanistic.

Parker Palmer

Palmer is a profound thinker whose passion for teaching is perhaps best summarized in his excellent study *The Courage to Teach* (1998). Here and in his other writings, a profound spirituality and morality are both evident. Indeed, he (Palmer, 1993) regards education as a spiritual journey. Teaching is a vocation, a calling, in which the teachers give themselves to their students in relationship. For him, teaching is a calling that demands the whole person since 'we teach who we are' (Palmer, 1998:1–3). In this sense it is an art rather than a science, but this does not deny that good teaching techniques should not prevail in the teaching and learning process; it merely says that they are not enough. At the heart of teaching is the teacher; good teaching depends on the integrity and identity of the teacher, and these are discovered by experimentation in living. At the heart of teaching is the teacher; the more we know ourselves, the better teachers we will be. As Buber taught, in the beginning is relationship. All teaching involves relationship, and knowing is loving. We might summarize Palmer's approach to teaching by saying that in teaching and learning the other's growth and development comes through the interrelationship of true selves (teacher and taught). Teachers always teach people – never subjects.

193

In relating with people, we, as teachers, are exposed to those in front of us, and this engenders fear – a fear that we often seek to hide by a performance of teaching. Often, however, the fear leads to loss of relationship and a form of didacticism that 'protects' us from the students. But here Palmer's insight can be seen when he points out that learners are also fearful. Palmer highlights the fact that often our fear prevents us from relating with our students in the way that we should. Nervousness is a disposition that many teachers exhibit, and we often long for the time when we will be so confident that we will not be afraid; but as Palmer points out, even as a well-established teacher he is still fearful when he teaches. This is certainly something that I can echo; throughout my teaching career I have always been nervous before I begin a session, and as I reflect upon my teaching career, my worst failures have been when I have let fear override what I have wanted for the class or the individuals with whom I have been working, or even the opportunity to truly relate with the learners in trust. Once we learn to trust in the relationship with the Other, we can both acknowledge our own fear and recognize their fear.

However, teaching is not really being out in front of the class occupying space; it is about using teaching techniques to create open space for others to explore, space in which the community of truth is practised (Palmer, 1993:xii, 69–87). It is about trusting the learners to overcome their fear and enjoy the exploration of learning together. With profound insight, Palmer (1998:63) summarizes the paradoxes of teaching:

- Whatever experience we have, we are beginners whenever we teach a new class.
- We know ourselves only in relationship with others.
- Good teaching is not about technique but about identity.
- Teaching takes place at the intersection of the private and the public.
- Intellect and feeling work together.

These points summarize the insights of his study of teaching and the teacher.

Teachers have to respect the integrity of the students, and it is this that underlies his philosophy of teaching. Teaching, he says, must be both structured and open, be friendly yet challenging, give support both to the individual and the group, and encourage both open discussion and silence. It is here that the morality of teaching is so important – for the teachers have the responsibility to enable growth and development in the quest for life and meaning.

Palmer is an inspirational writer about teaching. He opens himself and shows the lessons that he has learned from his teaching career. For him, more than any of the other perspectives on teaching that we have discussed in this chapter, there is a profound introspection about his role as a teacher.

Conclusion

This chapter has endeavoured to summarize the work of seven writers about teaching. Illich comes closest to Rogers, who maintained that teaching was not so important in the process of teaching and learning, but in Illich's case it was because he criticized the formal education system – but then so did Palmer, who wrote that he has spent the whole of his teaching career struggling against some of the things that he learned about teaching while he was in college. Each of these seven perspectives is different, but all of them, it could be claimed, offer a humanistic analysis of teaching. Bruner's approach is the most psychological and technical, Dewey's and Freire's the most philosophical and Palmer's and Brookfield's the most personal. Both Brookfield's and Knowles's approaches fall into the more traditional approaches used in adult education. Perhaps it is not surprising that through the dominant theme of these writers is that of relationship – a moral relationship between teacher and taught, recognizing as Freire does that the politics of teaching involves the democratic processes in which teachers learn from learners and learners learn from teachers. I think that all would agree with Bourdieu and Passeron when they assert that all pedagogic action 'is objectively, symbolic violence insofar as it is the imposition of a cultural arbitrary by an arbitrary power' (1977:5ff.) and that teachers' role is to deny this symbolic violence as they encourage learners to be curious, self-directed and critical. For students to acquiesce to teachers and to accept uncritically what we teach is a sign of bad teaching and mis-education rather than good teaching.

While teaching is clearly dominantly an art form of building personal relationships and the joint pursuit of 'truth', it is also a technology inasmuch as none of these writers would disregard the techniques of teaching; indeed, a part of both the professionalism and moral commitment of teachers is to be experts in teaching techniques so that we can best help our students in their quest to learn more, and learn it more efficiently.

Naturally, we could have turned to other exemplars of good teaching to include in this chapter but these seven highlight the humanistic nature of good teaching. Yet good teaching is a local phenomenon and we now live in a global world, so that teaching, in common with many other humanistic phenomena, has had to change and adapt to the new global economy. In the next chapter, therefore, we look at distance education.

10

DISTANCE EDUCATION AND OPEN LEARNING

This book started with a discussion of globalization, during which it was pointed out that one of the two main driving forces of this process is the development of information technology. It is not surprising, therefore, that educational systems have been affected by the changes in the substructure of the globe. It is unnecessary to rehearse all of these arguments again here, but we do need to recognize that nearly all forms of education are changing in response to the wider social pressures. Distance education has grown in popularity in recent years, popularized by Britain's Open University, although its history is far older, and even university distance education occurred long before the Open University was ever dreamed about (Rumble and Harry, 1982). Indeed, Peters (2009:226) suggests that '[t]he concept of distance education, although still practiced globally, is more than 150 years old and hence pedagogically and technologically outdated'. Peters focuses upon open learning now. At the same time, we should recall that despite its predominant place in the literature, the Open University was not the first distance education university: that honour belongs to the University of South Africa, which became a distance education university in 1923, although its own foundation as the University of the Cape of Good Hope, the oldest university in South Africa, goes back to 1873. This chapter first examines the nature of distance education/open learning and thereafter looks at the way in which it has developed and continues to develop, and examines some of its practices in contemporary society. Throughout this chapter it will be seen that among the major theorists of distance education is Otto Peters.

The nature of distance education and open learning

In one sense, perhaps, distance education in the United Kingdom actually began when James Stuart, the founder of university extra-mural adult education, experimented with correspondence education for women in the 1870s. There were societies for home study at about this time in both England and the United States. (See Garrison and Shale (1990) for a historical overview of distance education in the United States.) Correspondence education became a relatively popular form of education for adults in the early part of the twentieth century, although it was always regarded as second best. With the development of the wireless, there were many experiments with educational radio, especially in sparsely populated countries such as Australia, and developing societies such as Nigeria. Naturally, these approaches have now been replaced by more high-tech means of transmitting knowledge. However, it is only in more recent years that theories about distance education have begun to emerge. We can see, therefore, how distance education has moved from correspondence education, to hard-copy teaching and learning materials, to electronic communications techniques in the period of a half a century as a result of these forces for change.

One of most complete discussions of the meaning of the term 'distance education' is given by Keegan (1990:28–47). He (ibid.:44) characterizes distance education in the following manner:

- It involves a semi-permanent separation of teacher and learner.
- It is influenced by the educational organization in both the preparation of the teaching materials and the support of the students.
- It uses technical media.
- It is a two-way process.
- It has a semi-permanent absence of a learning group.

Naturally, these characteristics are open to certain criticisms. For instance, it may well be true that in many more recent forms of distance education there is a two-way relationship between teachers and taught so that the learners may also initiate teaching and learning situations. Consequently, this characteristic appears superfluous to any definition of the concept. Distance education is therefore defined here as those forms of education in which organized learning opportunities are usually provided through technical media to learners who normally study individually, and removed from the teacher in both time and space. As each educational institution has its own procedures and provides its own facilities, this definition seeks to be narrow enough to be meaningful and not wide enough to include almost any form of learning. Even so, with the development of the World Wide Web, the idea of the teacher begins to be unnecessary to the education; education and learning are now distinct phenomena. At this juncture, we can see that distance learning is different from distance education. The former is usually provided by educational institutions and is accredited by them, but now learning opportunities like those provided by the web can gain educational accreditation through the Accreditation of Prior Experiential Learning.

Consequently, we can see why Peters suggested that distance education is now a rather outmoded concept since the learning opportunities provided by the web open up the possibilities of a wide range of learning that lies beyond the control of any educational institution, so that the recognition and accreditation of learning that occurs beyond traditional education has become a necessity.

Just prior to the foundation of the Open University in the United Kingdom, however, Otto Peters (1984; see Sewart *et al.*, 1988:68–94 for analysis), who was a member of an important group of adult educators at the University of Tübingen in Germany, began to develop an influential theory about distance education as a typical form of education for the age. He regarded it as a rationalized form of industrial production – a division of labour with each individual in the course team having a different role in the production and dissemination of knowledge; mechanization, as the dissemination of knowledge was achieved through assembly-line production; and mass production, since there was theoretically no limit as to the number of copies of the same course that could be produced or students who could study the course once it was produced. He regarded this as a process of standardization and the beginnings of a monopoly of the educational market; see Keegan (1990) for a clear summary of Peters' position. This is a position consistent with the one being argued here for social change in general and education in particular. Perhaps the idea of the monopoly was premature, but it was at least being realistic. Indeed, we can see that this approach to education might eventually result in there being fewer educational institutions – and fewer academics – as face-to-face tuition becomes more expensive. Indeed, takeovers and mergers of educational institutions are already beginning.

Another significant theorist of distance education at the same time was Holmberg (1989), who regarded it as a form of guided didactic conversation and who considered that there are seven postulates to distance education:

1   There should be the creation of a personal relationship between the teaching and learning parties.
2   There needs to be well-developed self-instructional material.
3   There should be intellectual pleasure in the exercise.
4   The atmosphere, language and conventions should foster friendly conversation.
5   The message received by the learner should be conversational in tone, easily understood and remembered.
6   A conversational approach should always be used in distance education.
7   Planning and guiding are necessary for organized study.

Thus, Holmberg's approach is more humanistic than Peters' analysis, although Peters never claimed to approve of all that was occurring.

Indeed, Peters (2009:233) is at pains to point out that distance education should have a strong emphasis on the mission to reach those who have been disadvantaged in the traditional education system. Both Peters and Holmberg emphasize the need for learners to be self-directed in this form of education, although Holmberg's third point about intellectual pleasure may appear to be a little idealistic in some instances! Nevertheless, in order for it to work it is necessary to change the whole style of academic discourse and to a considerable degree the form of academic training in order to ensure that course writers are empathetic towards their readers. Indeed, it might well be argued that a Socratic approach to writing distance education material is much more useful since the learners are challenged to think for themselves rather than just being presented with teaching material that must be learned. However, it has been discovered that learners actually want to be given a lot of material. Indeed, there is a real sense in which learners want a great deal of information in distance education courses, so that they feel that they are getting a lot to learn – getting their 'money's worth' if it is self-funded.

One of the main differences about the preparation of teaching material for distance education and e-learning is that it involves a multidisciplinary team approach to teaching much more than does traditional teaching and learning.

Naturally, Holmberg's work is attractive to educators who have a humanistic approach to education, but there is a danger in making it all appear too friendly since the written word often assumes an aura of sanctity! The text appears to some readers as 'sacred knowledge' that cannot be criticized, and anything that is not included is regarded as less significant, or not important at all. Indeed, it is not uncommon to hear students studying distance education courses asking whether they should include material in their assignments that is not in the text – and occasionally poor tutors telling them that they should not do so! However learner-friendly the distance education might be, teachers and writers have to be aware that the curricula of the distance education courses are centralized and controlled, so that in this sense distance education has a tendency to be closed, and therefore it needs critical learners.

A theorist who was influential during the early years of the Open University was Charles Wedemeyer (1981). As with many American writers, his concerns were self-study, independent learning and individualism, and in this he comes closer to the point made above about distance learning. He regarded distance education as an optimistic enterprise in the provision of lifelong learning – one in which learners are independent of teachers.

However, there have been dramatic changes in the world in recent years and it is now possible to extend Peters' analysis, since it is being claimed that contemporary Western Europe is entering a period of late, or post, modernity. Basically, this means that the consequences of the

Enlightenment are being recognized and questioned, with some scholars asking whether it was actually a success (see, for example, Jarvis, 2008). This is not the place to pursue this discussion, but the success of distance education can clearly be seen as a sign of late modernity. Giddens (1990) suggests a number of features that typify contemporary society as being late-modern, such as its industrial-capitalistic nature, space–time distanciation, disembedded mechanisms and expert systems, reflexivity and individual responsibility. However, industrial capitalism is of a different order than the other four, being one of the driving forces of global change. In this sense, the shift towards distance learning is a response to the driving forces of global capitalism and information technology, and the other four are superstructural aspects that have been incorporated into the educational system as a result.

Distance education is, therefore, a form of education utilizing all forms of information technology to assist learners to learn. It has differing characteristics, depending upon the way in which different educational institutions utilize it. But space–time distanciation, disembedded mechanisms and expert systems, reflective learning and individual responsibility are central to them. It is important to note that Giddens's 'reflexivity' is changed here into reflective learning to indicate that the educational system here is dealing with human learning processes as well as social and system changes. It is clearly a contemporary phenomenon that epitomizes each of these four features of late-modern society, and so we shall now discuss them in the order in which they appear here.

Space–time distanciation

Giddens indicates that in 'pre-modern societies, space and place largely coincide, since the spatial dimensions of social life are, for most of the population, and in most respects, dominated by "presence" – by localised activities' (1990:18). In other words, students had to be in the presence of the teachers to hear their profound words. The history of the university is of students travelling to places where teachers expounded; in order to gain a degree from certain universities, residence qualifications were imposed, and so on. Now it is possible to study for, and be awarded, even higher degrees from some universities without ever being physically present either at the university itself or even in the country in which it is located. Now teachers record their lessons and they can be studied in the students' own time and place. The learning experience is no longer immediate and face to face, but mediated and secondary. Indeed, knowledge – like most other forms of capital – is now without boundaries (Walshok, 1995), and while Walshok's book is primarily about the United States, knowledge is not bounded in contemporary society. Consequently, distance education, by definition, symbolizes the process of space–time distanciation; we will return to this discussion in the next section when we examine space–time compression.

Disembedded mechanisms and expert systems

Disembedding implies a process of extracting the specific localized social relations and re-implanting them within a global context of space and time. Consequently, the distance teaching institutions can be experienced not as places to which learners travel for study with a teacher, but as the mechanisms through which the pursuit of their studies is facilitated wherever they study – new learning sites – and at whatever time they choose to undertake their work. The distance teaching institution is disembedded and needs no campus and no geographical location. In other words, the academy is now no longer a place, it is a process and a system; its educational offering is now a product guaranteed to provide specific learning for the purchasers. Now it is not only the teachers who are important, it is the whole system: producing, packaging, marketing, processing, support services for clients, and so on (Jochems et al., 2004). It is removed from its localized context, and the clients and learners have to be persuaded to trust in the efficiency and expertise of the whole system. This has progressed to such an extent that there are already virtual universities, to which we will return in the next section.

The idea of expert systems is also something with which we have become familiar over recent years; we do not need to know how a system functions in order to be serviced by it. The system processes its products, in this case both teaching and learning materials, and once students are registered, they receive the products – that is, the teaching and learning materials – without being aware of all the processes of production. But there is another sense in which the distance education institution is an expert system, since once students are registered as students, they are also processed. Each Open University student in the United Kingdom, for instance, is given a number on registration, and everything to do with that student is processed by the system number.

Reflective learning

The reflexivity of modernity, according to Giddens, involves a constant examination and re-examination of social practices which are 'reformed in the light of incoming information about those very practices' (1990:38). Consequently, the traditional mode of doing things is no longer sufficient justification for continuing a practice. Indeed, change in the mode of production and distribution of distance education materials will alter as new technologies initiate different ways of doing things. For instance, the interactive CD-ROM and the interactive computer program replace some of the traditional correspondence material as the market makes it a worth-while financial investment. However, hi-tech productions have become cheaper and the size of the market will increase, and it will be the cost of accreditation that inhibits some learners from gaining sufficient recognition for their learning for a few more years to come.

However, the concern here is much more with reflective learning. There are more opportunities when students operate at their own time and pace and in their own space for them to reflect upon the learning material with which they are presented. While there is a tendency to treat written material as 'sacred text', there is also a tendency to treat what teachers say as true, and in the teachers' presence that tendency is enhanced. Exercises can and should be provided in distance teaching in order to encourage reflective learning, but this reflective learning must also be critical learning since the autonomy of the learner can be much greater in e-learning.

Individuation

As the functioning of many elements of society has become organized and distanced from everyday life, there has been a new emphasis upon the individual rather than the group; on individual rights rather then human rights, and so on. Emphasis is also placed upon the existential questions of humankind: upon the self and upon self-identity. People do not always feel so constrained by the demands of organizations because they do not always have to attend them to be part of them – although they are actually controlled by the organizations' procedures in precisely the same way! Consequently, individuals feel able to follow their own pursuits at their own time and in their own way, and to some extent to be self-determining individuals. Distance education therefore provides the opportunity for people to continue their education individually in their own space, at their own time and pace, and have that learning serviced by a disembedded educational institution – an expert system (see Jochems *et al.*, 2004).

Distance education may therefore be seen to fit many of the characteristics of late modernity and it may be regarded as being a symbol of this form of society. This analysis highlights some of the contemporary issues that this form of education for adults raises. It is not considered important to pursue the consequences of these any further here, although it is necessary to recognize that some practitioners of distance education attempt to overcome some of the problems implicit in this discussion.

The continued development of distance education into open learning

As I have already argued, distance education is the product of industrial capitalism and information technology. There is a sense in which we have begun to look at the way in which changes in information technology have already affected the education system, and I shall suggest later in this section that more changes are occurring; but first we do need to return to the topic of global capitalism and to some of the points made in the opening chapters of this book. This section therefore will have two parts, dealing respectively with advanced capitalism and information technology.

Advanced capitalism

Peters has shown how thoroughly the production of distance education materials epitomizes industrial production, although he does not demonstrate its relation to the capitalist market in quite the same manner. However, inherent in capitalism are three features that can also now be discovered in distance education, namely privatization, commoditization and competition.

In recent times, education in most societies of the world has been provided by the state, although religious bodies have also been major providers. Private provision has been a small factor in what has generally been regarded as a welfare state responsibility. However, from the earliest days of distance education private organizations, such as Pitmans, have provided a small amount of education. When distance education really developed – especially in its university form, with the Open University in the United Kingdom, it was still partially state-provided. However, in more recent times there has been a proliferation of distance education 'universities' (Jarvis, 2001b) that have been totally private, and some have successfully sought to gain accreditation for their courses. At the same time, the state system has not been inactive and we have seen the emergence of the University for Industry, with LearnDirect and even more recent developments in the United Kingdom.

Once any commodity is technologically produced, it becomes an object, and, within a capitalist economy, a commodity that can be sold. A distance education package or an online course or an interactive CD-ROM is a marketable commodity and one that educational institutions have been encouraged to sell. However, if the programme is contained within an object that can be carried away from the vendor, or even mailed or transmitted electronically to the purchaser, then it becomes a more attractive marketable commodity. This is even more so if the language used is international, such as English or Spanish or Chinese, but Peters (2002) suggests that by about 2015, electronically retrievable information will be available in all the common languages of the world. Indeed, in more recent years the movement has extended from traditional electronic transmission to personal computers but also to mobile phones and iPods, so that we now have m-learning.

Even so, the capitalistic market is one of competition. The rhetoric of the market is that only the best-quality commodities will survive, but its reality is that only the strongest and largest organizations survive, irrespective of the quality of the product they sell. Distance education now advertises its wares, and buyers wish to know not only about the nature of the course being studied, but also the length of time that it will take, the qualification that will be awarded on successful completion, the number of assignments that have to be submitted and the fee that they will have to pay. Purchasers can then decide for themselves what their 'best buy' will be, depending on their own instrumental concerns. One of the obvious outcomes of this process is that unsuccessful institutions, irrespective of the quality of their product or of their potentiality, will lose out and may be forced to close. Hence, the large get larger at the expense of the small, unless, say, the small discover a gap in the market, but the consequences of this are self-evident: the innovative small will get taken over and incorporated into the larger.

But the market cannot be limited to the local area of the producing institution. The market is bounded only by the size of the globe! Hence, globalization has entered into distance education: for example, Britain's Open University has been opening offices throughout the world since the 1980s and has now become a mega-university (Daniel, 1996); the University of Surrey organized a Master's degree programme in post-compulsory education in the 1980s using hard copy which could be studied anywhere in the world; and now there are many universities offering similar programmes electronically. Now it is possible to study for a British university degree from many UK universities while still living in the farthest reaches of the world. Naturally, there are tremendous advantages to this – but it might also be wondered about the effect that this will have upon small indigenous universities of poor Third World countries, and once again it might lead to accusations of cultural imperialism. However, it might be much more a matter for some of trade or, as others would argue, of aid rather than anything else. Indeed, it could be argued that once education has embraced the market, then the logical outcome is that the large will get larger, and with it there will almost certainly be forms of cultural imperialism, hegemony of discourse and the impoverishment of many forms of local education. This can already be seen in many of the smaller countries of the world, where students feel forced to abandon their own language in order to be able to gain recognition in the wider world. There is, then, a danger that local cultural knowledge will be sidelined as the knowledge concerns of the dominant cultures become the focus of global distance education. The market has no intrinsic morals!

Information technology

We have already traced the development of distance education in conjunction with the developments in information technology. But the digital age has generated a new and major development in distance education, which can be associated with another aspect of space–time realignment: space–time compression (Harvey, 1990:240–259).

Harvey associates space–time compression with the Enlightenment, and while this in perfectly true, there is another sense in which the virtual age has exacerbated this process. It is now possible through electronic means to communicate interactively with people throughout the world. This development has given rise to the virtual classroom and the virtual university (Teare *et al.*, 1998). New private universities are beginning to emerge that are almost totally electronic and virtual, and there are tremendous advantages to such systems since there are no boundaries and it is still possible to communicate with tutors and peers around the world in a more personal manner than the one-way communication of more traditional distance education teaching.

With these developments there has been some questioning about the place of more traditional education. Katz and his associates (1999) called this 'dancing with the devil' – but they were serious when they asked whether the more traditional forms of education can compete in the learning market with these new developments. Clearly, traditional education has been forced to adapt to these social pressures, or else – following the inevitable law of the market – it will not survive. Aronowitz (2000), however, sees these new institutions as 'knowledge factories', which he condemns, arguing for a more humanistic approach to education. Irrespective of the fears of Aronowitz, it has to be acknowledged that education is moving in the direction of a greater degree of virtuality. Nevertheless, it is increasingly being recognized that there is still a need for the traditional face-to-face interaction, so that many institutions are developing mixed-mode delivery systems. This is especially true at higher degree (doctoral) level, where face-to-face interaction encourages critical and creative thought. Indeed, it could be argued that it is only in face-to-face interaction that creativity can flourish in education, so that there is some justification for Aronowitz's position. Yet Peters (2002:133) would argue that we are now presented with real opportunities for the development of autonomous learners but that we are faced with major challenges in developing new pedagogical models to utilize this new learning space effectively to empower them. Indeed, if we consider the developments in Asia, where a number of universities have well over 1 million registered students each, we can see just how widely electronic learning has developed and how it has offered greater opportunities to less privileged people.

As with most innovations, there are clearly advantages to distance education but, because it has been developed by market-driven forces, it is often associated with the good and the bad of the market, rather than the good and the bad of the delivery system per se. Obviously, there are many advantages in the system: people not having to travel to schools and colleges because of disadvantage or commitments, being able to study in their own time and at their own pace, and so on. But it can easily become an impersonal system that is open to all the criticisms that have been raised above, although it will no doubt continue to become an even more significant sector within the field of education and, like the capitalist market itself, it will continue to impose forms of cultural and linguistic imperialism on disadvantaged peoples and undermine local cultures and practices. Consequently, we have to see both the advantages and the disadvantages of distance education at the present time. The system does have many advantages in contemporary society but, unfortunately, it can hardly ever be neutral or even democratic.

Contemporary practices

As the times have changed, distance education has not just dropped one approach and adopted a new one; rather, new approaches have been added to what is already a very complex field, just leading to a greater degree of complexity. Indeed, I was recently introduced to an approach that a small faith-based educational institution is using in its new distance education courses that uses traditional written material sent electronically with references to the web, but also disks and small chips that enable learners to access a very wide range of learning material both from the web and specially prepared for the course in both audio and video modes. Thus, mixed methods of teaching and learning are now occurring since they are cheap to produce and disseminate, and provide a wide variety of learning opportunities.

Peters (2002:40–45) has suggested that there are at least seven different approaches to distance education today:

1   the 'examination preparation' model;
2   the correspondence education model;
3   the multiple (mass) media model;
4   the group distance education model;
5   the autonomous learner model;
6   the network-based distance education model;
7   the technology-extended classroom model.

In addition, he recognizes that there are hybrids of these taking a variety of forms. For instance, we still find educational institutions offering to prepare students for examination, offering 'model answers' to questions, and so on. There are still correspondence schools – and some universities, as they move into this new world, are adopting correspondence-type approaches but often combining them with more technological extensions of the classroom. In addition, there are other universities that combine the second and the third approaches. In the fourth approach, there are universities, such as the Chinese Open University, where the more formal third approach is used not with individual learners but with groups who have been released from work, etc. in order to follow the prescribed lecture, and so on. Institutions that seek to facilitate autonomous learners are sometimes criticized because they do not provide sufficient content, and distance education students (perhaps all students) do prefer to be given information, or at least led to it through careful Socratic approaches that are not necessarily conducive to creating autonomous learners. Increasingly, as knowledge expands and academic departments are not expanding at the same speed, students are enabled to network across the web and with each other, and also to use all forms of teaching and learning material through which they can create their own network of learning resources. This is being encouraged as different universities are putting whole courses online and allowing a wider public to access them. However, there are increasing dangers of plagiarism when this occurs since not all academic staff can be expected to know everything that is now available on the web in their subjects!

Finally, there is the technologically extended classroom. This can take a variety of forms. For instance, when Adult Learners Week was launched in Lithuania, the opening lectures in one university setting were teleconferenced to seven different centres throughout the country and the recipients enabled to dialogue with the lecturers in precisely the same way as did those who were present. In Taiwan there is at least one example of two universities sharing courses through teleconferencing, a phenomenon that can certainly be expected to be repeated as educational institutions are forced to network in order to cover the wider practical knowledge bases of different subjects and practices. Additionally, higher education in Singapore has been given government money to ensure that all new courses produced can be put online.

Naturally, as we continue to recognize the growing complexity of the learning process, there are many more possibilities to expand distance learning. At the same time, more mundane and everyday applications will continue to develop as corporations provide workstations for their employees that enable the employees to check every aspect of their job and also learn about new applications and situations as they are introduced in the wider corporation.

Basically, the World Wide Web has produced the most extensive 'library' of learning materials and opportunities that the world has ever known – more knowledge than anyone can imagine or learn – and this can all be accessed almost instantaneously at any individual's convenience in the home. Consequently, the opportunities that this offers are too many to number, but there is a fear that traditional institutions will find it hard to adapt to all these new approaches, as Katz and his associates warned, so that their functions may change from providers of learning to accreditors of learning – even to becoming examination centres through which individuals' learning may be tested and accredited. Then it has to be borne in mind that those who do not succeed in the market may perish, and this could be to the impoverishment of education generally and to some fields of study in particular.

However, producing all this material is also a very highly skilled and complex process. As we shall note later in this book, new roles for educators are rapidly emerging, and insufficient training exists that enables educators to become proficient at many of the skills required. For instance, it is widely recognized that the preparation of distance education materials places a greater emphasis on the creation of a course team of which the teacher is but one member. The style in which the material is written, if it is written, needs careful consideration, and Holmberg (1960:14) suggested that the material had to be conversational and almost two-way, which he later came to regard as guided didactic conversation. This is true also in the assessment of coursework that is to be returned to the distance education learners: comments might be regarded as an invitation to dialogue through the medium of the students' assignments and the tutors' comments.

The practice of distance education is now extremely common, especially with the development of desktop publishing, and this has resulted in many more people being involved in the preparation and assessment of distance education material. Naturally, the quality should be high since most aspects of it can be controlled before dissemination. The skills of becoming a distance educator are gradually being learned and taught, and slowly we are seeing degree courses emerge in distance education, as a separate field of study. There are not yet many such certificated courses in the techniques of distance education, but as children are now so adept at using such techniques, it is becoming increasingly important for teachers to be trained in ICT (see Chaib and Svensson, 2005) Indeed, some few people are beginning to suggest that practitioners should be trained before they become distance educators, in the same way as the training of educators of adults has emerged, and it will probably not be too long before initial training courses, and concurrently certificates, in distance education develop and become part of the educational scene.

Conclusion

Distance education's importance is recognized by such organizations as the Commonwealth of Learning as a means by which the First World can assist the Third, but it is only recently that theories of distance education have begun to emerge. The University for Industry, with its system of

LearnDirect, is a private–public partnership designed to help individuals learn so that they can improve their career prospects and competitiveness in the labour market. Hence, even the boundaries between the public and the private are beginning to disappear as more people seek to learn. Otto Peters (2002) has called one of his books *Distance Education in Transition*, which is a good reflection of the current state of play in this field as e-learning and even m-learning appear – but perhaps this transition is one that will not have an end product in the near future.

11

ASSESSING AND EVALUATING

The language of the marketplace has been familiar to liberal adult education for many years, but it is only in recent years that it has become a part of the vocabulary of other educators. Now education is a marketable commodity like other commodities, and educational institutions are more like other commercial organizations, so that more commercial methods of assessment and evaluation are beginning to appear. As educational organizations have been forced to seek new markets, they have become more competitive and flexible.

Continuing vocational education has become a rapidly expanding field, and with universities and colleges all seeking to offer additional education to those who are in work, functional degrees and diplomas, such as the MBA degree and the DBA and other taught doctorates, have become commonplace. Colleges and universities are striving to attract more students to their taught higher degrees (both Master's degrees and doctorates), and even engaging in competition to recruit more students by seeking to undercut their rivals in terms of the fees that they charge or even the amount of remission that they are prepared to award for prior educational experience. In addition, as potential students might not be able to gain educational release in working time, educational courses are now being offered during evenings and at weekends, and distance education and e-learning have become much more widely accepted, as I pointed out in the previous chapter. Courses are becoming modularized, irrespective of epistemological considerations, so that they can be more flexible and be marketed as independent units or as parts of wider qualifications. Flexibility and costs have become major concerns, and academic qualifications have become symbols of the education that has been purchased. Indeed, it is now common to find educational institutions advertising the symbol of the education – that is, the qualification to be gained, rather than the knowledge to be learned or the advantages of studying that specific field of knowledge. As early as 1993 a National Vocational Qualification advertisement for training read, 'If you're buying training, make sure you get a receipt' – and the receipt was the qualification! (*Guardian* (London), 19 October 1993).

Other forms of general adult education for adults, through adult education classes, have traditionally not been certificated and this has now all been 'lumped together' as informal learning (see Department for Innovation, Universities and Skills, 2009). Liberal adult education, for instance, has been a part of the educational provision for many years. Indeed, the folk high schools in Denmark, university extra-mural classes in the United Kingdom and the 150-hour programme in Italy have all tried to avoid certification, but if they are grant-aided, they have been subject to pressures to introduce certification. Indeed, the market ethos has now overtaken many of these systems, and there is discussion about certificated courses in Danish folk high schools. Some liberal adult education is rapidly moving towards a fully certificated form in the United Kingdom. Now, the educational qualification is a sign of the cultural capital possessed by individuals, and through the purchase of additional educational commodities the sign can be changed to demonstrate the amount of knowledge consumed through the institutionalized learning process. With the introduction of accreditation of prior experiential learning (APEL), the commodity can be bought at discount prices in the educational marketplace, and wise buyers seek the best purchases for their own purposes. It is significant that often the courses that are certificated are the same as, or similar to, those which were previously not certificated – change but no change – or, as Baudrillard suggests:

> Everything is in motion, everything is changing, everything is being transformed and yet nothing changes. Such a society, thrown into technological progress, accomplishes all possible revolutions but these are revolutions upon itself. Its growing productivity does not lead to structural change.
>
> (quoted in Kellner, 1989:11)

Educational institutions advertise their courses, just like other market providers. Indeed, the Further Education Unit in the United Kingdom, among others, recognized this trend in the 1990s and produced pamphlets on marketing strategy for adult and continuing education (Further Education Unit, 1990). Indeed, the educational market is now international, with many institutions of higher education advertising their courses throughout the world, and many of them adopting a variety of modes of delivery.

However, it is more often than not the sign that is advertised – Study for a University Degree – rather than the education itself. In order to attract the consumer, the commodity must become a sign, according to Baudrillard, who defines consumption as 'a systematic act of the manipulation of signs' (quoted in Poster, 1988:21). Individuals are therefore free to purchase their own education, if they can afford it, and develop in any direction they wish, or at least in one of the directions that they are offered through the market. They can reinforce their own understanding of themselves through the educational signs, among other signs, that they display. Indeed, the more prestigious the commodities, the greater the sign value. One should note that accreditation of prior experiential learning (APEL) and assessment of prior learning (APL) have been major advances to the education system that adult educators have advocated for many years. However, as with most educational reforms it took the social pressures generated by the globalization process and the marketplace to ensure that they were instigated and accepted.

Before the certificates are awarded, learners' work has to be assessed, and so the first part of this chapter looks at the processes and assessment, the second at certificates and credits, the third at evaluation. Finally, we ask about the public value of learning.

Assessing learners' work

In this section we will examine the nature of assessment, the rationale for assessment and some types of assessment. The concepts of assessment and evaluation raise issues about both value and correctness, and there is considerable confusion between them. In many ways they are similar processes but there is a tendency in education to use the term 'assessment' for the process of grading (evaluating, assessing) students' work and 'evaluation' for assessing the degree to which a curriculum fulfils its aims. But the process has many common features, and while I refer to assessment in this section, many of the points are valid for any discussion on evaluation.

The nature of assessment

Assessment is a complex process:

- We may regard it as assessing the level of correctness of facts – as if they are empirical, which raises questions about the nature of fact and perception.
- We may be seeking to assess the process rather than the answer – especially in essays – and in this sense we may be assessing the levels of logic as well as our perception of the degree of correctness of the writing, and so on, and this raises questions about the nature of rationality.
- If we are assessing the level of correctness of the language, we may well be assessing what society regards as correct – this is a cultural phenomenon.
- We may actually find ourselves assessing a response according to our own understanding of the phenomenon, and this raises questions about authoritarianism and subjectivity, and so on.

- When we assess a commodity, our assessment may be based not upon correctness at all, but on satisfaction; this sometimes, but not always, occurs when students assess teachers!

Assessment, then, is both an easy and an extremely difficult process. A socio-philosophical analysis of assessment is beyond the scope of this book, but it is important to raise some of the issues here.

For example, when we meet a person for the first time we may often comment afterwards, 'What a nice woman' or 'I didn't really think much of him', and so on. In a sense, as a result of our meeting we have assessed our own reactions to that person. What we are doing in this case is to assess how we have responded to the other person: we have assessed our reaction – others may have reached a different conclusion! This is important when we consider any form of assessment; it is our subjective reaction, although, as we shall see, there are bounds to the subjectivity of assessment. However, the most important first point to make is that assessment is natural and many, but not all, forms contain an element of subjectivity about them. Assessment, then, is placing a value on a phenomenon – and in this sense it has the same meaning as evaluation.

The point that I need to make here is that both assessment and evaluation tend to be subjective, and the only time when assessment can approach objectivity is when we mark work that involves fact – whether it be a scientific fact such as that 'O' is the symbol for oxygen or that 'Smith wrote this fact on p. 22 of the first edition of his book', and so on. But the question still remains as to whether we actually assess the fact or our perception of it. Our evaluation of the person whom we met is not like this at all; it is subjective and may be completely false! Many answers do not involve fact in this simple sense, and so we are engaged in a process of evaluating or assessing the degree of correctness rather than the absolute correctness of the answer. Indeed, we may actually end up assessing the degree to which the response conforms to our expectation – and this is a fundamental danger in education since it tends to be authoritarian. We often want learners to conform. It is easier for the markers to treat what is read as fact and the answers as correct or wrong than it is to admit to the fact that many assessments contain a great deal of subjectivity.

Not all assessment is subjective, however. We know that when we take a ruler and measure the height of a room, or the length of a piece of wood, we can get an accurate measurement. This measurement can be replicated whenever we wish. The same is true to a considerable extent when we check a mathematical calculation; we are able to award a mark that is more objective. We could say that it is a measurement of the learners' ability to solve the mathematical problems that have been set. However, it is rather different when we come to marking an essay. What will always remain the same is that we can measure how many paragraphs and words there are in the essay – that does not alter. But two markers may well disagree on the mark to be awarded for the content of the essay itself. This is not surprising because we are now no longer measuring but assessing, and we are often assessing the logic of the argument, the structure of the whole piece, and so on. Consequently, we are using our expertise to assess the work, but if there is feedback on the assessment, it should be constructive.

This problem is even greater when we assess practical performance. Unless the performance is recorded, it cannot be repeated in time, and so it is not something that can be repeated in order to check on the assessment. Assessing someone's teaching must be subjective, and the only way that we can generalize from the particular is to witness many different performances so that we gain an overall impression of the practice. This is something that can be used both in helping learners improve their performance and in making an assessment for credit. But it is difficult to put a percentage grade on practical performance, and many courses have broad grade categories, such as pass/fail or fail/pass/credit. This is more accurate and probably fairer to the learners.

Many educators are faced with a major problem in contemporary society: examination boards, governments and policy makers all want to treat assessment as if it is measurement. It is not! Assessment, as we have seen, is often a subjective process, rather like when we met that person; it is the same person but different people assess him or her differently. The same happens when assessing essays! During my career I have conducted many marking workshops in which groups of teachers or examiners have been asked to mark the same essay individually and simultaneously. Rarely has there been total agreement; rather, there has often been a difference of as much as 40 per cent! What the assessors were doing when they were marking those essays was placing their own value upon the essay – perhaps only on the content, but perhaps on the structure and level of analysis, or even the correctness of the spelling and grammar, and so on. But we all see something different in an essay, and what is a good point to one reader might not be such a novel one to another, and so on. Consequently, our assessments should not be authoritarian but questioning, suggestive and even seeking the learners to rethink their work in different ways. This by no means denies the fact that there may be correct and incorrect content in an essay, but it does emphasize the fact that it is not only the content that is assessed. And so we must see that assessment is not measurement – even though we might place a percentage grade on the piece of work. The idea of the percentage grade is only to give the appearance that the marking is objective and therefore to persuade the learners to accept it without question. However, morality demands that some form of dialogue ensue in subjective assessments – if not dialogue with the learners, dialogue between at least two markers.

Consequently, assessors ought to have a level of expertise that should enable them to make a more authoritative assessment of a piece of work than non-experts. However, the authority of the expert does not transform an assessment process to one of measurement. Our society is bedevilled with the idea of measurement because of the prevalence of the scientific measurement of inanimate and empirical phenomena. This is a problem for educators, and it is one that we have to confront. We need to be as fair as we can to learners; hence, we often double-mark to try to eradicate some of the subjectivity, and this is to be commended, so long as both markers mark the same script blind – that is, a clean script without any markings, or comments, from the other examiner appearing on the script. If the script is not blind, there is a tendency for the second marker to agree with the first.

The fact that so much assessing is subjective but that our society is often loath to acknowledge the fact is a real problem since we can see that a great deal of the educational examination system is seeking to provide an incorrect picture of the examining process – even though many techniques, such as double-blind marking, are put in place to try to reduce the level of subjectivity. However, reduction is not eradication! Therefore, we might need to ask ourselves why we assess at all.

A rationale for assessment

There are several reasons why we assess. In the teaching and learning process it is a diagnostic tool – that is, it is a way whereby teachers can discover the strengths and weaknesses of the learners and help them improve their work in the future. Teaching should always be a response to the learners' needs, and therefore it is necessary for teachers to try to diagnose what those needs are. Teachers therefore need to incorporate a variety of techniques, including assessing current needs of learners, in the teaching and learning process so that they are enabled to make their teaching even more relevant. Such techniques can vary from question-and-answer sessions, to open discussion and feedback, to tests and examinations. At this level, therefore, assessing is very important for the learners as well as the teachers because the learners can become aware of what they know and what they do not know, or what they can do acceptably and what needs to be improved. It is also at this point that it is necessary to remind ourselves that we are assessing learners' knowledge, skill and so on rather than assessing the learners themselves. Learners must not feel threatened by the process, and we as educators need to recognize the moral nature of the processes in which we are engaged.

Perhaps the most common reason given for assessment – especially in recent government policy – is the maintenance of standards. Schools, colleges and universities must be seen in this educational market to be

215

maintaining standards so that potential clients know the standard of the institutions in which they might enrol. At first sight this seems to be a laudable enterprise in which an open market is reinforced by transparency. Once we accept the subjectivity of the assessing process, however, we can see that it is not entirely possible for comparisons to be made unless the tests being taken are public and are all graded in the same way – which is precisely what the UK government has tried to do. But the approach still has flaws in it, since the learners in the schools and colleges start from different positions: they come into their educational institutions from different backgrounds, and so on. Therefore, the comparative nature of the exercise is problematic, although it is more possible to claim that standards in schools and colleges can be improved against the general picture using different teaching methods, different teachers, and so on – but we still do not overcome the subjective nature of assessment itself; we only see that in larger public examinations there are ways of making the process of assessing fairer.

A third reason for assessing is that it provides evidence of the learners' attainments and as such provides evidence that they may progress to another stage in their educational career or may enter the career itself. However, attainment does not necessarily equate with ability, and examination marks may not reflect intelligence. It was easier to make this claim when it was believed that there was only one form of intelligence, but with current research suggesting multiple intelligences it is harder to make it. Nevertheless, it is a convenient way for a college to judge entry and for a profession to assess someone's ability to enter the profession. Yet there is little research to suggest that the entry grade necessarily relates to career competence or attainment.

Overall, perhaps the best we can claim for assessment is that it provides a guide, an indication, rather than that it is an exact science of measuring. One could wish that this were more publicly acknowledged.

Types of assessment

In a book of this nature it is not possible to examine in detail every type of assessment and so Table 11.1 outlines some of the major types of assessment and explains briefly what they are.

Once we recognize the varieties of assessment techniques that are available and used, then it is necessary for examiners to be trained in the processes and able to utilize them in practice.

Total quality management

I have mentioned the fact that as education is now a commodity that has moved into the marketplace, quality might be regarded as having some-

Table 11.1 Types of assessment

Type of assessment	Description
Formative	This is the diagnostic form of assessment that occurs during the process of teaching and learning
Summative	The assessment that occurs at the end of the process – the final mark
Continuous	A process of assessment that involves an ongoing process throughout a course/module, etc. rather than relying entirely on a summative assessment
Analytical	This is also part of the diagnostic process since the marker carefully works through the piece of work, evaluating every aspect and, usually, commenting on it – as a form of teaching
Global	A technique of rapid-marking many scripts through reading a whole script and rank-ordering it against other similar scripts and then later awarding a grade on each script in relation to all the others
Self	An approach to assessing where the learners/practitioners assess themselves or their own work
Peer	An approach in which peers assess each other's work
Collaborative	When a number of people collaborate to agree a grade, usually involving the learner and the teacher

thing to do with customer satisfaction. Naturally, this might logically have no intrinsic connection with the standard of education; it might, for example, have to do with whether the learners enjoyed their studies. Hence, we find Parsons (1994:20) emphasizing the learners, or customers, as one of the four aspects of total quality management, the other three being the processes, the people and the culture. Not all writers on total quality management education emphasize the consumer quite so much, and Murgatroyd and Morgan (1993) have '3Cs' – culture, commitment and communication – as their baseline. Culture is about the ambience of the process, commitment is to the shared goals of the institution, and communication is about the ability to communicate effectively and efficiently. Clearly, the major baseline with some writers about total quality management is with success in the market rather than those other aspects of the teaching and learning process, and it is here where the lowering of standards might occur, since learners want a certificate and there is a chance that with lower standards, more learners might enrol on a course, knowing that they will almost certainly gain the award.

The need for training in assessment techniques

Many beginning teachers fear being involved in assessing, and in the marking workshops, which I referred to earlier, inexperienced teachers also fear revealing their grades to colleagues, and they are often likely to mark near to the average. This is because there is almost an aura of technical expertise applied to the process, whereas it is a natural process that is enhanced by our own learning experiences. Training teachers to understand this is important. But it is also important to help teachers understand the human nature of the process and how to present their reports to the learners. When we as educators make an assessment, we assess the learners' work; we do not assess them as people, but as people they actually emotionally experience the grade, so that assessments always need to be made in a humanistic manner. They actually feel that it is an assessment of them as persons. Hence, we have to treat the assessment process in quite a delicate manner, recognizing the humanistic and moral nature of education itself. We see this at every level – even at the level of publications, when assessors (reviewers) of papers are invited to write one report that can be returned to the author(s) of the paper and another that goes directly to the editor and may be less carefully phrased, and so on.

But the need for training goes much further than this: in my experience, my colleagues and I have run question-setting workshops, helping examiners recognize the need to set questions in precise ways, teaching them how the wording of the question needs to be consistent with its aims, since learners may actually see different meanings in questions, and so on. Ambiguous questions can, and should, be set when it is the intention of the examiner to create a situation in which the learners have to problem-solve. Setting questions is a skilled technique and should always be undertaken in conjunction with spelling out the aims of the question, what it is intended to assess, and so on. This means that it is wise to have questions double-checked if they are for classroom or college or national examinations.

However, there are different types of assessment process and it is necessary first to recognize that each form has its own demands as to the types of assessment, and as there are many different types, so it is necessary for assessors – and teachers, since assessment is part of the teaching process – to be familiar with a wide variety of techniques.

Certificates, credits, diplomas

Nearly all higher education is geared to the award of degrees, higher degrees, and so on. Indeed, nearly all forms of education for adults are now being certificated, and different approaches to qualifying certificates have emerged, three of which are discussed here: National Vocational Qualifications, diplomas, and credit accumulation and transfer.

National Vocational Qualifications (Scottish Vocational Qualifications – SVQs – in Scotland)

Not only has education become a commodity, it is one that has to be assessed in terms of its outputs. Considerable emphasis is now being placed upon the competences that are gained as a result of the learning – but the learning has to be both theoretical and practical if the qualification is to have vocational relevance. Consequently, in the 1980s, reflecting the idea that knowledge had to be performative, according to Lyotard (1984), new qualifications had to embody this perspective, and competences became significant. Competence is 'the possession and development of sufficient life skills, knowledge, appropriate attitudes and experience for successful performance in life roles' (Hermann and Kenyon, 1987:1). While knowledge, skills and attitudes might also be included within the general framework of competence, it is extremely difficult to assess all of these from the perspective of performance because individuals do not always perform consistently in accord with their own theoretical position, as Argyris and Schön (1974) have demonstrated. They argued that people had 'espoused theories' and 'theories in use'; the former are the perspectives which individuals will say guide their behaviour while the latter are those that may be detected from a close observation and analysis of their behaviour. The two are not necessarily consistent, and while the performance may be regarded as more important than the espoused theory, the coupling of knowledge and skills in any definition of competence is over-simple.

In vocational terms, a competence may be defined as 'a performance capability needed by workers in a specified occupational area' (Hermann and Kenyon, 1987:1). Different levels of competence have been designated in National Vocational Qualifications:

- Level 1 – performance of routine and predictable work activities.
- Level 2 – performance of work activities involving greater individual responsibility and autonomy than Level 1.
- Level 3 – skilled performance of activities, involving complex and non-routine work. Some supervisory activity may also be involved at this level.
- Level 4 – complex, technical, specialized and professional activities, including planning and problem solving. There is personal accountability at this level.
- Higher Level – competence in pursuit of a senior occupation, including the ability to apply fundamental principles and techniques. Extensive knowledge and understanding is necessary to underpin competence.

(summarized from Oakeshott, 1991:52)

Performance must be tested using valid assessment methods and endorsed by the best current practice. The standards, in the United Kingdom, are set by the Lead Industrial Bodies – that is, the organization, or occupational grouping, that has been given this responsibility. Since it is the performance being assessed, it is not necessary for individuals having their competences assessed to have attended a training course beforehand; it is the ability to perform the job that is important. This is regarded as the most efficient, since it allows for the shortest routes to be taken to the point of assessment, although the value of experience is not ruled out by this approach.

While it is clearly necessary to assess performance in the work situation, trying to categorize all performances into a few levels is a problematic undertaking, especially those which are demanded infrequently by the demands of the job. However, this approach has moved assessment away from the theoretical and artificial to the actual place of performance; but the assumptions underlying this approach are probably as problematic as those underlying more traditional modes of assessment, since successful performance on one day is no guarantee of it on another. Much more problematic, however, is the process of trying to subdivide an occupational performance into its competences and arriving at a complete list about which there is general agreement – indeed, the whole is always more than the sum of its parts!

However, a complex process of designating competences and testing them is being evolved at the present time, although the surrounding bureaucracy is clearly too great and some providers of courses seeking NVQ accreditation have expressed dissatisfaction with it. Even so, it is becoming possible to gain NVQs for participation in voluntary activities as well as vocational ones. Tiernan (1992) records how Britain's Royal Society of Arts recognized the skills involved in voluntary work and has introduced an Advanced Diploma in the Organization of Voluntary Groups, based on the NVQ model.

In addition, there is a movement towards introducing a more general set of qualifications that will relate to, but not replace, the current General Certificate qualifications; these are General National Vocational Qualifications (GNVQs). These qualifications are more work related than subject related, although it is anticipated that they will achieve compatibility with the normal General Certificate; it is claimed that level 3 GNVQ will be equivalent to an Advanced Level General Certificate of Education (Smith, 1993).

Diplomas

In 2008 the British government (www.direct.gov.uk) introduced a new qualification, the diploma, which emphasized even more the practical aspects of training and is specifically designed for the 14- to 19-year-old young person. In the first instance, diplomas will take two years to complete and will be available at three levels:

1   Foundation (level 1) – equivalent to five GCSEs at grades D to G;
2   Higher (level 2) – equivalent to seven GCSEs at grades A–C;
3   Advanced (level 3) – equivalent to three and a half A levels.

However, there is the possibility of breaking these down into progression diplomas in which the award is made for a part of the whole.

In 2008 it was intended to introduce these in five areas:

1   construction and built environment;
2   creative and media;
3   engineering;
4   information technology;
5   society, health and development.

It is anticipated that by 2013 there will be seventeen areas. In all of them, practical placements will be included in the training.

Credit accumulation and transfer

Once courses are modularized, it becomes possible to award some form of accreditation for each module. Standardized credits for educational achievement in continuing education were first discussed in the United States in the late 1960s. A National Task Force of the National University Continuing Education Conference in 1968 provided a definition of a continuing education credit as 'Ten contact hours of participation in an organized continuing education experience under responsible sponsorship, capable direction and qualified instruction' (Long and Lord, 1978:2). Long and Lord (1978) record how this idea developed and how the idea of accrediting experience developed from this, so that accreditation of prior experiential learning (APEL) emerged from within the same framework.

The movement towards standardized accreditation of modules developed much more slowly in the United Kingdom, although it was heavily influenced by the American experience. Eventually it was accepted by the Council for National Academic Awards, in 1986. Since the Council only accredited higher education courses, its credit scheme related to the different levels of the undergraduate degree and the taught Master's courses. It assumed that an undergraduate degree has three levels, relating to each of the three years, and that each year was equivalent to 1,200 hours of study. Consequently, the first year of an undergraduate degree was seen as a Certificate and worth 120 credits at level 1; completion of two years was equivalent to the Diploma of Higher Education and was the equivalent of the Certificate plus a further 120 credits at level 2; a bachelor's degree was worth 360 credits, at least 60 of which had to be obtained at level 3 and not more than 120 at level 1. An honours degree had to include 120 credits at level 3 and no more than 120 at level 1. A taught Master's degree consisted of 120 credits at M level, and herein lay one of the major mistakes that the Council made, since a taught Master's degree has always been the equivalent of one full year's study (i.e. 120 M-level credits) followed by a dissertation. This mistake by the Council effectively devalued the taught Master's degree by at least one-third.

Once a system that gradually achieved widespread acceptance had been produced, it became possible for students to study some modules in one educational institution and gain accreditation for that work and then to transfer to another institution to gain further credits. Many universities and colleges, while subscribing to the scheme, will award their own degrees only if at least a substantial proportion of the credits have been gained in their institution; this proportion is often as high as two-thirds of the whole. This is understandable, since there is not yet a national undergraduate or taught Master's degree, although there might have been if the Conservative government had not abolished the Council for National Academic Awards. The Open University now administers the remnants of the Council's scheme, and many of the Council's former 'clients' (the polytechnics) now have university status and award their own qualifications.

This principle has been used at lower-level courses and even in liberal adult education, where there has not been any assessment of achievement. For instance, in one or two places 'passport'-type schemes have been introduced whereby a record of attendance at courses has been retained by students, who could then produce their own record as part of their own learning portfolio in seeking credit for their previous learning experiences. Assessment of prior learning has become widely accepted in post-compulsory education in the United Kingdom, with two types appearing: a general and a specific credit. The former is often given as a general remission of part of a course for the overall learning experiences in which students have engaged, while the specific credit refers to remission of part of a course of study because of previous successful study in that specific area of knowledge. While assessment of prior learning in the general sense is recognition of the broad learning of adults, there is a danger that credit will be given to induce students to undertake specific courses because it will enable them to complete the courses sooner and more cheaply, etc. This danger becomes greater as education is being underfunded and colleges and universities are seeking to attract as many students as possible in order to make their courses viable. Specific credits are content based, and consequently there is a greater certainty that academic standards and subject coherence will be retained.

In almost precisely the same way, the European Union has introduced a transferable credit scheme – European Credit Transfer System (ECTS) – which stemmed from its concern to introduce study abroad programmes throughout the European Union, and it is regarded as a way by which the Union can help educational institutions to cooperate with each other. The programme began in 1988 in a selected number of universities, but by 1996 both universities and non-universities were involved in the project, and the number has been increasing each year; in 1997–8 there were 772 applications from new institutions to become involved, and this number continues to increase. The scheme is still largely based on the study abroad programme and, unlike the UK system, it awards 60 credits for an academic year, 30 for a semester and 20 for a term (trimester). Since this is a study abroad programme, institutions are required to agree on the programme before a student studies abroad, but as a result there is full academic recognition by participating institutions of each other's awards.

This is one of the major principles underlying the Bologna Process in higher education, which will, it is hoped, allow for credit recognition and transfer across Europe. While the policy is to be applauded, there are still major differences between countries, which means that such a transfer has not achieved automatic acceptance.

Accreditation is becoming a normal part of the education of adults, even of liberal adult education as it has become part of mainstream general education. The process of integration into mainstream education is something that adult educators would generally welcome, but the price for it has been high. In many ways, accreditation is contrary to the ethos of liberal adult education – an ethos that was being destroyed by the policies of the Conservative government of the early 1990s, although more recently its value has been recognized once again. At the same time, if education is to be regarded as a passport to an occupation or further study, it is necessary to have some form of recognition for the standards achieved in those courses, and accreditation is, therefore, a necessary part of this process.

As liberal adult education moved towards accreditation in order to continue to get some funding from the UK government, it was also being recognized that many people, especially the growing number of senior citizens returning to higher education, do not want to study for additional qualifications. Consequently, some courses are being offered that seek to combine both students seeking the award and others who are learning for learning's sake. This was something Houle (1961) researched, and the most recent further research undertaken, which is the *National Adult Learning Survey* (LaValle and Blake, 2001:14), notes that 20 per cent of all taught courses were non-vocational, although this does not mean that there was no award attached to them. However, we do know that the

University of the Third Age (U3A) retains the ethos of learning for learning's sake and that there are few awards given in the United Kingdom for completion of its courses. These are self-financing because of the voluntary nature of the U3A, but the provision of self-financing liberal adult education courses would result in decreasing provision as fewer individuals would be able to afford the fees, and therefore adult education would probably become even more open to the accusations that it is a middle-class leisure-time pursuit.

Naturally, there are a number of other reactions to this, and one of these is the emphasis being placed on self-directed learning, the study of which is becoming very prevalent throughout the United States and elsewhere (e.g. Candy, 1991). In addition, new forms of educational opportunities are emerging, such as free universities (Draves, 1980) and the University of the Third Age, where no credit is given since the learning is about human being and becoming rather than human having and consuming (Jarvis, 1992). Here people can learn, grow and develop, even within a market framework, without reference to qualifications.

It is becoming difficult to imagine that academic standards are being maintained with all the changes that are occurring, despite the valiant efforts of nearly all major educational institutions to introduce systems of quality control.

Curriculum/course evaluation

As I pointed out earlier, the term 'evaluation' tends to be used with reference to judging the quality of course or curriculum. Curriculum evaluation has been the normal manner through which educators assessed their work, although much of this was conducted in initial education. It was often assumed in adult education, for instance, that if tutors retained their students throughout the allocated duration of their course, then they must be acceptable. Another approach was that of elaborating upon the principles of good practice. Periodic reviews by both local and governmental inspectors were another sufficient check of the overall standard. However, this is now beginning to change under the influence of the market, and now the language of quality is appearing in adult and continuing education. Like the other underlying concepts of value, however, 'quality' is open to considerable discussion.

The definition of the concept is problematic. Quality has been defined as effectiveness, efficiency and even student or client satisfaction. However, to equate quality with any of these is to be guilty of the naturalistic fallacy, because quality simply cannot be equated to another value. Quality is quality and differs considerably from efficiency, since it is possible to be adjudged efficient even though the outcome is poor, and so on. Additionally, quality has been used in relation to quality teaching, quality learning, etc., but in these instances there is a tendency towards tautology. Quality is also used in relation to the outcomes of the teaching–learning transaction (see Müller and Funnell, 1991). Thus, it may be seen that this is by no means an obvious concept, although it does appear to be treated as rather self-evident at times. (See, for instance, Further Education Unit (1989), where the concept is assumed throughout rather than clarified.) The ideas of good practice and quality assurance were brought together in two research projects conducted by de Wit (1992, 1993), who wrote:

> Although there is no agreed definition of quality, there are several key themes in the current debate, which focus attention on the whole network of resources and procedures in CE. These themes are
>
> - fitness for purpose
> - need for a strategic approach
> - meeting customers' expectations
> - a cycle of continuous improvement
> - a cohesive system of interconnected processes
> (de Wit, 1993:7)

While any attempt to distil the main characteristics from such an abstract concept is fraught with danger, this approach is more correct than that of equating the concept with any specific characteristic, in the manner that some of the previous descriptions have done. De Wit's study drew together in a practical manner some of the main issues that are generally agreed to constitute quality in continuing education, and she produced a clear and practical checklist, under each of the following headings:

- Policy
- Staff
- Courses
- Marketing
- Teaching and Learning
- Outcomes.

Under each of these headings there are a number of questions that course teams and evaluators might ask about continuing education provision to ensure that good practice is being followed in all instances. Clearly, it does not overcome the conceptual problem, but this it acknowledges. It does, however, seek to provide practical guidelines within the limits it sets itself.

The public value of learning

There is a sense in which this section is a response to the fundamental question asked at the outset: why should education and learning opportunities be provided for adults? For years the answer to this question was assumed rather than discussed or researched rigorously, but in recent years the question has been addressed. At the very basic level it could be said that the driving force for the extension of education beyond school has been the needs of the economy, and a great deal of public investment has been made into forms of lifelong learning that are vocational in orientation, so much so that the concept of lifelong learning has been equated with work-life learning. But this is an over-simple response to the question, and more recently the question has been raised about the wider public value of learning.

Schuller et al. (2004:12–22) looked at the wider benefits of learning and conceptualized these benefits within a triangular framework – with human capital and social capital forming the base, and the apex of the pyramid being identity capital. Within human capital, there are qualifications, knowledge and skills; from the social capital side there are civic participation, friends and family, and these two meet where health, attitudes and values, and motivation to continue learning meet. Built upon this are the three aspects of identity capital: enjoyment, plans and the self-concept. The investigations of Schuller et al. have begun to show relationships between these as they have pointed to the way in which the person emerges through learning, and learning has a human, social and public value.

Once we begin to see that all forms of learning have benefits, major policy questions need to be asked about whose responsibility it is to provide learning opportunities, and even who should pay for them. Williams (2008:26) asked this question in the light of the fact that government had reduced the funding by 1.4 million places in the past two years. She notes that Leon Feinstein, head of the Centre for Research on the Wider Benefits of Learning, claimed that the Treasury wanted quantitative and statistically valid research data despite the fact that most of the research into learning must necessarily be of a qualitative nature. As she notes, perhaps the Commission of Inquiry into the Future of Lifelong Learning will provide more data that will influence government more effectively.

Conclusion

The whole nature of assessment and credit has been transformed with the advent of lifelong learning in a global market, but, as we shall see in the next chapter, the nature of the curriculum itself has been transformed as teaching and learning has become a marketable commodity.

12

CURRICULUM THEORY AND PROGRAMME PLANNING

'Curriculum' is a relatively common word in initial education but one used less frequently in the education of adults, 'programme' being more common. British writers, however, use both 'curriculum' and 'programme' reasonably interchangeably, while American writers also use the terms 'instructional design', 'design of learning' (Verner with Booth, 1964) or 'design of education' (Houle, 1972). In the United Kingdom the term 'programme' is beginning to assume greater significance since it has been recognized that in the learning market educational institutions offer a wide 'menu' of courses and modules and that it is now easier for learners to construct their own learning programme.

The concerns of adult education in the past have tended to be centred on the topics that have already been discussed, but without a great deal of explicit curriculum theory, perhaps because of its non-formal nature. Yet there has always been an implicit curriculum theory and also explicit statements of rationale for adult education. Some of these elements will be discussed in the first section of this chapter. At the same time, the curriculum theory implicit in the ideas already raised will also become apparent as adult education has become a marketable commodity. The second section will focus on the more explicit discussions about educational programmes that have emanated from the United States and will be constructed around the three types of programme described by Cervero and Wilson (1994).

Studies in curriculum theory

At the outset it is necessary to clarify the concept of curriculum itself, and thereafter the reasons why the term has not been employed widely in the education of adults until recently will be examined. Various types of curriculum models will then be discussed, and also the introduction of modularization. This will be followed by an analysis of the elements of the curriculum, including a discussion of the way that the concept of 'need' actually pointed to a market model of education long before the market was so prevalent: indeed, Illich (1977) actually claimed that needs were created by professionals.

The concept of curriculum

The word derives from the Latin *currere*, which means 'to run', and its associated noun, which has been translated as 'a course'. Hence, the word has been used to refer to following a course of study; but, as with many other terms, its meaning has been subtly changed over the years. Lawton noted that 'in the past definitions ... tended to emphasize the content of the teaching programme, now writers on the curriculum are much more likely to define it in terms of the whole learning situation' (1973:11). Similarly, Kelly suggested that it is necessary to 'distinguish the use of the word to denote the content of a particular subject or area of study from the use of it to refer to the total programme of an educational institution' (1977:3). From these two brief quotations it is possible to see that even these writers are referring to slightly different usages of the word. Perhaps Griffin's comment that curriculum refers to 'the entire range of educational practices or learning experiences' (1978:5) summarizes the problem. The word can mean almost anything from the content of what is taught to the total provision of an educational institution; it can also refer to the subject matter of a particular course of study or even to the learning that is intended. Hence, it relates to both the known and the intended – that is, the formal educational organization and provision – or to the unknown and unquantifiable – that is, the learning experiences. Traditionally it referred to the former, and in this sense to formal educational provision.

The term has been employed in a variety of different ways, especially in initial education, and we can look briefly at some of the terms that have been used synonymously with curriculum. 'Educational provision' is one: it refers either to what is organized and offered to students by the institutions or to what is organized and offered to the students by the teachers within those institutions. This might also be referred to as 'the total learning situation', referring to all the learning experiences, intended or unintended, provided by the educational institution since, as we have seen, the term 'learning' is replacing 'education' in some significant ways. The 'programme' may be either the prospectus provided by an educational institution, or a section of it, or it may refer to the actual number of courses that are organized after enrolment. A course may be the course of study followed by an individual within the institution or it may refer to a single course offered to a specific group of students, e.g. the nursing course. As modularization has developed, so the term 'course' has tended to refer to students' individual programmes of study. Modules, however, are individual courses.

There has been a subtle but nevertheless significant change with the development of modularization. Previously, individual courses were usually built around the epistemological demands of an area of knowledge, for example a course on the sociology of the family, by the end of which students were expected to have grasped the rudiments of the subject irrespective of the number of hours that they studied beyond the hours that they were taught. This was something of an open-ended commitment on behalf of the student, but it was not really quantifiable. A module, however, is usually designated by the number of hours of learning about a specific practice that a student is expected to undertake, so that, for instance, a 50-hour module might involve 15 hours of teaching in the classroom, 15 hours of private study and a 20-hour assignment – although the exact constitution of the 50 hours is a matter of college policy. The 50 hours might be designated to occur over a short period of time, say a few weeks (a 'short, fat' module) or over a longer period. A 100-hour module, on the other hand, might involve 40 hours of classroom teaching, 30 hours of private study and a 30-hour assignment, and this might occur over a period of 20 weeks (a 'long, thin' module). There are three important things to note about this change in curriculum design. First, more modules can be offered, so there is more student choice. Second, the length of the module has no relationship to the epistemological demands of the discipline. Third, there has been little or no research into the relative advantages of cramming a module into a short period of time, like a week, or holding it throughout a longer period, such as a semester. It is probable that the longer period is more effective for learning but the shorter one more useful for timetabling and marketing.

It is perhaps easy to recognize how the confusion in the use of the terms has arisen, since each of them has an affinity with the others. It is also important to note that the emphasis on learning is a comparatively recent addition and builds upon the ideas of the romantic curriculum and progressive education that were prevalent in the United Kingdom in the 1960s. At this stage it is clear that the term 'curriculum' tends to reflect the totality of the learning as if it is a comprehensive and coherent whole, whereas 'programme' implies that there are several parts to the whole, parts of which students might choose for themselves. This is an important distinction, and one that becomes more significant in any examination of the current situation in the education of adults. Certainly the scene has changed a great deal, and much of the discussion about curriculum theory that occurred in the 1970s and early 1980s now appears extremely dated. This chapter will look briefly at this earlier material now before moving on to analyse the contemporary situation.

A historical overview of curriculum theory

A great deal of curriculum theory that emerged was as a result of studies in initial education; in the United Kingdom, for instance, there was an obvious reference to this with specific reference to romantic and classical curriculum models. The same was not so true in the United States, where there has been a greater emphasis upon programme planning in adult education throughout the whole of this period, which we will discuss later in this chapter.

Many attempts have been made to produce a satisfactory model of the teaching and learning process in curriculum terms. Frequently, reference is made back to Tyler's (1949) classic study about school curricula, but Taba (1962:425), citing Giles *et al.* (1942), produced a model that, with slight adaptation, may be valid for the education of adults (see Figure 12.1). This model is a reasonably familiar one in curriculum theory since it contains the elements that occur in almost every learning and teaching process. Taba wrote:

> A curriculum usually contains a statement of aims and of specific objectives; it indicates some selection and organization of content; it either implies or manifests certain patterns of learning and teaching, whether because the objectives demand them or because the content organization requires them. Finally, it includes a programme of evaluation of the outcomes.
>
> (1962:10)

The model below may be applied to every course offered in an educational institution rather than to the overall programme, and thus there may be considerable variation in the elements of the curriculum between

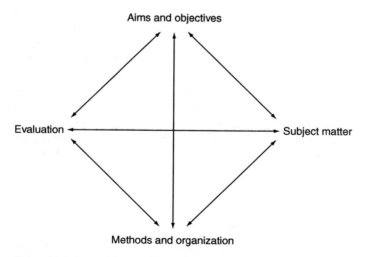

Figure 12.1 A teaching and learning process model for the teaching of adults.

different courses. Hence, discussion about the aforementioned elements must necessarily still remain at the level of generality.

British educators, claimed Davies, 'have been more interested in defining aims than in studying objectives, while American teachers have been more willing to think in terms of concrete objectives' (1976:11). Certainly this claim would be true of the curriculum models of both Verner and Houle discussed later. By contrast, British theorists focused upon the broader philosophical issues, as both Griffin (1978) and Mee and Wiltshire (1978) demonstrated in their respective ways. Yet the broad philosophy of educators of adults may also affect their attitude towards the concept, and the use of objectives in the design of a teaching and learning situation. Curriculum theorists have posited many types of objectives: instructional, teaching, learning, behavioural, expressive, etc. Davies (1976) discussed the whole area very thoroughly, so there is no need to expand on it here. Even so, it is useful to examine the relationship between aims and objectives and to see whether the latter actually reflect the overall aims as even the general philosophy of adult education. For instance, considerable emphasis has been given to behavioural objectives, and while these might be quite valid on some basic skills-based courses, their usefulness in cognitive learning courses is much more questionable and contrary to the overall philosophy of adult learning. They do, however, reflect this desire to measure rather than assess that we discussed in the previous chapter. Indeed, there is an argument that suggests that in seeking to achieve behavioural objectives, the autonomy of the learners might be quashed by the authority of the instructors, and the practice is, therefore, immoral. Objectives specified in behavioural terms always tend to imply that the human learner will learn and behave in a manner designated by the teacher, like a pigeon or a rat! Another implication of this approach is that teachers will adopt a didactic and authoritarian approach to teaching, and this is quite contrary to the philosophy of teaching. I maintain that any approach to teaching that designates how a learner will behave as a result of undergoing the teaching and learning process undermines the dignity of the learner and may be guilty of the charge of indoctrination; consequently, the process of teaching and learning then falls short of the high ideals of education. By contrast, Eisner (1969) regarded expressive objectives as evocative rather than prescriptive, which is much closer to the general philosophy of the education of adults that is advocated here. Nevertheless, behavioural objectives have a valid place in some forms of education and also in therapy, but while therapy might involve learning, it is not education.

The subject matter or content of some courses, especially those that are vocationally orientated or award-bearing, is usually prescribed by the examining or the validating body. This reflects the point that the curriculum may be regarded as a selection of culture made by those who have status or power in the profession or in education. Elsewhere, Jarvis (1983a:50–53) outlined other criteria for the selection of curriculum content in professional education, including the demands of professional practice, the relevance of the topic, and its worthwhileness. However, there are courses in which the subject matter may actually be negotiated between tutor and students, but these courses tend to be exceptions rather than everyday occurrences since validating bodies tend to require the content of courses to be specified at validation. In liberal adult education these occurrences may have been much more frequent in the past since the subject matter depended on the interests of the students and might be negotiated between tutor and students.

Negotiated subject content may be much more common in continuing professional education since practitioners, being aware of their strengths and weaknesses in practice, will probably know what they need to learn during in-service education in order to improve the quality of their practice. Diagnosis of learning needs should occur either prior to a course or at the very least at its outset, so it is essential for the teacher to join with the students in planning a teaching and learning programme. Often in continuing professional education it is useful to spend a planning day a few weeks prior to the commencement of the course, mapping out the areas of the subject matter that should be covered during it. Diagnosis should always precede learning and teaching, as we discussed in the previous chapter.

The location of the teaching, the organization of the room in which the teaching and learning is to occur, the content of the session and the methods to be employed are all part of the educational process. They should all relate to the learners, to their learning needs or wants and to their learning styles, but they are also dependent upon the expertise of the tutorial staff. The organization of the environment relates to the adulthood of the learners and to the teaching methods employed. Similarly, the actual methods employed by the teacher are important considerations in the educational process. Bourdieu and Passeron claimed that all 'pedagogic action is, objectively, symbolic violence in so far as it is the imposition of a cultural arbitrary by an arbitrary power' (1977:5). It is important to recognize the symbolic significance of the teaching method. Moreover, the symbolism becomes an immoral reality if the teaching methods employed in any teaching and learning transaction inhibit the development, or undermine the dignity and humanity, of the learners; but it becomes moral and good curriculum practice when they encourage their growth and expression of humanity.

The philosophical issues involved in teaching are important considerations, especially in the education of adults, but the methods employed must also relate to the ethos of the group and the content of the session. Hence, the skill of the teacher is not only about techniques but also about social skills in human interaction, and it is a combination of these various factors that can lead to teaching and learning becoming an effective and stimulating process.

Clearly, the aims and objectives that have been set for any single teaching and learning session or for a course as a whole provide one basis for its evaluation. Yet these may prove to be too restrictive since the class may have deviated from the selected aims and even from the content decided upon in order to follow up ideas that arise during the process itself. This may have resulted in effective learning and class satisfaction, with all the participants regarding it as successful. Hence, if learning and understanding has occurred, within a humanistic context, then the education may be assessed as successful.

Evaluation should not be undertaken by teachers by themselves since in the education of adults the students should be full participants in the process. In non-compulsory education this occurs in any case, since as Newman forcibly reminded his readers:

> Adult education is a cruel test of a tutor's skills. It is a sink or swim business. If the tutor does not have what it takes, people stop coming. His students vote with their feet, unobtrusively transferring to other classes or simply staying away. The class dwindles week by week, leaving him all too well aware that he has been found wanting.
>
> (1979:66)

Perhaps this is a rather dramatic portrayal of the manner by which students are actually involved in the process of evaluation. Indeed, many students are very kind to their tutors and encourage inexperienced ones. Even so, students do evaluate their tutors and the process of teaching and learning that has occurred, and so it is beneficial to all concerned to involve them in the more formal process. However, this form of student evaluation is less frequent on certificated courses as the students need the certificate. In this sense, certification is kind to the teacher!

Classical and romantic models of the curriculum

The models just discussed owe their origin to theorists whose main concern was initial education, but many developments in school education curriculum theory were mirrored in the developments in adult education at this time. The classical curriculum reflected the teacher-centred approach while the 1960s emphasis on student-centred learning is reflected in the development of the romantic curriculum model.

The concepts of classical and romantic curriculum reflect contrasting educational ideologies, the latter coming to prominence in initial education

Table 12.1 The classical and romantic curricula

Elements of the classical curriculum	Elements of the romantic curriculum
Subject-centred	Child-centred
Skills	Creativity
Instruction	Experience
Information	Discovery
Obedience	
Conformity	Originality
Discipline	Freedom
Objectives	Processes
• acquiring knowledge	• 'living' attitudes and values
Content	Experiences
• subjects	• real-life topics and proposals
Method	Method
• didactic instruction	• involvement
• competition	• cooperation
Evaluation	Evaluation
• by tasks (teacher-set)	• self-assessment (in terms of
• by examinations (public and competitive)	self-improvement)

Source: Lawton (1973:22–23).

in the 1960s, which has been regarded as a period of romanticism. These positions have been summarized by Lawton in two different tables, and his argument is summarized here in Table 12.1.

Most models must necessarily overemphasize their salient points, so Table 12.1 presents a polarization of the two curriculum models. Yet the fact that the major features are highlighted means that it is possible to see immediately the significance of these for a deeper understanding of the education of adults. Clearly, the romantic curriculum, as formulated here, approximates to the more traditional forms of adult education, and there is a sense in which it has a 'superior' sense about it since the learners are treated as persons. Earlier it was pointed out that both continuing and recurrent education are based upon two philosophies of lifelong education; Griffin (1978) examined these from the perspective of a curriculum theorist. His basic premise was that continuing education is related to the classical curriculum while recurrent education has a romantic curriculum foundation. His analysis, while revealing, basically illustrated the affinity between what was called continuing education and mainstream education, while recurrent education had a greater conceptual affinity with adult education.

Knowles: andragogy

As we saw in an earlier chapter, Knowles suggested that andragogy has four premises that distinguish it from pedagogy: the learner is self-directed; the learner's experiences are a rich resource for learning; the learner's readiness to learn is increasingly orientated to the developmental tasks of social roles; and the learner's time perspective assumes an immediacy, so that learning is problem centred – and performance centred – rather than subject centred. Knowles (1989:83–84) later added two other premises to this list, and his new list is as follows: adults need to know why they are learning; adults' self-concept is of being responsible for their own lives; adults bring greater quality and quantity of experience to their new learning; adults are ready to learn what they need to know; their learning is life centred; and adults have intrinsic motivations to learn. Clearly, Knowles did not formulate andragogy in curricular terminology, and perhaps his failure to do so has been a major reason why the debate about his work has been confused and so wide-ranging. Can andragogy be equated with the romantic curriculum? In many ways the response to this must be in the affirmative.

Jarvis (1993b) also returned to the andragogy–pedagogy debate, seeking to see why Knowles's work, which is so obviously wrong when applied to children and adults, has retained so much currency. It seemed that the major variable distinguishing andragogy from pedagogy is experience, not chronological age. If this argument is accepted, it is now possible to formulate the andragogy–pedagogy debate within the framework of the education for adults, which is a rather different perspective from that initially presented by Knowles. Indeed, individuals having little experience in a subject might want a more pedagogic approach while those having a lot of experience might prefer an andragogic approach. This leads on to the possibility of conceptualizing the initial vocational education curriculum in pedagogic terms and the continuing vocational education programme in andragogic terms. From this it can be seen that it is more possible to discuss initial vocational education in traditional curriculum terms but much clearer to discuss continuing vocational education in programme terms. In both cases it must be recognized that the process occurs within the humanistic perspective on education for adults.

Without a humanistic student-centred approach it is maintained here that learning and human development may be impaired, and this is the crux of Macfarlane's analysis of literacy education in terms of these two types of curricula, as Table 12.2 demonstrates.

Once again, this type of approach overemphasized some of the differences, but he suggested that the student-centred approach aids the learner's development and growth. Macfarlane noted that the two approaches demand quite different methods and organization to be successful in any way. He also maintained that these different approaches have ramifications for policy, staff recruitment, training and resource development. Yet it is clear from his analysis that the student-centred approach is closer to the humanistic ideals mentioned earlier in this study, which are at the

Table 12.2 Macfarlane's analysis of adult literacy education in terms of two curricular models

	Curricular attitudes among advocates of the traditional curriculum	*Curricular attitudes among advocates of a student-centred curriculum*
Role of the student process	Passive recipient of externally formulated and needs	Active participant in defining own goals
The literacy process	Hierarchies, centred upon skills and stages of progress	Holistic, task centred
Tutor's view of student	One who is deprived and handicapped (and hence inferior)	An equal who is not to blame for failure
Impact on student's self-image	Relatively unimportant, a by-product of progress in skills	Purposefully enhanced
Student's view of tutor	'The expert who will cure me'	'The friend who helps me sort things out'
Dangers	Maintains dependency Transfer of skills to real-world usage very doubtful	Threatens student and structure and lack of perception of progress

Source: Macfarlane (1978:156).

heart of adult education. Even so, this does not mean that all teaching need be of a facilitative style.

Implicit in the debate about continuing and recurrent education and in the distinction between classical and romantic curricula is the matter of control: who should control the learning activities? Who should control the learning outcomes? And so on. Since romantic education was student centred there is a sense in which control moved in the students' direction. This is even more evident in programme models that appeared at about the same time.

In more recent writings there has been a movement away from the terminology about curriculum produced by initial educational theorists. One example of this is Bines's (1992) threefold typology of professional education training models: apprenticeship, technocratic and post-technocratic models of initial professional education. Bines suggests that the apprenticeship model is one that involves on-the-job instruction with some day release in order to acquire some 'cookbook knowledge' – basically, practical knowledge. Technocratic curricula consist of a threefold approach to professional preparation: transmission of some systematic knowledge; the interpretation of that knowledge as it is applied to practice; and practical placements. The third model, which is a response to the weakness of the positivist approaches contained in the second model, is built upon both the experience of practice and reflection on it, so that its focus is on professional competence, and the practical experience becomes the centre of the professional preparation. She recognizes, however, that as resources become scarce, it becomes more difficult to staff practical training adequately. However, this model does not really develop a systematic epistemology (although it has a basis upon which one might be built), but it does reflect the concerns of writers like Schön (1987).

The quality of practice, however, is a most difficult phenomenon to assess, as one experiment at the University of Surrey demonstrates. In general nurse training a few years ago it was expected that student nurses would successfully pass four practical assessments during their training. A student nurse was videotaped undertaking one of these assessment procedures, and the ward sister in whose ward she was working adjudged that she had actually failed the practical assessment at the time when the video was made. It was then shown to a group of thirty experienced nurses who were on an assessment training course. About one-third of those watching would have passed the student on the performance that they witnessed, while two-thirds agreed with the ward sister and would have failed her. However, the student had already successfully passed that assessment a number of months previously! Professional competence is not necessarily an easy thing to assess. Another problem with the competence-based approach to practice is that sometimes good practitioners are good because they know when not to act, as well as when to act, and it is difficult to assess the competence of active inactivity! Consequently, it appears that the post-technocratic approach that is currently in use is one which, while it seeks to overcome some of the problems of the previous curriculum approach, still requires a great deal more refinement.

Even so, the significant thing about Bines's approach is that it sought to reconceptualize curriculum theory in terms of professional preparation and to produce models that are appropriate for education beyond school. In addition, she has made a distinction between curricula for initial professional education and programmes for professional continuing education. She did not develop this latter aspect, although there are instances of this in Bines (1992). However, this approach comes much closer to the American literature on programme development, which is explored in the second part of this chapter.

The hidden curriculum

Bourdieu and Passeron's explicit discussion of the power involved in the process of teaching and learning may also be found in the hidden curriculum. Every institution evolves its own procedures, many of which contain values that are recognized and intended but some of which may be unrecognized and unintended by those who formulate them. Some of these

237

values have been highlighted in this chapter, such as those implicit in the teachers or students selecting the curriculum content, or in the use of various types of teaching. Yet there are others, and some of those that are unintended or recognized by the educators of adults may be apparent to the students who attend the institution, and it may be some of these that are learned, and affect their attitudes towards adult or continuing education. Hence, for instance, the differing status accorded to different types of class may be very clear to students, and those whose class is given low status may feel deprived. Vocational classes will, at present, always be given precedence over non-examinable leisure-time study, even though the latter may sometimes be more academic. Courses that bring in funds to the institution will be given preference over other forms of education. Power shows in other ways such as the fact that students may not be treated as adults in the organization, in the teaching methods employed, or in the evaluation of the life and work of the institution. By contrast, other institutions may create such an ethos that the hidden curriculum purveys the humanistic ideals of education itself. The ethos of the institution is, therefore, the carrier of a message that may be received and learned by adult students who attend, and the carrier's subculture is contained within the hidden curriculum; it reflects its, and often wider society's, philosophy, social power and attitudes towards both individuals and people.

Thus, there are many different elements in the curriculum, and the final sub-section of this first section of the chapter briefly discusses some of these.

Elements in curriculum planning

The traditional curriculum in adult education was needs based. This reflected the welfare orientation of early adult education; it existed either to meet the needs of those who had lost out in the schooling system or to meet the needs or wants of those who wished to continue learning long after they had completed their initial schooling and higher education. It was learner centred and its curriculum was romantic/andragogic in orientation. But there is a strange sense in which this welfare curriculum is also a market model. Adult education did not respond either to the epistemological imperatives of an academic discipline or to the practical demands of a professional practice; it responded to the needs and wants of the potential clients. Discovering those needs and instituting courses for them was an entrepreneurial enterprise without financial profit being the motive. Courses were designed to meet the needs of potential participants and were assessed by such criteria as students staying the course and wanting to continue their studies, students feeling that their needs had been met and the adult centre staff's sense that they were providing a service to the people in the community. It is no wonder that as continuing professional education emerged, it was adult educators who were most happy responding to these demands and creating courses to meet the new emerging demands; many universities failed to recognize the expertise that was at their disposal in extra-mural departments, departments that had often been distrusted because of their entrepreneurial skills. Some few universities recognized those skills; and some leading adult educators found themselves in senior management positions in universities and colleges.

However, as the market continued to develop and gradually began to dominate the scene, post-compulsory education became regarded as a commodity to be marketed. At the same time, there was another important movement: education had to become more practical, so that epistemological demands had less emphasis placed upon them. Lyotard (1984) had claimed that knowledge that gained legitimation would necessarily be performative, and the British government claimed that there was no major difference between academic and vocational knowledge. This meant that courses were not constructed around epistemological demands but around the demands for practice, and practice has different mixtures of the practical and the theoretical, taking different amounts of time to master. Courses became bounded by units of time and were competence based – so modules of learning emerged. These were of different lengths of time and made different intellectual demands on the students, but planning such programmes demanded much the same skills as planning traditional adult education programmes, as Figure 12.2 illustrates.

Figure 12.2 represents a complicated system that incorporates those aspects of the curriculum referred to above, and at the same time anticipates something of the programme planning models that are to be discussed in the second part of this chapter, since it seeks to demonstrate how the educational process is exposed to the influence of the market and the wider society and its governing bodies, as well as being affected by the philosophy of the educator. In fact, the philosophy of the educator has certainly been relegated in importance as the demands of the institution, especially the financial demands, have assumed priority in the knowledge economy. An uneasy tension may exist as a result of the interplay of the forces stemming from factors mentioned in the first three boxes and those in the following two. Each of these elements will be elaborated upon in a subsequent section of this chapter, but it is clear from Figure 12.2 that the curriculum is always located in wider social systems. This is a systems model, similar to other systems models, produced by organization theorists in order to assess the functioning of other types of organizations (e.g. J. Child, 1977:144–178), so it may be seen how the sociological study of the education of adults may benefit from similar sociological analyses conducted in other areas of organizational life, and many studies of learning occur in organizational settings.

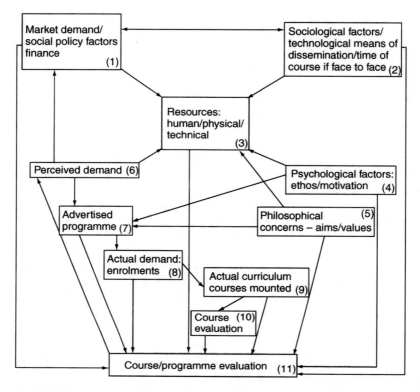

Figure 12.2 A market curriculum planning model for the education of adults.

Market and policy

There has been considerable debate about the legitimacy of education becoming a commodity, with writers such as Aronowitz claiming that universities have become knowledge factories. Such concerns are very legitimate in contemporary society but the usefulness of knowledge has a long history in education: societies like the Society for Really Useful Knowledge existed in the nineteenth century. At the same time, the commodification of knowledge and commercialization of education have lessened the need for critical awareness about the nature of knowledge and the effects of its utilization. But the market still reigns supreme, and so nearly every educational institution needs to consider the potential market for the learning opportunities that it might offer.

Education is rarely free from the decisions of national and local government, and so policy factors also affect the curriculum in any educational establishment. Indeed, examining the development of educational policy decisions in the United Kingdom shows that continuing vocational education was distinguished from liberal adult education, and then continuing professional education became lifelong learning and endeavoured to incorporate liberal adult education within it. It then became a major focus of educational policy (see Further Education Unit, 1992; Fryer, 1997, 1998), but in more recent years there has been a division again and liberal adult education has become certificated as part of the mainstream provision, while lifelong learning has been vocationalized. By 2008 (Department for Innovation, Universities and Skills, 2008) the only liberal adult education that stood outside of the vocational ambit was included in the term 'informal education'.

Not only have macro-curriculum decisions been affected by governmental policy, but even the content of curriculum has been affected in this way. As long ago as 1859, John Stuart Mill (1962:239) deprecated state involvement in the content of education since he regarded it as an infringement on human liberty, but when the Manpower Services Commission was established in the United Kingdom, it forbade the inclusion of any political material in the curricula, claiming that 'inclusion in the course of political or related activities "could be regarded as a breach of ... agreement with the MSC and could result in the immediate closure of the course"' (Harper, 1982). This example shows that even in a relatively democratic country like the United Kingdom, government policy can and does exercise considerable control over the curriculum content.

Despite the government's claim that it wishes to leave a great deal to the market, it has constantly intervened in education, sometimes in a way that many educationalists consider to be detrimental to education, although often with very good intent. Nevertheless, it should be recognized that even the policy decision to 'leave things to the market' has tremendous effects upon curriculum content since the market ensures 'the survival of the fittest' but not 'the survival of the best', or in this case the more popular subjects, and enables the less popular ones to be offered at a higher fee in order to make them financially viable.

Sociological factors

It was recognized above that the curriculum itself may be regarded as a selection from culture, so that the social forces that operate upon the educational process are quite profound. Culture is changing rapidly and various aspects of knowledge are changing rapidly. Yet knowledge itself is not value-free: some has high status without being very practical, while other knowledge has low status but is most useful (Young, 1971). The relevance of knowledge is also significant in its inclusion in any curriculum (Jarvis, 1978b). If curricula contain socially organized knowledge selected from culture, then it is significant to know where, why and by whom such a selection of knowledge is made. Clearly, in self-directed learning and in some forms of adult education it is the learners who make the selection, but Griffin (1978) suggested that this may not occur in continuing education. However, it has long been recognized that when students make the choice of what they wish to study, if it is not based on vocational need it is most likely to be based on social class – a point made by Westwood (1980:43) about liberal adult education many years ago. No curriculum in lifelong learning can escape the social pressures exerted upon it, and so it is necessary that more sociological analyses of the educational processes undertaken by adults should be conducted (see Jarvis, 1985, 2006; Elsey, 1986). Indeed, the situation of the learners is also an important factor in curriculum planning since it affects their learning (see Lave and Wenger, 1991).

The time when the course is programmed is an important factor: for instance, more working people who cannot get time off work to study will need to attend in the evenings, but older people tend not to like attending any educational course in the dark, and so on. Weekends are becoming much more prevalent than ever before, although many educational institutions tend not to offer courses on Saturday afternoons and Sundays, out of respect for academic staff's weekends. However, as education becomes a 'service industry' it may have to utilize all the windows of opportunity. Naturally, the use of flexi and distance education is helping overcome some of these problems, and the modular structure of modern courses lends itself to distance education.

Resources

Resources may be classified as financial, technical, accommodation and staff. Little more needs to be written about the first of these since it plays a self-evidently important part in curriculum planning and we discussed it earlier.

As education is becoming increasingly more technical, technology becomes an important resource in curriculum planning: not only the overhead projector, the laptop and the projector but the technical equipment to make PowerPoint displays and other forms of audio-visual aid – such as chips being built into teaching material and CDs. In addition, as more courses become electronic, the technological resources for preparing professional electronically transmitted courses becomes increasingly significant, which means that skilled electronics specialists become part of the course teams.

Mainstream education for adults now demands proper adult accommodation in universities and colleges, which means that lecture rooms need to be redesigned and that other facilities on the campus and in the college buildings need to remain open for as long as the students are present. Accommodation for informal adult education was the subject of a report by the Advisory Council for Adult and Continuing Education (1982c) in which it was recognized that day schools should continue to form the main accommodation resource for adult education, and while this remains the case, they are much less significant these days as colleges run a great many adult education classes. The Advisory Council report also recommended that every adult should have access to prime-use accommodation, even though this may not be as close to their homes as the local school, but this has not happened, as a great deal of lifelong learning is now located in higher education, and university and college accommodation is now used.

The main resources in education of most kinds are the tutor and the technicians. There has been considerable discussion in this study about the tutor's role in the education of adults, so it is unnecessary to cover this ground again. There are a number of issues that should be mentioned here: the use of staff untrained in the art of teaching adults and the use of part-time staff to mount classes in minority subjects and interests. One of the recommendations of the Dearing Report (1997), something that was strikingly obvious to anybody involved in the training of teachers, was that university teachers needed training. Teaching is a skilled occupation, and educational institutions should ensure that their staff are highly trained or experienced professional teachers.

A second point to note about the academic staff is that they should be given sufficient time to prepare their teaching material and also to mark the written work that follows. The amount of time to mark assignments needs to be fully costed in the planning of the curriculum, and in the desire to offer courses on the market at competitive prices it is things like time for marking that is insufficiently costed. As an example, when I ran a distance education Master's course in adult education, I paid part-time tutors on a basis of forty-five minutes to mark a single essay assignment, and full-time staff reckoned on a similar period of time for this exercise.

Third, part-time staff are often treated as a reserve army of labour – used when their courses are full and dropped if their courses do not recruit sufficiently well. Yet unless the educational institution treats its part-time staff well, the result will be decreased job satisfaction.

As the library has always been a resource, so the web is becoming an even more significant and easily accessible one. However, many items on the web are not necessarily factual, and so learners might need 'guiding' through some of them so that they learn to read them critically. This requires careful work, and time, by the tutor. At the same time, not everybody has access to the web as yet, and so there is a sense in which the underprivileged are doubly underprivileged if they cannot gain access to some of the most important teaching material. However, it is increasingly easy to incorporate a lot of material on CDs, and so on, which can be produced extremely cheaply.

Psychological factors

One of the strengths of Knowles's formulation of andragogy is that it focused upon some of the psychological factors that need to be taken into consideration in planning adults' learning. If adults are, for instance, problem centred rather than subject based, then more courses should be planned that have relevance to the everyday life environment. If they are going to respond to the rapidly changing socio-cultural milieu with active questioning, then the programme should include courses or sessions that provide opportunities for them to seek answers. If some adults have developed an aversion to education as a result of their experiences in initial education, everything must be done to overcome the problem from the outset, including the employment of tutors able to put adults at their ease, the way the accommodation is used and the way the programme is advertised. However, one has to appreciate that some of the psychological factors may not be fully responded to in planning because of the limited nature of the available resources.

Philosophical factors

Underlying every programme of education there is a philosophy, whether it is explicit or implicit, considered or rarely thought about, consistent or inconsistent. It may be a philosophy constrained by other factors, such as social policy, but it remains a philosophy. At the outset of this study a rationale for the education of adults was produced which argues that every human being has a basic need to learn and that in a rapidly changing society each individual may need to make many adjustments in order to be in harmony with the socio-cultural milieu. Most individuals will develop as a result of their experiences, although it was recognized that growth is not inevitable, since there can be forms of mis-education. This approach, however, reflects Dewey's (1916) assertion that education is a means to human growth and that growth continues throughout the whole of life. Therefore, I maintain that underlying every curriculum should be a concern about the development of the learners as persons. This is a humanistic, progressive perspective and one that is prevalent in adult education.

As society is changing rapidly, it has to be recognized that some types of knowledge change so rapidly that they appear artificial and fleeting. It is essential that some people keep abreast with these developments, and so society has the need to produce lifelong learners. Education is frequently accused of being a process that moulds and controls people so that they fit into a niche in society without disrupting it very greatly. The lifelong learner must be flexible and adaptable.

If educators see their role in terms of responding to the economic needs of the wider society primarily, they clearly have a different philosophical perspective upon education than the one that sees education as fundamentally about human growth and development. This does not mean that the humanistic, progressive approach to education has no concern about the economic needs of society, only that it sees the development of the learners as persons as they acquire a critical awareness, knowledge and understanding as more significant in educational terms.

Other philosophical perspectives may also underpin the whole of an educational programme. Elias and Merriam (1980) point out that both liberal and radical philosophies are significant in curriculum design. Hence, it is possible to see that the literacy programme devised by Freire was considerably influenced by his own philosophy and that of his co-workers, and that this approach was totally different from literacy education in societies, such as the United Kingdom, in which this radical philosophical perspective is not prevalent. Even so, Freire's own programme was not free to operate without influences upon it, such as the forces operating in the wider society.

Perceived demands

The demands for certain forms of education may emanate from government, professional bodies, local chambers of commerce, business and industry, and so on. It is therefore necessary for educational institutions to have their antennae attuned to the articulation of these demands; institutions need liaison officers who work with these different groups and both hear the demands and test whether there is sufficient demand to justify organizing a specific course.

Liberal adult education has also had a market model having a welfare dimension since it used the language of needs (wants, demands) and practised supply and demand. Newman wrote:

> Adult education is designed in the simplest possible way to respond to demand. It is the other side of the numbers game. If classes can be closed on the basis of attendance, then they can also be set up. That is to say, if you have a group of people eager to pursue some activity, or if you have evidence of sufficient community interest you can approach your local adult education agency or centre and ask that a course be arranged, a room and basic facilities provided, and a tutor paid.
>
> (1979:35)

The term 'need' should be distinguished from the idea of a basic need to learn, which was discussed in the opening chapters, but since it has played such a significant part in adult education thinking it should be analysed and related to 'wants', 'interests' and 'demands'. It will have become clear from the previous discussion that education has become a commodity in the market, so that needs are becoming 'wants' and 'demands', and consequently the whole of these new considerations about curriculum in relation to both modularization and the market have already been discussed.

The planning of courses is based upon this point – that the educational institution is responding to a demand – but since the preparation of this response is a costly business it is not surprising that there is a degree of conservatism in many colleges. They will not take the risk unless they can be reasonably well assured that they will make a return on the investment of their resources. In this sense, the previous year's evaluation generates a revised perception of the market demand, which in its turn tends to inhibit innovation.

Advertised programmes

The prospectus is a major tool inasmuch as it is the outcome of planning of the curriculum. Prospectuses need professional design so that they can compete in the market, where many other providers may also be offering their courses. In such cases the prospectus needs to be designed to be interesting, eye-catching, easy to negotiate, and so on. The prospectus is the symbol of the institution, and so the medium itself tells its potential students something about its own standards and expectations.

Courses and programmes must themselves be advertised as prospectuses, and two issues need to be considered here: to advertise successfully is a professional undertaking in both design and distribution, but to advertise too successfully might once have been contrary to the high ideals of education itself. Such a claim can no longer be made, and educators have to change from the time when Rogers and Groombridge (1976:76) could claim that adult education is

> a service needing constant promotion and visibility [but] it remains largely unpromoted and directly invisible; where sympathetic understanding of all modern media is needed, it continues hopelessly to rely on methods which would have looked out of place in the late nineteenth century.

They suggested a variety of approaches that might be employed, including focused distribution, a supplement in a local newspaper, direct mailing, skilful cultivation of the local press in order to ensure good coverage of newsworthy items, and militant publicity. Obviously, post-compulsory education must reach out to the wider populace, and many of these techniques are now included in the marketing process. However, much of this now lies outside of the concern of the educators themselves as many educational institutions have their own marketing departments. With this market orientation, educational institutions compete against one another for students, and advertising has become more professional and commercial. Indeed, it is perhaps now necessary for education to take stock of what is occurring and ask itself whether it is really happy with the route down which it has been forced to travel in recent years.

Advertising, as an occupation, is often accused of employing immoral, or at least questionable, methods (Jarvis, 2008). While the accusation is rarely substantiated, it is important that education should not be seen to use methods to promote its courses that create a sense of need in potential students, or manipulate them. These techniques may be regarded as immoral and certainly fall short of the high ideals of education. It is nevertheless important to prepare good publicity and to disseminate it widely, but the means used to persuade people to enrol on courses must always be in accord with the ideals of education; other means do not justify the ends.

Actual demand

At the commencement of the academic year, semester or term, the enrolment period brings the preparatory work into focus. The extent to which the advertised programme prepared by the educators actually responds to the demands of the potential students may now be revealed. In one study, Sargant (1990) discovered that 36 per cent of the adult population had been involved in some form of academic study over the previous three years, but a few years later (Sargant *et al.*, 1997) the figure was closer to 40 per cent. In 2008, Aldridge and Tuckett (2008) recorded a figure of 38 per cent. They (2008:11) also make the following point:

> Since 2007, participation in learning among both men and women has declined by three percentage points. Since 1996 however, when the survey series began, the gender gap has reversed and become narrower with participation among men falling from 43 to 38 per cent, while among women it has increased from 38 to 39 per cent.

Unsurprisingly, they also record that participation varies with socio-economic class, with some 51 per cent of classes A and B and only 26 per cent of classes D and E participating in current or recent learning. There was a similar decline by age from 79 per cent of 17- to 19-year-olds to 11 per cent of 75-plus-year-olds in 2008 (2008:16).

Sargant *et al.* (1997:ix) also discovered that there was a considerable variation in the places where the learners studied, with: at a university (21 per cent), at a college (21 per cent), at the workplace (15 per cent), at home (11 per cent) and at adult learning centres (9 per cent) being the most popular. Compared with the 1991 study, universities have assumed a much more prominent role, indicating how they have been forced to change to the demands of the global learning market, but studying at home has declined considerably.

The subjects studied varied considerably but have also changed a great deal in a very few years. Sargant *et al.* (1997:37) wrote:

> Some jobs and functions have changed over the last 15 years, the most obvious changes being brought by the computer. The ... demise of the shorthand and copy-typist, with the increasing multi-skilling in offices, has reduced the proportion learning secretarial/office skills from 8% ... in 1980 to 6% in 1990 and 2% in 1996. The same skill needs are now met by computer studies, which does not just achieve the same percentage as it did in 1990 (8%), but has doubled it to 17%. In 1980, computer systems were a male subject and presumably studied by people such as programmers and systems analysts. In 1990, men and women took computer studies in similar number, but shorthand/typing was also still important for women (12%). By 1996, shorthand/typing has virtually disappeared and computer-related studies has taken over, but more men (18%) than women are studying it!
>
> The decline in the study of all forms of engineering from 16% in 1980 to 7% in 1990 and 4% in 1996 is clearly a function of the decline of manufacturing industry. It is balanced by increases in the professional, managerial and administrative areas, where participating by women is now at a more encouraging level.

Similar changes have been recorded in a variety of other subjects and crafts, but Sargant *et al.* suggested that it is not that studying such crafts is declining so much as that people no longer consider them as learning. This may be because no credit may be gained from following them.

Clearly, the programme may not respond to everybody's learning needs, and so in recent years there have arisen educational advisory services that can help potential students to find another course in the prospectus that responds to their interests or to discover another educational institution offering the course that the student requires. This is a national service coordinated by the National Association of Educational Guidance for Adults (NAEGA); it is an association that brings together organizations and individuals who provide work and lifelong learning guidance for adults. The association has its own publications and organizes its own conferences. The aims of NAEGA are:

- to promote the formation and development of lifelong learning guidance for adults;

- to promote high standards of practice;
- to promote the understanding and acceptance of lifelong guidance for adults;
- to promote the training of all those involved in providing lifelong learning guidance for adults;
- to provide feedback at regional and national levels on issues affecting access to opportunities for adults;
- to assist in the exchange of information between services and practitioners.

The actual curriculum

The actual content of the teaching and learning programme of any educational institution must therefore to some extent rely on the response to the prospectus. Yet as we have seen, demand itself is hardly sufficient reason for inclusion in the curriculum of any particular topic, so that there must be a place for some minority interests. Even so, the extent to which economically unviable courses may be continued does depend upon the philosophy underpinning the educational institution's curriculum and upon the social policy factors that affect the funding arrangements for specific courses.

The actual curriculum of an educational institution is more than its programme of courses, as will be recognized from the above discussion about the way in which the term is employed. Because it can refer to the total learning situation, the whole ethos of the institution, its hidden curriculum and the teaching and learning curriculum are all united at this point.

Course evaluation

The basis of course evaluation is now often a questionnaire given to students to evaluate the course that they have studied. There is a danger with this form of evaluation, based on the fact that in business and industry a good product is one with which the customer is satisfied. Criteria such as these may provide little or no genuine evaluation about the content of the course in relation to what might have been provided, or the ability of the course leader, and so on. Satisfaction might well be one criterion in course evaluation, but there are others, including the course leader's evaluation, independent evaluation, and outcomes in terms of examination results.

Examination results are included here as one criterion, but it is a crude behaviouristic evaluation tool because it tells us little about what actual learning has occurred. But 'league tables' are increasingly used to assess the level of a school or college, rather than being as seen as one criterion in a complex process.

Course and programme evaluation

Evaluation of a whole curriculum is a very time-consuming and complex process, and there is a danger that some inspection visits tend to be little more than paper-chasing. For instance, I once heard an inspector describing a teacher as excellent. When asked how he knew, he replied, 'The tutor's notes are really first class.' The notes became a substitute for the reality, and many an inspection visit tends to focus upon the paper rather than the actual curriculum as implemented. To be fair, inspectors are aware of both the strengths and the shortcomings of this form of inspection, as are curriculum teams when they carry out their own evaluations. Their evaluation should look at all the factors in curriculum planning, as the above model indicates.

This form of systems analysis, although very useful, contains a fundamental danger: that it becomes functionalist and merely seeks to describe and explain the system rather than to reveal the strengths and the weaknesses of each element within the whole. Senge (1990) discusses systems analysis in his famous *Fifth Discipline*, and while such an approach is valid, it still runs the dangers of the weaknesses of functionalist analysis.

Programme planning

American adult education, by contrast, has rarely used the term 'curriculum'. I well remember talking to Malcolm Knowles about this and he said, 'We don't have a curriculum, we have a programme.' Thus, it is to the American literature that we turn our attention briefly – but we also need to recognize that more recently the American literature has also tended to employ the term 'curriculum' (Wang, 2008). Cervero and Wilson (1994), who provide a theoretical basis for curriculum planning, suggest that there are three broad programme planning models: the classical, the naturalistic and the critical. We shall examine each in turn.

The classical model

As was pointed out in the earlier chapters on Knowles, perhaps andragogy is better understood as a curriculum, or programme, planning model than as a model for either teaching or learning. Indeed, Knowles (1980b: 26–27) suggests six stages in the process:

1 helping learners diagnose their learning needs;
2 planning with learners a sequence of learning experiences to answer them;
3 creating conditions conducive to learning;
4 using appropriate methods for learning;

250

5 providing the necessary resources;
6 helping learners measure the outcomes of the learning.

It is clear from the above sequence that there is little difference here from the traditional models of curriculum that relate it to the teaching and learning process. Underlying it is a humanistic philosophy but one lacking a theory of curriculum and a discussion of teaching style, and also the sociological factors that also underlie the programme. For instance, there is no recognition of the critical debate that was discussed in the previous part of this chapter.

There were a number of programme planning models produced at this time, including Verner with Booth's (1964) one, but in 1985 Boone produced a comprehensive overview of programme planning. In this case he used the term in rather the same way as British educators tend to use the term 'workshop' or 'specially designed course'. In his approach he examined many of the major American theories and then proceeded to produce his own model in which he recognized two stages in programme planning (the organization and its renewal processes, and linking the organization to its publics), two stages of design and implementation, and a final stage of evaluation. This is a classical, practical approach in which he listed in each of these five stages the essential elements to consider, as Table 12.3 (overleaf) indicates. Clearly, this is a behaviourist and empirical model, but it is quite realistic about how educational activities have to offer themselves on the market and seek to demonstrate their usefulness.

Boone's model comes close to what Cervero and Wilson call the naturalistic model, as we shall see when we look at the work of Houle.

About the same time, Langenbach (1988) also wrote on the subject, and is one of the few American adult educators who used the term 'curriculum'. He examined a variety of curricula prevalent in adult education. He defined a curriculum model as 'a plan that creates access to education and training' (1988:2), which illustrates that his major concern is with elements of programme planning. Nevertheless, he does examine a variety of the American approaches to adult education, plus the work of Freire, from a curriculum perspective.

Finally, in this section one of the more classical approaches is that known as ADDIE – the Instructional Systems Development (ISD) or ADDIE model:

- Analyze
- Design
- Develop
- Implement
- Evaluate.

(Bierema, 2008:25)

251

Table 12.3 Summary of Boone's model of programme planning

Stage 1 – Understanding the organization and its renewal processes, including:
- commitment to its function
- commitment to its structures
- its processes
- its commitment to using a tested framework for programme planning
- its commitment to renewal

Stage 2 – Linking the organization to its publics, including:
- mapping its publics
- identifying its target publics
- interfacing with leaders of these publics
- collaborative assessment of needs

Stage 3 – Designing the planned programme, including:
- translating expressed needs to macro-needs
- translating these into objectives
- identifying educational strategies
- specifying intended outcomes

Stage 4 – Implementing the programme, including:
- developing action plans
- developing and implementing strategies for marketing the plans
- following through on plans
- training leaders
- monitoring and reinforcing the teacher–learner transaction

Stage 5 – Evaluation and accountability, including:
- determining and measuring programme outcomes
- assessing programme inputs
- using results for programme revision and organizational renewal
- using results as appropriate in accounting to sponsors, etc.

Source: Boone (1985).

This simple summary almost returns us to Tyler's four points of the curriculum but in this instance it is much more practical and is not based upon a philosophical foundation – which is one of its fundamental weaknesses. Indeed, it takes for granted the foundation since it may appear self-evident. However, in any form of planning, self-evidency is a dangerous precept that tends to conservativism and forms of social and cultural reproduction.

The naturalistic approach

Cervero and Wilson (1994:17) distinguish the naturalistic approach from the previous one by suggesting that that was based on idealized principles while this is based on an examination of the actual process. However, this is a very difficult distinction to sustain, since Boone's model could also have been located here. Indeed, many of the classical approaches have come from practical concerns, although it is true that the classical models do not indicate the influence of the educator on the planning and implementation process. Cervero and Wilson suggest that Houle's (1972) work does provide this perspective. He was one of the best-known of writers on this topic in the United States, and sought to illustrate the design of education.

While recognizing the complexity of designing an educational programme, Houle produced two different types of models. He recognized that there are a variety of different educational situations in which a programme may be designed, and Table 12.4 illustrates the eleven different ones that he considered significant.

It will be seen that these various situations listed by Houle encapsulate a variety of adult learning situations, so that it is possible to fit within this framework self-directed learning, on the one hand, and planning an informative documentary television programme for a mass audience, on the other. Houle discussed each of these situations very fully in his writing, which is a most valuable exercise in the study of the design of education. Nevertheless, such a classification records nothing of the actual process that underlies the production of these educational situations, and so he also produced a second systems approach, which is summarized in Table 12.5.

Houle also recognized that in the design of the format it is necessary to consider the following points: resources, leaders, methods, schedule,

Table 12.4 Houle's major categories of educational design situations

Individual
    c1 An individual designs an activity for himself
    c2 An individual or group design an activity for another individual

Group
    c3 A group (with or without a continuing leader) designs an activity for itself
    c4 A teacher, or a group of teachers, designs an activity for, and often with, a group of students
    c5 A committee designs an activity for a larger group
    c6 Two or more groups design an activity which will enhance their combined programmes of service

Institution
    c7 A new institution is designed
    c8 An institution designs an activity in a new format
    c9 An institution designs a new activity in an established format
    c10 Two or more institutions design an activity which will enhance their combined programmes of service

Mass
    c11 An individual, group or institution designs an activity for a mass audience

Source: Houle (1972:44).

Table 12.5 Summary of Houle's decision points in programme planning

1 Identification of possible educational programme
2 Decision taken to proceed
3 Identification of objectives
4 Refining the objectives
5 Designing the format
6 Contextualizing the format
7 Putting the plan into operation
8 Measuring the results
9 Evaluating the results

Source: Houle (1972:47).

sequence, social reinforcement, individualization, roles and relationships, criteria for evaluation, and clarity of design. In addition, he suggested that in contextualizing the format, programme planners should also consider guidance or counselling, lifestyle, finance and interpretation. This model has become quite widely cited as a clear approach to programme planning, as indeed it is, but it does omit a number of issues, some of which will be discussed later in this chapter.

Houle stated that in 'applying the model to a situation, one may begin with any component and proceed to others in any order' (1972:46–47). However, this is not really what the actual diagram in his study suggests since it is a sequential cycle which, while the process may begin at any point in the process, takes the programme designer through seven stages. The fourth and fifth stages have a number of individual facets. This model is meticulous in its production and Houle's discussion admirably thorough but it does adopt the perspective of the adult educator who is able to design an educational programme free from external constraint, which may not actually reflect the reality of what happens during the process. It is therefore necessary to include external factors as a variable in the process.

At about the same time as Houle was producing his model, Verduin (1980) wrote a book in which he discussed curriculum building. The book claims to produce the first curriculum model for adult education, although this is rather a problematic claim in the light of the programme planning books that were already published. While he used the term 'curriculum', he did not produce a theoretical discussion of the concept, although he outlined five elements in his model: aim (which he called direction), outside political forces, goals, instruction and evaluation. In addition, he was very concerned with practical processes of planning instruction, with a behaviourist orientation. For instance, in one place he (ibid.:102) produced a fivefold chart: assess entering behaviour; specific behavioural objectives; specify learning unit and procedures; present learning unit and tasks; student performs and learns. This was an early book in this field and one which at least recognizes the possibility that adult education could have a curriculum.

The critical perspective

Throughout this work it has been recognized that education cannot be removed from the social and political context within which it occurs, and Cervero and Wilson point in the direction of more critical thinkers, such as Freire, Habermas and Griffin, whose work has already been cited. Once again this discussion reverts to the idealized and theoretical, and does not look at either the constraints or the practicalities of programme planning in a market situation. Consequently, this discussion then takes us back to the earlier chapters of this book where we examined globalization and the market in a critical manner – but it does have to be recognized that there is frequently a conflict between what the educators might want to do and what the market will sustain, the reality being that educational programmes need learners who are also fee-payers.

Conclusion

Perhaps, therefore, even the more practical approach of Houle is not really a practical one and more research needs to be undertaken in order to demonstrate this, as the research of Martin (1999) illustrates. His study was of art teachers in the United Kingdom who wished to teach creative art but whose learners wanted to learn to copy pictures, and so on. The lecturers recognized that if they taught the type of creative art that they wished to teach, encouraging the learners to be original and creative, they were in danger of their learners leaving their class, whereas if they taught the learners what they wanted, they would keep them. The market was bound to prevail – they could not implement a providers' model of the curriculum – but it did create the possibility of role strain and declining job satisfaction for the lecturers. Such studies as this take us beyond the critical theoretical perspective and back to the practicalities of the teaching and learning situation, and also demonstrate that most curriculum theory and programme planning are in the realms of grand theory and are illustrations of the gap between theory and practice.

Beisgen and Kraitchman (2003:98) have offered a list of things that programme organizers might do to generate creativity among older learners:

- provide the right environment;
- provide opportunities to create;
- encourage ideas;
- provide challenges;
- help older adults not to be afraid to fail;

- provide time and resources;
- develop expertise;
- provide positive, constructive feedback;
- encourage a spirit of play and experimentation;
- provide opportunities for group interaction;
- provide a safe place for risk taking;
- offer rewards that recognize achievement;
- provide opportunities for brainstorming;
- help older adults develop thinking patterns to create new ideas;
- stimulate all the senses;
- provide opportunities to recognize and display creative work by older people.

While their work points us forward to the need to prepare adult educators professionally, it also illustrates that practical programmes might point the way to theorizing about curriculum and programme planning.

13

PRACTICE, THEORY, RESEARCH
AND POLICY

The relationship between theory and practice and research is one that has been touched upon elsewhere in this book, without the main terms being defined. Theory is usually taken to be the body of knowledge that a professional occupation regards as essential in order to practise. However, I have already raised problems about this in at least three ways: first, the role of the educator has become much more complex, so that the knowledge necessary to practise may relate only to a specialized part of the whole professional role; second, our understanding of knowledge itself has become much more complex so that, third, we now question the extent to which theory can actually be applied to practice since practice is a site for learning (Jarvis, 1999). Practice is a more self-evident term but its significance both as a site for learning and as being at the heart of practical knowledge has made it more significant in recent years. Research is also a learning concept but it is a process of learning conducted under stringent scientific conditions, and researching practice is usually a matter of case study rather than being in a position to generate generalized theory. Indeed, I have argued that in many situations a personal theory is generated from practising rather than the other way around. Additionally, I shall show that the interrelationship between these three and policy is also very complex. This chapter, therefore, has three main parts: the relationship between practice and theory, the interrelationship between research and practice, and the relationship between research and policy. Finally, the conclusion points the way forward with a forthcoming policy document from NIACE, the National Institute of Adult Continuing Education.

Practice and theory

In 1974, Argyris and Schön also raised one of the basic issues of this chapter when they distinguished between espoused theory and theory in use, the former being the theory to which practitioners give allegiance while the latter is that theory which can be constructed as a result of observing their performance. They recognized that there was not always congruency between the two; indeed, they (1974:7) actually claimed that there may, but need not, be compatibility between them at all. However, what the practitioners espouse may relate to what they learn during their professional preparation in the classroom while what they practise may relate to what they learn in practice. At the same time, Argyris and Schön's concern was not really with the body of knowledge as theory, but only the manner by which practitioners made sense of the world and increased their effectiveness within it.

The relationship between the body of knowledge, as theory, and practice re-emerged in the United Kingdom (Bright, 1989; Usher and Bryant, 1989) and in the United States (Cervero, 1991) in the 1980s and 1990s, with many papers in professional journals questioning the idea that theory could be applied to practice. If we think of the speed of knowledge change in contemporary society and we recognize how rapidly things are actually changing in practice, we can see that before research data can be gathered, interpreted and disseminated, the world of practice might have changed considerably and so the theory has already become history! Hence, it is unwise to think that theory should be applied to practice in adult education and lifelong learning.

The other issue that we raised in our discussion about the nature of knowledge is that we are concerned with practical knowledge that is integrated rather than theoretical knowledge that is academic discipline-based. This raises a question: what is educational knowledge? This was a topic of concern in adult education in the United States as early as 1964 (Jensen *et al.*, 1964), when Jensen thought that adult education borrowed from the foundation disciplines and was a combination of them. Hence, the foundation disciplines have long been regarded as one of the academic bases of educational knowledge, but they do not help us understand the practical aspects of education, so this discussion gives rise to a subsequent one: what is the nature of the study of education? We need to answer this before we respond to the first question about the nature of educational knowledge.

Adult education and lifelong learning as fields of practice and study

Adult education is a field, or many fields, of practice. This appears to be a fairly unproblematic claim, but it is not so self-evident with lifelong learning, since lifelong learning can refer simply to learning throughout the lifespan – and this relates to human existence. It is the other aspect, the provision of learning opportunities throughout life, that can be treated as a field, or fields, of practice. However, both adult education and lifelong learning may also be fields of study, and when we examine fields of study it is quite easy to interpret the phenomenon that we investigate from the perspective of the disciplines – from a sociological, psychological, economic perspective, and so on. It is also possible that we undertake that interpretation from a more critical perspective (Carr and Kemmis, 1986), a feminist perspective, and so on. But then we are actually producing feminist, sociological, psychological or economic knowledge rather than educational knowledge. In other words, we are producing philosophy of adult education, sociology of lifelong learning, and so on. Educational knowledge, in contrast, is about the fields of practice, and this is practical knowledge. But as we can see from this discussion of adult education and lifelong learning, the education of adults is not about one field of practice, but about many. They can occur in educational institutions or outside of them; in professional or community settings; they can be vocational or leisure-time occupations, etc. The only common phenomenon is the educational process, so that a major conceptual problem that now arises is not 'What is education?' but 'What is educational knowledge?' No attempt will be made here to resolve this problem since its complexity demands a full-length study.

Nevertheless, it is clear that the common feature of all of these fields of practice is the practical activity, and the educational is practical. In order to practise it, some practical knowledge is necessary, which can only be learned in practice and which will continue to be learned for as long as the practitioners seek to problematize their practice. Usher (1989) called for more analysis of practical knowledge, and in many ways this has occurred, although its implications still need to be worked out. Jarvis (2009c) has begun to look at learning in this way, and many studies have sought to understand learning in the workplace, and so on (e.g. Olesen, 2009; Watkins and Marsick, 2009). The implications of these studies for teaching and learning are still being developed.

Practical knowledge and information about practice

Teachers of adults, then, are practitioners, and education is a practice. In order to be an expert teacher of adults it is necessary to know how to teach. As an educational practice, there are considerable similarities with school teaching, and we have highlighted this relationship elsewhere. However, Ryle (1963 [1949]:40–41) made the point that knowing how to play chess does not mean that the player has to be able to articulate the rules, only that he or she observes them during the game. He suggested, in rather the same way as Argyris and Schön (1974) did about theory in use, that as the chess player is seen to obey the rules, onlookers know that the chess player knows how to play the game. In a similar manner, Nyiri (1988:19) discussed the knowledge necessary to know how to ride a bicycle. He pointed out that this ability is learned not through knowing the theories of dynamics underlying the riding of a bicycle, but rather by trial and error.

Consequently, it is necessary at this point to ask what relationship exists between the actual performance of the action and the knowledge in the mind: that is, what makes practical knowledge? What is clear is that this is not simply a matter of applying theory to practice! This is a much more difficult question to answer because the chess player might not always be able to articulate the rules of chess and the bicycle rider might not know the scientific rules that explain how balance can be maintained and the bicycle be ridden. Is it just the ability and the confidence to perform the correct actions, because they have been habitualized and memorized? Is *knowledge how* no different from *being able to*? In some ways it is. The instructor might be able to tell student teachers how to teach, but until they have actually taught, they do not know that they are able to do so. The instructor's information is information, some of which might then become part of the learners' practical knowledge at a later date. Knowing how to perform the action is not the same as having the skill to do it, and so learners can be taught the procedures about how to perform a skill, but they still have to learn how to do it for themselves. This they cannot be taught in the classroom, although they can be coached, or mentored, by an expert in the practice situation. In addition, learners can be taught that if they perform a skill in a certain manner, there are most likely to be certain outcomes; in other words, they can learn *knowledge that* in the classroom but then they have to learn in practice how to practise – and they only know that they can do it, when they do it.

However, the chess player knows when the rules are being broken and the cyclist is aware when someone else has not got the confidence to ride the bicycle. Naturally, this gives rise to the idea that some elements of practical knowledge are tacit (Polanyi, 1967; Baumard, 1999), or even that it is merely a matter of confidence that the skill performance is correct, and so no actual thought need go into why it is correct until such time as an action does not quite fit the situation. At this point of disjuncture, actors have to think about it and perhaps devise (learn) some new ideas that need to be tried out in practice. If they work, then they can be internalized, but their precise formulation may be forgotten, for expert practical knowledge is fundamentally subjective, pragmatic and presumptive upon the world, and the relationship between this form of personal theory and practice is pragmatic. In fact, practical knowledge is not only *knowing how*, in Ryle's terms; it is also *knowing that* something will most likely occur given certain conditions and having the *tacit knowledge* that develops through experience. Practical knowledge consists of a personal combination of certain forms of knowledge.

How then is practical knowledge learned? Nyiri suggested that

> [o]ne becomes an expert not simply by absorbing explicit knowledge of the type found in textbooks, but through experience,

that is, through repeated trials, 'failing, succeeding, wasting time and effort ... getting a feel for a problem, learning when to go by the book and when to break the rules'. Human experts thereby gradually absorb 'a repertory of working rules of thumb, or "heuristics", that, combined with book knowledge, make them expert practitioners'. This practical heuristic knowledge, as attempts to simulate it on the machine [computer] have shown, is 'hardest to get at because experts – or anyone else – rarely have the self-awareness to recognize what it is. So it has to be mined out of their heads painstakingly one jewel at a time'.

(Nyiri, 1988:20–21; all quotations from Feigenbaum and McCorduck, 1984)

Education occurs in many fields of practice, of which the education of adults – whether it is adult education or lifelong learning – is one. Knowledge of the practice of education can be learned partly by doing it in the classroom and also from watching the practice of experts; it is grounded in the field of practice. This is confirmed from students' reports on teaching practice; they say that they try things out to see if they work, they observe other teachers performing and they learn from experience. They learn the process by direct participation in it. They have developed their own practical knowledge of teaching as well as having been taught knowledge about practice. Clearly, practice is an important area for learning, and Schön (1983) highlighted the fact that practitioners are not necessarily mindless in the performance of their occupation, although they can presume upon repetitive situations, but rather are responsive to new situations and reflective in practice in order to improve their overall performance.

Such analyses have led to calls to reintroduce the apprenticeship model of training school teachers in the United Kingdom, and this could also be extended to the preparation of educators of adults as well. However, there are some fundamental questions to be raised about this claim, namely:

- If there is no research into, or agreement about, what constitutes good practice, then what every practitioner learns from any experienced practitioner must be acceptable if it works, even though not all experienced practitioners are experts. But I have also argued that education must be humanistic, which is a belief perspective, and that beliefs and values, as well as efficiency, underlie the idea of 'good' practice.
- Not all aspects of practice can be learned through observing the expert because unusual situations are likely to occur in most forms of professional practice, and so all practitioners are likely to experience something in the course of their practice that they have not been able to observe in their apprenticeship with the expert – but working with the expert does allow practitioners to learn practical knowledge itself.

- If there is only apprenticeship, then every new practitioner needs to reinvent every aspect of the wheel, which might be an even greater waste of time than learning some aspects of practice in the classroom first!

The apprenticeship model does not rule out classroom learning, although the latter is only one form of learning and is not superior to learning in practice. Hence, it is advantageous to have a body of knowledge about how the education of adults is undertaken, whether this be about teaching, curriculum design, management, etc. in the field. This body of knowledge should be gathered from observation of practice rather than from theoretical explication of how a procedure should be performed, a teaching method practised or a lesson prepared.

Preparation for teaching adults should therefore include classroom instruction into the knowledge of practice, but this remains information for the practitioners, and it only becomes knowledge when it becomes embedded within their own understanding of their own practice – their own practical knowledge. Preparation for practice is providing information about practice both in the classroom situation and in practice, and the opportunity to learn practical knowledge in practice. Exposure to experts in practice is a useful aspect of learning practical knowledge. Nyiri (1988) claimed that a great deal of practical knowledge is learned through exposure to custom, convention and ritual. But it also has to be recognized that exposure to bad practice is also a way of learning because learners not only learn from experts, but learn from the mistakes of others. Naturally, this approach is traditional, but the transmission of the ethos of practice is necessarily conventional and conservative. Social change is gradual, and a great deal of practice adapts to, rather than initiates, change.

Hence, it is possible to construct what we might call a body of practical knowledge to be included in a curriculum for the preparation of educators of adults, but which is actually only information about practice, and this is its status when it is taught. Theory in this sense – and it is not the only definition of theory – is information about practice rather than practical knowledge. It is about the practice of the education of adults, and it might be applicable to the practice of both adult education and lifelong learning – but it is not necessarily always so. Once this body of information about education has been constructed, it might be called a body of educational knowledge or even a body of adult educational knowledge, etc., and this is confusing because what we call a body of knowledge is not knowledge in the sense of being known by the practitioners; it is actually potential information – that is, theory – that might become an element in practitioners' practical knowledge.

Does having a body of knowledge (information about practice) mean that education is a discipline like other social sciences? The response to such a question must be negative. The body of educational knowledge is a body of information that is drawn from practice, but once we interpret practice (knowledge why), we will always be forced to use knowledge that is drawn from the social sciences, and even the pure sciences, because practice is itself interdisciplinary. The point about this is that in everyday life actions are performed that, if they are ever analysed, might be seen to be an integration of distinct but applied disciplines – such as psychology or sociology or philosophy, or even as being from beliefs and ideologies such as Marxism or feminism, etc. However, in everyday life people do not, when they think about how they are going to behave, always consciously decide that they are going to use a little bit of psychological, a lot more philosophical, some sociological knowledge, etc. and mix it together to constitute the practical knowledge underlying a specific behaviour – although they may well be guided by their cultural and ideological beliefs. These are times when actors are aware that they have applied some philosophical ideals, etc. to their behaviour, so that it would be untrue to claim that the foundations of practical everyday knowledge are never recognized (see Heller, 1984:185–215). The same is true of educational knowledge: it is a unique constellation of applied knowledge that falls within the ambit of the other social science disciplines. It is only independent inasmuch as it relates to the fields of practice, and this can be demonstrated in the following manner: it is possible to have a philosophy of adult education or a sociology of continuing medical education, but it is not possible to have an adult education of sociology or a lifelong learning of psychology, and so on. In this sense, education is not an academic discipline but a field of practice that can be studied from a wide variety of perspectives.

There is necessarily a close link between the body of practical knowledge (information about practice) and practice. However, it is necessary to explore this relationship a little more specifically here. Traditionally, it has been argued that the body of knowledge (or theory) of practice should be taught before the new recruits enter the field, so that they can implement what they have learned in the classroom when they get into practice. This rather positivist approach, however, is flawed, as Schön (1983) showed when he pointed out that practitioners do learn in and from practice and when he argued for an end to technical rationality. Indeed, this body of practical knowledge does not determine practice. If it did, it would imply that practitioners mindlessly perform their professional duties in a totally unchanging world. Consequently, theory does not, or should not, determine practice, but neither does practice totally determine theory. Rather, as Lukes (1981:396ff.) suggested, it is a relationship of underdetermination. If it were not such a relationship, then actions would be predetermined and the social world would be regarded as unchanging and unchangeable. Such a view of both society and humankind is unacceptable, and so I suggest that there must always be incongruence between even the body of practical knowledge and practice itself. Indeed, it would constitute a much bigger problem if there were congruency between them.

Research and practice

Research is generally regarded as researching practice, but clearly research per se is much broader than this since it can also relate to researching in theoretical perspectives, historical approaches, and so on. At its heart, research is an exercise in learning. Research is also generally divided into two camps: quantitative and qualitative. There has been a tendency in the past, and it still exists in some uninformed circles, for some advocates and practitioners of quantitative research to dismiss a great deal of qualitative research as anecdotal. This is a view that can also be found in governmental policy: quantitative research is regarded as scientific, and policy can be built upon it more easily than upon qualitative evidence. Yet while the predominance of the quantitative is wrong, it is understandable, and qualitative research should be regarded as a different but valid form of research.

Quantitative and qualitative research

Quantitative research, as its name suggests, is about measuring things. However, once we have measured something, this still tells us only about the phenomenon being measured – the what; it tells us nothing about the why. But not all 'facts' are measurable in any case and, above all, facts have no meaning. For instance, we can count the number of words, paragraphs and sections in this chapter and we will have measured it. But it tells us nothing about the meaning of what is written here. The meaning can only be arrived at by interpretation of facts – that is, we give them meaning. Meaning is not self-evident, and there are many instances where experts have disagreed about the meaning of facts. In some cases this has had disastrous consequences – when an expert in a court of law, for instance, gives an interpretation of facts that is later shown to be wrong. Meaning is not quantitative!

Another aspect of quantitative facts about which we have to be sure before we undertake interpretation is that what we are saying we are measuring we are actually measuring. We have all seen this with intelligence testing. For instance, if Gardner's (1983) theory of multiple intelligences is correct, then there is no way that an intelligence test can measure intelligence; it can only tell us how an individual performs in answering the questions in a specific test paper on a given day. Indeed, it cannot even be used for comparative purposes since individuals may have different strengths in different intelligences and will therefore perform differently in response to the same paper. However, there is a tendency to give a score to intelligence testing – an IQ – or to give a grade to an essay. This gives the interpretation an appearance of being objective and scientific and therefore indisputable, and for as long as the policy makers accept it (as in examinations, for instance), the appearance of being objective will be treated as if is a fact rather than something not quite so empirically factual. This phenomenon is something that is part of the hegemony of the pure sciences.

However, I am not claiming that quantitative research has no validity; only that its validity – like that of qualitative research – is limited. In the pure sciences it is necessary to measure, and measurements, when interpreted by experts, enable us to know more about the nature of phenomena. In fields of practice, like adult education and lifelong learning, we can measure enrolments, participation in some forms of formal and non-formal learning, and so on. We can also measure the number of people who are affected by certain barriers or opportunities to continue their learning, and so on. This does enable us to interpret facts, and perhaps those interpretations may affect both policy and practice. But it must be emphasized at this point that since the meaning of facts is not self-evident, there is always an element of qualitative interpretation even in the most quantitative of research; data need interpretation to have meaning and become knowledge. But in education, for instance, we cannot measure good teaching. We can measure the number of good teachers, but only on days when lessons are observed!

Qualitative research is a different form of research – it is about assessing and understanding rather than measuring – and in recent years it has assumed a greater significance as the social sciences are beginning to gain greater acceptability. Adult education and lifelong learning fall within the field of the social sciences but, as I have said, there is still a place for quantitative research in education.

There are many different methods of qualitative research, each with its strengths and weaknesses, and since this is not a research methods book, we shall not go into them here. Suffice it to say, these approaches tend to be interactive, between the researcher and those individuals being researched, which has given rise for greater concern about the ethics of research than ever before, as regards the protection of personal data but also in the way that the researchers conduct their research. Ethical concerns are also very important when personal quantitative data are being collected. There is a real sense in which research is always an intrusion into people's privacy. The researcher has no rights of intrusion; he or she can intrude only with the consent of those being researched.

One of the features about qualitative research, which may be one of the reasons why it is seen as anecdotal, is that it is nearly always local and small scale. To the quantitative researcher this is a fundamental weakness, but in the complexity of contemporary society there is a danger that large-scale research projects fail to uncover the diversity of the potential respondents.

However, this does mean that results of small-scale qualitative research projects – which can and do probe more deeply into the beliefs, attitudes and lives of the respondents – cannot be conclusive about a wider population. Generally we can see that the particular cannot be generalized. Crudely, we can say that quantitative research starts with hypotheses that it tests and from which conclusions may be drawn whereas qualitative research starts with research questions or problems and ends with hypotheses that the findings might have some significance beyond what have been discovered.

Research has now become very complex indeed and so it is not surprising that more training is being offered in research methods than ever before. Most Master's degrees in adult education and lifelong learning contain at least one, and often two, modules in research methods, and these are often compulsory. In the United Kingdom, the Economic and Social Research Council (ESRC) has also introduced a new structure for many PhDs, what is commonly known as the 1 + 3 – that is, a one-year Master of Research degree plus three years of research for the PhD. Some universities and departments have mistakenly claimed that all PhDs should be like this, rather than that doctoral researchers should be experts in research methods. A Master of Research degree might be very important for someone entering the field of research, or for young academics who are going to enter teaching in higher education and who will be supervising PhD work in the future. It is more questionable whether more mature individuals who are seeking to undertake PhD research on a part-time basis need to undertake the whole of a Master's degree in research before undertaking the research that concerns them, but all individuals undertaking research do need some training in research technique since poorly conducted research lowers the reliability of the findings and lowers the status of the field in the eyes of professional academic researchers.

Part-time researchers are often practitioner or action researchers, which points to the need for a properly developed and regulated practitioner doctorate, of equal but different status to the PhD. Some practitioner doctorates are being developed, although the distinction between them is not always clearly enunciated. Such an approach should ensure that it is a field of practice that is being researched, and that practical knowledge and its relationship to the disciplines are well understood. An award of a Doctor of Education (EdD), or even one in lifelong learning or human resource development, would recognize the developments.

The effects of research on practice

The question now needs to be asked whether research findings do affect practice, and while there are many instances where this remains an open question, Volkoff (2009) records an instance where two research findings conducted for the Board of Adult and Community Education Board in Victoria, Australia, had a profound effect on the life of the community. She records the fact that this research was grounded in practice and supported by the state government. She shows how the findings were used to produce publications, give advice to government, give conference presentations, were used in professional development programmes with both management and practitioners, and were also used in regional stakeholder briefings. Finally, Volkoff argued that part of the strength of this was that the practitioners were themselves involved in the research, so that they were practitioner researchers rather than practitioners being researched. That the research was grounded in practice and involved practitioners was a major part of the success of the project, but, as she also said, it was successful because of the enthusiasm and commitment of the research team.

Practitioner and action research

Practitioner researchers (Jarvis, 1999) are usually individuals involved in researching their own practice for no other reason than that they want to understand it better. In this sense, research is a focused and disciplined approach to learning under supervision – but it is still a form of learning and may be understood from within the model of learning discussed earlier in this book. In this sense, research has been democratized and is something in which practitioners can be involved while they are still carrying out their daily work. Research grants are not so necessary for this approach to research, so that it is little wonder that in this knowledge society there are an increasing number of such research projects, especially in adult education and continuing learning.

Action research is often like practitioner research (McNiff, 1988) inasmuch as it is the practitioner who undertakes the research, but this need not always be the case. The objective of action research is seeking to understand some field of practice so that it can be changed to improve it in some way.

The relationship between theory, practice and research

Having analysed theory, practice and research, we have begun to explore their interrelationship. Perhaps Usher and Bryant's (1989) study has undertaken this most consistently thus far in the literature of adult education. Their contention that this is a triangular relationship in which each affects the other is recognized as having some validity, but, as I have already pointed out, the relationship is even more complex than this. Traditionally, the data discovered from research about practice were regarded as the new theory, or then the new theory was taught and put into practice and then researched, but this is now insufficient. The concepts are much more complex than this and we need to see that this interrelationship has a number of possibilities:

- Research into practice becomes the personal practical knowledge of the practitioner researcher and, possibly, any publication from the research might become information (theory) that is taught to others, who might in their turn, but need not, use it in practice.
- Personal knowledge (personal theory – practical knowledge) might be used, but not applied, in practice and the practice might be researched, and so on.
- Research data might be interpreted and incorporated into a curriculum that might be used in practice, but if the practice is undergoing rapid change, then the research data will themselves be out of date before they have been learned. In other words, the data are already history!

It is clear from this discussion that the relationships between these three are not automatic or predetermined in any way and, as I said earlier, the case is one of underdetermination.

The relationship between research and policy

It has been traditionally believed over the years that policy is based on research findings, but this is too strong a claim for the relationship. Rather, research findings may be used if they fit into the already existing policies and ideological belief systems of government. For instance, if a government department will only accept quantitative research, then it will tend to ignore qualitative data, however well researched. Neither is government likely to suddenly reverse its already existing policies, which may be based on its ideological systems, just because some research findings contradict those belief systems or the policies. Research findings may be like water dripping onto a rock in that they may have some effects in the long run, whereas if the research findings are popularized in some way, so that they have some effect on public opinion, government might actually respond more rapidly – which is ironic when we consider the fact that within the academic and research communities research gains status if it is published in peer-reviewed journals whose only, very limited, circulation is among fellow academics! In this sense, research might actually form the basis of future policy statements.

Consequently, there are differing perspectives about the extent to which there is a relationship between the two: Nutley *et al.* (2007) use the idea of evidence-based policy. But in a more recent paper, Field (2009) discusses this relationship very cogently. He noted that there are a number of difficulties in the relationship between the two, such as the facts that:

- policy makers and researchers occupy different institutional cultures;
- institutional complexities are not always obvious to the researcher;
- research is not neutral since there are always selection processes involved;
- costs spiral, and the state's role may be to steer rather than direct;
- often research voices challenge policy from outside rather than engaging with it.

This does lead to the question of who are the advocates for adult and continuing education and lifelong learning; who are those who engage with the policy makers? In the United Kingdom one of the clear answers is that the National Institute of Adult Continuing Education (NIACE), mainly through its director, currently Alan Tuckett, but also through other leading members, successfully engages with the policy makers – and it does this with the leaders of all the major political parties. If the advocates are engaged in the debate at a sufficiently high level, they can actually help set the research agenda as well as influence its outcomes. Field (2009) shows how the work in which he was involved in the Foresight programme did influence a government White Paper, *The Learning Revolution,* and in this way policy could influence both research and practice.

Policy

Since 1995 the European Union has published a series of policy statements about lifelong learning (European Commission, 1995, 2000, 2001a, 2006). The primary concern of the first three was twofold: generating a learning society capable of producing a Europe fit to take its place in the competitive global economy. The second focused on citizenship since Europe needs to create a political union that is significant to the population. These were the two dominant aims of lifelong learning, although two others were often specified: social inclusion and personal development. However, the second of these papers was a consultation, the outcome of which was the recognition that lifelong learning is more than vocational learning, so that in the third document the European Union specified that lifelong learning was not totally about economics; in *Making a European Area of Lifelong Learning a Reality,* in which it was more specifically recognized that the Europe of Knowledge threatens to bring about 'greater inequalities and social exclusion' (European Commission, 2001a:6), it is claimed that lifelong learning

> is much more than economics. It also promotes the goals and ambitions of European countries to become more inclusive, tolerant and democratic. And it promises a Europe in which citizens

have the opportunity and ability to realise their ambitions and to participate in building a better society.

(ibid.:7)

However, it was not until the final one (European Commission, 2006), on adult learning that the themes varied. There were five 'messages' in this document:

1   The barriers to participation should be lifted so that there is a degree of equality about it.
2   The quality of adult education should be improved by further professional training of teachers.
3   There should be recognition and validation of learning outcomes in all forms of adult education – formal, non-formal and informal – based on common European principles.
4   Greater investment should be made in the education of older people and migrants.
5   The quality and comparability of data about education and learning must be improved.

In a sense, the European Commission recognized that it needed to break away from the all-too-familiar themes of vocation and citizenship and to include all forms of adult education within its considerations. Once we recognize that all forms of education are important, this does mean that the emphasis on vocationalism and citizenship is important, but it is not the only significant outcome of adult learning.

In precisely the same way, the British government's own policies and practices about post-compulsory education, and to some extent even school education, were vocational, and this produced considerable protest, especially from those involved in liberal education. The British government issued a consultation paper, *Informal Adult Learning: Shaping the Way Ahead* (Department for Innovation, Universities and Skills, 2008) in which this was admitted, and it went on to talk about the future of informal adult learning. Although the consultation was well received, the document itself was thoroughly criticized: 'I am afraid that this is a poor paper. It gets off to a very bad start: the historical introductions should have been omitted. It is superficial, partial, inaccurate, and complacent; and it lacks all analytical depth' (Taylor, 2008:8). However, it listed five points for discussion:

1   understanding and improving provision;
2   the government's contribution;
3   Department for Innovation, Universities and Skills-funded informal learning;

270

4   equality of access;
5   broadcasting and information technology.

The consultation generated over 5,000 replies and also provided a basis for a new lobby: CALL, the Campaigning Alliance for Lifelong Learning. This led to a new government policy paper on informal adult learning entitled *The Learning Revolution* (Department for Innovation, Universities and Skills, 2009). Clearly, this paper was an attempt by the government to recognize that adult learning is more than vocational training in precisely the same way as the European Union had been forced to do just a few years previously. But – a revolution it was not! In my own work (Jarvis, 2008) I have called for a revolution in learning which located the revolution in the recognition that the modernity project has failed and was logically bound to fail, and that we need not only a new approach but advocates, teachers and leaders. The revolution proposed by the British government certainly did not lead us very far outside the traditional lines of thought about learning, but it is to be welcomed because it did break away from the vocational mould. Once more there were five emphases:

1   government's recognition that adult learning can make a profound contribution to people's lives;
2   that government must make a virtue out of necessity;
3   that all government departments should pledge themselves to support a learning revolution;
4   that we should be inspired about learning;
5   that government can provide a framework for life-enriching adult learning.

And so the government claimed that it was setting out to:

• build a culture of learning;
• increase access to informal adult learning;
• transform the way people learn through technology;
• make it happen.

It actually did seek to respond to some of the European Union points, especially about the education of senior citizens, by recognizing the place that organizations such as the University of the Third Age play in society. It also recognized that many of the traditional sites of learning which were not regarded as mainstream education, such as museums, are now to be included within the remit of adult learning – something adult educators had long accepted. There was a great deal of rhetoric in the document but it remains to be seen whether the statement will have any real effect on future developments. Certainly there is promise there and, significantly, it is possible to see that some earlier research, such as *The Benefits of Learning* (Schuller *et al.*, 2004), has been recognized within this policy statement.

Nevertheless, the overall reaction to this White Paper has been mixed – from rhetoric to over-generalization and lack of significant proposals; visionary but short on funding; inclusive but lacks recognition of the place of practitioners, and so on. Clearly, there is nothing revolutionary in the policy document, but then government policy rarely is revolutionary. Its aim was to sow the seeds for a new movement in learning, but it was rather late in this, although it must be hoped that it will help all government departments focus on the need for recognition of the informal in adult learning.

Conclusion

The purpose of this chapter has been to open up some of the questions about research, policy and practice rather than to write a chapter about each. It starts with a concern about the growing complexity of research itself and indicates that it is necessary for practitioners in adult education and lifelong learning to be aware of the academic debates about research as well as their being researchers themselves since in the contemporary climate there is a sense in which they are already practitioner researchers learning in their own practice. It also points to the necessity of researchers engaging in both practice and policy. We can see that the relationship between research, policy and practice is much more complicated than it might appear on the surface, and we can see how it is necessary for practitioners to enter a critical debate about government policy about adult learning.

However, this text was completed and sent to the publishers a month or so before the National Institute of Adult Continuing Education published the results of its consultation (*Learning through Life*, Schuller and Watson, 2009), which aims at producing an analysis of the state of adult education in the United Kingdom and a strategic framework for future developments of lifelong learning. At the same time, this book is written for an international readership and so it was not considered appropriate to await its publication in order to write more about it here, but the following brief list of the themes is intended as a guide to those readers who are interested in seeing what aspects of lifelong learning the National Institute of Adult Continuing Education has used as a framework:

- prosperity, employment and work
- demography and social structure
- well-being and happiness
- migration and communities
- technological change

- poverty reduction
- citizenship and belonging
- crime and social exclusion
- sustainable development
- the roles of the public, private and voluntary sectors.

In addition, many of the thematic papers are available on the web.

There are two significant things, at least, that emerge from this: the extent to which the report will influence government policy in the coming years, and whether this report will be used more widely in the international community.

This chapter has raised a number of questions about the nature of the relationship between research, practice and policy but it also points to the need for practitioners to receive professional preparation for their role, which is the subject of the next and final chapter.

14

THE PROFESSIONAL
PREPARATION OF TEACHERS OF
ADULTS

When this book was first written, there was considerable concern and interest in getting adult educators trained, and I discussed this within the framework of the professionalization of an occupation. However, there has been a vast change in adult education in the United Kingdom and elsewhere in the world, as has become apparent by the increasing number of degree courses and so on that are being mounted on the subject of continuing education, lifelong learning, and so on. To a considerable extent this has followed the introduction of lifelong learning into the world of policy, as we saw earlier in this text. In the United Kingdom, perhaps the biggest stimulus for increased training was the Dearing Report (1997). In the remainder of Europe there was a report from the Education Council to the European Council (European Commission, 2001b), and during the Swedish presidency of the European Union three strategic goals were adopted for European education and training:

1   improving the quality and effectiveness of education and training systems in the European Union;
2   facilitating the access of all to education and training systems;
3   opening up education and training systems to the wider world.

(European Commission, 2002:8)

This was the first time that a document had sketched out a comprehensive education and training system for the whole of Europe. These three aims were then subdivided into thirteen objectives – five for the first objective, three for the second and five for the last.

Following the adoption of this project, the European Commission issued a work programme, and this was followed by a further policy document on the need to invest efficiently in education and training in Europe (European Commission, 2003) since it was claimed there has been a significant underinvestment in human resources within the European Union.

It is beyond the scope of this chapter to examine all of these objectives, but it is significant that the first objective is improving education and training for teachers – which is about both their initial and their continuing education. It will be recalled that education and training in the European documents includes both higher education and lifelong learning and that both sectors are included in this discussion. Consequently, it is on this objective that we focus here since for educators in both lifelong learning and higher education it is claimed that

> [t]eachers and trainers are the most essential actors in the overall strategy towards a knowledge-based economy ... Europe needs to improve the ways in which teachers and trainers are prepared for, and supported in their profoundly changing role in the knowledge society.
>
> (European Commission, 2002a:14)

We can see, therefore, that training and continuing professional development are regarded as an essential stage in the development of the knowledge society; they are also an indicator of being professional, or of professionalism. Consequently, we see that in an educational marketplace, one of the indicators of quality is the professionalism of the teachers: paradoxically, the market has had some beneficial effects on education!

Consequently, it is also significant that the document from the European Commission specifies that among the key issues to be addressed are:

- identifying the skills that teachers and trainers should have, given their changing roles in a knowledge society;
- providing the conditions which adequately support teachers and trainers as they respond to the challenges of the knowledge society, including through initial and in-service training in the perspective of lifelong learning.

> (European Commission, 2002:14)

The aims of this chapter are to contextualize the process of change by, initially, examining the process of professionalization, providing a brief historical picture of what occurred in the United Kingdom in the 1970s and 1980s and examining recent UK developments, and finally to look more broadly at the training of educators of adults.

The process of professionalization

The introduction of training schemes for adult and further education was a step in the process of professionalization, but it also reflected something of the changes that were beginning to occur in society, as more adults were returning to education. But as I argued earlier (Jarvis, 1985), adult education at that time was a semi-profession – that is, an occupation that has the following characteristics: no firm theoretical base; no monopoly of exclusive skills nor special area of competence; the existence of rules to guide practice; less specialization than occupations generally regarded as professions; control exercised by non-professionals; a service ethic. Space rules out any full discussion of each of these points, although it is essential to note that the development of a theoretical curriculum about the education of adults received a stimulus from the introduction of training courses for adult educators. Whether adult education could have ever actually professionalized along the classic lines of professionalization is doubtful. However, there never has been a complete and agreed typology of a profession, nor an agreed definition, so that it was easy in those early days of training for writers to treat adult education as a profession (see, for example, Mee, 1980:105). Yet Illich's (1977) analysis of disabling professions should also serve as a salutary warning to educators that while there may be advantages in pursuing this process, there are also dangers.

Even if it were possible to agree on a definition and characteristics of a profession, it might be argued that in a time of rapid change it is unrealistic to try to achieve a static and unchanging definition by which to decide what occupations are professions. Indeed, such an approach appears to have little value. Using the term 'profession' also gives the impression that an occupation to which it is applied is a homogeneous 'whole', but many years ago Bucher and Strauss (1966:186) developed the idea that professions are 'loose amalgamations of segments pursuing different objectives in different manners and more or less deliberately held together under a common name at a particular period in history'. The following different roles suggest that adult education was a loose amalgamation of roles in teaching adults, subdividing and forming new occupations. I want to suggest that there are at least eighteen such roles:

1 teacher/facilitator;
2 teaching assistant;
3 supervisor;
4 trainer/coach;
5 mentor;
6 counsellor/adviser;
7 administrator;
8 assessor;
9 researcher;
10 trainer of teachers/trainers;
11 author of learning materials;
12 programme/curriculum planner;
13 educational policy maker;
14 programme administrator;
15 programme technical staff;

16 consultant and evaluator;
17 retailer/marketer;
18 manager.

The first ten roles are those that have direct contact with the learners, while the second group are at least one stage removed from them. Moreover, the education of adults has always demanded many different roles from its practitioners, as early writers on the subject also suggested. For instance, Newman (1979) characterized the multifarious roles of adult educators as:

- entrepreneurs – they have to establish courses and then ensure that there are sufficient students to make them viable;
- wheeler-dealers – they have to overcome all the problems of entrepreneurs employed in a bureaucratic education service;
- administrators – they are responsible for planning programmes and employing staff;
- managers – their job is to manage the part-time staff and the educational premises;
- animators – they have to make things happen;
- troubleshooters – they have to deal with the multitude of problems that complex organizations like adult education institutes create;
- experts on method – they might be called upon to provide guidance and assistance to part-time adult education staff;
- campaigners – since adult education, as a marginal branch of education, is always under threat.

It is quite significant that Newman did not include teaching among these roles. Hence, it may be concluded that for some full-time staff in local education authority adult education, teaching was a fairly insignificant part of their work.

However, models about the process of professionalization might also be useful in order to guide our thinking about what happened in education towards the end of the twentieth century. Following a number of attempts to describe the process of professionalization, for example Caplow (1954) and Greenwood (1957), one that was very widely accepted was Wilensky's (1964). He suggested that as occupations professionalize, they undergo a sequence of structural changes that, while not invariant, form a progression:

- The occupation becomes full-time.
- It establishes a training school, which it later seeks to associate with universities.
- It forms its own professional association, which seeks:
  i to define the core tasks of the occupation;

    ii   to create a cosmopolitan perspective to the practice of the occupation;

    iii to compete with neighbouring occupations in order to establish an area of exclusive competence;

    iv to seek legal support for the protection of the job territory.

- It publishes its own code of ethics to assure the public that it will service its needs.

Since the growth of lifelong learning and the incorporation of a great deal of continuing education in mainstream education, together with the impetus of the Dearing Report, we can see that the more traditional picture of adult education has been replaced by one in which educators of adults are certainly undergoing a process of professionalization – and the focus is on the central tenets of teaching. Many of these points are now quite central to the everyday practice of higher and further education. Most universities and colleges run their own in-house training and have staff development officers who are responsible for it. There are now other occupations that fill the roles that traditional adult educators carried out a quarter of a century ago, such as counsellors and advisers, marketing officers, managers, troubleshooters, and so on

From semi-profession to the beginnings of professionalization

The education of adults, like most other branches of education in the United Kingdom, except initial education, was slow to produce a national pre-service teacher training scheme. While it was hoped that this would arise from developments in the United Kingdom, which we shall discuss shortly, it now appears to have been rather idealistic even when in-service training was beginning to occur nationally. Campbell (1977) and Caldwell (1981) both indicate that a similar situation prevailed in North America. Indeed, many who entered adult education on a full-time basis, let alone those who are part-time teachers, had no qualification in the education of adults at all – their teaching qualifications, if they had any, being in the education of children. Hence, it is possible to see that the discussions that emerged about the differences between andragogy and pedagogy had practical relevance since, while there are common elements, there were enough significant differences to raise questions about the appropriateness of a pedagogic qualification for teaching adults.

Training for adult education teachers was raised as early as the 1919 report (Smith, 1919), when it was suggested that more opportunities should be provided for training (para. 261) and that such teachers 'should have adequate remuneration and a reasonable degree of financial security' (para. 271). Thereafter, tutor training occupied the minds of adult educators on a number of occasions (see Legge, 1991:59–73 for a summary). Peers also noted that

> [t]he matter was raised again by the Adult Education Committee of the Board of Education in a report published in 1922 (The Recruitment, Training and Remuneration of Teachers). In a report published by the Carnegie United Kingdom Trust in 1928, the result of an enquiry undertaken jointly by the British Institute of Adult Education and the Tutor's Association, the problem of training was discussed more fully and an account was given of existing experiments. Finally, after some years of discussion by a subcommittee of the Universities Council for Adult Education, the whole ground was surveyed again with some thoroughness in a report published in 1954 (Tutors and their Training).
>
> (1958:217)

Peers (ibid.:223) claimed that training for adult education should be a major activity for all university extra-mural departments, but this suggestion was slow to be adopted and for a while after the 1954 report, tutor training ceased to occupy a significant place in the concerns of adult education. However, there were movements in the late 1960s to initiate training schemes, and the East Midlands Regional Advisory Council for Further Education introduced the first in 1969, which had three stages (Elsdon, 1970): an introduction, a more advanced course and, finally, a certificate course which was to be validated by the University of Nottingham. In 1973 the Russell Report actually made reference to the need for adult education staff to receive training. This scheme was introduced, a description of which was provided by Bestwick and Chadwick (1977). It subsequently assumed greater significance since it was the model that the Advisory Council for the Supply and Training of Teachers used for its recommendations. Until this time there was little research into the training needs of part-time adult education staff, but by the early 1980s this topic had become a more significant issue, as was apparent from the number of research publications on the topic (see L.C. Martin, 1981; Handley, 1981; Graham *et al.*, 1982).

It was also at this time that the UK government created the Advisory Committee on the Supply and Training of Teachers under the chairmanship of Professor N. Haycocks, which issued three reports. The first, in late 1977, concerned itself with the training of full-time further education staff and recommended a two-year part-time Certificate of Education (Further Education) course, with a qualification to be awarded at the end of the first year for those who did not wish to progress to the second year. This first year was to be more practical but was intended to be planned in conjunction with the second-year centre in order to ensure continuity.

There was a similar movement in the United States although by no means as comprehensive (see Brookfield, 1988). Lindeman (1938), for instance, advocated that all students training to be school teachers should also study 'one unit of adult education covering one whole academic year' (quoted in Brookfield, 1988:96). Overstreet and Overstreet (1941) noted that most adult educators had been trained by experience, and by the end of the 1940s there was concern being expressed about the extent to which adult education was a profession and the type of training necessary for this (Hallenbeck, 1948). By 1964, Houle could write about the emergence of graduate study in American adult education in the United States, although it is still clear that the greater part of this study was in-service rather than pre-service, and theoretical rather than practical.

In March 1978 the Haycocks Committee published its second report, the subject of which was the training of part-time staff in further and adult education and the training of full-time staff in adult education. This report commenced by reviewing the then current provision for training for adult educators and noted that the College of Preceptors and the City & Guilds of London Institute courses provided a considerable amount of training at that time. This was especially true of the City & Guilds of London Institute further education teachers' course (CGLI 730), which had attracted some 3,000 candidates in 1975 and 1976. About half of those were tutors in branches of education outside further and adult education, notably the health service professions, Her Majesty's Forces and industry. Nursing certainly took advantage of this course for many years, although the Panel of Assessors for District Nursing withdrew recognition of it as a qualifying route for practical work teachers since it tended to be orientated towards further education rather than specifically orientated towards the professional clinical situation. Nevertheless, this course did attract 700 from the ranks of the part-time staff of further and adult education, but it was recognized that it was predominantly a further education course, and the City & Guilds of London Institute subsequently devised a new course (CGLI 942) that was piloted in London in 1982.

The Advisory Committee's second report focused upon the East Midlands Regional scheme and noted that this was already being regarded as a model upon which the North West Region was considering constructing its own training programme. Finally, the committee recommended that there should be a coherent scheme of initial training for all teachers working at post-school level, which should lead to the award of Certificate of Education (Further Education) and to qualified teacher status, although this was more fully developed in a subsequent report.

The Haycocks Committee then went on to outline its proposal for this scheme, which was a three-stage scheme similar to the East Midlands scheme. The first stage, it was recommended, should be widely available, as an induction, and should preferably be undertaken prior to employ-

Table 14.1 The recommended content for Stage I courses

- Motives and expectations of teachers and students
- Setting aims and objectives
- Introduction to learning theory
- Planning learning situations
- Introduction to teaching aids
- Introduction to lesson
- Evaluation

ment. However, it was recognized that this was perhaps idealistic, and so it was suggested that this initial stage might be offered during the first two terms of teaching. While this proposal appeared more realistic, it had to be recognized that new teachers do find preparation time-consuming, so it might not be as realistic as it appeared. Table 14.1 records the suggested content of this initial course, which was to involve thirty-six hours of attendance. In addition, it was suggested that new part-time teachers should have a mentor who would work closely with them.

The second stage of the recommended course was to be more advanced and involve the classroom and thirty-six hours of supervised teaching practice. This amount of supervised teaching practice certainly placed the emphasis of the course on practical teaching but there was little doubt that it was both an expensive and a time-consuming recommendation. Each of the teaching modules required between eight and twelve hours of attendance at lectures and seminars, etc. Initially it was considered that some of this might actually be reduced by using resource-based packages, which was clearly an interesting suggestion, although the final report did not include this suggestion. The Open University did, however, propose such a distance education course; the draft scheme was published in 1982 and its content included three booklets:

1 adult learners: needs, motivations and expectations;
2 adult learners: responding to need;
3 a further reference booklet containing fifteen short papers on different but relevant topics.

The Stage II courses were to be pitched at about the same level as the well-established City & Guilds of the London Institute Further Education Teachers' Certificate course 730. The revised course (City & Guilds, 1978) included the topic areas shown in Table 14.2. This course also had a supervised teaching practice, so that it approximated even more closely to the Stage II courses. While the City & Guilds actually piloted a new course (CGLI 942) at this time that was specifically orientated to Stage II of training for adult education, the curriculum for the 730 course remained substantially unaltered over the next ten years.

Table 14.2 The recommended content for Stage II courses

- Setting objectives for teaching
- Psychology of learning in post-adolescent stages of life
- Teaching methods with post-school students
- Audio-visual aids
- Teaching specialist subjects
- Context of further and adult education
- Principles of learning
- Principles of teaching strategy
- Learning resources
- Course organization and curriculum development
- Assessment
- Communication
- The teacher's role in relation to students in further education

The third stage of this training, the Advisory Committee recommended, should lead to full certification, equivalent to a full-time first year of an undergraduate course of study, and should be provided by institutions in which 'there is a substantial nucleus of experienced staff who had both the experience and the qualification to teach it'. In addition, the Advisory Committee recognized the diversity of adult education and made the following recommendations for the training of full-time staff:

- new, untrained teachers entering full-time teaching in adult education should embark upon the first stage of the full-time Further Education Certificate recommended in the first Haycocks Report;
- for those trained as teachers in sectors other than further education, a six-week part-time conversion course;
- for part-time adult educators who have taken Stages I and II, a Stage III course leading to a Certificate in Education (FE);
- a one-year full-time, or equivalent part-time, course for those who possess the Certificate in Education (FE) and who wish to work as organizers and administrators in adult education – leading to an advanced diploma in adult education or higher degree.

Thus, it may be seen that no division between further education and adult education existed in the recommendations for initial training at all three levels and that it was only at post-certificate level that adult education was regarded as a specialism. This was one of the criticisms made by the Advisory Council for Adult and Continuing Education (1978) in its formal response to the recommendations, but in retrospect it is clear that adult education was not regarded as a separate sector of education. In addition, it criticized the Haycocks Committee for being too narrow, for trying to combine forms of training that ought to be separated and for omitting any consideration of using the university departments of adult education in initial training. These were all valid criticisms of an important but conceptually confused report and also reflect the level of concern about training in adult and further education at this period, something from which the European Council's 2002 proposals might learn.

As a result of these reports, colleges, once they had been approved by their Regional Advisory Council, were able to submit their courses to the Council for National Academic Awards (the Council was disbanded during the period in which the polytechnics were being granted university status) for validation. Initially, the Further Education Board received mainly submissions that led to a certificate of education, but during the first four or five years, courses were developed and submitted leading to first degrees, postgraduate certificates and higher degrees. All these courses concentrated on full-time staff, or at least upon those who were teaching at least ten hours per week, although a few demanded only five hours' class contact, but this tended to be the exception. Since the courses were devoted almost exclusively to further education, many adult educators were excluded by the teaching requirement.

In the first instance, only one university (the University of Surrey) began offering postgraduate training in the education of adults. Surrey allowed for teachers of adults to be trained together irrespective of whether they came from adult, further or higher education or from the professions. Surrey was also the first university to include teaching in higher education in its courses, something that was not to happen more widely until after the Dearing Committee's recommendations. This university also introduced both Master's and doctoral programmes in the education of adults from this period. Only a few years later, other universities were embarking on the same route. Basically, Surrey's innovation was to introduce a set of qualifications for teachers in post-compulsory education parallel to those for school education.

Much of the preceding discussion reflects developments that occurred before a greater emphasis was placed on competency and National Vocational Qualifications. Even universities considered adopting a National Vocational Qualification approach. Consequently, the training of adult educators could not remain outside these developments, as the City & Guilds showed by undertaking pilot studies of a competence-based 730 course, although at that time it did not have a National Council of Vocational Qualifications approval. However, this was the direction that training had been taking from the outset, since most of the curricula described above had been framed in terms of behavioural objectives.

However, as Last and Chown (1993:234–236) reported, the Further Education Unit was to produce 'an entirely new competence based qualification framework for the sector' which did have NCVQ approval. While they were not entirely happy with the approach, they reported that they were preparing their own curriculum for the training of adult educators, which would be much more orientated to the current competence-based approach. They suggested that this was in accord with some of the best practices in adult education, such as reflective learning, in a manner espoused by Schön (1983), and so it might well be asked what were considered to be the best practices of educators of adults. Many of the answers came from analyses of the roles that they were actually performing, although it might have been better to train new recruits into the role that they might play in the future, rather than the one that current practitioners were actually performing. However, there were a multitude of such lists, and Campbell wrote:

> Such lists are well nigh endless, indeed tiresome – but useful to a degree. Out of this formidable, though by no means exhaustive array of analyses it is possible to identify three distinct, significant clusters of competences marking the ideal adult educator which can be taken as generalized goals for training. The first is a conviction within the adult educator of the potentiality for growth of adults, and a strong personal commitment to adult education exemplified by the extension of his own education. The willingness to accept others' ideas, the encouragement of freedom of thought and expression is fundamental as is a dynamic rather than a static view of the field of adult education. The second is the possession of certain skills – of writing and speaking, certainly – but also the capacity to lead groups effectively, to direct complex administrative activity, and to exercise a flair in the development of programs. Finally, the adult educator must understand the conditions under which adults learn, their motivation for learning, the nature of the community and its structure. Underlying all of these, and essential, is an understanding of oneself undergirded by a sustaining personal philosophy.
>
> (1977:58)

Tough (1979:181–183) echoed many of these points in his discussion of the characteristics of the ideal helper as warm and loving, having confidence in the learner's ability, being prepared always to enter into a genuine dialogue with the learner, having a strong motivation to help and being an open and growing person. Both Campbell and Tough reflected the humanistic tradition, which was prevalent in adult education but less strong in other areas of the education of adults. For instance, Gibbs and Durbridge (1976) asked Open University full-time staff tutors what they looked for in effective part-time tutors. The replies were reported under the following headings: knowledge of the subject matter; ability to handle the subject matter; general teaching skills; classroom skills; correspondence skills; social competence; academic suitability; values and work rate;

Table 14.3 Competences of an adult educator

- communicate effectively with learners
- develop effective working relationships with learners
- reinforce positive attitudes towards learners
- develop a climate that will encourage learners to participate
- establish a basis for mutual respect with learners
- adjust rate of instruction to the learners' rate of progress
- adjust teaching to accommodate individual and group characteristics
- differentiate between teaching children and teaching adults
- devise instructional categories that will develop the learners' confidence
- maintain the learners' interest in classroom activities
- adjust a programme to respond to the changing needs of learners
- use classrooms and other settings that provide a comfortable learning environment
- recognize learners' potentiality for growth
- place learners at their instructional level
- summarize and review the main points of a lesson or demonstration
- participate in a self-evaluation of teaching effectiveness
- provide continuous feedback to the learners on their educational progress
- select those components of a subject area that are essential to learners
- coordinate and supervise classroom activities
- determine those principles of learning that apply to adults
- demonstrate belief in innovation and experimentation by willingness to try new approaches in the classroom
- plan independent study with learners
- apply knowledge of material and procedures gained from other teachers
- relate classroom activities to the experience of learners.

Source: Mocker and Noble (1981).

administrative competence; interesting style; systematic style; understand-ing style; informal, flexible style. Hence, it may be seen that more empha-sis was placed on teachers and their competences by Open University staff than on the adult educator as a human being who facilitated adult learn-ing. In the United States, Mocker and Noble (1981:45–46) sought to con-struct a full list of competences (Table 14.3), but even they warned their readers that it was neither exhaustive nor a blueprint for training.

At first sight, Mocker and Noble's list appears full and exhaustive, and yet on closer scrutiny there are points that some adult educators may wish to dispute. The values of the person who constructs such an inventory must always be apparent, so that no such list could provide an undisputed basis for devising a curriculum of training. If many lists were consulted, it might be possible to distil out the common factors that might provide something of a foundation, but without an agreed theoretical perspective this approach still fails to provide a problem-free approach.

Recent developments in the professional preparation of educators in both adult education and lifelong learning

The professionalization of educators of adults is no longer a sufficiently significant issue to merit much more than a mention in the British submission to the UNESCO world conference on adult education (National Institute of Adult Continuing Education, 2008b), but it does include the ten pedagogic principles of effective adult pedagogy:

1 It equips learners for life.
2 It engages in valued forms of knowledge.
3 It recognizes prior experience and learning.
4 Learning should be scaffolded, e.g. supported in various ways.
5 Assessment should be congruent with learning.
6 It promotes the active engagement of the learners.
7 It fosters both individual and social processes and outcomes
8 It recognizes the significance of informal learning.
9 It depends on the continuing development of all who are engaged in pedagogic practice.
10 It demands consistent policy frameworks with support for learning as their primary focus.

(summarized from National Institute of Adult Continuing Education, 2008b:129–130)

These principles have emerged from an Economic and Social Research Council research programme on teaching and learning. This programme is an indicator of how far the professionalization process has progressed in the United Kingdom since the Dearing Report (1997) focused on the lack of professionalization of university teachers and the Kennedy Report (1997) focused on the need for greater training in educational guidance and counselling for teachers in further education.

However, there was considerable initial resistance in higher education to the introduction of pre-service or in-service preparation for teaching, and when the National Committee of Inquiry into Higher Education (Dearing, 1997) reported, it focused on the need for higher education to professionalize. Among its recommendations was the following:

> We recommend that the representative bodies, in consultation with the Funding Bodies, should immediately establish a professional Institute for Learning and Teaching in Higher Education. The functions of the Institute would be to accredit programmes of training for higher education teachers; to commission research into learning and teaching practices; and to stimulate innovation.
>
> (Dearing, 1997, Recommendation 14)

286

It recommended that all lecturers should, during their probationary period, be expected to become a member of the Institute as 'higher education teaching needs to have higher status and be regarded as a profession of standing' (para. 14.28). The Institute was expected to accredit programmes of teacher training for higher education. The report recommended not only that these qualifications should be gained during the probationary period but that this should be followed by appropriate in-service training as academics' careers progressed, which should be recognized by the award of a fellowship. Universities have also been encouraged to establish their own centres for teaching and learning, which some have done. However, this is also happening elsewhere in the world; the University of Singapore, for instance, has established a centre that has already run two international conferences on teaching and learning in higher education (Wang *et al.*, 2000, 2002).

In a sense, these recommendations almost premised the separation of teaching and research as university academic responsibilities, something that universities have long resisted – but, as I have argued elsewhere (Jarvis, 1983a), it is difficult to straddle two professions. Consequently, the Institute's development has been slow since many university staff have tended to ignore, or are unaware of, its existence. Nevertheless, we can see how the Dearing Committee returned to the issue of professionalization in its consideration of teaching in higher education and that the roles of teaching and research are themselves being separated in this professionalization process.

In 2003 the government's White Paper *The Future of Higher Education* returned to the subject of professionalism yet again:

> At present, there are no nationally recognized professional standards for teachers in higher education; and many of those who teach have never received any training to do so. In order that teaching in higher education is treated seriously as a profession in its own right, and that teachers are given the skills that they need, we expect that national professional standards will be agreed by 2004–5, through the proposed new teaching quality academy.
>
> (Department for Education and Skills, 2003: para. 4.14)

These standards are to be competence based, and as from 2006 the government expected all new teaching staff to obtain a teaching qualification. The government is asking the Higher Education Funding Council for England to make more funding available 'to those institutions that can demonstrate that it will be spent on rewards for their best teaching staff' (para. 4.23). Indeed, those departments that produce quality teaching will be declared centres of excellence (para. 4.28), and many such centres have been given this accolade. The roles of teaching and research have now been completely divided, since we are also seeing the development of Master's degrees in research being supported by research councils.

The rationale for this emphasis on good teaching is clearly outlined in the White Paper:

> All students have the right to good teaching, and some may not be able to exercise their choices as easily as others – perhaps because they want to study a very specialized course, or because they want to live at home. So as well as making sure that students can make well-informed choices, we must guarantee good-quality teaching for everybody. This means being clearer about the teaching and learning practices and students and governments, as the principle funders, have the right to expect from all higher education providers. All providers should set down their expectations of teachers with reference to national professional standards; should ensure that staff are trained to teach and continue to develop professionally; should have effective quality assurance systems and robust degree standards; and should value good teaching and reward good teachers.
>
> (para. 4.13)

Despite a confusion of logic in respect to choice of courses in the above quotation, it is clear that the professionalization of teaching is very much part of the government's agenda. Rewarding of good teaching has been practised in some higher education institutions in the United Kingdom for some time. For instance, I attended an award ceremony for good teaching at the University of Maryland in the mid-1980s and it is interesting that my memorandum to my own university vice-chancellor at that time commending the practice did not even merit a reply, but now the university has a Centre of Excellence in Teaching and Learning.

In the same way as the universities have been developing their training programmes, so has the emphasis on professionalization of further education teachers been strengthened, and this has also been assisted by the fact that closer cooperation between further education and the schools sector has necessitated the former developing a system of professional preparation that would lead to a recognized teacher status. From 2007 the Institute for Learning is conferring Qualified Teacher Learning and Skills (QTLS) status on appropriately qualified teachers. The Institute of Learning has also issued its own principles of continuing professional development, which can be summarized as follows:

- Professional development is a continuous process that adds value to a teacher practitioner's career.
- Professional practice requires reflective practice.

288

- Teacher practitioners should identify their own professional needs.
- Teacher practitioners should set measurable objectives in conjunction with the needs of their employer.
- There should be a balance between formal and informal continuing professional development activities.
- Professional development is an integral part of employment.

In order to gain qualified status, teachers must have completed not only the first two years of the initial training course, like the City & Guilds initial further education teacher training programmes, but also a level 3 course. The City & Guilds has introduced a 7303 course which prepared teachers to teach in the lifelong learning sector. The course objectives are:

- to have an integrative approach to theory and practice;
- to be able to reflect on past experience;
- to build up knowledge of the principles of teaching, learning, assessment and evaluation;
- to develop communication and interpersonal skills;
- to develop an awareness of one's own professional role and the value and legal requirements for practising it.

This course requires at least thirty hours' class contact time plus two written assignments. There are also other City & Guilds qualifications at the fourth and even fifth levels in teaching, learning and development, such as a Certificate in Delivering Learning (City & Guilds 7402), one in Learning and Development, Awards, Roles and Responsibilities (City & Guilds 7318) and the Certificate in Further Education Teaching (City & Guilds 7407).

The concern for the professional preparation of educators of adults is something that is occurring throughout the world of education. Not only has there been the ESRC programme in the United Kingdom, there have been Grundtvig programmes funded by the European Union, and conferences on the professional preparation of educators of adults have also been organized.

However, there is one major question that has to be debated when we examine this process of professionalization. In order to make awards, most of the qualifications gained come as a result of the amount of teaching and learning, and now it is time to return to the questions about the nature of good teaching.

It is significant to note that while the terminology of professionalization of teaching has been frequently employed, some of the main characteristics of professionalization have not been focused upon greatly, such as ethics. The focus in this age of managerialism and targets has been on pedagogy and teaching competency – although there are now opportunities to recognize the expertise of teachers in annual award ceremonies for good teaching.

Conclusion

The theme running through this chapter has been that educating adults might be conceptualized as an occupation that is continually in process of professionalization. However, the role has never been a single, homogeneous 'whole'; rather, it has been a variety of different roles that have been held together at a moment in history. As the demands of the role have become greater, it has been impossible for the segments to remain together, so that we have witnessed segmentation, the creation of new occupations and the generation of a multitude of opportunities for professional preparation and development of educators in all the new occupations formed. Now teaching is being regarded as a single role, but the United Kingdom's Open University is already offering courses in the preparation and development of distance educators, so that teaching itself is subdividing. The wheel is continually reinventing itself, and in each instance the customers are becoming a more clearly defined target. The process will no doubt continue for some time to come. However, what continues to be central to a quality educational service for adults is a professional staff who are sufficiently funded to be able to respond to the learning needs of all the people who wish to enhance their learning throughout their lives.

SELECTED FURTHER READING

General

Jarvis, P. (1999) *An International Dictionary of Adult and Continuing Education*, 2nd ed. London: Routledge
A thorough introduction to many of the major concepts in the field. It contains over 3,500 references and provides a background against which adult and continuing education may be studied.

Jarvis, P. (2006, 2007, 2008) *Lifelong Learning and the Learning Society*. London: Routledge (a trilogy)
The first of these volumes is on human learning, the second on the relationship between the learning society and globalization, and the third is an examination of citizenship and democracy in the light of a critical evaluation of the Enlightenment project.

Jarvis, P. (ed.) (2001) *Twentieth Century Thinkers in Adult and Continuing Education*, 2nd ed. London: Routledge
This book contains studies of some of the work of some of the most influential writers of the twentieth century in adult and continuing education.

Jarvis, P. with Griffin, C. (ed.) (2003) *Adult and Continuing Education: Major Themes in Education*. London: Routledge (5 vols)
These five volumes present a picture of the whole field of adult and continuing education from the time of the Enlightenment to the end of the twentieth century: 164 extracts from original texts plus editorial comment.

Jarvis, P. (ed.) (2009c) *The Routledge International Handbook of Lifelong Learning*. London: Routledge
This book contains forty-five chapters, written by leading specialists in the field, about every aspect of lifelong learning. It is the most comprehensive volume produced on the subject.

1 The person as learner

Hall, E. (1976) *Beyond Culture*. New York: Random House
This is a nicely written book from an anthropological perspective that throws a lot of light on relationships and learning. It questions commonly accepted ideas.

Jarvis, P. (2009a) *Learning to be a Person in Society*. London: Routledge
Once we accept that learning is about the whole person, it is possible to understand that learning can also find a place within all the human sciences. This book begins to explore the idea that whole persons are learned beings and that learning is both a lifelong and life-wide process.

Nelson, K. (2007) *Young Minds in Social Worlds*. Cambridge, MA: Harvard University Press
A very clear introduction to learning in early childhood – well written and extremely informative. It is a book that will help educators of adults understand some of the basics of learning in society.

O'Loughlin, M. (2006) *Embodiment and Education*. Dordrecht: Springer
This is a very clear book on the place of the body and the physical sense in the learning process.

Schuller, T., Preston, J., Hammond, C., Bassett-Grundy, A. and Bynner, J. (2004) *The Benefits of Learning*. London: RoutledgeFalmer
This is an excellent contemporary study of human learning and the way individuals benefit from learning itself. Based on recent research in the United Kingdom, it points to some of the contemporary debates in educational policy.

Tomasello, M. (1999) *The Cultural Origins of Human Cognition*. Cambridge, MA: Harvard University Press
This book recognizes the evolutionary and historical aspects of the human being while it examines the cognitive processes. It is a good introduction to locating learning within a cultural and psychological context.

2 The learning society

Beck, U. (2000) *What Is Globalization?* Cambridge: Polity
A clear sociological introduction to the process of globalization illustrating both its threats and opportunities. An important introduction, and easy to read.

Coffield, F. (2000) *Differing Visions of a Learning Society* (2 vols). Bristol: Polity
These two volumes contain thirteen research reports and two essays. The former are reports from the United Kingdom's Economic and Social Research Council research projects on the learning society and the latter are introductions by the editor. They cover a wide range of material and provide an excellent picture of a wide variety of activities in contemporary society.

Field, J. (2002) *Lifelong Learning and the New Educational Order.* Stoke-on-Trent: Trentham
A nice, clear introduction to lifelong learning in society raising some significant questions.

Held, D., McGrew, A., Goldblatt, D. and Perraton, J. (1999) *Global Transformations.* Cambridge: Polity
A more advanced sociological study of the globalization process. It raises many issues and points the reader to some of the complexities of the process.

Husen, T. (1974) *The Learning Society.* London: Methuen
One of the earliest books about the learning society. It was much more idealistic than the world that has emerged; Husen thought that this society would be brought about through the introduction of computers.

Hutchins, R. (1968) *The Learning Society.* Harmondsworth, UK: Penguin
The first book on the learning society – idealistic and humanistic. Hutchins thought that part-time education would be available for everybody as a result of recent technological innovations.

Jarvis, P. (2007) *Globalisation, Lifelong Learning and the Learning Society: Sociological Perspectives.* London: Routledge
This is the second volume of a trilogy based on lifelong learning and the learning society; the first book was concerned with human learning and the third with democracy. Many of the ideas in this second chapter were first worked out for the book on globalization, where there is a much more developed argument than the one contained in this chapter.

Lengrand, P. (1975) *An Introduction to Lifelong Education.* London: Croom Helm
The author of this book was at the forefront to promoted lifelong education both in UNESCO and in Europe. It is an easy book to read and raises, quite succinctly, many important questions.

Longworth, N. (1999) *Making Lifelong Learning Work: Learning Cities for a Learning Century*. London: Kogan Page

Longworth, N. (2006) *Learning Cities, Learning Regions, Learning Communities*. London: Routledge
Longworth writes extremely well and clearly. He has examined many cities and regions that call themselves learning cities and learning regions and he reports on the way that they have developed. He explains fully the processes of development and explains fully the characteristics of learning communities.

3 Education and learning

Delors, J. (chair) (1995) *Learning: The Treasure within Paris*. Paris: UNESCO
Produced at a time when lifelong education was becoming regarded as little more than an instrument for the knowledge economy, this was an important corrective. It claimed that there are four pillars of learning: learning to know, to do, to be and to live together. Unfortunately, it omitted the ecological dimension – but this is a very clear and important document.

Department for Innovation, Universities and Skills (2009) *The Learning Revolution*. London: The Stationery Office
This is the British government's White Paper on informal learning. It seeks to combine all informal learning opportunities in one category which is separate from vocational education. There is little revolutionary here; it is a recognition that despite the government's vocational concerns, there has been a great deal of innovation in informal education in the United Kingdom – some of it, it must be said, with active government support.

Faure, E. (chair) (1972) *Learning to Be*. Paris: UNESCO
This was UNESCO's first report on lifelong education. It is an important document that laid the foundations for much thought about lifelong education thereafter, and it was not until the Delors Report that UNESCO produced another of comparable standard.

Freire, P. (1972) *Pedagogy of the Oppressed*. Harmondsworth, UK: Penguin
This was one of the earliest of Freire's writings and perhaps the most incisive. Here he focuses on the poor and how they can learn, become conscientized and learn to play an active part in the world. It reflects Freire's radical Christian philosophy and demonstrates the place of education in the community.

Horton, M. (1990) *The Long Haul.* New York: Anchor Books
This is Horton's autobiography – assisted by Judith and Robert Kohl. It contains an exciting story of a leading radical adult educator whose teaching was to influence the civil rights movement in the United States.

The Edinburgh Papers: Reclaiming Social Purpose in Community Education (2008) University of Edinburgh, Learning for Democracy Group
These are the papers that were produced for a conference in Scotland on the state of community education. They illustrate how weak it has become, and examine some relevant policy issues.

4 Learning

Belenky, M., Clinchy, B., Goldberger, N. and Tarule, J. (1986) *Women's Ways of Knowing.* New York: Basic Books
This is a thorough study of 135 women and their ways of knowing. It throws considerable light on the social context of learning, and while all the respondents are women, the conditions discussed could also refer to men.

Illeris, K. (2007) *How We Learn.* London: Routledge
This is the update of an earlier book, Illeris's *Three Dimensions of Learning* (2002), and he examines the work of a number of contemporary theorists as he seeks to explain how we learn. It is an excellent study of learning.

Jarvis, P. (2006) *Towards a Comprehensive Theory of Human Learning.* London: Routledge
This is the first volume of the trilogy mentioned at the beginning of this section. It updates my work on learning and seeks to contextualize it in the light of other theories of learning. In another sense, it is the beginnings of a philosophical study of learning that will be pursued in great detail in subsequent work.

Jarvis, P., Holford, J. and Griffin, C. (2003) *The Theory and Practice of Learning*, 2nd ed. London: Routledge
This is a basic textbook that provides an introduction to all the major contemporary theories of learning.

Jarvis, P. and Parker, S. (2005) *Human Learning: An Holistic Approach.* London: Routledge
In this book the editors have asked a number of theorists from different disciplines to write about learning from the perspective of their own discipline. Not all the relevant disciplines were included but this was the first time any book endeavoured to examine learning from a multidisciplinary perspective.

Kolb, D. (1984) *Experiential Learning*. Englewood Cliffs, NJ: Prentice Hall
This book highlights Kolb's thinking about experiential learning, tracing the history of the idea through Dewey and Lewin. It is a clearly written book that has become quite seminal.

Sennett, R. (2008) *The Craftsman*. London: Penguin
This book is not by a learning theorist and neither is it specifically about learning but there are many important discussions here about learning skills and contextualizing this within discussions of the Enlightenment.

Sternberg, R. (1997) *Thinking Styles*. Cambridge: Cambridge University Press
This is a carefully constructed study of how we think, written by a leading psychologist. We have noted his styles in this text of the chapter, but the whole book repays careful study.

5 Perspectives on learning theory

Illeris, K. (ed.) (2009) *Contemporary Theories of Learning*. London: Routledge
Illeris has edited a book in which sixteen theories (one chapter double-authored), including his own, are written by leading contemporary theorists; not all of the chapters were new for this volume. Illeris lets the authors speak for themselves.

Vygotsky, L. (1986) *Thought and Language*. Cambridge, MA: MIT Press
This is an important book about the foundations of learning as researched by Vygotsky. While it is not specifically about adult learning, it does help develop our understanding of his work.

6 Developments in learning theory

Blakemore, S.-J. and Frith, U. (2005) *The Learning Brain*. Oxford: Blackwell
A readable introduction to the relationship between learning and our knowledge of the brain.

Gardner, H. (2007) *Five Minds for the Future*. Boston, MA: Harvard Business Press
This is an easy-to-read, quite personal book in which Gardner explores that the way that he believes thought will develop in the coming years.

Goleman, D. (1995) *Emotional Intelligence*. London: Bloomsbury
Goleman writes extremely well; he is a journalist as well as an academic.

This is the first of his studies of the emotions and it begins to open up for our thinking ways in which we learn emotionally. The book also recognizes the neurological implications of the emotions.

Housden, S. (2007) *Reminiscence and Lifelong Learning*. Leicester: National Institute of Adult Continuing Education
This is a clear discussion of memory as a major resource for learning in later life; it is both theoretical and practical.

Jarvis, P. (2001) *Learning in Later Life*. London: Croom Helm
This is a succinct introduction to a broad range of topics relating to later life including retirement, wisdom, meaning and spirituality, mental fitness and the fourth age.

Jarvis, P. (2009a) *Learning to be a Person in Society*. London: Routledge
This book utilizes a great deal of current research into learning and, in a sense, demonstrates ways in which studies of learning could develop. It is also philosophical, and this points the way to a future study in the philosophy of learning. It is comprehensive.

Withnall, A. (2010) *Improving Learning in Later Life*. London: Routledge
This is a research report from the Teaching and Learning Research Programme; it is one of eighteen projects in the programme. This is a clear research report of the fact that older people learn, and in this book we can hear them talking about their learning. The book is well written and clear, although its referencing to the wider field could have been more thorough. It is an important study in this field.

7 Teaching adults

Jarvis, P. (1997) *Ethics and the Education of Adults in Late Modern Society*. Leicester: National Institute of Adult Continuing Education
This book is an introduction to the ethics of teaching. It introduces the reader to some of the basic theories of ethics and shows how teaching is a moral activity.

Macfarlane, B. (2004) *Teaching with Integrity*. London: RoutledgeFalmer
This book explores the nature of integrity and applies it to many different teaching activities. It is clearly written and accessible.

Strain, J., Barnett, R. and Jarvis, P. (eds) (2009) *Universities, Ethics and the Professions*. London: Routledge
This book has four discrete parts, each examining an aspect of the place of universities and teaching in contemporary society. Each part has an introduction that highlights the points it covers. There are a wide variety

of perspectives that illustrate the difficulties in looking and the ethical nature of education itself.

Strike, K. and Soltis, J. (1985) *The Ethics of Teaching*. New York: Teachers College
A philosophical introduction to the ethics of teaching starting with a long chapter about the nature of this inquiry and then examining four major issues. The book concludes with two sets of case studies and disputes.

8 The processes of teaching

Brookfield, S. (1995) *Becoming a Critically Reflective Teacher*. San Francisco: Jossey-Bass
This is a well-written, practical book – informative, insightful and experiential. There is a lot of worthwhile material in this volume.

Freire, P. (1998) *Pedagogy of Freedom*. Lanham, MD: Rowman & Littlefield
This is one of Freire's best books – published posthumously – and it is an excellent introduction to Freire's philosophy of teaching in which we are introduced to the humanity and democracy of the teaching and learning relationship.

Jarvis, P. (ed.) *The Theory and Practice of Teaching*, 2nd ed. London: Routledge
This edited version covers a very wide range of teaching approaches and methods and is written by practitioners who have been involved in the education of adults for the whole of their careers.

Newman, M. (2006) *Teaching Defiance*. San Francisco: Jossey-Bass
Michael Newman represents traditional critical adult education, and this book is about the way in which he worked with trade unions and other groups to help them learn active citizenship. It is extremely well written.

Palmer, P. (1993) *To Know as We Are Known*. New York: HarperCollins
This is an excellent introduction into teaching, showing profound insight in which the author sees education as a spiritual journey. While he has written this from a Christian perspective, it has attracted readers of all faiths and of no faith at all.

Rogers, J. (2001) *Adults Learning*, 4th ed. Buckingham, UK: Open University Press
This is an informative, easy-to-read and practical book about teaching adults. The fourth edition brings up to date a well-established introductory textbook.

9 Theoretical perspectives on teaching

Brookfield, S. (1990) *The Skillful Teacher*. San Francisco: Jossey-Bass
This is a rather personalized approach to teaching in which Brookfield describes the way that he plays his role as an educator of adults. It is well written, easy to read and contains a full bibliography

Bruner, J. (1968) *Toward a Theory of Instruction*. New York: W.W. Norton
This is a short book that became something of a classic. While it is orientated to the teaching of children, there is much insight here that is also valuable to educators of adults.

Dewey, J. (1938) *Experience and Education*. London: Collier Macmillan
This short book was written after Dewey's own experiments with progressive education. While it is orientated towards initial education, the foundation of experiential education can be discovered here and many ideas appropriate to the education of adults are embedded in this work.

Illich, I. (1973) *Deschooling Society*. Harmondsworth, UK: Penguin
This is one of Illich's many books illustrating his concerns with institutionalization and professionalization. It is not a 'methods book', but it does outline some very early thinking about the learning society, as well as providing a critical perspective on teaching.

Palmer, P. (1998) *The Courage to Teach*. San Francisco: Jossey-Bass
Perhaps the most moving and profound book about teaching that I have ever read; the humanity of the writer comes across in every word. It is a very personal and challenging book.

10 Distance education and open learning

Holmberg, B. (1989) *Theory and Practice of Distance Education*. London: Routledge
This is an excellent introduction to many of the issues about distance education. It is practical and introduces readers to Holmberg's own attempts to make distance education a two-way interactive process.

Jochems, W., van Merrienboer, J. and Koper, R. (eds) (2004) *Integrated E-Learning*. London: RoutledgeFalmer
This is one of a series on the developments in open and distance education. The editors are all based at the Open University of the Netherlands and they explore a number of relevant issues about the relationship between technological and social changes and about how these changes can contribute to teaching and learning. The book is also both theoretical and practical.

Peters, O. (2002) *Distance Education in Transition*. Oldenburg, Germany: Bibliotheks- und Informationssystems der Universität Oldenburg
Otto Peters has always been one of the leading theorists in distance education and in this book he develops his thinking into the realms of e-learning. This is an important study.

Selwyn, N., Gorard, S. and Furlong, J. (2006) *Adult Learning in the Digital Age*. London: Routledge
This is a book written around a research report about adults and the way that they learn through the use of information and communication technology (ICT). It is a study worth reading to get a feeling of the rather intermittent use of ICTs in the present world.

11 Assessing and evaluating

Mehrens, W. and Lehmann, I. (1991) *Measurement and Evaluation in Education and Psychology*, 4th ed. Fort Worth, TX: Holt, Rinehart and Winston
This is a full, technical text about the ways to measure and evaluate. It is written as a textbook with many examples and illustrations.

Rowntree, D. (1977) *Assessing Students: How Shall We Know Them?* London: Harper & Row
A well-written and comprehensive book. Despite its date, it still raises very many significant issues for those of us who have to assess.

12 Curriculum theory and programme planning

Cervero, R. and Wilson, A. (1994) *Planning Responsibly for Adult Education*. San Francisco: Jossey-Bass
This is an excellent introduction to American thinking about programme planning. Realistically, it includes discussion about power, politics and funding, and its relevance is wider than just the American scene.

Wang, V.C.X. (ed.) (2008) *Curriculum Development for Adult Learners in the Global Community* (Vol. 1 of 2 vols). Malabar, FL: Krieger
This is a basic book that introduces readers to the basic theories of curriculum current in US adult education; it is not really global.

13 Practice, theory, research and policy

Black, T. (1999) *Doing Quantitative Research in the Social Sciences*. London: Sage
This is a very thorough statistically orientated textbook in six parts and twenty-two chapters in which the research design, the actual measurement techniques and the statistics are all integrated.

Denzin, N. and Lincoln, Y. (eds) (1989) *Handbook of Qualitative Research.* Thousand Oaks, CA: Sage
This is a very comprehensive introduction to qualitative research. It has thirty-five chapters covering almost every aspect of qualitative research. Any educational researcher will find this book invaluable.

Jarvis, P. (1999) *The Practitioner Researcher.* San Francisco: Jossey-Bass
This is a small basic book that uses experiential learning theory to question the relationship between theory and practice; it also demonstrates a relationship between research and teaching. It is a practical text for those wishing to undertake research in their own practice situation.

National Institute of Adult Continuing Education (2008) *CONFINTEA VI: United Kingdom National Report.* Leicester: NIACE
Every country participating in the 2009 World Conference on Adult Education will have produced a national report about the state of adult education in that country. This report is given as an example; it is a select research report.

Nutley, S., Walter, I. and Davies, H. (2007) *Using Evidence.* Bristol: Policy Press
This book discusses the use of evidence and the extent to which it can inform the public services. It is a comprehensive and very thorough study of the ways in which research evidence can be used, but it draws out principles about the ways in which the use of research evidence might be enhanced.

Schuller, T. and Watson, D. (2009) *Learning through Life.* Leicester: NIACE
A report prepared by the National Institute of Adult Continuing Education looking at the future of lifelong learning in the United Kingdom. It provides a strategic framework through which we may assess the development of lifelong learning in the coming years.

Usher, R. and Bryant, I. (1989) *Adult Education as Theory, Practice and Research.* London: Routledge
This book explores the relationship between theory, practice and research. It is an important textbook although slightly dated now.

14 The professional preparation of teachers of adults

Brookfield, S. (ed.) (1988) *Training Educators of Adults.* London: Routledge
This book contains some of the most important essays written in American adult education about the development of training of adult educators in the United States.

Jarvis, P. and Chadwick, A. (eds) (1991) *Training Adult Educators in Western Europe*. London: Routledge
This book contains essays by sixteen adult educators about the development of training of adult educators in their countries. It is now a historical study in the light of the many projects that have been developed in different countries in recent years, and it would be necessary to consult national reports now.

BIBLIOGRAPHY

Abercrombie, NB., Hill, S. and Turner, B. (2000) *Dictionary of Sociology*, 4th ed., London: Penguin.

Adult Learning Australia (updated 23 January 2003) *Learning Towns and Learning Cities*, www.ala.asn.au/cities.html.

Adult Literacy and Basic Skills Unit (n.d.) *Guidelines for Special Development Projects*, London: Adult Literacy and Basic Skills Unit.

Advisory Council for Adult and Continuing Education (1978) *The Training of Adult Education and Part Time Further Education Teachers – A Formal Response from the Advisory Council for Adult and Continuing Education*, Leicester: ACACE.

—— (1979a) *Towards Continuing Education*, Leicester: ACACE.

—— (1979b) *A Strategy for the Basic Education of Adults*, Leicester: ACACE.

—— (1979c) *Links to Learning*, Leicester: ACACE.

—— (1980) *Regional Provision for the Training of Part Time Adult Education Staff*, Leicester: ACACE.

—— (1981) *Protecting the Future for Adult Education*, Leicester: ACACE.

—— (1982a) *Continuing Education from Policies to Practice*, Leicester: ACACE.

—— (1982c) *Prime Use Accommodation for Adult Education*, Leicester: ACACE.

—— (1982d) *Education for Unemployed Adults*, Leicester: ACACE.

—— (1982e) *The Case for a National Development Body for Continuing Education in England and Wales*, Leicester: ACACE.

Aldridge, F. and Tuckett, A. (2008) *Counting the Cost*, Leicester: NIACE.

Alford, H.I. (ed.) (1980) *Power and Conflict in Continuing Education*, Belmont, CA: Wadsworth.

Alheit, P., Bron-Wojciechowska, A., Brugger, E. and Dominicé, P. (eds) (1995) *The Biographical Approach in European Adult Education*, Vienna: Verband Wiener Volksbildung.

Allaway, A.I. (1977) *The Educational Centres Movement, 1909–1977*, NIAE in association with the Educational Centres Association.

Allman, P. (1982) 'New perspectives on the adult: an argument for lifelong education', *International Journal of Lifelong Education* 1 (1): 41–52.

—— (1984) 'Self-help learning and its relevance for learning and development in later life', in Midwinter, E. (ed.) *MutualAid Universities*, London: Croom Helm.

Apps, J.W. (1979) *Problems in Continuing Education*, New York: McGraw-Hill.

Apter, M. (1989) 'Negativism and the sense of identity', in Breakwell, G. (ed.) *Threatened Identities*, London: Wiley.

Argyle, M. (1974) *The Social Psychology of Work*, Harmondsworth, UK: Penguin.

Argyris, C. (1982) *Reasoning. Learning and Action*, San Francisco: Jossey-Bass.

Argyris, C. and Schön, D. (1974) *Theory in Practice: Increasing Professional Effectiveness*, San Francisco: Jossey-Bass.

—— (1978) *Organizational Learning: A Theory of Action Perspective*, Reading, MA: Addison-Wesley.

Aristotle (1925) *Nichomachean Ethics* (trans. David Ross), Oxford: Oxford University Press.

Armstrong, P.F. (1982) 'The "needs-meeting" ideology in liberal adult education', *International Journal of Lifelong Education* 1 (4): 293–321.

Aronowitz, S. (2000) *The Knowledge Factory*, Boston: Beacon Press.

Asia–Europe Meeting (ASEM) (2002) *Lifelong Learning in ASEM Countries: The Way Forward*, Copenhagen: Ministry of Education.

Aslanian, C.B. and Brickell, H.H. (1980) 'Americans in transition: life changes and reasons for adult learning', in *Future Directions for a Framing Society*, New York: College Board.

Ausubel, D.E., Novak, I.S. and Hanesian, E. (1978) *Educational Psychology: A Cognitive View*, New York: Holt, Rinehart & Winston.

Bandura, A. (1977) *Social Learning Theory*, 2nd ed., Englewood Cliffs, NJ: Prentice Hall.

—— (1989) 'Human agency in social cognition theory', *American Psychologist* 44: 1175–1184.

Baptiste, I. (2001) 'Educating lone wolves: pedagogical implications of human capital theory', *Adult Education Quarterly* 51 (3): 184–201.

Barbalet, J. (1988) *Citizenship*, Milton Keynes, UK: Open University Press.

Barlow, S. (1991) 'Impossible dream: why doesn't mentorship work in UK nurse education?', *Nursing Times* 87 (1): 53–54.

Baskett, M. and Marsick, V. (eds) (1992) *Professionals' Ways of Knowing: New Findings on How to Improve Professional Education*, San Francisco: Jossey-Bass.

Battersby, D. (1990) 'From andragogy to gerogogy', in Glendenning, F. and Percy, K. (eds) *Ageing, Education and Society*, Association for Educational Gerontology, University of Keele, UK.

Bauman, Z. (1987) *Legislators and Interpreters*, Cambridge: Polity.

—— (1988) *Freedom*, Milton Keynes, UK: Open University Press.

—— (1992) *Intimations of Postmodernity*, London: Routledge.

—— (1998) *Globalization*, Cambridge: Polity.

—— (1999) *In Search of Politics*, Cambridge: Polity.

—— (2002) *Society under Siege*, Cambridge: Polity.

Baumard, P. (1999) *Tacit Knowledge in Organizations*, London: Sage.

Beard, R. (1976) *Teaching and Learning in Higher Education*, 3rd ed., Harmondsworth, UK: Penguin.

Beck, U. (1992) *Risk Society*, London: Sage.

—— (1994) 'The reinvention of politics', in Beck, U., Giddens, A. and Lash, S. (eds) *Reflexive Modernization*, Cambridge: Polity.

—— (2000) *What Is Globalization?* Cambridge: Polity.

Becker-Schmidt, R. (1987) 'Dynamik sozialen Lernens: Geschlechterdifferenz und Konflickte aus der Perspecktive von Frauen', in Becker-Schmidt, R. and Knapp, G.-A. (eds) *Geschlechtertrennung – Geschlechterdiffenenz – Suchbewegungen sozialen Lernens*, Bonn: Dietz Nachf.

Becker-Schmidt, R. and Knapp, G.-A. (eds) (1987) *Geschlechtertrennung – Geschlechterdifferenz – Suchbewegungen sozialen Lernens*, Bonn: Dietz Nachf.

Beinart, S. and Smith, P. (1998) *The National Learning Survey, 1997*, London: Department for Education and Science.

Beisgen, B. and Kraitchman, M. (2003) *Senior Centers: Opportunities for Successful Aging*, New York: Springer.

Belbin, C. and Belbin, R.M. (1972) *Problems in Adult Retraining*, London: Heinemann.

Belenky, M., Clinchy, B., Goldberger, N. and Tarule, J. (1986) *Women's Ways of Knowing*, New York: Basic Books.

Bell, D. (1973) *The Coming of Post-industrial Society*, New York: Basic Books.

Berger, P.L. (1974) *Pyramids of Sacrifice*, Harmondsworth, UK: Pelican.

Berger, P.L. and Luckmann, T. (1966) *The Social Construction of Reality*, Harmondsworth, UK: Penguin.

Bergevin, P., Morris, D. and Smith, R.M. (1963) *Adult Education Procedures*, New York: Seabury Press.

Bergson, H. (2004) [1912]) *Matter and Memory*, New York: Dover Publications.

Bestwick, D. and Chadwick, A. (1977) 'A co-operative training scheme for part-time teachers of adults', *Adult Education* 50 (4): 238–242. Leicester: NIAE.

Bierema, L. (2008) 'Principles of instructional design and adult learners', in Wang, V.C.X. (ed.) *Curriculum Development for Adult Learners in the Global Community*, vol. 1: *Strategic Approaches*, Malabar, FL: Krieger.

Biesta, G. (2007) *Beyond Learning: Democratic Learning for Human Future*, Boulder, CO: Paradigm Publishers.

Bines, H. (1992) 'Issues in course design', in Bines, H. and Watson, D. (eds) *Developing Professional Education*, Buckingham, UK: SRHE and Open University Press.

Black, T. (1999) *Doing Quantitative Research in the Social Sciences*, London: Sage.

Blackwell, L. and Bynner, J. (2002) *Learning, Family Formation and Dissolution*, London: Institute of Education, Centre for Research on the Wider Benefits of Learning.

Blakemore, S.-J. and Frith, U. (2005) *The Learning Brain*, Oxford: Blackwell.

Bligh, D.A. (1971) *What's the Use of Lectures?* Exeter: D.A. and B. Bligh, Briar House.

Bloom, B. (ed.) (1956) *Taxonomy of Educational Objectives*, vol. 1: *The Cognitive Domain*, London: Longman.

Boone, E.J. (1985) *Developing Programs in Adult Education*, Englewood Cliffs, NJ: Prentice Hall.

Boone, E.J., Shearon, R.W., White, E.E. *et al.* (1980) *Serving Personal and Community Needs through Adult Education*, San Francisco: Jossey-Bass.

Borger, R. and Seaborne, A.E.M. (1966) *The Psychology of Learning*, Harmondsworth, UK: Penguin.

Boshier, R. (1980) *Towards a Learning Society*, Vancouver: Learning Press.

Botkin, J., Elmandjra, M. and Malitza, M. (1979) *No Limits to Learning*, Oxford: Pergamon Press.

Bottomore, T. and Reubel, M. (eds) (1963) *Selected Writings in Sociology and Social Theory*, Harmondsworth, UK: Pelican.

Boud, D. and Bridge, W. (1974) *Keller Plan: A Case Study in Individualized Learning*, Institute of Educational Technology, University of Surrey, Guildford, UK.

Boud, D. and Miller, N. (eds) (1996) *Working with Experience*, London: Routledge.

Boud, D.J., Bridge, W.A. and Willoughby, L. (1975) 'P.S.I. now – a review of progress and problems', *Journal of Educational Technology* 6 (2): 15–34.

Boud, D., Keogh, R. and Walker, D. (eds) (1983) *Reflection: Turning Experience into Learning*, London: Kogan Page.

Bourdieu, P. (1973) 'Cultural reproduction and social reproduction', in Brown, M. (ed.) *Knowledge, Education and Social Change*, London: Tavistock.

Bourdieu, P. and Passeron, J.-C. (1977) *Reproduction in Education, Society and Culture*, London: Sage.

—— (1994) 'Language and the teaching situation', in Bourdieu, P., Passeron, J.-C. and Saint Martin, M. *Academic Discourses*, Cambridge: Polity.

Bourner, T., Martin, V. and Race, P. (eds) (1993) *Workshops that Work*, Maidenhead, UK: McGraw-Hill.

Bowles, S. and Gintis, H. (1976) *Schooling in Capitalist America*, London: Routledge & Kegan Paul.

Boyle, C. (1982) 'Reflections on recurrent education', *International Journal of Lifelong Education* 1 (1): 5–18.

Bradshaw, J. (1977) 'The concept of social need', in Fitzgerald, M., Malmos, P., Muncie, J. and Zeldin, D. (eds) *Welfare in Action*, London: Routledge & Kegan Paul/OUP.

Brassett-Grundy, A. (2002) *Parental Pespectives on Family Learning*, London: Institute of Education, Centre for Research on the Wider Benefits of Learning.

Bright, B. (ed.) (1989) *Theory and Practice in the Study of Adult Education*, London: Routledge.

Brinkerhoff, R. (1987) *Achieving Results from Training*, San Francisco: Jossey-Bass.

Brockett, R. (ed.) (1988) *Ethical Issues in Adult Education*, New York: Teachers College Press.

Brockett, R. and Hiemstra, R. (1991) *Self-Direction in Adult Learning*, London: Routledge.

Brookfield, S. (1986) *Selecting and Facilitating Adult Learning*, San Francisco: Jossey-Bass.

—— (1987) *Developing Critical Thinkers*, San Francisco: Jossey-Bass.

—— (ed.) (1988) *Training Educators of Adults*, London: Routledge.

—— (1990) *The Skillful Teacher*, San Francisco: Jossey-Bass.

—— (1995) *Becoming a Critically Reflective Teacher*, San Francisco: Jossey-Bass.

—— (2009) 'On being taught', in Jarvis, P. (ed.) *Learning to be a Person in Society*, London: Routledge.

Brown, G. and Atkins, M. (1988) *Effective Teaching in Higher Education*, London: Methuen.

Brown, H. (ed.) (1973) *Knowledge, Education and Social Change*, London: Tavistock.

Brown, V. (1992) 'The emergence of the economy', in Hall, S. and Gieben, B. (eds) *Formations of Modernity*, Cambridge: Polity.

Brundage, D.H. and Mackeracher, D. (1980) *Adult Learning Principles and Their Application to Program Planning*, Toronto: Ontario Institute for Studies in Education.

Bruner, J.S. (1968) *Toward a Theory of Instruction*, New York: W.W. Norton.

—— (1979) *On Knowing*, Cambridge, MA: Belknap Press of Harvard University Press.

—— (1990) *Acts of Meaning*, Cambridge, MA: Harvard University Press.

Brunner, E. da S., Nicholls, W.L. and Sieber, S.D. (1959) *The Role of a National Organization in Adult Education*, New York: Bureau of Applied Social Research, Columbia University.

Bryant, I. (1983) 'Paid educational leave in Scotland', *International Journal of Lifelong Education* 2 (1): 55–62.

Buber, M. (1959) *I and Thou*, Edinburgh: T&T Clark.

—— (1961) *Between Man and Man*, London: Fontana.

Bucher, R. and Strauss, A. (1966) 'Professional associations and the process of segmentation', in Vollmer, H. and Mills, D. (eds) *Professionalization*, Englewood Cliffs, NJ: Prentice Hall.

Burgess, P.D. (1974) 'The educational orientations of adult participants in group educational activities', unpublished doctoral thesis, University of Chicago.

Burnard, P. (1990) 'The student experience: adult learning and mentorship revisited', *Nurse Education Today* 10: 349–354.

Caffarella, R. (1988) 'Ethical issues in the teaching of adults', in Brockett, R. (ed.) *Ethical Issues in Adult Education*, New York: Teachers College Press.

Caldwell, P.A. (1981) 'Preservice training for instructors of adults', in Grabowski, S. and Associates, *Preparing Educators of Adults*, San Francisco: Jossey-Bass.

Campbell, C. (1987) *The Romantic Ethic and the Spirit of Modern Consumerism*, Oxford: Blackwell.

Campbell, D.D. (1977) *Adult Education as a Field of Study and Practice*, Vancouver: Centre for Continuing Education, University of British Columbia.

—— (1984) *The New Majority*, Edmonton, University of Alberta Press.

Candy, P.C. (1981) *Mirrors of the Mind*, Manchester Monographs 16, University of Manchester, Department of Adult and Higher Education.

—— (1991) *Self-Direction for Lifelong Learning*, San Francisco: Jossey-Bass.

Cantor, L.M. (1974) *Recurrent Education – Policy and Developments in OECD Member Countries; United Kingdom*, Paris: OECD.

Cantor, L.M. and Roberts, I.F. (1972) *Further Education in England and Wales*, 2nd ed., London: Routledge & Kegan Paul.

Caplow, T. (1954) *The Sociology of Work*, Minneapolis: University of Minnesota Press.

Cardy, E. and Wells, A. (1981) *Adult Literacy Unit: Development Projects 1978–80*, London: Adult Literacy and Basic Skills Unit.

Carlton, S. and Soulsby, J. (1999) *Learning to Grow Older and Bolder*, Leicester: NIACE.

Carnivale, A., Gainer, L. and Villet, J. (1990a) *Training in America*, San Francisco: Jossey-Bass.

—— (1990b) *Training the Technical Workforce*, San Francisco: Jossey-Bass.

Carp, A., Peterson, R. and Roelfs, P. (1974) 'Adult learning interests and experiences', cited in Cross, K. (ed.) (1981) *Adults as Learners*, San Francisco: Jossey-Bass.

Carr, W. and Kemmis, S. (1986) *Becoming Critical*, London: Falmer.

Cashdan, A. and Whitehead, J. (eds) (1971) *Personality, Growth and Learning*, London: Longman.

Casner-Lotto, J. and Associates (1988) *Successful Training Strategies*, San Francisco: Jossey-Bass.

Castells, M. (1996) *The Information Age: Economy, Society and Culture*, vol. 1: *The Rise of the Network Society*, Oxford: Blackwell.

Cell, E. (1986) *Learning to Learn from Experience*, Albany: State University of New York Press.

Cervero, R. (1988) *Effective Continuing Education for Professionals*, San Francisco: Jossey-Bass.

—— (1991) 'Relationships between theory and practice', in Peters, J., Jarvis, P. and Associates, *Adult Education: Evolution and Achievements in a Developing Field of Study*, San Francisco: Jossey-Bass.

Cervero, R. and Wilson, A. (1994) *Planning Responsibly for Adult Education*, San Francisco: Jossey-Bass.

Chadwick, A.F. (1980) *The Role of the Museum and Art Gallery in Community Education*, Department of Adult Education, University of Nottingham.

Chaib, M. and Svensson, A.-K. (2005) *ICT in Teacher Education*, Jönköping, Sweden: Jönköping University Press and Encell.

Chalmers, D. (1996) *The Conscious Mind*, Oxford: Oxford University Press.

Charnley, A., Osborn, M. and Withnall, A. (1980) *Review of Existing Research in Adult and Continuing Education*, vol. 1: *Mature Students*, Leicester: NIAE.

—— (1982) *Review of Existing Research in Adult and Continuing Education*, vol. 8: *Training the Educators of Adults*, Leicester: NIAE.

Charters, A.N. *et al.* (1981) *Comparing Adult Education Worldwide*, San Francisco: Jossey-Bass.

Child, D. (1977) *Psychology and the Teacher*, 2nd ed., London and New York: Holt, Rinehart & Winston.

—— (1981) *Psychology and the Teacher*, 3rd ed., New York: Holt, Rinehart & Winston.

Child, J. (1977) *Organization: A Guide to Problems and Practice*, London: Harper & Row.

City & Guilds of London Institute (1978) *730 Further Education Teachers' Certificate*, London: CGLI.

Clark, A. (2001) *Learning Organisations*, Leicester: NIACE.

Clark, C. (1990) 'The teacher and the taught: moral transactions in the classroom', in Goodlad, J.L., Soder, R. and Sirontik, K.A. (eds) *The Moral Dimensions of Teaching*, San Francisco: Jossey-Bass.

Clarke, J. (2002) 'Deconstructing domestication: women's experience and the goals of critical pedagogy', in Harrison, R., Reeve, F., Hanson, A. and Clarke, J. (eds) *Supporting Lifelong Learning*, London: RoutledgeFalmer.

Coare, P. and Cecil, L. (eds) (2009) *Really Useful Research? Proceedings of the 39th Annual Conference of SCUTREA*, Brighton: University of Sussex and SCUTREA.

Coates, K. and Silburn, R. (1967) *St Ann's: Poverty, Deprivation and Morale in a Nottingham Community*, Department of Adult Education, University of Nottingham.

Coffield, F. (ed.) (2000) *Differing Visions of a Learning Society*, Bristol: Policy Press.

Cohen, N. (2002) 'One way to get very rich', *Observer* (London), 24 February.

Coleman, A. (1982) *Preparation for Retirement in England and Wales*, Leicester: NIAE.

Coleman, J. (1990) *Foundations of Social Theory*, Cambridge, MA: Belknap Press of the Harvard University Press.

Collins, M. (ed.) (1995) *The Canmore Proceedings*, Saskatoon: University of Saskatchewan.

Coombs, P. and Ahmed, M. (1974) *Attacking Rural Poverty*, Baltimore: Johns Hopkins University Press.

Cooper, C.L. (ed.) (1975) *Theories of Group Processes*, London: Wiley.

Cooper, D. (1983) *Authenticity and Learning: Nietzsche's Educational Philosophy*, London: Routledge.

Council for National Academic Awards (1991) *Handbook 1991–1992*, London: CNAA.

Council on the Continuing Education Unit (1984) *Principles of Good Practice in Continuing Education*, Silver Spring, MD: CCEU.

Courtney, S. (1981) 'The factors affecting participation in adult education: an analysis of some literature', *Studies in Adult Education* 13 (2): 98–111.

—— (1992) *Why Adults Learn*, London: Routledge.

Cox, R. and Pascall, G. (1994) 'Individualism, self-evaluation and self-fulfilment in the experience of mature women students', *International Journal of Lifelong Education* 13 (2): 159–173.

Crabbe, J. (ed.) (1999) *From Soul to Self*, London: Routledge.

Crane, J.M. (1982) 'Individualized learning: an analysis of the theoretical principles with illuminative references from the experientially-evolved practices of an individualized learning system developed in an adult basic academic upgrading programme', unpublished MSc dissertation, University of Surrey, Guildford, UK.

Crawford, J. (2005) *Spiritually Engaged Knowledge*, Aldershot, UK: Ashgate.

Cross, K.P. (1981) *Adults as Learners*, San Francisco: Jossey-Bass.

Cusack, S. (1996) 'Developing a lifelong learning program: empowering seniors in lifelong learning', *Educational Gerontology* 21 (4): 305–320.

Cusack, S. and Thompson, W. (1998) 'Mental fitness: developing a vital aging society', *International Journal of Lifelong Education* 17 (5): 307–317.

Dadswell, G. (1978) 'The adult independent learner and public libraries', *Adult Education* 51 (1): 5–11, Leicester: NIAE.

Dahlgren, L.-O. (1984) 'Outcomes of learning', in Marton, F., Hounsell, D. and Entwistle, N. (eds) *The Experience of Learning*, Edinburgh: Scottish Academic Press.

Dale, S.M. (1980) 'Another way forward for adult learners: the public library and independent study', *Studies in Adult Education* 12 (1): 29–38.

Dale, S. and Carty, J. (1985) *Finding Out about Continuing Education*, Milton Keynes, UK: Open University Press.

Daloz, L. (1986) *Effective Teaching and Mentoring*, San Francisco: Jossey-Bass.

Danaher, G., Schirato, T. and Webb, J. (2000) *Understanding Foucault*, London: Sage.

Daniel, J. (1996) *Mega-universities and Knowledge Media*, London: Kogan Page.

Dave, R.H. (ed.) (1976) *Foundations of Lifelong Education*, Oxford: Pergamon Press for UNESCO Institute for Education.

Davies, D. and Robertson, D. (1986) 'Open college: towards a new view of adult education', *Adult Education* 59 (2): 106–114.

Davies, I.K. (1971) *The Management of Learning*, London: McGraw-Hill.

—— (1976) *Objectives in Curriculum Design*, London: McGraw-Hill.

Dawkins, R. (1976) *The Selfish Gene*, Oxford: Oxford University Press.

Day, C. and Baskett, H.K. (1982) 'Discrepancies between intentions and practice: re-examining some basic assumptions about adult and continuing professional education', *International Journal of Lifelong Education* 1 (2): 143–155.

de Wit, P. (1992) *Quality Assurance in University Continuing Vocational Education*, London: HMSO.

Dearden, R.F. (1972) '"Needs" in education', in Dearden, R.F., Hirst, P.H. and Peters, R.S. (eds) *Education and the Development of Reason*, vol. 1: *A Critique of Current Educational Aims*, London: Routledge & Kegan Paul.

Dearden, R.F., Hirst, P.H. and Peters, R.S. (eds) (1972) *Education and the Development of Reason*, vol. 1: *A Critique of Current Educational Aims*, London: Routledge & Kegan Paul.

Dearing, R. (chair) (1997) *Higher Education in the Learning Society*, London: HMSO.

Delanty, G. (2000) *Citizenship in a Global Age*, Buckingham, UK: Open University Press.

Delors, J. (chair) (1996) *Learning: The Treasure Within*, Paris: UNESCO.

Denzin, N. and Lincoln, Y. (eds) (1989) *Handbook of Qualitative Research*, Thousand Oaks, CA: Sage.

Department for Education and Employment (1998a) *The Age of Learning*, London: DfEE.

—— (1998b) *Learning City Network: Practice, Progress and Value*, London: DfEE.

Department for Education and Skills (2003) *The Future of Higher Education*, Cm 5735, London: HMSO.

Department for Innovation, Universities and Skills (2008) *Informal Adult Learning: Shaping the Way Ahead*, London: DIUS.

—— (2009) *The Learning Revolution*, Cm 7555, London: DIUS.

Devereux, W. (1982) *Adult Education in Inner London 1870–1980*, London: Shepheard-Welwyn/ILEA.

Dewey, J. (1916) *Education and Democracy*, New York: The Free Press.

—— (1938) *Experience and Education*, London: Collier Macmillan.

—— (ed.) (1958) *Experience and Nature*, New York: Dover Publications.

—— (1991 [1910]) *How We Think*, New York: Prometheus Books.

—— (1993) *Approaches to Good Practice in Quality Assurance in University Continuing Education*, Universities Association for Continuing Education Working Paper 3, University of Birmingham.

Directgov, www.direct.gov.uk/en/EduvationAndLearningQualicationsExplained/DG_07 (downloaded 25 June 2009).

Directorate-General for Education and Culture (2002) *Education and Training in Europe: Diverse Systems, Shared Goals for 2010*, Brussels: European Commission.

Dohman, G. (1996) *Lifelong Learning: Guidelines for a Modern Education Policy*, Bonn: Federal Ministry of Education, Science, Research and Technology.

Dominicé, P. (2000) *Learning from Our Lives*, San Francisco: Jossey-Bass.

Donald, M. (2001) *A Mind So Rare*, New York: W.W. Norton.

Dovey, K. and Onyx, J. (2001) 'Generating social capital at the workplace: a South African case of inside-out social renewal', *International Journal of Lifelong Education* 20: 151–168.

Draves, W. (1979) 'The free university network', *Lifelong Learning: The Adult Years* 3 (4): 4–5.

—— (1980) *The Free University: A Model for Lifelong Learning*, Chicago: Association Press.

Duke, C. (1992) *The Learning University*, Buckingham, UK: Open University Press in association with the Society for Research in Higher Education.

Durkheim, E. (1933) *The Division of Labor in Society*, New York: The Free Press.
—— (1956) *Education and Sociology* (trans. S.D. Fox), New York: The Free Press.
Edinburgh Papers, The: Reclaiming Social Purpose in Community Education (2008) University of Edinburgh, Learning for Democracy Group.
Eisner, E.W. (1969) 'Instructional and expressive educational objectives', in Popham, W.J., Eisner, E.W., Sullivan, H.J. and Tyler, L.L. (eds) *Instructional Objectives*, Chicago: Rand McNally.
Elbe, K. (1988) *The Craft of Teaching*, 2nd ed., San Francisco: Jossey-Bass.
Elias, J.L. (1979) 'Andragogy revisited', *Adult Education* 29: 252–256.
Elias, J.L. and Merriam, S.B. (1980) *Philosophical Foundation of Adult Education*, Malabar, FL: Krieger.
Ellwood, C. (1976) *Adult Learning Today*, London: Sage.
Elsdon, K.T. (1970) 'The East Midlands Scheme', *Adult Education* 46 (4). Leicester: NIAE.
—— (1975) *Training for Adult Education*, Department of Adult Education, University of Nottingham in conjunction with the NIAE.
—— (1981) *New Directions: Adult Education in the Context of Continuing Education*, London: Department of Education and Science.
Elsey, B. (1980) 'Volunteer tutors in adult education', *Studies in Adult Education* 12 (2).
—— (1986) *Social Theory Perspectives on Adult Education*, Department of Adult Education, University of Nottingham.
Engestrom, Y. (1987) *Learning by Expanding*, Helsinki: Orienta-Konsultit.
—— (1990) *Learning, Working and Imagining*, Helsinki: Orienta-Konsultit.
Entwistle, N. (1981) *Styles of Learning and Teaching*, Chichester, UK: Wiley.
Eraut, M. (1994) *Developing Professional Knowledge and Competence*, London: Falmer.
Eurich, N. (1985) *Corporate Classrooms*, Princeton, NJ: Carnegie Foundation for the Advancement of Teaching.
European Commission (1995) *Teaching and Learning: Towards the Learning Society*, Brussels: European Commission.
—— (1997) *Towards a Europe of Knowledge*, COM(97)563 final, Brussels: European Commission.
—— (1998) *Education and Active Citizenship*, Brussels: European Commission.
—— (2000) *A Memorandum on Lifelong Learning*, SEC(2000)1832, Brussels: European Commission.
—— (2001a) *Making a European Area of Lifelong Learning a Reality*, COM(2001)678 final, Brussels: European Commission.
—— (2001b) *The Concrete Future Objectives of Education Systems*, COM(2001)59 final, Brussels: European Commission.
—— (2001c) *European Governance: A White Paper*, COM(2001)428 final, Brussels: European Commission.
—— (2002) *Education and Training in Europe: Diverse Systems, Shared Goals for 2010*, Brussels: European Communities.
—— (2003) *Investing Efficiently in Education and Training: Imperative for Europe*, COM(2002)779 final, Brussels: European Communities.
—— (2006) *Adult Learning: It Is Never Too Late to Learn*, COM(2006)614 final, Brussels: European Commission.
Fairbairn, A.N. (1971) *The Leicestershire Community Colleges*, London: NIAE.

—— (1978) *The Leicestershire Community Colleges and Centres*, University of Nottingham, Department of Adult Education.

Faure, E. (1972) *Learning to Be*, Paris: UNESCO.

Feigenbaum, E. and McCorduck, P. (1984) *The Fifth Generation*, New York: Signet.

Feinstein, L. (2002a) *Quantitative Estimates in the Social Benefits of Learning, 1: Crime*, London: Institute of Education, Centre for Research on the Wider Benefits of Learning.

—— (2002b) *Quantitative Benefits of the Social Benefits of Learning, 2: Health*, London: Institute of Education, Centre for Research on the Wider Benefits of Learning.

Field, J. (2009) 'Reflecting from the front-line: research on lifelong learning and policies of well-being', in Coare, P. and Cecil, L. (eds) *Really Useful Research? Proceedings of the 39th Annual Conference of SCUTREA*, Brighton: University of Sussex and SCUTREA.

Finch, J. (1984) *Education as Social Policy*, London: Longman.

Fitzgerald, M., Halmos, P., Muncie, J. and Zeldin, D. (1977) *Welfare in Action*, London: Routledge & Kegan Paul/Open University Press.

Fletcher, C. (1980a) 'The theory of community education and its relation to adult education', in Thompson, J.L. (ed.) *Adult Education for a Change*, London: Heinemann.

—— (1980b) 'Community studies as practical adult education', *Adult Education* 53 (2). Leicester: NIAE.

—— (1982) 'Adults in a community education centre', *International Journal of Lifelong Education* 1 (3): 261–271.

—— (n.d.) *The Challenges of Community Education*, Department of Adult Education, University of Nottingham.

Fletcher, C. and Thompson, N. (1980) *Issues in Community Education*, Lewes, UK: Falmer.

Flude, R.A. (1978) 'A course in rural community action', *Adult Education* 51 (3). Leicester: NIAE.

Flude, R. and Parrott, A. (1979) *Education and the Challenge of Change: A Recurrent Education Strategy for Britain*, Milton Keynes, UK: Open University Press.

Fordham, P., Poulton, G. and Randle, L. (1979) *Learning Networks in Adult Education*, London: Routledge & Kegan Paul.

Fowler, J. (1981) *Stages of Faith*, New York: Harper & Row.

Fraser, W. (1995) *Learning from Experience*, Leicester: NIACE.

Freire, P. (1971) 'A few notions about the word "concientization"', *Hard Cheese* no. 1. Reprinted in Dale, R., Esland, U. and MacDonald, M. (eds) *Schooling and Capitalism* (1976) London: Routledge & Kegan Paul/Open University Press.

—— (1972a) *Cultural Action for Freedom*, Harmondsworth, UK: Penguin.

—— (1972b) *Pedagogy of the Oppressed* (trans. M.B. Ramer), Harmondsworth, UK: Penguin.

—— (1973a) *Education for Critical Consciousness*, London: Sheed & Ward. Reprinted under the title *Education: The Practice of Freedom*, London: Writers and Readers Publishing Cooperative.

—— (1973b) 'Education, liberation and the Church', *Study Encounter* 9 (1): 1–16.

—— (1973c) 'By learning they can teach', *Convergence* 6 (1): 78–84.

—— (1978) *Pedagogy in Process: The Letters to Guinea-Bissau*, London: Writers and Readers Publishing Cooperative.

—— (1985) *The Politics of Education*, London: Macmillan.

—— (1996) *Pedagogy of Hope*, New York: Continuum.

—— (ed.) (1997) *Mentoring the Mentor*, New York: Peter Lang.

—— (1998) *Pedagogy of Freedom*, Lanham, MD: Rowman & Littlefield.

Freire, P. and Faundez, A. (1989) *Learning to Question: A Pedagogy of Liberation*, Geneva World Council of Churches.

Freire, P. and Macedo, D. (1987) *Literacy: Reading the Word and the World*, London: Routledge.

Freire, P. and Shor, I. (1987) *A Pedagogy for Liberation*, London: Macmillan.

Fromm, E. (1984 [1942]) *The Fear of Freedom*, London: ARK Paperbacks.

Fryer, R. (chair) (1997) *Learning for the Twenty First Century*, London: Department for Education and Employment.

—— (1998) *Creating Learning Cultures*, London: Department for Education and Employment.

Further Education Unit (1989) *Supporting Quality in YTS*, London: FEU.

—— (1990) *Developing a Marketing Strategy for Adult and Continuing Education*, London: FEU.

—— (1992) *Quality Education and Training for the Adult Unemployed*, London: FEU.

Gagné, R.M. (1977) *The Conditions of Learning*, 3rd ed., New York: Holt, Rinehart & Winston.

Gagné, R.M., Briggs, L. and Wager, W. (1992) *Principles of Instructional Design*, 4th ed., Fort Worth, TX: Harcourt Brace Jovanovich.

Galbraith, M. (ed.) (1990) *Adult Learning Methods*, Malabar, FL: Krieger.

Gardner, H. (1983) *Frames of Mind*, New York: Basic Books.

—— (1999) *Intelligence Reframed*, New York: Basic Books.

—— (2005) *Five Minds for the Future*, Boston: Harvard Business School Press.

Garrison, R. and Shale, D. (eds) (1990) *Education at a Distance*, Malabar, FL: Krieger.

Gelpi, E. (1979) *A Future for Lifelong Education* (2 vols) (trans. R. Ruddock), Manchester Monographs 13, University of Manchester.

Gerhardt, S. (2004) *Why Love Matters*, London: Routledge.

Gibbons, M., Limoges, C., Nowotny, H., Schwartzman, S., Scott, P. and Trow, M. (1994) *The New Production of Knowledge*, London: Sage.

Gibbs, U. (1981) *Teaching Students to Learn*, Milton Keynes, UK: Open University Press.

Gibbs, U. and Durbridge, N. (1976) 'Characteristics of Open University tutors (Part 2): Tutors in action', *Teaching at a Distance* 7: 7–22. Milton Keynes: Open University.

Giddens, A. (1990) *The Consequences of Modernity*, Cambridge: Polity.

—— (1991) *Modernity and Self-Identity*, Cambridge: Polity.

Giles, H.H., McCutcheon, S.P. and Zechriel, A.N. (1942) *Exploring the Curriculum*, New York: Harper.

Glendenning, F. (ed.) (1985) *Educational Gerontology: International Perspectives*, London: Croom Helm.

Glendenning, F. and Percy, K. (eds) (1990) *Ageing, Education and Society*, Association for Educational Gerontology, University of Keele, UK.

Goleman, D. (1995) *Emotional Intelligence*, London: Bloomsbury.

—— (1998) *Working with Emotional Intelligence*, New York: Bantam Books.

Goodlad, J., Soder, R. and Sirotnik, K. (eds) (1990) *The Moral Dimensions of Teaching*, San Francisco: Jossey-Bass.

Gould, A. (1979) *Towards Equality of Occupational Opportunity*, Association of Recurrent Education. Discussion Paper 5, Centre for Research into Education for Adults, University of Nottingham.

Grabowski, S.H. and Associates (1981) *Preparing Educators of Adults*, San Francisco: Jossey-Bass.

Graham, T.B., Dames, J.H., Sullivan, T., Harris, P. and Baum, F.E. (1982) *The Training of Part-Time Teachers of Adults*, University of Nottingham, Department of Adult Education.

Gray, J. (1995) *Enlightenment's Wake*, London: Routledge.

Greenfield, S. (1999) 'Soul, brain and mind', in Crabbe, J. (ed.) *From Soul to Self*, London: Routledge.

Greenwood, E. (1957) 'Attributes of a profession', *Social Work* 2: 44–55.

Griffin, C. (1978) *Recurrent and Continuing Education: A Curriculum Model Approach*, Association of Recurrent Education, University of Nottingham, School of Education.

—— (1979) 'Continuing education and the adult curriculum', *Adult Education* 52 (2): 81–85. Leicester: NIAE.

—— (1982) 'Curriculum analysis of adult and lifelong education', *International Journal of Lifelong Education* 1 (2): 109–121.

—— (1987) *Adult Education as Social Policy*, London: Croom Helm.

Griffit, W. (1980) 'Coordination of personnel, programs and services', in Peters, J. and Associates, *Building an Effective Adult Education Enterprise*, San Francisco: Jossey-Bass.

Groombridge, B. (1972) *Television and the People*, Harmondsworth, UK: Penguin.

Gross, R. (1977) *The Lifelong Learner*, New York: Touchstone Books, Simon & Schuster.

Grossman, M. and Kaestner, R. (1997) 'Effects of education on health', in Behrman, J. and Stacey, N. (eds) *The Social Benefits of Education*, Ann Arbor: University of Michigan Press.

Gurnah, A. (1992) Editorial, *Adults Learning* 3 (8).

Habermas, J. (1972) *Knowledge and Human Interests*, London: Heinemann.

—— (2006) *Time of Transitions* (ed. and trans. C. Cronin and M. Pensky), Cambridge: Polity.

Hall, A. (1985) *The Adult School Movement in the Twentieth Century*, University of Nottingham, Department of Adult Education.

Hall, C. (1954) *A Primer of Freudian Psychology*, New York: Mentor Books.

Hall, E. (1976) *Beyond Culture*, New York: Anchor Books.

Hall, R.H. (1969) *Occupations and the Social Structure*, Englewood Cliffs, NJ: Prentice Hall.

Hallenbeck, W.C. (1948) 'Training adult educators', in Ely, M. (ed.) *Handbook of Adult Education in the United States*, Center for Adult Education. Republished in Brookfield, S. (ed.) (1988) *Training Educators of Adults*, London: Routledge.

Halmos, P. (1978) 'The concept of social problem', *Social Work and Community Course DE206*, Block 1, Milton Keynes, UK: Open University Press.

Handley, J. (1981) 'An investigation into the training needs of part-time tutors, with particular reference to the development of courses at ACSTT Stage IL level', unpublished MSc dissertation, University of Surrey, Guildford, UK.

Hargreaves, A. (2003) *Teaching in the Knowledge Society*, Maidenhead, UK: Open University Press.

Hargreaves, P. and Jarvis, P. (2001) *The Human Resource Development Handbook*, rev. ed., London: Kogan Page.

Harper, K. (1982) 'Colleges warned against "politics" in YOP courses', *Guardian* (London), 29 November: 22.

Harré, R. (1998) *The Singular Self*, London: Sage.

Harris, W.J.A. (1980) *Comparative Adult Education: Practice, Purpose and Theory*, London: Longman.

Harrop, S. and Woodcock, G. (1992) 'Issues in the construction of a modular curriculum for university professional adult education courses', *Studies in the Education of Adults* 24 (1): 86–94.

Hartree, A. (1984) 'Malcolm Knowles' theory of andragogy: a critique', *International Journal of Lifelong Education* 3 (3): 203–210.

Harvey, B., Dames, J., Jones, D. and Wallis, J. (1981) *Policy and Research Adult Education*, Department of Adult Education, University of Nottingham.

Harvey, D. (1990) *The Condition of Postmodernism*, Oxford: Blackwell.

Haslam, N. (2007) *Introduction to Personality and Intelligence*, London: Sage.

Haycocks, J.N. (1978) *The Training of Adult Education and Part-Time Further Education Teachers*, Advisory Committee on the Supply and Training of Teachers, London.

Heater, D. (1999) *What Is Citizenship?* Cambridge: Polity.

Hegarty, T.B. (1976) 'Education for the legal profession', in Turner, J.R. and Rushton, I. (eds) *Education for the Professions*, Manchester: Manchester University Press.

Held, D. and McGrew, A., Goldblatt, D. and Perraton, J. (1999) *Global Transformations*, Cambridge: Polity.

Heller, A. (1984) *Everyday Life*, London: Routledge & Kegan Paul.

—— (1988) *General Ethics*, Oxford: Blackwell.

Henry, J. (1989) 'Meaning and practice in experiential learning', in Weil, S. and McGill, I. (eds) *Making Sense of Experiential Learning*, Buckingham, UK: Open University Press in association with SRHE.

—— (1992) 'Creativity, capability and experiential learning', in Mulligan, J. and Griffin, C. (eds) *Empowerment through Experiential Learning*, London: Kogan Page.

Hermann, U. and Kenyon, R. (1987) *Competency Based Vocational Education*, London: FEU.

Hetherington, J. (1980) 'Professionalism and part-time staff in adult education', *Adult Education* 52 (5). Leicester: NIAE.

Hilgard, E.R. and Atkinson, R.C. (1967) *Introduction to Psychology*, 4th ed., New York: Harcourt, Brace and World.

Hilgard, E.R., Atkinson, R.L. and Atkinson, R.C. (1979) *Introduction to Psychology*, 7th ed., New York: Harcourt Brace Jovanovich.

Hirst, P.H. and Peters, R.S. (1970) *The Logic of Education*, London: Routledge & Kegan Paul.

Holmberg, B. (1960) *On Methods of Teaching by Correspondence*, Lund: Gleerup.

—— (1981) *Status and Trends of Distance Education*, London: Kogan Page.

—— (1989) *Theory and Practice of Distance Education*, London: Routledge.

Holt, R. (1982) 'An alternative to mentorship', *Adult Education* 55 (2): 152–156. Leicester: NIAE.

Hopper, E. and Osborn, M. (1975) *Adult Students: Education, Selection and Social Control*, London: Frances Pinter.

Horton, M. and Freire, P. (1990) *We Make the Road by Walking*, ed. Bell, B., Gaventa, J. and Peters, J., Philadelphia: Temple University Press.

Horton, M. with J. Kohl and H. Kohl (1990) *The Long Haul*, New York: Anchor Books.

Hostler, J. (1977) 'The education of adults', *Studies in Adult Education* 9 (1). Leicester: NIAE.

—— (1978) 'Liberal adult education', *Studies in Adult Education* 10 (2).

Houghton, V. (1974) 'Recurrent education: a plea for lifelong learning', in Houghton, V. and Richardson, K. (eds) *Recurrent Education: A Plea for Lifelong Learning*, London: Ward Lock Educational/Association of Recurrent Education.

Houghton, V. and Richardson, K. (eds) (1974) *Recurrent Education: A Plea for Lifelong Learning*, London: Ward Lock Educational/Association of Recurrent Education.

Houle, C.O. (1960) 'The education of adult educational leaders', in Knowles, M. (ed.) *Handbook of Adult Education in the United States*, Washington, DC: Adult Education Convention of the USA.

—— (1961) *The Inquiring Mind*, Madison: University of Wisconsin Press. Republished as a second edition in 1988 by the Oklahoma Research Center for Continuing and Professional Higher Education, University of Oklahoma.

—— (1964) 'The emergence of graduate study in adult education', in Jensen, U., Liveright, A.A. and Hallenbeck, W. (eds) *Adult Education: Outlines of an Emerging Field of University Study*, Washington, DC: Adult Education Association of the USA.

—— (1972) *The Design of Education*, San Francisco: Jossey-Bass.

—— (1979) 'Motivation and participation with special reference to non-traditional forms of study', in OECD 1977, Vol. 3.

—— (1980) *Continuing Learning in the Professions*, San Francisco: Jossey-Bass.

Housden, S. (2007) *Reminiscence and Lifelong Learning*, Leicester: NIACE.

Houston, R.P., Bee, H., Hatfield, E. and Rimm, D.C. (1979) *Invitation to Psychology*, New York: Academic Press.

Howe, M.J.A. (1977) *Adult Learning*, Chichester, UK: Wiley.

Hoy, J.D. (1933) 'An enquiry as to interests and motives for study among adult evening students', *British Journal of Educational Psychology* 3 (1).

Huang, C.-S. (2006) 'The University of the Third Age in the UK: an interpretive critical study', *Educational Gerontology* 32 (10): 825–842.

Hughes, K. and Mayo, M. (1991) 'Opening up personal development', *Adults Learning* 3 (4).

Hughes, M. (1977) 'Adult education on the cheap: an extension of adult education provision into the school classroom', *Adult Education* 50 (4): 226–232. Leicester: NIAE.

Husen, T. (1974) *The Learning Society*, London: Methuen.

Husserl, E. (ed.) (1973) *Experience and Judgment*, London: Routledge & Kegan Paul.

Hutchins, R.M. (1970) *The Learning Society*, Harmondsworth, UK: Penguin.

Hutchinson, E. and Hutchinson, E.M. (1978) *Learning Later*, London: Routledge & Kegan Paul.

Hutchinson, E.M. (ed.) (1970) 'Adult education – adequacy of provision', *Adult Education* 42 (6). Leicester: NIAE.

Illeris, K. (2002) *The Three Dimensions of Learning*, Roskilde, Denmark: Roskilde University Press.

—— (2007) *How We Learn*, London: Routledge.

—— (ed.) (2009a) *Contemporary Theories of Learning*, London: Routledge.

—— (ed.) (2009b) *International Perspectives on Competence Development*, London: Routledge.

Illich, I. (1973a) *Deschooling Society*, Harmondsworth, UK: Penguin.

—— (1973b) *After Deschooling, What?* London: Writers and Readers Publishing Cooperative.

—— (1977) 'Disabling professions', in Illich, I., Zola, I.K., McKnight, J., Caplan, J. and Shanken, R. (eds) *Disabling Professions*, London: Marion Boyars.

Illich, I. and Verne, E. (1976) *Imprisoned in a Global Classroom*, London: Writers and Readers Publishing Cooperative.

Illich, I., Zola, I.K., McKnight, J., Caplan, J. and Shanken, R. (eds) (1977) *Disabling Professions*, London: Marion Boyars.

Jarvis, P. (1975) 'The parish ministry as a semi-profession', *Sociological Review* 23: 911–922. University of Keele, UK.

—— (1977) 'A profession in process: the relationship between occupational ideology, occupational position and the role strain, satisfaction and commitment of Protestant and Reformed ministers of religion', unpublished PhD thesis, University of Aston, UK.

—— (1978a) 'Students' learning and tutors' marking', *Teaching at a Distance* 13: 13–17. Milton Keynes, UK: Open University Press.

—— (1978b) 'Knowledge and the curriculum in adult education: a sociological approach', *Adult Education* 51(4). Leicester: NIAE.

—— (1980) 'Pre-retirement education: design and analysis', *Adult Education* 53 (1). Leicester: NIAE.

—— (1981) 'The Open University unit: andragogy or pedagogy?', *Teaching at a Distance* 20: 27–28. Milton Keynes, UK: Open University Press.

—— (1982a) 'What's the value of adult education?' *Adult Education* 54 (4). Leicester: NIAE.

—— (1982b) *Adult Education in a Small Centre: A Case Study in the Village of Lingfield*, Department of Adult Education, University of Surrey, Guildford, UK.

—— (1983a) *Professional Education*, London: Croom Helm.

—— (1983b) 'Education and the elderly', *Adult Education* 55 (4). Leicester: NIAE.

—— (1983c) 'The lifelong religious development of the individual and the place of adult education', *Lifelong Learning: The Adult Years* 6 (9).

—— (1984) 'Andragogy: a sign of the times', *Studies in the Education of Adults*, 16: 32–38.

—— (1985) *The Sociology of Adult and Continuing Education*, London: Croom Helm.

—— (1987) *Adult Learning in the Social Context*, London: Croom Helm.

—— (ed.) (1988) *Britain: Policy and Practice in Continuing Education*, San Francisco: Jossey-Bass.

—— (1990) *International Dictionary of Adult and Continuing Education*, London: Routledge.

—— (1992) *Paradoxes of Learning*, San Francisco: Jossey-Bass.

—— (1993a) *Adult Education and the State*, London: Routledge.

—— (1993b) 'Pedagogy, andragogy and professional education', paper presented at the International Conference on the Training of Adult Educators, Wadham College, Oxford.

—— (1994) 'Learning practical knowledge', *Journal of Further and Higher Education* 18 (1): 31–43.

—— (1996) 'The public recognition of lifetime learning', *Lifelong Learning in Europe* 1 (96): 10–17.

—— (1997) *Ethics and the Education of Adults in Late Modern Society*, Leicester: NIACE.

—— (1999) *The Practitioner Researcher*, San Francisco: Jossey-Bass.

—— (2000) 'Globalization, the learning society and comparative education', *Comparative Education* 36 (3): 342–355.

—— (2001a) *Learning in Later Life*, London: Kogan Page.

—— (2001b) *Universities and Corporate Universities*, London: Kogan Page.

—— (ed.) (2001c) *Twentieth Century Thinkers in Adult and Continuing Education*, 2nd ed., London: Kogan Page.

—— (2002a) 'Learning from experience', unpublished paper presented at the Danish Pedagogical University, as the opening of the academic year lecture (September).

—— (2002b) 'Lifelong learning, governance and active citizenship', unpublished lecture delivered at the ASEM Conference, Copenhagen.

—— (2002c) 'The implications of lifelong learning for lifewide learning', unpublished lecture delivered to the European Union Presidency Conference on Lifelong Learning, Copenhagen.

—— (ed.) (2002d) *The Theory and Practice of Teaching*, London: Kogan Page.

—— (2006) *Towards a Comprehensive Theory of Human Learning*, London: Routledge.

—— (2007a) *Globalisation, Lifelong Learning and the Learning Society*, London: Routledge.

—— (2007b) 'Working with elders: mapping a field of practice through publications?', seminar paper presented at the University of Leicester ESRC seminar sponsored series on educational gerontology.

—— (2008) *Democracy, Lifelong Learning and the Learning Society: Active Citizenship in a Late Modern Age*, London: Routledge.

—— (2009a) *Learning to be a Person in Society*, London: Routledge.

—— (2009b) 'The end of the sensate age – what next?' *Fortieth Annual International Sorokin Lecture*, Saskatoon: University of Saskatchewan.

—— (ed.) (2009c) *The Routledge International Handbook of Lifelong Learning*, London: Routledge.

Jarvis, P. and Chadwick, A. (eds) (1991) *Training Adult Educators in Western Europe*, London: Routledge.

Jarvis, P. with Griffin, C. (eds) (2003) *Adult and Continuing Education: Major Themes in Education* (5 vols), London: Routledge.

Jarvis, P. and Parker, S. (eds) (2005) *Human Learning: An Holistic Approach*, London: Routledge.

Jarvis, P. and Walker, J. (1997) 'When the process becomes the product: summer universities for elders', *Education and Ageing* 12: 60–68.

Jarvis, P. and Walters, N. (eds) (1993) *Adult Education and Theological Interpretations*, Malabar, FL: Krieger.

Jarvis, P., Holford, J., Griffin, C. and Dubelaar, J. (1997) *Towards a Learning City*, Corporation of the City of London Education Department.

Jayagopal, R. (1990) *Human Resource Development: Conceptual Analysis and Strategies*, New Delhi: Sterling Publishers.

Jennings, B. (ed.) (n.d.) *Community Colleges in England and Wales*, Leicester: NIAE.

Jensen, G., Liveright, A.A. and Hallenbeck, W. (eds) (1964) *Adult Education: Outlines of an Emerging Field of University Study*, Washington, DC: Adult Education Association of the USA.

Jessup, F.W. (ed.) (1969) *Lifelong Learning: A Symposium on Continuing Education*, Oxford: Pergamon Press.

Joas, H. (1996) *The Creativity of Action*, Cambridge: Polity.

Jochems, W., van Merrienboer, J. and Koper, R. (eds) (2004) *Integrated E-Learning*, London: RoutledgeFalmer.

Johnstone, J.W.C. and Rivera, R.J. (1965) *Volunteers for Learning*, Chicago: Aldine.

Joll, J. (1977) *Gramsci*, Glasgow: Fontana/Collins.

Jones, B. (2009) 'A perfect storm', *Adults Learning* 20 (8): 28–29. Leicester: NIACE.

Kagan, I. (1971) 'Developmental studies in reflection and analysis', in Kidd, A.H. and Rivoire, I.E. (eds) *Perceptual Development in Children*, New York: International Universities Press. Reprinted in Cashdow, A. and Whitehead, I. (eds) (1971) *Personality, Growth and Learning*, London: Longman.

Kallen, D. (1979) 'Recurrent education and lifelong learning: definitions and distinctions', in Schuller, T. and Megarry, I. (eds) *World Yearbook on Education 1979: Recurrent Education and Lifelong Learning*, London: Kogan Page.

Katz, D. (1960) 'The functional approach to the study of attitudes', *Public Opinion Quarterly* 24: 163–177.

Katz, R. and Associates (1999) *Dancing with the Devil*, San Francisco: Jossey-Bass.

Keddie, N. (1980) 'Adult education: an ideology of individualism', in Thompson, J.C. (ed.) *Adult Education for a Change*, London: Heinemann.

Keegan, D. (1990) *Foundations of Distance Education*, London: Routledge.

—— (ed.) (1993) *Theoretical Principles of Distance Education*, London: Routledge.

Keller, E.S. (1968) 'Good-bye, teacher...', *Journal of Applied Behavior Analysis* 1: 79–89.

Kellner, D. (1989) *Jean Baudrillard: From Marxism to Postmodernism and Beyond*, Cambridge: Polity.

Kelly, A.V. (1977) *The Curriculum: Theory and Practice*, London: Harper & Row.

Kelly, G.A. (1955) *The Psychology of Personal Constructs*, New York: Norton.

Kelly, T. (1970) (3rd ed. 1990) *A History of Adult Education in Great Britain*, Liverpool: Liverpool University Press.

Kennedy, H. (chair) (1997) *Learning Works*, Coventry: Further Education Funding Council.

Kenny-Wallace, G. (2000) 'Plato.com: the role and impact of the corporate universities in the third millennium', in Scott, P. (ed.) *Higher Education Reformed*, London: Falmer.

Kerr, C., Dunlop, J., Harbison, F. and Myers, C. (1973) *Industrialism and Industrial Man*, Harmondsworth, UK: Penguin.

Kett, J. (1994) *The Pursuit of Knowledge under Difficulties*, Stanford, CA: Stanford University Press.

Kidd, J.R. (1973) *How Adults Learn*, Chicago: Association Press.

Killeen, J. and Bird, M. (1981) *Education and Work*, Leicester: National Institute of Adult Education.

Kim, A. and Merriam, S. (2004) 'Motivations for learning among older adults in a learning in retirement institute', *Educational Gerontology* 30 (6): 441–455.

Kingwell, M. (2000) *The World We Want*, Toronto: Penguin, Canada.

Kirk, P. (1976) 'The loneliness of the long distance tutor', *Teaching at a Distance* 7: 3–6. Milton Keynes: Open University.

Kirkwood, C. (1978) 'Adult education and the concept of community', *Adult Education* 51 (3): 145–151. Leicester: NIAE.

Kirkwood, G. and Kirkwood, C. (1989) *Living Adult Education*, Milton Keynes, UK: Open University Press.

Knapper, C.K. and Cropley, A.J. (1985) *Lifelong Learning and Higher Education*, London: Croom Helm.

Knowles, M.S. (1970) *The Modern Practice of Adult Education: Andragogy versus Pedagogy*, Chicago: Association Press.

—— (1978) *The Adult Learner: A Neglected Species*, 2nd ed., Houston: Gulf Publishing Co.

—— (1979) 'Andragogy revisited II', *Adult Education* (Washington, DC) 3: 52–53.

—— (1980a) *The Modern Practice of Adult Education*, Chicago: Association Press.

—— (1980b) 'The growth and development of adult education', in Peters, J. and Associates, *Building an Effective Adult Education Enterprise*, San Francisco: Jossey-Bass.

—— (1986) *Using Learning Contracts*, San Francisco: Jossey-Bass.

—— (1989) *The Making of an Adult Educator*, San Francisco: Jossey-Bass.

Knowles, M. and Associates (1984) *Andragogy in Action*, San Francisco: Jossey-Bass.

Knox, A.B. (1977) *Adult Development and Learning*, San Francisco: Jossey-Bass.

Knudson, R.S. (1979) 'Andragogy revisted: humanagogy anyone?', *Adult Education* (Washington, DC) 29: 261–264.

Kohlberg, L. (1981) *The Philosophy of Moral Development*, vol. 1: *Essays in Moral Development*, San Francisco: Harper.

Köhler, W. (1947) *Gestalt Psychology*, New York: Liveright.

Kolb, D.A. (1984) *Experiential Learning*, Englewood Cliffs, NJ: Prentice Hall.

Kolb, D.A. and Fry, R. (1975) 'Towards an applied theory of experiential learning', in Cooper, C.L. (ed.) *Theories of Group Processes*, London: Wiley.

Korten, D. (1995) *When Corporations Rule the World*, London: Earthscan.

Krech, D., Crutchfield, R.S. and Ballachery, E.L. (1962) *Individual in Society*, New York: McGraw-Hill.

Kulich, I. (ed.) (1977) *Training of Adult Educators in East Europe*, Vancouver: Centre for Continuing Education, University of British Columbia.

—— (1982a) *Adult Education in Continental Europe: An Annotated Bibliography of English Language Materials 1975–9*, Vancouver Centre for Continuing Education, University of British Columbia.

—— (1982b) 'Lifelong education and the universities: a Canadian perspective', *International Journal of Lifelong Education* 1 (2): 123–142.

Kumar, K. (1978) *Prophecy and Progress*, Harmondsworth, UK: Penguin.

Kwan, C.-Y. (2000) 'Problem-based learning in medical education: from McMaster to Asia Pacific Region', in C. Wang *et al.* (eds) *Teaching and Learning in Higher Education Symposium*, Singapore: National University of Singapore.

Labouvie-Vief, G. (1978) 'Models of cognitive functioning in the old adult: research needs in educational gerontology', in Sherron, R.H. and Lumsdon, D.B. (eds) *Introduction to Educational Gerontology*, Washington, DC: Hemisphere.

Lacey, A.R. (1989) *Bergson*, London: Routledge.

Laksamba, C. (2005) 'Policies and practices of lifelong learning in Nepal', unpublished PhD thesis, Department of Political, International and Policy Studies, University of Surrey, Guildford, UK.

Langenbach, M. (1988) *Curriculum Models in Adult Education*, Malabar, FL: Krieger.

Last, I. and Chown, A. (1993) 'Teacher training in adult education', *Adults Learning* 4 (9): 234–236.

Lave, J. and Wenger, E. (1991) *Situated Learning*, Cambridge: Cambridge University Press.

Lawson, K.H. (1975) *Philosophical Concepts and Values in Adult Education*, Department of Adult Education, University of Nottingham. Reprinted in a 2nd edition and published by the Open University Press.

—— (1977) 'Community education: a critical assessment', *Adult Education* 50 (1): 6–13. Leicester: NIAE.

—— (1982) 'Lifelong education: concept or policy?', *International Journal of Education* 1 (2): 97–108.

Lawton, D. (1973) *Social Change, Educational Theory and Curriculum Planning*, London: Hodder & Stoughton.

Learmouth, J. with Maidments, L. (eds) (1993) *Teaching and Learning in Cities*, Whitbread Educational Partnership Paper.

Learning City Network, *LCN eNews*, published regularly, Nottingham.

—— (2000) *LCN Conference Report*, LCN: Nottingham.

Learning Lives Project, www.learninglives.org.

Learning Towns and Cities, *The Toolkit – Practice, Progress and Value.*

Lebel, I. (1978) 'Beyond andragogy to gerogogy', *Lifelong Learning: The Adult Years* 1 (9): 16–18, 24–25.

Legge, D. (1968) 'Training adult educators in the United Kingdom', *Convergence* 1 (1).

—— (1971a) 'The use of the talk in adult classes', in Stephens, M.D. and Roderick, G.W. (eds) *Teaching Techniques in Adult Education*, Newton Abbot, UK: David & Charles.

—— (1971b) 'Discussion methods', in Stephens, M.D. and Roderick, G.W. (eds) *Teaching Techniques in Adult Education*, Newton Abbot, UK: David & Charles.

—— (1981) 'The training of teachers of adults', in Harvey, B., Daines, I., Jones, D. and Wallis, I. (eds) *Policy and Research Adult Education*, Department of Adult Education, University of Nottingham.

—— (1982) *The Education of Adults in Britain*, Milton Keynes: Open University Press.

—— (1991) 'Educators of adults in England and Wales', in Jarvis, P. and Chadwick, A. (eds) *Training Adult Educators in Western Europe*, London: Routledge.

Leithäuser, T. (1976) *Formen des Alltagsbuwusstseins* (The Forms of Everyday Consciousness), Frankfurt am Main: Campus.

Lengrand, P. (1975) *An Introduction to Lifelong Education*, London: Croom Helm.

Lester-Smith, W.O. (1966) *Education: An Introductory Survey*, Harmondsworth, UK: Penguin.

Levinas, E. (1991) *Totality and Infinity* (trans. A. Lingis), Dordrecht: Kluwer.

Leung, A., Chi, I., Chow, N., Chan, K.-S. and Chou, K.-L. (2006) 'Construction and validation of a Chinese value of learning scale', *Educational Gerontology* 32 (10): 907–920.

Leytham, G. (1971) 'The principles of programmed learning', in Stephens, M.D. and Roderick, G.W. (eds) *Teaching Techniques in Adult Education*, Newton Abbot, UK: David & Charles.

Li Herzhong (1997) 'The university for old people in China', *Third Age Learning International Studies* 7: 91–95.

Li Zhi, Du Zicai and Chan Yuan (1997) 'The Chinese characteristics of and prospects for China's education for the aged in Wuhan', *Third Age Learning International Studies* 7: 71–77.

Light, G. and Cox, R. (2001) *Learning and Teaching in Higher Education*. London: Paul Chapman.

Lindeman, E. (1938) 'Preparing leaders in adult education' (speech given to Pennsylvania Association for Adult Education, 18 November). Published in Brookfield, S. (ed.) *Training Educators of Adults*, London: Routledge.

—— (1961 [1926]) *The Meaning of Adult Education*, Montreal: Harvester House.

Lippitt, R. and White, R.K. (1958) 'An experimental study of leadership and group life', in Maccoby, E.E., Newcomb, T.M. and Hartley, E.L. (eds) *Readings in Social Psychology*, New York: Holt.

Little, A., Willey, R. and Gundara, J. (1982) *Adult Education and the Black Communities*, Leicester: ACACE.

London, J. (1973) 'Reflections upon the relevance of Paulo Freire for American adult education', *Convergence* 6 (1), 48–61, 73.

Long, H. and Lord, C. (eds) (1978) *The Continuing Education Credit Unit: Concept, Issues and Use*, Athens, GA: University of Georgia Center for Continuing Education.

Long, H. and Associates (1988) *Self-Directed Learning: Application and Theory*, Athens, GA: University of Georgia, Department of Adult Education.

—— (1993) *Emerging Perspectives of Self-Directed Learning*, Norman: University of Oklahoma, Research Center for Continuing and Professional Higher Education.

—— (1997) *Expanding Horizons in Self-Directed Learning*, Norman: University of Oklahoma, College of Education.

—— (1998) *Developing Paradigms for Self-Directed Learning*, Norman: University of Oklahoma, College of Education.

Longworth, N. (1999) *Making Lifelong Learning Work: Learning Cities for a Learning Century*, London: Kogan Page.

Lovell, B.R. (1980) *Adults Learning*, London: Croom Helm.

Lovett, T. (1975) *Adult Education, Community Development and the Working Class*, London: Ward Lock Educational.

—— (1980) 'Adult education and community action', in Thompson, J.L. (ed.) *Adult Education for a Change*, London: Heinemann.

Lovett, T. and Mackay, L. (1978) 'Community based study groups', *Adult Education* 51 (1): 22–29. Leicester: NIAE.

Lovett, T., Clarke, C. and Kilmurray, A. (1983) *Adult Education and Community Action*, London: Croom Helm.

Lucent Technologies (1996) *Distance Education: The Vision*, www.lucent.com/cedl/.

Luckmann, T. (1967) *The Invisible Religion*, London: Collier Macmillan.

Lukes, S. (1981) 'Fact and theory in the social sciences', in Potter, D. *et al.* (eds) *Society and the Social Sciences*, London: Routledge & Kegan Paul/Open University Press.

Lyotard, J.-F. (1984) *The Postmodern Condition*, Manchester: University of Manchester Press.

McAdam, D. (2001) *The Person*, Fort Worth, TX: Harcourt.

Maccoby, E.E., Newcomb, T.M. and Hartley, E.L. (eds) (1958) *Readings in Social Psychology*, 3rd ed., New York: Holt.

McCullough, O. (1980) 'Analyzing the evolving structure of adult education', in Peters, I. and Associates, *Building an Effective Adult Education Enterprise*, San Francisco: Jossey-Bass.

Mace, I. and Yarnit, M. (eds) (1987) *Time Off to Learn*, London: Methuen.

Macfarlane, B. (2004) *Teaching with Integrity*, London: RoutledgeFalmer.

Macfarlane, T. (1978) 'Curriculum innovation in adult literacy: the cost of insularity', *Studies in Adult Education* 10 (2).

McGill, I. and Beaty, L. (1995) *Action Learning*, 2nd ed., London: Kogan Page.

McGill, I. and Brockbank, A. (2004) *The Action Learning Handbook*, London: RoutledgeFalmer.

McGivney, V. (1990) *Access to Education for Non-participant Adults*, Leicester: NIACE.

McGregor, D. (1960) *The Human Side of Enterprise*, New York: McGraw-Hill.

McIntosh, N. (1974) 'The Open University student', in Tunstall, I. (ed.) *The Open University Opens*, London: Routledge & Kegan Paul.

McIntosh, N.E. (1979a) 'To make continuing education a reality', *Oxford Review of Education* 5 (2): 169–182. Republished by ACACE, Leicester.

—— (1979b) 'Andragogy revisited: response to Elias', *Adult Education* (Washington, DC) 29: 256–261.

McKenzie, L. (1977) 'The issue of andragogy', *Adult Education* (Washington, DC) 27: 225–229.

—— (1979) 'Andragogy revisited: response to Elias', *Adult Education* (Washington, DC) 29: 256–261.

McLagan, P.A. (1978) *Helping Others Learn*, Reading, MA: Addison-Wesley.

MacMurray, J. (1961) *Persons in Relation*, Atlantic Highlands, NJ: Humanities Press.

McNiff, J. (1988) *Action Research: Principles and Practice*, London: Routledge.

Mager, C. (1991) 'Open college networks', *Adults Learning* 3 (4): 97–98.

Mannings, R. (1986) *The Incidental Learning Research Project*, Bristol Folk House, Adult Education Centre.

Mannion-Watson, C. (1982) 'An evaluation of a pilot course on the teaching of study skills to Sixth Form students', unpublished MSc dissertation, University of Surrey, Guildford, UK.

Marcuse, H. (1964) *One Dimensional Man*, reprinted in 1986 by ARK paperbacks, London.

Marshall, T.H. (1950) *Citizenship and Social Class and Other Essays*, Cambridge: Cambridge University Press.

Marsick, V. (ed.) (1987) *Learning in the Workplace*, London: Croom Helm.

Martin, B. (1981) *A Sociology of Contemporary Cultural Change*, Oxford: Blackwell.

Martin, L.C. (1981) 'A survey of the training needs of part-time tutors in a region', *Studies in Adult Education* 13 (2).

Martin, P. (1999) 'Art teachers in contemporary adult education', unpublished PhD thesis, University of Surrey, Guildford, UK.

Marton, F. and Booth, S. (1997) *Learning and Awareness*, Mahwah, NJ: Lawrence Erlbaum Associates.

Marton, F., Hounsell, D. and Entwistle, N. (1984) *The Experience of Learning*, Edinburgh: Scottish Academic Press.

Maslin, K.T. (2001) *An Introduction to the Philosophy of Mind*, Cambridge: Polity.

Maslow, A.H. (1968) *Toward a Psychology of Being*, 2nd ed., New York: Van Nostrand.

Mee, G. (1980) *Organisation for Adult Education*, London: Longman.

Mee, G. and Wiltshire, H. (1978) *Structure and Performance in Adult Education*, London: Longman.

Mehrens, W. and Lehmann, I. (1991) *Measurement and Evaluation in Education and Psychology*, 4th ed., Fort Worth, TX: Holt, Rinehart & Winston.

Meister, L. (1998) *Corporate Universities*, 2nd ed., New York: McGraw-Hill.

Merriam, S. and Caffarella, R. (1991) *Learning in Adulthood*, San Francisco: Jossey-Bass.

Merriam, S.B. and Cunningham, P. (1989) *Handbook of Adult and Continuing Education*, San Francisco: Jossey-Bass.

Merton, R.K. (1968) *Social Theory and Social Structure*, New York: The Free Press.

Mezirow, J. (1977) 'Perspective transformation', *Adult Education Quarterly* 9 (2): 100–110.

—— (1981) 'A critical theory of adult learning and education', *Adult Education* (Washington, DC) 32 (1): 3–24.

—— (1991) *Transformative Dimensions of Adult Learning*, San Francisco: Jossey-Bass.

Mezirow, J. and Associates (1990) *Fostering Critical Reflection in Adulthood*, San Francisco: Jossey-Bass.

—— (2000) *Learning as Transformation*, San Francisco: Jossey-Bass.

Midwinter, F. (1975) *Education and the Community*, London: Allen & Unwin.

—— (ed.) (1984) *Mutual Aid Universities*, London: Croom Helm.

Mill, J.S. (1962 [1859]) *On Liberty*. Reprinted in *Utilitarianism*, London: Fontana Library Collins.

Miller, N. and Dollard, J. (1941) *Social Learning and Imitation*, New Haven, CT: Yale University Press.

Mocker, D.W. and Noble, F. (1981) 'Training part-time instructional staff', in Grabowski, S. (ed.) *Preparing Educators of Adults*, San Francisco: Jossey-Bass.

Moemeka, A.A. (1981) *Local Radio: Community Education for Development*, Zaria, Nigeria: Ahmadu Bello University Press.

Molyneux, F., Low, U. and Fowler, G. (ed.) (1988) *Learning for Life*, London: Croom Helm.

Monbiot, G. (2000) *The Captive State*, London: Macmillan.

—— (2007) 'Don't listen to what the rich world's leaders say – look at what they do', *Guardian* (London), 5 June: 33.

Morris, H. (1956) 'Architecture, humanism and the local community', paper read at the Royal Institute of British Architects (RIBA) on 15 May, and published in

Fletcher, C. and Thompson, N. (eds) (1980) *Issues in Community Education*, Lewes, UK: Falmer Press.

Morrison, J. and Meister, J. (2002) 'e-Learning in the corporate university: an interview with Jeanne Meister', *Commentary*, http://ts.mivu.org/default.asp?show=article&id=888.

Morstain, B.R. and Smart, J.C. (1974) 'Reasons for participation in adult education courses: a multivariate analysis of group difference', *Adult Education* (Washington, DC) 24 (2): 83–98.

Müller, D. and Funnell, P. (eds) (1991) *Delivering Quality in Vocational Education*, London: Kogan Page.

Murgatroyd, S. and Morgan, C. (1993) *Total Quality Management and the School*, Milton Keynes, UK: Open University Press.

Murray, M. with Owen, M. (1991) *Beyond the Myths and Magic of Mentoring*, San Francisco: Jossey-Bass.

National Institute of Adult Continuing Education (1993a) *Yearbook of Adult Continuing Education 1993–4*, Leicester: NIACE.

—— (1993b) *Draft Strategic Plan 1993/6*, Leicester: NIACE.

—— (2008a) *Shaping the Way Ahead*, Leicester: NIACE.

—— (2008b) *CONFINTEA VI: United Kingdom National Report*, Leicester: NIACE.

Nelson, K. (2007) *Young Minds in Social Worlds*, Cambridge, MA: Harvard University Press.

Newman, M. (1973) *Adult Education and Community Action*, London: Writers and Readers Publishing Cooperative.

—— (1979) *The Poor Cousin*, London: Allen & Unwin.

—— (2006) *Teaching Defiance: Stories and Strategies for Activist Educators*, San Francisco: Jossey-Bass.

Newman, M. (2009) 'Give students smart drugs on demand to aid study', *Times Higher Education*, 1 January: 10.

NICEC (n.d.) *Adult Guidance in Community Settings*, www.gla.ac.uk/avg/avgrd2_2.htm.

Nutley, S., Walter, I. and Davies, H. (2007) *Using Evidence*, Bristol: Policy Press.

Nyiri, I. (1988) 'Tradition and practical knowledge', in Nyiri, I. and Smith, B. (eds) *Practical Knowledge: Outlines of a Theory of Traditions and Skills*, London: Croom Helm.

Nyiri, I. and Smith, B. (eds) (1988) *Practical Knowledge: Outlines of a Theory of Traditions and Skills*, London: Croom Helm.

Oakeshott, M. (1933) *Experience and Its Modes*, Cambridge: Cambridge University Press.

Oakeshott, M. (1991) *Educational Guidance for Adults: Identifying Competences*, London: Further Education Unit.

Olesen, H.S. (2009) 'Workplace learning', in Jarvis, P. (ed.) *The Routledge International Handbook of Lifelong Learning*, London: Routledge.

Oliveira, R. and Oliveira, M. (1976) *Guinea-Bissau: Reinventing Education*, Geneva: Institute of Cultural Action.

O'Loughlin, M. (2006) *Embodiment and Education*, Dordrecht: Springer.

O'Neill, C. (2003) 'Learning to be a person', unpublished PhD thesis, University of Surrey, Guildford, UK.

Organisation for Economic Co-operation and Development (1973) *Recurrent Education: A Strategy for Lifelong Learning*, Paris: OECD.

—— (1996) *Lifelong Learning for All*, Paris: OECD.

—— (2001) *Cities and Regions in the New Learning Economy*, Paris: OECD.

—— (2007) *Understanding the Brain: The Birth of a Learning Science*, Paris: OECD.

Overstreet, H. and Overstreet, B. (1941) 'The making of the makers', in Overstreet, H. and Overstreet, B. (eds) *Leaders for Adult Education*, New York: American Association of Adult Education.

Palmer, P.J. (1993) *To Know as We Are Known*, New York: HarperCollins.

—— (1998) *The Courage to Teach*, San Francisco: Jossey-Bass.

Parker, S. (1976) *The Sociology of Leisure*, London: Allen & Unwin.

Parsons, C. (1994) *Quality Improvement in Education: Case Studies in Schools, Colleges and Universities*, London: Fulton.

Paterson, R.W.K. (1979) *Values, Education and the Adult*, London: Routledge & Kegan Paul.

Pavlov, I.P. (1927) *Conditioned Reflexes*, New York: Oxford University Press.

Payne, J. (1993) 'Too little of a good thing? Adult education and the workplace', *Adults Learning* 4 (10): 274–275.

Pedler, M., Burgoyne, J. and Boydell, T. (1997) *The Learning Company*, 2nd ed., London: McGraw-Hill.

Peers, R. (1958) *Adult Education: A Comparative Perspective*, London: Routledge & Kegan Paul.

Peters, J.M. and Gordon, S. (1974) *Adult Learning Projects: A Study of Adult Learning in Urban and Rural Tennessee*, Knoxville: University of Tennessee.

Peters, J.M. and Associates (1980) *Building an Effective Adult Education Enterprise*, San Francisco: Jossey-Bass.

Peters, J.M., Jarvis, P. and Associates (1991) *Adult Education: Evolution and Achievements in a Developing Field of Study*, San Francisco: Jossey-Bass.

Peters, O. (1984) 'Distance teaching and industrial production: a comparative interpretation in outline', in Sewart, D., Keegan, D. and Holmberg, B. (eds) *Distance Education: International Perspectives*, London: Croom Helm.

—— (1998) *Learning and Teaching in Distance Education*, London: Kogan Page.

—— (2002) *Distance Education in Transition*, Oldenburg, Germany: Bibliotheks- und Informationssystems der Universität Oldenburg.

—— (2009) 'The contribution of open and distance education to lifelong learning', in Jarvis, P. (ed.) *The Routledge International Handbook of Lifelong Learning*, London: Routledge.

Peters, R.S. (1966) *Ethics and Education*, London: Allen & Unwin.

—— (1972) 'Education and the educated man', in Dearden, D.F., Hirst, P.H. and Peters, R.S. (eds) *A Critique of Current Educational Aims*, vol. 1: *Education and the Development of Reason*, London: Routledge & Kegan Paul.

Peterson, R.E. and Associates (1979) *Lifelong Learning in America*, San Francisco: Jossey-Bass.

Peterson, S. (1989) 'Reducing student attrition', in Weil, S. and McGill, I. (eds) *Making Sense of Experiential Learning*, Buckingham, UK: SRHE/Open University Press.

Phillipson, C. and Strang, P. (1983) *The Impact of Pre-retirement Education*, University of Keele, UK, Department of Adult Education.

Piaget, J. (1929) *The Child's Conception of the World*, London: Routledge & Kegan Paul.

Polanyi, M. (1967) *The Tacit Dimension*, London: Routledge & Kegan Paul.

Poole, R. (1990) *Morality and Modernity*, London: Routledge.

Popham, W.J., Eisner, E.W., Sullivan, H.J. and Tyler, L.L. (1969) *Instructional Objectives*, Chicago: Rand McNally.

Poster, C. and Kruger, A. (eds) (1990) *Community Education in the Western World*, London: Routledge.

Poster, M. (ed.) (1988) *Jean Baudrillard: Selected Writings*, Cambridge: Polity Press.

Potter, D. *et al.* (eds) (1981) *Society and the Social Sciences*, London: Routledge & Kegan Paul/Open University Press.

Pratt, D. and Associates (1998) *Five Different Approaches to Teaching in Adult and Higher Education*, Malabar, FL: Krieger.

Press Release (November 2002) 'Ireland to become a Nation of "Learning Cities and Learning Counties"', http://www/dublincity.ie/profile/pressr/201119.htm.

Preston, J. and Hammond, C. (2002) *The Wider Benefits of Further Education: Practitioner Views*, London: Institute of Education, Centre for Research on the Wider Benefits of Learning.

Pursaill, J. (1989) *National Vocational Qualifications and Further Education*, London: Further Education Unit.

Putnam, R. (2000) *Bowling Alone: The Collapse and Revival of American Community*, New York: Simon & Schuster.

Ranson, S. (1994) *Towards the Learning Society*, London: Cassell.

Reason, P. and Rowan, J. (eds) (1981) *Human Inquiry*, Chichester, UK: Wiley.

Redmann, D. (ed.) (2000) *Defining the Cutting Edge*, St Paul, MN: Academy of Human Resource Development.

Reischmann, J. (1986) 'Learning en passant', paper presented at AAACE, Hollywood, CA.

Revans, R. (1980) *Action Learning: New Techniques for Action Learning*, London: Blond & Briggs.

—— (1982) *The Origins and Growth of Action Learning*, Bromley, UK: Chartwell-Bratt.

Richardson, M. (ed.) (1979) *Preparing to Study*, Milton Keynes, UK: Open University Press.

Riegel, K. (1973) 'Dialectic operations: the final period of cognitive development', *Human Development* 16: 346–370.

Riesman, D. (1950) *The Lonely Crowd: A Study of Changing American Character*, New Haven, CT: Yale University Press.

Robertson, R. (1995) 'Glocalisation', in Featherstone, M., Lash, S. and Robertson, R. (eds) *Global Modernities*, London: Sage.

Rodd, M. (1992) 'Change for the better? Recent developments in adult literacy', *Adults Learning* 4 (2).

Roderick, G.W., Bell, J., Dickenson, R., Turner, R. and Wellings, A. (1981) *Mature Students in Further and Higher Education*, University of Sheffield, Division of Continuing Education.

Rogers, A. (ed.) (1976) *The Spirit and the Form*, University of Nottingham, Department of Adult Education.

—— (1986) *Teaching Adults*, Milton Keynes, UK: Open University Press.

Rogers, C.R. (1969) *Freedom to Learn*, Columbus, OH: Charles F. Merrill.

—— (1983) *Freedom to Learn for the 80's*, New York: Merrill-Macmillan.

Rogers, C.R. and Freiberg, H.J. (1994) *Freedom to Learn*, 3rd ed., New York: Merrill.

Rogers, F.M. (1962) *Diffuision of Innovations*, Glencoe, IL: The Free Press.

Rogers, J. (ed.) (1973) *Adults in Education*, London: British Broadcasting Corporation.

—— (1977) *Adults Learning*, 2nd ed., Milton Keynes, UK: Open University Press.

—— (1989) *Adults Learning*, 3rd ed., Milton Keynes, UK: Open University Press.

Rogers, J. and Groombridge, B. (1976) *Right to Learn*, London: Arrow Books.

Rorty, R. (1982) *Consequences of Pragmatism*, New York: Harvester Wheatsheaf.

Rose, S. (2005) *The 21st-Century Brain*, London: Jonathan Cape.

Rowntree, J. and Bins, H. (1986 [1903]) *History of the Adult School Movement*, University of Nottingham, Department of Adult Education.

Rumble, G. (1982) *The Open University of the United Kingdom*, Distance Education Research Group, The Open University, Milton Keynes, UK.

Rumble, G. and Harry, K. (1982) *The Distance Teaching Universities*, London: Croom Helm.

Russell, L. (1973) *Adult Education: A Plan for Development*, London: HMSO.

Ryle, G. (1963 [1949]) *The Concept of Mind*, Harmondsworth, UK: Penguin.

Ryle, M. (1993) 'A case for collaboration', *Adults Learning* 4 (9): 240–241.

Sargant, N. (1990) *Learning and Leisure*, Leicester: NIACE.

Sargant, N. with Field, J., Francis, H., Schuller, T. and Tuckett, A. (1997) *The Learning Divide*, Leicester: NIACE.

Scheler, M. (1926) *Die Wissensformen und die Gesellschaft*, Leipzig: Der Neue-Geist Verlag.

—— (1980) *Problems of a Sociology of Knowledge* (trans. M.S. Frings), London: Routledge & Kegan Paul.

Schiller, H. (1981) *Who Knows: Information in the Age of the Fortune 500*, Norwood, NJ: Ablex.

Schön, D.A. (1973) *Beyond the Stable State*, Harmondsworth, UK: Penguin.

—— (1983) *The Reflective Practitioner*, New York: Basic Books.

—— (1987) *Educating the Reflective Practitioner*, San Francisco: Jossey-Bass.

Schuller, T. and Megarry, I. (eds) (1979) *World Yearbook on Education 1979: Recurrent Education and Lifelong Learning*, London: Kogan Page.

Schuller, T. and Watson, D. (2009) *Learning through Life*, Leicester: NIACE.

Schuller, T., Brassett-Grundy, A., Green, A., Hammond, C. and Preston, C. (2002) *Learning, Continuity and Change in Adult Life*, London: Institute of Education, Centre for Research on the Wider Benefits of Learning.

Schuller, T., Preston, J., Hammond, C., Bassett-Grundy, A. and Bynner, J. (2004) *The Benefits of Learning*, London: RoutledgeFalmer.

Schultz, T. (1961) *Investment in Human Capital*, Basingstoke, UK: Macmillan, cited from Jarvis, P. with Griffin, C. (eds) (2003) *Adult and Continuing Education: Major Themes in Education*, vol. 5, London: Routledge.

Schutz, A. (1974) *The Phenomenology of the Social World*, London: Heinemann.

Schutz, A. and Luckmann, T. (1974) *The Structures of the Life World*, London: Heinemann.

Searle, J. (1992) *The Rediscovery of the Mind*, Cambridge, MA: MIT Press.

Selwyn, N., Gorard, S. and Furlong, J. (2006) *Adult Learning in the Digital Age*, London: Routledge.

Senge, P. (1990) *The Fifth Discipline*, New York: Doubleday.

Senior, B. and Naylor, J. (1987) *Educational Responses to Adult Unemployment*, London: Croom Helm.

Sennett, R. (1986) *The Fall of Public Man*, London: Faber & Faber. (First published by Alfred A. Knopf in New York in 1977.)

—— (2008) *The Craftsman*, London: Penguin.

Sewart, D., Keegan, D. and Holmberg, B. (eds) (1984) *Distance Education: International Perspectives*, London: Routledge.

Sheridan, A. (1980) *Michel Foucault: The Will to Truth*, London: Tavistock.

Sherron, R.H. and Lumsden, D.B. (eds) (1978) *Introduction to Educational Gerontology*, Washington, DC: Hemisphere.

Shilling, C. (1993) *The Body and Social Theory*, London: Sage.

Shirasha, I. (1995) 'Japan, a developing country in the field of lifelong learning as well as ageing: its new perspectives and barriers', *Third Age Learning International Studies* 5: 101–104.

Skinner, B.F. (1951) 'How to teach animals', *Scientific American* 185 (6): 26–29.

—— (1968) *The Technology of Teaching*, New York: Appleton Century Crofts.

—— (1971) *Beyond Freedom and Dignity*, Harmondsworth, UK: Penguin.

Sless, D. (1981) *Learning and Visual Communication*, London: Croom Helm.

Small, N. (ed.) (1992) *The Learning Society: Political Rhetoric and Electoral Reality*, University of Nottingham, Association for Lifelong Learning.

Smith, A.L. (1919) 'Adult Education Committee Final Report', reprinted in 'The 1919 Report', University of Nottingham, Department of Adult Education.

Smith, G. (1993) 'BTEC GNVQs and developments in vocational education', *Adults Learning* 4 (5). Leicester: NIACE.

Smith, J. and Spurling, J. (1999) *Lifelong Learning: Riding the Tiger*, London: Cassell.

Smith, M. (1994) *Local Education*, Buckingham, UK: Open University Press.

Socias, C., Brage, L. and Garma, C. (2004) 'University programs for seniors in Spain: analysis and perspectives', *Educational Gerontology* 30 (4): 315–328.

Sommer, R. (1989) *Teaching Writing to Adults*, San Francisco: Jossey-Bass.

Srinivasan, L. (1977) *Perspectives on Non-formal Adult Learning*, New York: World Education.

Stanistreet, P. (2009) 'Mind the funding gap', *Adults Learning* 20 (8): 22–27. Leicester: NIACE.

Stationery Office, The (1998) *Learning Towns and Learning Cities*, London: The Stationery Office.

—— (2006) *Social Trends 2006*, London: The Stationery Office.

Stehr, N. (1994) *The Knowledge Society*, London: Sage.

Stenhouse, L. (1975) *An Introduction to Curriculum Research and Development*, London: Heinemann.

Stephens, M.D. (1981) 'The future of continuing education', *Adult Education* 54 (2): 134–138. Leicester: NIAE.

Stephens, M.D. and Roderick, G.W. (eds) (1971) *Teaching Techniques in Adult Education*, Newton Abbot, UK: David & Charles.

Sternberg, R. (1997) *Thinking Styles*, Cambridge: Cambridge University Press.

Stock, A. (1971) 'Role playing and simulation techniques', in Stephens, M.D. and Roderick, U.W. (eds) *Teaching Techniques in Adult Education*, Newton Abbot, UK: David & Charles.

—— (1982) *Adult Education in the United Kingdom*, Leicester: NIAE.

Strain, J., Barnett, R. and Jarvis, P. (eds) (2009) *Universities, Ethics and the Professions*, London: Routledge.

Strike, K. and Soltis, I. (1985) *The Ethics of Teaching*, New York: Teachers College Press.

Surridge, R. and Bowen, J. (1977) *The Independent Learning Project: A Study of Changing Attitudes in American Public Libraries*, Brighton: Public Libraries Research Group.

Taba, H. (1962) *Curriculum Development: Theory and Practice*, New York: Harcourt, Brace and World.

Tabberer, R. and Allman, J. (1981) *Study Skills at 16 Plus*, Slough, UK: National Foundation for Educational Research.

Taylor, C. (1991) *The Ethics of Authenticity*, Cambridge, MA: Harvard University Press.

Taylor, J. (1978) 'The Advisory Council for Adult and Continuing Education', *Adult Education* 51 (4): 209–215. Leicester: NIAE.

Taylor, P.V. (1993) *The Texts of Paulo Freire*, London: Routledge.

Taylor, R. (2008) 'The future of informal adult learning', *Adults Learning* 19 (6): 8–9.

—— (2009) 'Self-directed learning in the modern context', in Jarvis, P. (ed.) *The Routledge International Handbook of Lifelong Learning*, London: Routledge.

Teare, R., Davies, D. and Sandelands, E. (1998) *The Virtual University*, London: Cassell.

Tennant, M. (1986) 'An evaluation of Knowles' theory of learning', *International Journal of Lifelong Education* 5 (2): 113–122.

—— (1988) *Psychology and Adult Learning*, London: Croom Helm.

Tett, L. (2008) 'Rearticulating professional identity', in *The Edinburgh Papers: Reclaiming Social Purpose in Community Education*, University of Edinburgh, Learning for Democracy Group.

Thompson, J.L. (ed.) (1980) *Adult Education for a Change*, London: Heinemann.

Thompson, J. (1993) 'Learning, liberation and maturity: an open letter to whoever's left', *Adults Learning* 4 (9): 244. Leicester: NIACE.

Thorndike, E.L. (1928) *Adult Learning*, London: Macmillan.

Thornton, A.H. and Stephens, M.D. (eds) (1977) *The University in Its Region*, University of Nottingham, Department of Adult Education.

Tiernan, K. (1992) 'Taking credit for voluntary work', *Adults Learning* 4 (2): 38–39. Leicester: NIACE.

Tight, M. (1982) *Part-Time Degree Level Study in the United Kingdom*, Leicester: ACACE.

—— (1991) *Higher Education: A Part-Time Perspective*, Buckingham, UK: Society for Research into Higher Education/Open University Press.

Titmus, C. (1981) *Strategies for Adult Education: Practices in Western Europe*, Milton Keynes, UK: Open University Press.

—— (1989) *Lifelong Education for Adults: An International Handbook*, Oxford: Pergamon Press.

Tomasello, M. (1999) *The Cultural Origins of Human Cognition*, Cambridge, MA: Harvard University Press.

Tönnies, F. (1957) *Community and Society* (trans. C.P. Loomis), East Lansing: Michigan State University Press. Published in the United Kingdom as *Community and Association* by Routledge & Kegan Paul, London.

Torres, C. (2009) *Globalizations and Education*, New York: Teachers College Press.

Tough, A. (1979) *The Adult's Learning Projects*, 2nd ed., Toronto: Ontario Institute for Studies in Education.

—— (1981) *Learning without a Teacher*, 3rd ed., Educational Research Series no. 3, Toronto: Ontario Institute for Studies in Education.

Tremlin, T. (2006) *Minds and Gods*, Oxford: Oxford University Press.

Tuckett, A. (2005) 'Enough is enough', *Adults Learning* 17 (1): 6–7. Leicester: NIACE.

Tuijnman, A. (1989) *Recurrent Education, Earnings and Well-being*, Stockholm: Almqvist & Wiksell International.

Tuijnman, A. and van der Kamp, M. (eds) (1993) *Learning across the Lifespan*, Oxford: Pergamon Press.

Tunstall, J. (ed.) (1974) *The Open University Opens*, London: Routledge & Kegan Paul.

Tuomi, I. (1999) *Corporate Knowledge*, Helsinki: Metaxis.

Turner, B. (1990) 'Outline of a theory of citizenship', *Sociology* 24 (2): 189–217.

Turner, J. and Stets, J. (2005) *The Sociology of Emotions*, Cambridge: Cambridge University Press.

Turner, R. (1962) 'Role taking: process versus conformity', in Rose, A. (ed.) *Human Behavior and Social Processes*, London: Routledge & Kegan Paul.

Turner, V. (1969) *The Ritual Process*, Harmondsworth, UK: Penguin.

Tyler, R.W. (1949) *Basic Principles of Curriculum and Instruction*, Chicago: University of Chicago Press.

UNESCO (n.d.) *Creative Learning and Ageing*, Hamburg: UNSECO and NIACE.

Usher, R. (1989) 'Locating adult education in the practical', in Bright, B. (ed.) *Theory and Practice in the Study of Adult Education*, London: Routledge.

Usher, R. and Bryant, I. (1989) *Adult Education as Theory, Practice and Research*, London: Routledge.

Vaill, P. (1996) *Learning as a Way of Being*, San Francisco: Jossey-Bass.

Venables, P. (1976) *Report of the Committee on Continuing Education*, Milton Keynes: Open University Press.

Verduin, J. (1980) *Curriculum Building for Adult Learning*, Carbondale: Southern Illinois University Press.

Vermilye, D.W. (ed.) (1977) *Relating Work and Education*, San Francisco: Jossey-Bass.

Verner, C. with Booth, C. (1964) *Adult Education*, Washington, DC: Center for Applied Research in Education.

Vignuda, J.-L. (2009) 'Tourism development in the Asia-Pacific Region: opportunities for lifelong learning', in Jarvis, P. (ed.) *The Routledge International Handbook of Lifelong Learning*, London: Routledge.

Volkoff, V. (2009) 'Permeating policy and practice: research into adult learning with a view to the future', in Coare, P. and Cecil, L. (eds) *Really Useful Research? Proceedings of the 39th Annual Conference of SCUTREA*, Brighton: University of Sussex and SCUTREA.

Vygotsky, L. (1978) *Mind and Society*, Cambridge, MA: Harvard University Press.

—— (1986) *Thought and Language* (rev. and ed. A. Kozulin), Cambridge, MA: MIT Press.

Wallace, D. (2008) 'Community education: a mirror and a shield', in *The Edinburgh Papers: Reclaiming Social Purpose in Community Education*, University of Edinburgh, Learning for Democracy Group.

Wallerstein, I. (1974) *The Modern World System*, New York: Academic Press.

Walshok, M. (1995) *Knowledge without Boundaries*, San Francisco: Jossey-Bass.

Wang, C., Mohanan, K., Pan, D. and Chee, Y. (eds) (2000) *Proceedings of the First Symposium on Teaching and Learning in Higher Education*, National University of Singapore.

Wang, C., Mohanan, K. and Pan, D. (eds) (2002) *Proceedings of the Second Symposium on Teaching and Learning in Higher Education*, National University of Singapore.

Wang, V.C.X. (ed.) (2008) *Curriculum Development for Adult Learners in the Global Community* (2 vols), Malabar, FL: Krieger.

Watkins, D. and Biggs, J. (eds) (1996) *The Chinese Learner*, Hong Kong: University of Hong Kong; Canberra: Australian Research Council.

Watkins, K. and Marsick, V. (1993) *Sculpting the Learning Organization*, San Francisco: Jossey-Bass.

—— (2009) 'Trends in lifelong education in the US workplace', in Jarvis, P. (ed.) *The Routledge International Handbook of Lifelong Learning*, London: Routledge.

Webster, F. (2002) *Theories of the Information Society*, London: Routledge.

Wedemeyer, C. (1981) *Learning at the Back Door*, Madison: University of Wisconsin Press.

Weil, S.W. and McGill, I. (eds) (1989) *Making Sense of Experiential Learning*, Buckingham, UK: Open University Press/SRHE.

Wenger, E. (1998) *Communities of Practice*, Cambridge: Cambridge University Press.

West, C.K., Fowler, J.A. and Wolf, P.M. (1991) *Instructional Design: Implications from Cognitive Science*, Englewood Cliffs, NJ: Prentice Hall.

Westwood, S. (1980) 'Adult education and the sociology of education: an exploration', in Thompson, J.L. (ed.) *Adult Education for a Change*, London: Heinemann.

Wilensky, H.A.L. (1964) 'The professionalization of everyone?', *American Journal of Sociology* 70: 137–158.

Williams, E. and Heath, A.E. (1936) *Learn and Live*, London: Methuen.

Williams, G. (1977) *Towards Lifelong Education: A New Role for Higher Education Institutes*, Paris: UNESCO.

Williams, G.L. (1980) 'Adults learning about adult learning', *Adult Education* 52 (6): 386–391. Leicester: NIAE.

Williams, J. (2008) 'The public value debate', *Adults Learning* 19 (7): 26–27. Leicester: NIAE.

Wilson, S. (1980) 'The school and the community', in Fletcher, C. and Thompson, N. (eds) *Issues in Community Education*, Lewes, UK: Falmer.

Wiltshire, H. (1973) 'The concepts of learning and need in adult education', *Studies in Adult Education* 5 (1): 26–30. (Reprinted in Rogers, A. (1976) *The Spirit and the Form*, University of Nottingham, Department of Adult Education.)

—— (1976) 'The nature and uses of adult education', in Rogers, A. (ed.) *The Spirit and the Form*, University of Nottingham, Department of Adult Education.

—— (1981) 'Changing concepts of adult education', in Elsdon, K. (ed.) *New Directions: Adult Education in the Context of Continuing Education*, London: Department of Education and Science.

Winch, C. (1998) *The Philosophy of Human Learning*, London: Routledge.

Withnall, A. (2010) *Improving Learning in Later Life*, London: Routledge.

Witkin, H.A. (1965) 'Psychological differentiations', *Journal of Abnormal Psychology* 70 (5): 317–336. (Reprinted in Cashdan, A. and Whitehead, J. (1971) *Personality Growth and Learning*, London: Longman.)

Wlodkowski, R. (1985) *Enhancing Adult Motivation to Learn*, San Francisco: Jossey-Bass.

Wood, D. (1982) *Continuing Education in Polytechnics and Colleges*, University of Nottingham, Department of Adult Education.

Woodhall, M. (1980) *The Scope and Costs of the Education and Training of Adults in Britain*, Leicester: ACACE.

—— (1988) 'Economic and financial implications of recurrent and continuing education', in Molyneux, F., Low, G. and Fowler, G. (eds) *Learning for Life*, London: Croom Helm.

Woodley, A., Wagner, L., Slowey, M., Hamilton, M. and Foulton, O. (1987) *Choosing to Learn: Adults in Education*, Buckingham, UK: Open University Press/SRHE.

Workers' Education Association (1982) *The Robert Tressell Papers: Exploring 'The Ragged Trousered Philanthropists'*, obtainable from Robert Tressell Workshop, c/o Robert Tressell House, 25 Wellington Square, Hastings, East Sussex.

Yarrington, R. (1979) 'Lifelong education trends in community colleges', *Convergence* 12 (1–2): 86–94.

Yeaxlee, B.A. (1925) *Spiritual Values in Adult Education* (2 vols), London: Oxford University Press.

—— (1929) *Lifelong Education*, London: Cassell.

Young, M.F.D. (1971) 'Curricula as socially organized knowledge', in Young, M.F.D. (ed.) *Knowledge and Control*, London: Collier Macmillan.

Ziegler, M. (2008) 'Expanding curriculum development models', in Wang, V.C.X. (ed.) *Curriculum Development for Adult Learners in the Global Community*, vol. 1: *Strategic Approaches*, Malabar, FL: Krieger.

Zimmerman, F.E. (1979) 'Elderhostel '78 at Adelphi University', *Lifelong Learning: The Adult Years* 3 (3): 10, 22–23.

INDEX

Page numbers in *italic* refer to tables, numbers in **bold** refer to figures.

334